TECHNIQUES OF
FINANCIAL ANALYSIS

TECHNIQUES OF FINANCIAL ANALYSIS

Erich A. Helfert, D.B.A.

Eighth Edition

IRWIN

Burr Ridge, Illinois
Boston, Massachusetts
Sydney, Australia

A professional version of this text is published by
IRWIN PROFESSIONAL PUBLISHING.

© RICHARD D. IRWIN, INC., 1963, 1967, 1972, 1977, 1982, 1987, 1991, and 1994

Executive editor:	Michael W. Junior
Marketing manager:	Ron Bloecher
Project editor:	Karen M. Smith
Production manager:	Laurie Kersch
Cover designer:	Laura Gunther
Art coordinator:	Mark Malloy
Compositor:	Graphic Sciences
Typeface:	12.5/14 Caledonia
Printer:	R. R. Donnelley & Sons Company

Library of Congress Cataloging-in-Publication Data

Helfert, Erich A.
    Techniques of financial analysis / Erich A. Helfert. — 8th ed.
        p.   cm.
    Includes bibliographical references and index.
    ISBN 0-256-12025-0
    1. Corporations—Finance.   2. Cash flow.   3. Financial statements.
4. Ratio analysis.   I. Title.
HG4026.H44   1994
658.15′1—dc20   93–31832

Printed in the United States of America
    4 5 6 7 8 9 0 DO 0 9 8 7 6

To Anne

PREFACE

For the past 30 years, the seven editions of this book have served to give the student, analyst, or business executive a concise, practical, usable, and up-to-date overview of key financial analysis tools. The presentation is carefully structured to help the reader understand the relationship between management decisions and financial results, interpret financial reports, develop basic financial projections, evaluate capital investment decisions, assess the implications of financing choices, and derive the value of a business or a security. Every technique and measure is described and demonstrated in the context of important underlying financial concepts, but without delving into theoretical abstraction.

All analytical tools and related financial concepts are discussed from a *decision-making* standpoint; that is, they are linked to the three basic *types of decisions* made continuously by the management of any ongoing business: *investment, operating, and financing.* The presentation is also structured around the *viewpoints* of the major parties interested in the analysis and performance of a business: *managers, owners, and creditors.*

In all this, however, practicality is paramount. Any issues and concepts going beyond what is essential are left to the more specialized texts and articles identified in the references. Self-study exercises and problems are provided after each chapter so the reader can practice applying the analytical tools and check the results against solutions in Appendix VI.

The book has consistently maintained a unique appeal for both students and practitioners because of its clarity and common sense presentation. Originally an outgrowth of the compact technical briefing materials used in the MBA program at the Harvard Business School, which supplement practical case study discussion with essential background, the book has been regularly updated and modified approximately every five years. This eighth edition reflects not only the latest practice in the use of the various financial techniques but also the experience gained over seven editions from the widespread use the book has enjoyed. It has been used as a resource in university finance courses, both graduate and undergraduate, and in hundreds of executive development seminars and in-company programs in the United States, Canada, Latin America, and overseas, including the author's own numerous client companies. Translated into seven foreign languages over the years, the book has transcended the confines of American business practice on which it is built, because the way in which the analytical methods are described makes them almost universally applicable.

The current edition has been reinforced and updated to emphasize the logical, integrated flow of the materials beginning with an overview of the "business system" and the financial analysis concepts, all the way to the development of business valuation and the meaning of shareholder value. The added graphics supporting the materials were tested in numerous executive development courses over the past several years.

The first five chapters, which form an integrated set, are built around the conceptual overview of the business system, its decisional context, and its relationship to financial statements and analytical tools as presented in Chapter 1. The coverage of analytical methods begins in Chapter 2 with funds flow analysis, moves on to financial performance analysis, covers financial projections, and culminates in a discussion of the financial dynamics useful in modeling financial conditions.

The last five chapters deal with more specialized topics such as investment analysis, the cost of capital, financing choices, and valuation of securities and businesses. The new final chapter contains some integrated case materials in which the application of the various analytical techniques is demonstrated.

The existing appendixes were also updated, including the recent addition of object-oriented analysis concepts. Two new appendixes were added; one provides some international perspective on performance analysis, and the other is a glossary of key concepts. Solutions to all problems were again included in the last appendix, making the book truly self-contained for individual study.

The revision process has not, however, affected the book's primary focus on the doable and practical—in effect an "executive briefing" concept—and on building the reader's basic ability to grasp financial relationships and issues. As before, the book only presupposes that the user has some familiarity with basic accounting concepts.

I would again like to express my appreciation to my former colleagues at the Harvard Business School for the opportunity to develop the original concept of the book. My thanks also go to my business associates and to my colleagues at universities and in executive development programs here and abroad (too numerous to mention individually) for their continued extensive use of the book and for the many expressions of interest and constructive suggestions that have supported the book's evolution.

I am grateful to Bill Ault, National University (San Diego); Susan Shalagan, University of Hartford (Connecticut); Harold Fletcher, Loyola College (Baltimore); and Lee Gunnels, Muskingum Area Technical College (Ohio), who reviewed the manuscript of this edition and suggested refinements and revisions.

Finally, I continue to be most gratified by the positive responses from so many individual users, past and current, who have found the book helpful in their studies and in their professions.

Erich A. Helfert

CONTENTS

A NOTE
FROM THE EDITOR

Over the past 30 years, thousands of managers and managers-in-training have read *Techniques of Financial Analysis*. For most, it was their first exposure to understanding the relationship between finance concepts and daily decisions. It remains, for many, a valuable reference called upon for day-to-day performance.

Frequently, I talk with readers proclaiming the value of this great resource. My colleague Mike Allison, the Business Manager for our editorial group here at Irwin, confessed, "When I was in manufacturing, I would refer to *(Techniques of Financial Analysis)* two or three times a week. I still do!"

I am confident you will also utilize this great resource for years to come.

Michael W. Junior
Publisher

INTRODUCTION

When a student, analyst, or business executive is dealing with a financial problem or wishes to understand an economic issue related to business investment, operations, or financing, a wide variety of analytical techniques—and sometimes rules of thumb—are available to generate quantitative answers. Selecting the appropriate tools from these choices is clearly an important part of the analytical task. Yet, experience has shown again and again that developing a proper perspective for the problem or issue is just as important as the choice of the tools themselves.

Therefore, this book not only presents the key financial tools generally used, but also explains the broader context of how and where they're applied to obtain meaningful answers. To this end, the first chapter provides an integrated conceptual backdrop both for the financial/economic dimensions of business management and for understanding the nature of financial statements, data, and processes underlying financial analysis techniques.

While the tools and techniques covered in this book are discussed and demonstrated in detail, the user must not be tempted to view them as ends in themselves. It's simply not enough to master the techniques alone! Financial analysis is both an analytical and a judgmental process which helps answer questions that have been carefully posed in a managerial context. The process is at its best when the analyst's efforts are focused as much on structuring the issue and its context as they are on data manipulation. We can't stress enough that the basic purpose of financial analysis is to help those responsible for results to make sound business decisions.

Apart from providing specific numerical answers, the "solutions" to financial problems and issues depend significantly on the points of view of the parties involved, on the relative importance of the issue, and on the nature and reliability of the information available. In each situation the objective of the analysis must be clearly understood before pencil is put to paper or computer keys are touched—otherwise, the process becomes wasteful "number crunching."

Management has been defined as "the art of asking significant questions." The same applies to financial analysis, which should be targeted toward finding meaningful answers to these significant questions—whether or not the results are fully quantifiable. In fact, the qualitative judgments involved in finding answers to financial/economic issues can often count just as heavily as the quantitative results, and no analytical task is complete until these aspects have been carefully spelled out and weighed.

The degree of precision and refinement to which any financial analysis is carried also depends on the specific situation. Given the uncertain nature of many of the estimates used in calculations, it's often preferable to develop ranges of potential outcomes rather than precise "answers." At the same time, it's wasteful to further refine answers that clearly suggest the choice of particular alternatives—there's no need to belabor the obvious! Moreover, common sense dictates that most of the analytical effort should be directed at areas where the likely payoff from additional analysis is largest—to match the amount of energy expended with the significance of the results.

The following points are a suggested checklist for review and consideration before any financial analysis task is begun. This list should be helpful to the person actually doing the work as well as to the manager who may have assigned the question or project to an associate:

1. What's the exact nature and scope of the issue to be analyzed? Have the problem and its relative importance in the overall business context been clearly spelled out, including the relevant alternatives to be considered?

2. Which specific factors, relationships, and trends are likely to be helpful in analyzing the issue? What's the order of their importance, and in what sequence should they be addressed?

3. Are there possible ways to obtain a quick "ballpark" estimate of the likely result to help decide (1) what the critical data and steps might be and (2) how much effort should be spent on refining these?

4. How precise an answer is necessary in relation to the importance of the problem itself? Would additional refinement be worth the effort?

5. How reliable are the available data, and how is this uncertainty likely to affect the range of results? What confirmation might be possible, and at what degree of effort?

6. What limitations are inherent in the tools to be applied, and how are these likely to affect the range of

results? Are the tools chosen truly appropriate to the problem?

7. How important are qualitative judgments in the context of the problem, and what's the order of their significance? Which analytical steps might be obviated by such considerations?

Only after having thought through these questions should specific analytical work on a problem proceed. The relatively small amount of effort expended on taking this critical first step at the beginning will pay off in much more focused and meaningful work. In effect, we're talking about using a rational approach to problem solving in financial/economic analysis. In the end, this is what effective support of decision making in a company's investments, operations, and financing is all about.

1 BUSINESS AS A FINANCIAL SYSTEM

This introductory chapter lays the conceptual foundation for discussing the analytical tools and financial/economic concepts presented throughout this book.

First, we'll use a systems perspective to introduce a broad overview of the typical business and the pattern of its activities. The underlying concept is simple: Any business can be viewed as an interrelated system of financial resource movements, all of which are activated by management decisions, large and small. Such a systems approach is useful here because it reflects the dynamic nature of all business activities and also represents them effectively in financial/economic terms.

Visualizing the total business in such a graphic way provides a consistent overall context for understanding both the purpose and nature of analytical methods, and for assessing the meaning of analytical results. Moreover, the systems approach serves as an introduction to financial modeling and improves the reader's ability to appreciate the judgmental aspects of financial/economic analysis that go beyond mere technical methodology.

Second, we'll present two additional conceptual overviews, again to reinforce the larger context and meaning of financial/economic analysis. The first of these overviews gives a broad perspective of the nature and meaning of commonly used financial statements that are a necessary formal reflection of the status and results of the business system:

- Balance sheets.
- Operating (income) statements.
- Statements of changes in owners' (shareholders') equity.
- Funds flow statements.

We'll address the major attributes and limitations of these statements and their relationships to each other. We'll also highlight the judgments necessary to interpret the information presented in these statements for use in financial/economic analysis.

The second overview presents the various objectives of the key analytical processes that can be applied to interpreting the performance of the business system. These objectives are grouped by three major analytical viewpoints:

- Financial accounting.
- Investor analysis.
- Managerial economics.

We present this overview as a useful backdrop for choosing and evaluating the analytical techniques and results discussed throughout this book.

In all of our discussions we deliberately refer to "financial/economic" analysis. The intent is to recognize that the task of the business analyst or manager who analyzes, judges, and guides a firm's activities has to be broader than mere manipulation of financial data. Ultimately, the performance and value of any business must be judged in economic terms.

At the same time, however, much of the available data and many of the analytical techniques are based on financial accounting and its special conventions, which don't necessarily reflect current and future economic performance and value of the business. Therefore, any analyst engaged in financial/economic analysis must do a great deal of interpretation and even translation of available data to properly match the context of the analysis. As we'll see, it's the analyst's duty to make sure that the process and results of any analysis clearly fit the desired objectives, whether these are purely financial in nature or whether they call for economic judgments.

A DYNAMIC PERSPECTIVE OF BUSINESS

Decision Context

Successful operation, performance, and long-term viability of any business over time depend on a continuous sequence of sound individual or collective decisions made by the management team. Every one of these decisions ultimately causes an economic impact, for better or worse, on the business. In essence, the process of managing any enterprise requires an ongoing series of economic choices. These choices in turn activate movements of the financial resources supporting the business.

For example, hiring an employee results in a future series of salary or wage payments in return for services provided. Selling merchandise on credit releases goods from inventory to the customer and creates a documented obligation by the customer to remit payment 30 or 60 days hence. Investing in a new manufacturing facility causes, among other effects, a potentially complex set of future financial obligations to be fulfilled. Successful negotiation of a line of credit with a lender brings an inflow of funds into the business, to be repaid in future periods.

Some decisions are major, such as investing in a new manufacturing plant, raising large amounts of debt, or adding a new line of products or services. Most other decisions are part of the day-to-day processes through which every functional area of a business is managed. Common to all, however, is the basic concept of "economic trade-offs," that is, before every decision the manager must weigh the benefits obtained against the costs incurred.

In normal day-to-day decisions the underlying trade-offs may be quite apparent. In complex situations, however, careful analysis is usually required to evaluate whether resources committed directly or indirectly by the decision are likely to be profitably recovered. Periodically the combined effect of all these trade-offs and decisions can be observed when performance and value of the business are judged either by means of financial statements or with the help of special economic analyses.

Fundamentally, managers make all decisions on behalf of the owners of the business, as they deploy available internal and external resources to bring about economic gain for the owners. Despite the great variety of issues managers of different businesses face every day, their tasks have sufficient similarity that we can say that all business decisions, large and small, can effectively be grouped into just three basic areas:

- The investment of resources.
- The operation of the business using these resources.
- The proper mix of financing that funds these resources.

Figure 1–1 shows the continuous interrelationship of these three areas.

FIGURE 1–1
The Three Basic Business Decisions

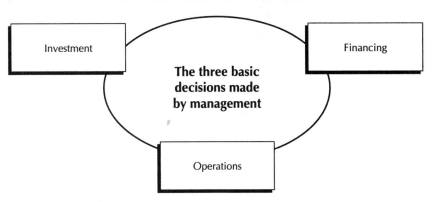

Today's business world is one of infinite variety. Enterprises of all sizes engage in areas such as manufacturing, trade, finance, and myriad services, using widely different legal and organizational structures, and often involving international operations and far-flung investments.

Common to all businesses, however, is the following definition of the basic economic purpose of sound management:

> Planned deployment of selected resources in order to create, over time, economic value sufficient to recover all resources employed while earning an acceptable return on these resources under conditions that match the owners' expectations of risk.

Over the long run, successful resource deployments should result in a net improvement in the economic position of the owners—including their ability to make further resource investments if they choose. Only if such an economic net improvement is achieved has additional shareholder value been created, as we'll discuss in more detail in later chapters. The primary effect of such value creation will normally be a higher valuation of the business. If the company's stock is traded publicly, such value is judged by the securities markets; if the company is privately held, value creation will tend to be reflected in the price offered by potential buyers of the business. If no value increment is achieved over time, the firm's economic viability is in doubt.

In the end, creating shareholder value at any level depends on properly managing the three basic decisional areas common to all organizations:

- Selecting and executing *investments* based on sound economic analysis and management.
- Guiding the *operations* of the business profitably by making effective use of all resources employed.
- Prudently *financing* the business by consciously trading off the rewards expected against the risk exposure from using external credit.

Making successful economic trade-offs in arriving at these decisions is the fundamental driving force of the value creation process. These trade-offs must be explicitly managed in a consistent way to achieve long-run success. Figure 1–2 depicts the interrelationship of the three decision areas.

FIGURE 1–2
The Process of Value Creation

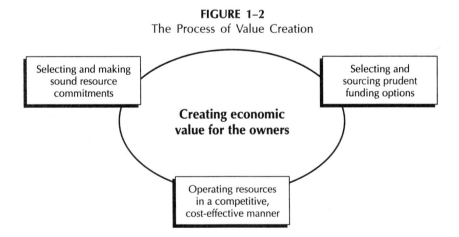

The basic task—and also the challenge—of financial/economic analysis thus amounts to constructing a reasonably consistent and meaningful set of data and relationships that can be effectively used in appropriate analytical frameworks and tools. If this is done well, applying the frameworks and tools should enable the manager and the analyst to judge various decision trade-offs, financial condition, operational effectiveness, and outlook for the business in terms of financial and economic performance and value.

Figure 1–3 adds, in the form of background layers, the analytical framework and tools, data sources, and general backdrop of competitive and economic conditions to reflect an integrated set of concepts within which the interplay of management decisions and interpretation of results should ideally take place.

FIGURE 1–3
The Broad Context of Financial/Economic Analysis

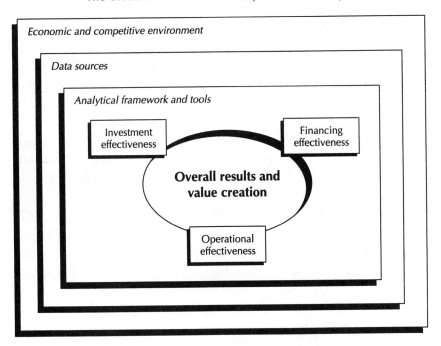

The Business System

As managers operate a business—any business—their daily decisions impact the resources under their control in one way or another in a dynamic interrelationship. As we said earlier, all decisions cause resource movements of various degrees. These movements are best characterized by the term *funds flows*. *Funds* is a common financial concept which denotes resources, whether they're committed by the business in the form of cash balances, receivables, inventories, and plant and equipment, or obtained by the business in the form of loans, vendor credit, bonds, or shareholder capital.

All management decisions cause changes in the magnitude and pattern of funds flows, both in the form of funds committed (uses) and in the form of funds obtained (sources). In any successful business these movements' combined effect over time leads to the desired buildup of economic value.

Eventually any funds movement causes a change in cash—and the combined changes in cash from all decisions over time are the basis of the long-term economic viability of a business. In fact, the simple principle of relating "cash in" to "cash out" is the driving force behind many forms of financial/economic analysis. It's the basis of the economic trade-offs that lead to the creation of shareholder value. As we'll see in Chapter 2, there are formal ways of tracking and analyzing funds flow patterns and their cash impact that assist the manager or analyst in judging a business's results and prospects.

Let's now take a conceptual view of how a typical business operates. With the help of a simplified systems diagram we can demonstrate the basic funds flow patterns and the key relationships involved. We can also establish an overview of key management decision areas in each of the three decisional segments. This will lead to a display of financial analysis measures and key business strategies as they relate to the business system and to management decisions. Every one of these measures and concepts will, of course, be discussed in greater depth in the appropriate chapters of this book.

Figure 1–4 presents a basic flow chart containing all major elements necessary to understand the broad funds flow patterns of a typical business. The arrangement of boxes and arrows is designed to show that we're dealing with a closed system in which all parts are interrelated with each other. The system is organized in three segments that match the three major decision areas: investment, operations, and financing.

The top segment represents the three components of business investment: the investment base already in place, the addition of new investments, and any disinvestment (divestment) of resources no longer deemed necessary.

The center segment represents the operational interplay of three basic elements: price, volume, and related costs of products and/or services. It recognizes that costs usually are partly fixed and partly variable.

The bottom segment represents the basic financing options open to a business in two parts. The first part represents the normal disposition of the operating profit achieved for a period. It reflects a three-way split between dividends paid to owners, interest paid to lenders, and earnings retained for reinvestment in the business. The second part displays the available choices for a company's long-term capital sources. It shows ownership (shareholders') equity (augmented by any retained earnings) and long-term debt held by outsiders. Trade-offs and decisions that affect retained profits or long-term capital sources impact the company's funding potential which, as the arrow on the left indicates, supports the level of any additions to the investment base at the top of the chart.

We'll now examine each part of the system in some

FIGURE 1–4
The Business System: An Overview

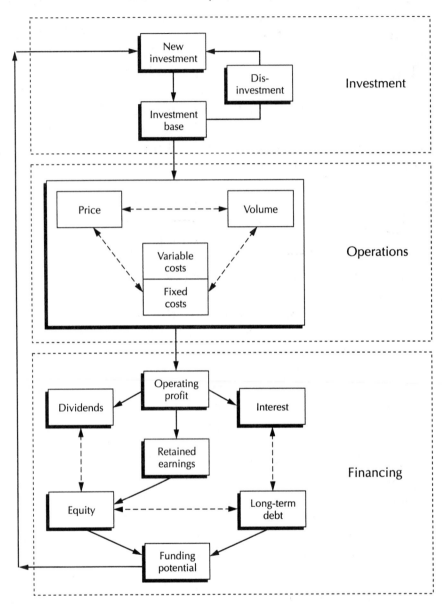

detail to highlight both the types of decisions made and the interrelationship of their effects.

Investment Decisions

Investment is the basic driving force of any business. It supports the competitive strategies developed by management and is based on plans (capital budgets) for committing existing or newly obtained funds to three main areas:

- Working capital (cash balances, receivables due from customers, and inventories, less trade credit from suppliers and other normal current obligations).
- Buildings, machinery and equipment, office furnishings, and so on.
- Major spending programs (research and development, product or service development, promotional programs, etc.).

Figure 1–5 shows the investment portion of the systems diagram, with the addition of applicable yardsticks and key strategies that can be identified in this area.

FIGURE 1–5
The Business System: Investment Segment

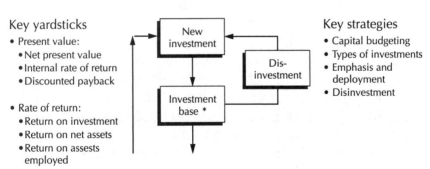

Key yardsticks
- Present value:
  - Net present value
  - Internal rate of return
  - Discounted payback
- Rate of return:
  - Return on investment
  - Return on net assets
  - Return on assests employed

New investment

Dis-investment

Investment base *

Key strategies
- Capital budgeting
- Types of investments
- Emphasis and deployment
- Disinvestment

* Assumes that an amount equal to depreciation and amortization of assets is continuously reinvested here, in order to maintain all existing facilities and equipment in good operating condition; but cost increases in such replacement assets may, of course, actually require a greater amount of reinvestment.

During the annual planning process in which capital budgets are formulated, management normally chooses from a variety of options those new investments that are expected to achieve desired economic returns for the shareholders. At the same time, sound practice requires that the deployment of the existing investment base be revalidated periodically to see if continued commitment is warranted by the operations' performance and outlook.

If it can be shown that, for example, withdrawal from a particular market or activity is economically justified, the opposite of investment, *disinvestment*, becomes a significant option. Disposing of the assets involved or selling the operating unit as a going concern will permit more advantageous redeployment of these funds. Also, any sale of equipment being replaced by newer facilities will provide funds for other purposes.

The various linkages in the overall diagram in Figure 1–4 take on major importance here. They suggest that investments or disinvestments should match not only the firm's operational characteristics and needs, but also the financial policies that management deems acceptable. For example, selection of current and potential markets (a strategic choice) will affect how and where new facilities will be deployed. The characteristics of these markets, such as an outlook for rapid growth, might require significant future investments that could be constrained by the company's funding potential under restrictive financial policies.

Whether investments involve plant and equipment, various physical resources (such as mineral deposits), intangibles (such as proprietary technology), deployment of human resources, incremental working capital, or other outlays, all these resource commitments represent the operational "trigger" for action in almost every kind of business.

Yardsticks that are helpful in selecting new investments and disinvestments are generally based on present value concepts, which measure the economic trade-off between investment funds committed and operational cash flow benefits gained. These measures are detailed in Chapter 6. Yardsticks for measuring the effectiveness with which the existing investment base is employed basically utilize rate of return concepts, which are based on financial accounting data (Chapter 3).

Operations Decisions

Here key strategies and decisions involve the effective utilization of the funds invested in serving selected markets as well as setting appropriate pricing and service policies that are competitive in filling customers' needs. These choices invariably amount to economic trade-offs in which management must balance the impact of competitive prices and competitors' actions on sales volume and on the profitability of products or services. At the same time all operations of the business must be made cost effective and maintained as such to achieve competitive success. Figure 1–6 highlights key elements of the operations segment of the financial system.

Sound results depend in part on understanding and exploiting operating leverage, that is, the effect on the company's profitability of the level and proportion of fixed (period) costs committed to the operations, versus the amount and nature of variable (direct) costs incurred in manufacturing, service, or trading operations. This concept will be expanded in Chapter 5. The interplay of all these forces and decisions results in the net operating profit for a period.

The key yardsticks in the operations segment include a variety of operating ratios that measure the effectiveness with which funds are employed, as well as specific expense and profit indicators. Also, there are measures for the relative profit contribution margin of different products and services, and a variety of comparative operating data against which to benchmark the cost

FIGURE 1–6
The Business System: Operations Segment

Key yardsticks
- Operating ratios
- Contribution analysis
- Activity analysis
- Comparative data
- Benchmarking

Key strategies
- Utilization of resources
- Market selection
- Competitive position
- Pricing strategy
- Cost effectiveness
- Operating leverage
- Core capabilities

* Assumes that all legally required income taxes have been paid after deducting interest, and therefore operating profit is shown here net of such income taxes.

effectiveness of particular operations. A newer concept is activity-based analysis, which in essence amounts to an economic analysis of specific areas of the business. These measures are detailed in Chapters 3 and 4.

Financing Decisions

This segment represents the various choices available to management to fund the investments and operations of the business over the long term. Two key areas of strategy and decisions are identified: the disposition of profits and the shaping of the company's capital structure. Normally this set of trade-offs and decisions is made at the highest levels of management and endorsed by the board of directors of a corporation because the choices are crucial to the firm's long-term viability. Figure 1–7 displays the relationships, yardsticks, and strategies in the financing segment.

The first strategy area, disposition of profits, involves the basic three-way split of operating profit after taxes

FIGURE 1-7
The Business System: Financing Segment

Key yardsticks
- Earnings per share
- Cash flow per share
- Payout ratio
- Interest coverage

Key strategies
- *Disposition of operating profit:*
  - Dividends to owners
  - Interest to lenders
  - Retention of profits

- Return on equity
- Return on capitalization
- Debt/equity ratio
- Debt service
- Cost of capital
- Shareholder value

- *Capital structure proportions:*
  - Types of equity
  - Types of debt
  - Financial leverage
  - Risk/reward trade-off

* Assumes a continuous rollover of debt (refinancing), that is, there is no reduction in existing debt levels from repayments, as new funds are raised to cover these. It does not specifically provide for off-balance sheet debt, such as leases.

between (1) owners, (2) lenders, and (3) reinvestment in the business. Each element is affected by current or past management policies, trade-offs, and decisions. For example, payment of dividends to owners is at the discretion of a corporation's board of directors. Here the critical trade-off choice is the relative amount of dividends to be paid out, which directly impacts the alternative use of these funds for reinvestment and growth.

The payment of interest to lenders is a matter of contractual obligation. The level of interest payments incurred relative to operating profit, however, is a direct function of management policies and actions regarding the use of debt—the higher the proportion of debt in the capital structure, the greater will be the demand for profit dollars to be used for paying interest and also the greater will be the firm's risk exposure.

Retained earnings represent the residual profit for the period, after payment of interest and dividends and after providing for applicable income taxes. Combined with any new funds provided by investors and lenders, retained earnings expand the funding potential for additional investment and growth.

Key measures in the area of earnings disposition are earnings and cash flows on a per share basis, which are broad indicators of the company's ability to compensate both lenders and owners. In addition, there are specific ratios measuring the proportion of dividends paid out, coverage of interest on debt, and coverage of total debt service requirements. (See Chapter 3.)

The second area, the planning of capital structure proportions, involves selecting and balancing the relative proportions of funds obtained over time from ownership sources and from long-term debt obligations which, after taking into account business risk and debt service requirements, should result in an acceptable level of overall profitability.

Again, this requires a series of economic trade-offs, including the assessment of the rewards obtained versus the risks involved in different alternatives open to management. Numerous types of equity can be employed as ownership funding, and the choices of debt instruments are similarly varied. (See Chapter 8.)

The key concept in choosing funding methods is the impact of financial leverage. (See Chapter 5.) In essence, financial leverage can be defined as prudent use of funds obtained from fixed-cost debt obligations for financing those investment opportunities that promise potential earnings higher than the cost of the interest on the borrowed funds. A positive difference between earnings and cost will enhance ownership equity and thus shareholder value. If the opposite holds true, however, earnings lower than the interest cost will penalize ownership equity and shareholder value. Management decisions here amount to a conscious economic trade-off between risk and reward expectations.

Key measures in the area of capital structure strategy include ratios measuring return on equity and return on capitalization (equity and long-term debt combined), various debt service coverage ratios (Chapter 3), ratios for relative levels of debt and equity (Chapter 5), measures of the cost of various forms of capital as well as the combined cost of capital for the company as a whole (Chapters 7 and 8), and shareholder value creation concepts (Chapter 9).

Internal Assumptions

Our very simplified model of the business system contains three key assumptions as stated in the footnotes to Figures 1–5, 1–6, and 1–7. They cover:

- Depreciation.
- Taxes.
- Rollover of debt.

Depreciation expense isn't recognized as such anywhere in the system because we've assumed that an amount equal to the annual depreciation write-off made against operating profit will be automatically reinvested each year in the investment base in order to maintain the firm's productive capacity, but without providing any incremental profits.

This is why the diagrams show operating profit as the ultimate operating result. The assumption reflects a common rule of thumb used in financial analysis, namely, that an ongoing operation needs to spend approximately the amount of depreciation to keep facilities in proper repair. If there were no plans to do this, any uncommitted depreciation funds would have to be added to the operating profit and would thus become available for new investment. (Chapter 2 discusses the funds aspects of depreciation.)

Next, we assume that all statutory income taxes for every period have been calculated, paid, and subtracted in arriving at operating profit and that all appropriate deductions have been taken in the process, including the interest expense recognized in the system diagram.

Finally, we assume that the amount of existing long-term debt outstanding remains unchanged; that is, no provision was made for paying off this debt as long as the business is operating and growing. Instead, a continuous "rollover" of debt is assumed; that is, new financing is arranged as repayments of existing blocks of debt become due. This assumption in effect permits keeping the relative proportion of funding from debt and equity sources stable over time.

Normally, as the amount of owners' equity grows with every period of profitable operations, management will likely wish to match, in proportion, such incremental retained earnings with an incremental amount of new debt—unless management decides that a change in debt policy is appropriate for a variety of reasons. Under the latter conditions, specific assumptions would have to be made about the pattern of repayments planned, which of course would change the relative proportions of debt and equity outstanding.

Interrelationships of Key Strategic Areas

It should be obvious by now that our concept of the basic business system (Figure 1–4) forces us to recognize and deal with the many dynamic interrelationships of the key management strategies, policies, and decisions and the basic funds movements they cause. Consistency among these variables is an important aspect of a firm's long-term success. For example, it would be ineffective for a company to set aggressive growth objectives for its operations while at the same time restricting itself to a set of rigid and conservative financial policies. Similarly, paying out high levels of current operating profit in the form of dividends while maintaining a restrictive debt policy would clash with an objective to hold market share in a rapidly expanding business. Under such circumstances adequate funds for new investment simply wouldn't be available.

The basis for successful management is a consistent set of business strategies, investment objectives, operating goals, and financial policies that reinforce each other rather than conflict. They must be chosen through conscious and careful analysis of the economic trade-offs involved, both individually and in combination. Our simplified systems diagram has provided a way to recognize these interrelationships in an initial broad context of decisions and funds flows.

THE NATURE OF FINANCIAL STATEMENTS

To apply our insights gained from the conceptual overview, we must now look for information that will (1) allow the manager or analyst to track the condition and results of a business and (2) assist in understanding the funds flow patterns in more specific terms. The process of financial analysis involves review of a great variety of formal or informal data relevant to the specific purpose of the analysis. Some data are common to most types of financial analysis, while others are developed to provide specialized information.

The most common form in which basic financial information about a business is available publicly—unless a company is privately held—is a set of financial statements issued under guidelines of the public accounting profession (Generally Accepted Accounting Principles) and under the supervision of the Securities and Exchange Commission. Such a set of statements usually contains balance sheets as of given dates, operating statements for given periods, and funds flow statements for the same periods. A special statement highlighting changes in owners' equity on the balance sheet is commonly provided as well.

Since financial statements are the basis for most analytical efforts pertaining to a business, we must first understand their nature, coverage, and limitations before we can use the data and observations derived from these statements for our analytical judgments. Financial statements, which are prepared according to commonly accepted accounting principles, reflect effects of management's past and current decisions. They involve considerable ambiguity, however. Financial statements are governed by financial accounting rules that attempt to consistently and fairly account for every business transaction using the following conservative principles:

- Transactions are recorded at costs prevailing at the time.
- Adjustments to current values are made only if values decline.
- Revenues and costs are recognized when committed, not when cash changes hands.
- Periodic matching of revenues and costs is achieved via accruals, deferrals, and accounting allocations.
- Allowances for negative contingencies are required, thus reducing profits and recorded value via estimates.

These rules by their very nature leave the financial accounting results open to considerable interpretation, especially if the analyst seeks to understand a company's economic performance and value.

The Balance Sheet

The balance sheet as of any given date describes the categories and amounts of assets employed by the business (i.e., the funds committed) and the offsetting liabilities incurred to lenders and owners (i.e., the funds obtained). Also called the *statement of financial condition* or *statement of financial position,* it must always balance because the total assets invested in the business at any point in time by definition are matched precisely by the liabilities and owners' equity supporting these assets.

The major categories of assets, or uses of funds, are:

- Current assets (items that in the normal course of business turn over within a relatively short period of time, such as cash, marketable securities, accounts receivable, and inventories).
- Fixed assets (such as land, mineral resources, buildings, equipment, machinery, and vehicles), all of which are used over the long term.
- Other assets, such as deposits, patents, and various intangibles like goodwill that arose from an acquisition.

Major sources of funds are:

- Current liabilities, which are obligations to vendors, tax authorities, employees, and lenders due within one year.
- Long-term liabilities, which are a variety of debt instruments repayable beyond one year, such as mortgages and bonds.
- Owners' equity, which represents the funds contributed by various classes of owners of the business as well as accumulated earnings retained in the business.

Balance sheets are static in that, like a snapshot, they reflect conditions on the date of their preparation. They're also cumulative in that they represent the effects of all decisions and transactions that have taken place and have been accounted for up to the date of preparation.

26

As we indicated earlier, financial accounting rules require that all transactions be recorded at costs and values as incurred at the time, and retroactive adjustments to recorded values are made only in very limited circumstances. As a consequence, balance sheets (being cumulative) display assets and liabilities acquired or incurred at different times. Because the current economic value of assets can change, particularly in the case of longer-lived items (such as buildings and machinery) or resources (such as land and minerals), the costs stated on the balance sheet may not reflect true economic values. Moreover, changes in the value of the currency in which the transactions are recorded can, over time, distort the balance sheet. Ultimately, the residual book value of owners' equity reflects all of these value differentials.

Finally, a number of relatively recent rules require the estimation and recording of contingent liabilities arising from a variety of future obligations such as pensions and health care costs, further introducing a series of value judgments.

The accounting profession, through its Financial Accounting Standards Board, is expending a great deal of effort to resolve these and other issues affecting the meaning of the balance sheet, but with only partial success. Accounting standards continue to evolve, and a manager or analyst must be aware of the underlying principles and processes when reviewing and analyzing this statement. We'll discuss the most important of these issues specifically as we examine analytical techniques in later chapters.

In our decisional context of investment, operations, and financing, the balance sheet can be viewed as a cumulative listing of the impact of past investment and financing decisions. It's a historical record of all transactions affecting the current business. In addition, the net effect of operations in the form of periodic profit or loss is reflected in the changing ownership equity account. Figure 1–8 is a simple conceptual picture of the

FIGURE 1–8
Balance Sheet in Decisional Context

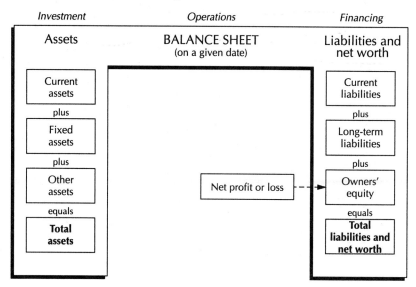

Management Decision Area

balance sheet as it relates to the three areas of management decisions.

The major categories normally found on the balance sheet are listed here. However, this is an oversimplification. In actual practice, the analyst encounters a large variety of detailed asset, liability, and net worth accounts because balance sheets reflect the unique nature of a given company and the sector it's in. But the actual accounts can always be grouped into the basic categories listed.

As an example of the balance sheet of a major corporation, Figure 1–9 shows TRW Inc.'s consolidated balance sheet for December 31, 1992, and December 31, 1991, as published in its 1992 annual report, but presented here without accompanying notes.

TRW Inc. is a major international company headquartered in Cleveland, Ohio. It focuses on products and services with a high technology or engineering content

FIGURE 1–9
TRW INC. AND SUBSIDIARIES
Consolidated Balance Sheets at December 31, 1992, and 1991
($ millions)

Assets	*1992*	*1991*
Current assets:		
Cash and cash equivalents	$ 66	$ 75
Accounts receivable	1,289	1,356
Inventories	422	512
Prepaid expenses	69	61
Deferred income taxes	270	258
Total current assets	2,116	2,262
Property, plant, and equipment at cost	5,052	5,010
Less: Allowances for depreciation and amortization	2,741	2,686
Total property, plant, and equipment—net	2,311	2,324
Intangible assets:		
Intangibles arising from acquisitions	552	561
Capitalized data files and other	464	420
	1,016	981
Less: Accumulated amortization	299	266
Total intangible assets—net	717	715
Other assets	314	334
Total assets	$5,458	$5,635
Liabilities and shareholders' investment		
Current liabilities:		
Short-term debt	$ 260	$ 407
Accrued compensation	286	298
Trade accounts payable	583	567
Other accruals	752	620
Dividends payable	30	28
Income taxes	85	32
Current portion of long-term debt	16	30
Total current liabilities	2,012	1,982
Long-term liabilities	804	251
Long-term debt	941	1,213
Deferred income taxes	222	440
Minority interests in subsidiaries	63	64
Shareholders' investment:		
Serial preference stock II	1	1
Common stock	39	38
Other capital	222	184
Retained earnings	1,105	1,377
Cumulative translation adjustments	53	98
Treasury shares—cost in excess of par	(4)	(13)
Total shareholders' investment	1,416	1,685
Total liabilities and shareholders' investment	$5,458	$5,635

Source: Adapted from TRW Inc. 1992 annual report.

to the space and defense, automotive, and information systems markets, serving segments in which the company typically holds leading positions. Founded in 1901, the company employs about 64,000 people in 21 countries. It ranked 64th in sales in the 1992 Fortune 500 listing. We'll use TRW's published financial statements as examples in Chapters 2 and 3 and demonstrate the use of analytical techniques on their data.

The Operating Statement

The operating statement reflects the effect of management's operating decisions on business performance and the resulting profit or loss for the owners of the business *over a clearly specified period of time.* The profit or loss calculated in the statement increases or decreases owners' equity on the balance sheet. The operating statement is thus a necessary adjunct to the balance sheet in explaining the major component of change in owners' equity and it provides essential performance assessment information.

The operating statement—also referred to as the *income statement, earnings statement,* or *profit and loss statement*—displays the revenues recognized for a specific period as well as costs and expenses charged against these revenues, including write-offs (e.g., depreciation and amortization of various assets) and taxes. Revenues and costs involve elements such as sales for cash or credit, purchases of goods or services for resale or manufacture, payment of wages, incurring trade credit, and scheduling production for inventory. The operating statement represents the firm's accountants' best effort to match the relevant items of revenue with the relevant items of expense.

Again, these efforts are governed by generally accepted accounting principles. How certain costs and expenses are handled involves accounting judgments. Among these are the depreciation of assets being used over more periods than the current reporting period, the cost of goods purchased or manufactured in previous periods, and proper allocation of general expenses to a specific period. We'll take up the more critical judgment areas as we apply the analysis techniques in later chapters.

When viewed in our decisional context, the operating statement in the center column of Figure 1–10 expands the details of the transactions and allocations that make up one of the key performance elements, profit or loss.

Again we're providing an actual example of an operating statement in Figure 1–11, TRW's consolidated statement of earnings for the years ending December 31, 1991, and December 31, 1992.

The combined use of a balance sheet and an operating statement provides more basic insights than the balance sheet alone. But because the operating statement covers a period of time, while the balance sheet describes conditions at the end of a period, it's useful

FIGURE 1–10
Operating Statement in Decisional Context

Management Decision Area

Investment	Operations	Financing
Assets	BALANCE SHEET (on a given date)	Liabilities and net worth

	OPERATING STATEMENT	
Current assets	Revenues	Current liabilities
plus		plus
Fixed assets	less Cost of sales	Long-term liabilities
plus	equals Gross margin	plus
Other assets	less Operating expenses	Owners' equity
equals	equals Operating earnings/loss	equals
Total assets	less Income taxes	Total liabilities and net worth
	equals Net profit or loss	

FIGURE 1–11
TRW INC. AND SUBSIDIARIES
Statement of Earnings
For the Years Ended December 31, 1992, and 1991
($ millions)

	1992	1991
Sales	$8,311	$7,913
Cost of sales	6,617	6,307
Gross profit	1,694	1,606
Administrative and selling expenses	826	841
Research and development expenses	393	346
Restructuring expense (income)	(29)	343
Interest expense	163	190
Other expenses (income) net	(7)	15
Total expenses	1,346	1,735
Earnings (loss) before income taxes and cumulative effect of accounting changes	348	(129)
Income taxes	154	11
Earnings (loss) before cumulative effect of accounting changes	194	(140)
Cumulative effect to January 1, 1992, of accounting changes, net of income taxes	(350)	–
Net earnings (loss)	$ (156)	$ (140)
Per share of common stock:		
Fully diluted earnings:		
Before cumulative effect of accounting changes	$ 3.09	$ (2.30)
Cumulative effect of accounting changes	(5.60)	–
Net earnings (loss) per share	$ (2.51)	$ (2.30)
Primary earnings:		
Before cumulative effect of accounting changes	$ 3.09	$ (2.30)
Cumulative effect of accounting changes	(5.60)	–
Net earnings (loss) per share	$ (2.51)	$ (2.30)
Other data:		
Average number of common shares outstanding (millions)	62.3	61.2

Source: Adapted from TRW Inc. 1992 annual report.

to have balance sheets for both the beginning and the end of the period covered by the operating statement.

When we use balance sheets that bracket the period under analysis, the net effects of investment, operating, and financing decisions can be related to the specific period, be it a month, quarter, year, or any other time interval represented by the operating statement.

The Funds Flow Statement

Over a period of time the profit and loss account won't be the only area affected by management's operating decisions. There will also be changes in most assets and liabilities, particularly in the accounts making up working capital, such as cash, receivables, inventories, and current payables. The statement that displays such changes in terms of funds movements is called a *funds flow statement* or *statement of cash flows*. It provides the basis for a dynamic analysis that focuses on the changes in financial condition resulting from the decisions made during a given period.

The statement is prepared from a comparison of the beginning and ending balance sheets, and is also linked to the operating statement for the period. It reflects decisions involving uses and sources of funds; that is, (1) commitments of funds to invest in assets or to repay liabilities or (2) raising of funds through additional borrowing or through reducing asset investments. One major source of funds, of course, is profitable operations in which revenues exceed costs and expenses. In contrast, unprofitable operations are a use of funds. The importance of the funds flow statement to the analysis of business performance should be clear.

The amount of detail in the funds flow statement can vary widely, depending on the nature of the business and the different funds movements emphasized. In the past, basic formats for these statements differed as well. Beginning with recent years, however, the Financial Accounting Standards Board has required that all published funds flows statements follow a common format listing uses and sources by the familiar three decision areas: investments, operations, and financing. This was a recognition of funds flow statements' usefulness in understanding dynamics of the business system as discussed earlier. Figure 1–12 shows the funds flow statement in terms of our management decision context.

One aspect of the funds flow statement that requires some explanation is the treatment of accounting write-offs. From a funds flow standpoint, write-offs such as depreciation and amortization merely represent book-keeping entries that don't affect funds. The reason is simply that the assets being amortized by these entries represent funds committed in past periods. Consequently, the write-off categories, insofar as they had reduced net profit, must be added back here as a positive funds flow, thus restoring the funds from operations to their original level before the write-off. Handling this adjustment is detailed in Chapter 2.

The funds flow statement has the same inherent limitations as the balance sheet and the operating statement because it's derived from the accounting data contained in these statements. Another limitation is the need to display the net change from the beginning to the end of the period in each asset, liability, and ownership account reported, which may "bury" major individual transactions that occurred during the period and perhaps offset each other.

As we said before, management decisions are made in

FIGURE 1–12
Funds Flow Statement in Decisional Context

Management Decision Area

Investment	Operations	Financing
FUNDS FLOW STATEMENT		
Investments	**Operations**	**Financing**
Investments (increases) in all types of assets are uses of funds; disinvestments (reductions) in all types of assets are sources of funds.	Profitable operations are a source of funds; losses drain funds from the system. Accounting write-offs or write-ups do not affect funds; their profit impact must be adjusted for.	Trade credit and new financing (increases in liabilities and equity) are sources of funds; repayments of liabilities, dividends, and returns of capital are uses of funds.

a continuous sequence, and the balance sheets and operating statement for a period capture only their net effect. But if there were material transactions (such as major investments, acquisitions, or divestitures), they're generally noted specifically in the company's funds flow statement.

TRW's consolidated funds flow statement for the years ended December 31, 1992, and December 31, 1991 (Figure 1–13) shows how the various elements are listed in practice. A number of adjustments based on internally available information have been made by TRW to show more clearly the nature of funds movements during the periods covered.

The Statement of Changes in Owners' (Shareholders') Equity

The fourth financial statement commonly provided by a business is an analysis of the main changes, during a specific period, in the owners' capital accounts, or net worth. We know from the earlier discussion that one of these changes is the profit or loss for the period, as displayed in the operating statement. But other management decisions may have affected owners' equity.

For example, many corporations, including TRW, pay dividends on a quarterly basis. Such dividends are normally paid in cash, reducing both the cash balance and owners' equity. Another decision may be to provide additional capital through sale of new shares of common stock. A third area may involve write-offs or adjustments of asset values connected with disposition of assets or with business combinations. A fourth area involves the complex adjustments related to the exchange of foreign currencies by companies doing business internationally.

The net change in owners' equity may thus be selectively split into its major components to highlight the impact of these decisions. Figure 1–14 provides a conceptual view of the statement. The limitations of this

FIGURE 1–13
TRW INC. AND SUBSIDIARIES
Statement of Cash Flows
For the Years Ended December 31, 1992, and 1991
($ millions)

	1992	1991
Operating activities:		
Net earnings (loss)	$(156)	$(140)
Adjustments to reconcile net earnings (loss) to		
net cash provided by operating activities:		
Cumulative effect of accounting changes, net		
of taxes	350	–
Depreciation and amortization	481	469
Restructuring	(96)	227
Dividends received from affiliated companies	5	7
Deferred income taxes	5	27
Other—net	20	40
Changes in assets and liabilities, net of effects		
of businesses acquired or sold:		
Accounts receivable	(104)	(56)
Inventories and prepaid expenses	(46)	22
Accounts payable and other accruals	227	30
Other—net	(38)	(7)
Net cash provided by operating activities	648	619
Investing activities:		
Capital expenditures	(530)	(537)
Proceeds from divestitures	371	52
Acquisitions, net of cash acquired	(12)	(5)
Investments in other assets	(62)	(95)
Proceeds from sales of property, plant, and equipment	11	51
Other—net	19	(27)
Net cash used in investing activities	(203)	(561)
Financing activities:		
Increase (decrease) in short-term debt	(229)	69
Proceeds from debt in excess of 90 days	198	462
Principal repayments in excess of 90 days	(351)	(495)
Dividends paid	(114)	(111)
Other—net	18	4
Net cash provided by (used in) financing activities	(478)	(71)
Effect of exchange rate changes on cash	24	16
Increase (decrease) in cash and cash equivalents	(9)	3
Cash and cash equivalents at beginning of year	75	72
Cash and cash equivalents at end of year	$ 66	$ 75

Source: Adapted from TRW Inc. 1992 annual report.

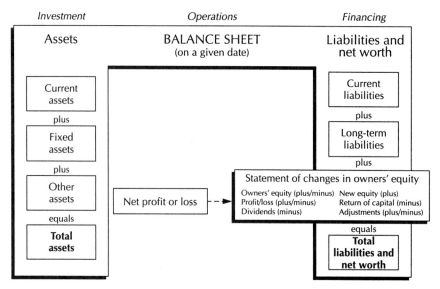

FIGURE 1–14
Statement of Changes in Owners' Equity
in Decisional Context

Management Decision Area

special analytical statement largely depend on how much the issuing company chooses to disclose beyond what's legally required.

Unless a company decides to provide specific information related to ownership accounts, the analyst may find it difficult to reconstruct the components of financial change from published data alone. Viewed in our context of performance assessment, the statement of changes in owners' equity thus can be clearly recognized as subsidiary information that helps us understand the financing sector of the balance sheet.

Again, TRW's consolidated statement of changes in owners' (shareholders') equity for the years ended December 31, 1992, and December 31, 1991, is given as an actual example in Figure 1–15. The format used by the company clearly displays the principal changes.

This portion of the chapter has provided an overview

FIGURE 1–15

TRW INC. AND SUBSIDIARIES

Statement of Changes in Shareholders' Investment

For the Years Ended December 31, 1992, and 1991

	1992 Shares (millions)	*Millions of Dollars*	*1991 Shares (millions)*	*Millions of Dollars*
Serial preference stock II:				
Series 1:				
Balance at January 1 and December 31	.1	$ –	.1	$ –
Series 3:				
Balance at January 1 and December 31	.1	1	.1	1
Common stock:				
Balance at January 1	61.6	38	60.8	38
Sale of stock and other	1.3	1	.8	–
Balance at December 31 ...	62.9	39	61.6	38
Other capital:				
Balance at January 1		184		185
Sale of stock and other		38		(1)
Balance at December 31 ...		222		184
Retained earnings:				
Balance at January 1		1,377		1,628
Net earnings (loss)		(156)		(140)
Dividends declared:				
Preference stock		(1)		(1)
Common stock ($1.84 and $1.80 per share)		(115)		(110)
Balance at December 31 ...		1,105		1,377
Cumulative translation adjustments:				
Balance at January 1		98		98
Translation adjustments		(45)		–
Balance at December 31 ...		53		98
Treasury shares—cost in excess of par value:				
Balance at January 1		(13)		(43)
ESOP funding		12		26
Purchase of shares		(6)		(1)
Sold under stock options ...		3		5
Balance at December 31 ...		(4)		(13)
Total shareholders' investment:		$1,416		$1,685

Source: Adapted from TRW Inc. 1992 annual report.

38

of the nature and relationships of the four major financial statements as the background for analysis of the results of management decisions and their impact on funds movements. Within our decisional framework these four statements can be combined to help us visualize their coverage and relationship as an integrated whole.

Note that Figure 1–16's generalized overview

FIGURE 1–16
Generalized Overview of Financial Statements

Management Decision Area

| Investment | Operations | Financing |

| Assets | BALANCE SHEET (on a given date) | Liabilities and net worth |

Current assets	OPERATING STATEMENT	Current liabilities
plus	Revenues	plus
Fixed assets	less — Cost of sales	Long-term liabilities
plus accounting write-offs	equals — Gross margin	plus
Other assets	less — Operating expenses	Statement of changes in equity
	equals — Operating earnings/loss	Owners' equity
equals		equals
Total assets	less — Income taxes	**Total liabilities and net worth**
	equals — Net profit or loss	

FUNDS FLOW STATEMENT

| **Investments** | **Operations** | **Financing** |
| Investments (increases) in all types of assets are uses of funds; disinvestments (reductions) in all types of assets are sources of funds. | Profitable operations are a source of funds; losses drain funds from the system. Accounting write-offs or write-ups do not affect funds; their profit impact must be adjusted for. | Trade credit and new financing (increases in liabilities and equity) are sources of funds; repayments of liabilities, dividends, and returns of capital are uses of funds. |

displays not only what the four statements cover in terms of key information, but also how they're related, being derived from the same basic information. The dotted lines indicate the impact of any accounting write-offs.

To summarize, the balance sheet describes a firm's financial condition at a point in time. It shows the cumulative effect of previous decisions and includes profits or losses for preceding periods. The operating statement matches revenues and expenses for a specific period, including write-offs and allocations. It provides more detail about the elements making up the aftertax net profit and loss that was recorded in arriving at the owners' equity on the balance sheet. In contrast to the two previous statements, the funds flow statement is a dynamic look in that it highlights the *net changes* in assets, liabilities, and ownership accounts over a specific period. It allows the analyst to see the pattern of funds uses and sources that resulted from management's decisions concerning investments, operations, and financing. The statement recognizes and corrects for the fact that write-offs and amortization of assets acquired in the past are bookkeeping entries and don't affect funds. Finally, the statement of changes in owners' equity gives more details concerning the change in ownership accounts as recorded on the beginning and ending balance sheets.

Within the limitations of accounting rules and accountant's judgments, financial statements are an effort to reflect, with reasonable consistency, all business transactions that, over time, result in a net improvement or worsening of the economic value of owners' equity. As ensuing chapters will relate, the manager or analyst must review these statements, carefully interpret their meaning, and apply standard techniques as well as explicit judgments in evaluating the financial and economic performance of the company under review.

THE CONTEXT OF FINANCIAL ANALYSIS

Now that we've explored the broad background of business system dynamics and the nature of financial statements describing performance and values, it's useful to provide one more context that allows us to put this book's materials into proper perspective. It will reinforce a number of the references we've made earlier to the judgmental aspects of financial analysis.

Managers or analysts performing various kinds of financial analysis normally do so with a specific purpose in mind. During the process of analysis, they use financial statements, special analyses, data bases, and other information sources to derive reasonable judgments about past, current, and prospective conditions of a business and the effectiveness of its management.

We must recognize that not only the person performing the analysis and interpretation has a purpose and viewpoint, but so do the preparers and providers of the various types of information on which the analysis is based. During our discussion of the nature of financial statements, we referred to the accounting rules and principles governing the compilation of these documents, and to the need to allow for the specific biases introduced by them. This isn't to say that financial statements are right or wrong in an absolute sense, but rather that the information may have to be adjusted in some cases or even discarded in others to suit the purpose of the analysis.

Figure 1–17's descriptive overview represents the key objectives of three major financial/economic processes as a context for understanding the differences in data generation and analytical orientation involved in each. The table identifies financial accounting, investor analysis, and managerial economics as processes whose objectives differ, but which frequently have to draw on each other for information and data. We must consider the orientation and focus of these processes when

FIGURE 1–17
The Different Objectives of Financial/Economic Processes

Financial Accounting	*Investor Analysis*	*Managerial Economics*
Profit determination	**Financial information**	**Activity economics**
• Revenue recognition	• Adjustment process	• Task analysis
• Expense recognition	• Trend analysis	• Economic allocation
• Cost allocation	• Profit projection	• Contribution analysis
• Profit definition	• Cash flow projection	• Trade-off determination
Value determination	**Comparative data**	**Resource effectiveness**
• Historical costs	• Industry analysis	• Investment base
• Conservatism	• Competitor analysis	• Capital investments
• Equity as residual value	• Economic conditions	• Capital divestments
• Contingency recognition	• Adjustment areas	• Human resources
Tax determination	**Market analysis**	**Shareholder value**
• Legal data requirements	• Share price patterns	• Cash flow patterns
• Income/expense timing	• Market trends	• Cost of capital
• Tax management issues	• Value drivers	• Investor expectations
• Statement adjustments	• Market models	• Risk/reward trade-off

information is shared between them, or exchanged for use by any one of them. Our ultimate aim is to analyze and judge business problems, company performance, and shareholder value in *economic* terms, which requires careful adjustment of data and analyses that often were prepared with different objectives in mind.

When we speak of financial analysis within the scope of this book, our emphasis is on the objectives of the middle column (investor analysis), but we must include many aspects of the right column (managerial economics) because the two areas are related. But a large portion of the data we use are originated on the left, by financial accounting, while some are obtained from the right, from internal data bases on which managerial economics depends.

As we implied earlier, there are three major objectives in financial accounting as governed by professional standards and SEC regulations:

- Profit determination.
- Value determination.
- Tax determination.

42

Profit determination focuses on recognizing when revenue is earned during a period, and how to determine matching costs and expenses. A clear distinction must be drawn between the recording of a revenue or expense transaction, and the actual receipt or disbursement of cash, which may lag the recognition of the revenue or expense item by days or months. Similarly, costs incurred in the past may be allocated to current or future periods with the objective of determining a profit figure that matches only "recognized" revenue and expense elements. This has significant implications for funds flow analysis, as we'll see.

Value determination rests on the principle of historical costs, a conservative concept using transaction evidence as the value criterion. When economic values of assets change, adjustments in these recorded values are made for reductions only, in readily identifiable areas such as accounts receivable that have become uncollectible, or inventories where market value has declined below cost. Increases are recognized only when assets are sold, not while they're being held. The business's residual value—that is, its recorded ownership equity (book value)—therefore may over time bear little resemblance to the equity's market value (economic value). In addition, the growing emphasis on recording contingencies of all kinds introduces a bias in value because only potential liabilities are established, but not potential gains. Examples are long-term pension and benefit obligations, and potential liabilities arising from all types of operational, legal, and contractual issues.

Meanwhile, appreciation of assets like land, buildings, natural resources, and technological advances is left unrecognized until they're disposed of. As the wave of takeovers in the 1980s demonstrated, careful analysis of the target companies' balance sheets uncovered massive unrecorded potential gain to be realized in the eventual breakup of the acquired companies.

Tax determination is governed by the legal requirements of the current tax code, which often involves
modified principles of income and expense recognition,
including disallowance of certain costs and expenses.
Tax rules tend to speed up the timing of revenue recognition versus financial accounting rules, and also to
spread out expense recognition. The rules are clearly
intended to enhance current tax receipts. Differences
between financial accounting for reporting purposes
and tax accounting give rise to tax management issues in
companies and industries where the amounts involved
are significant enough to affect actual decisions on investments, operations, and financing.

From the standpoint of financial analysis, the important question is tax accounting's effect on the financial
statements used for analysis. As we'll see, the amount of
taxes actually paid versus the amount shown on the
operating statement can differ materially; adjustments
made on the balance sheet in the form of deferred taxes
to compensate for this situation may signal significant
funds movements.

Investor analysis in this context has three objectives:

- Interpretation of financial information.
- Use of comparative data.
- Analysis of financial markets.

Interpretation of financial information essentially involves analysis of financial statements and other financial data about a company to assess and project its
performance and value. The key judgments focus on the
adjustment process through which data reported under
accounting principles are modified or converted into information that permits economic and funds flow judgments to be made. Only rarely can financial data as
generally provided be used in their exact form to derive
analytical judgments. Applying the various ratios and
relationships discussed in Chapter 2, for example, often

leads to significant questions and actual adjustments during the process of analysis.

Trend analysis uses various series of adjusted past data to look for and analyze significant changes in magnitudes and ratio relationships over time, and becomes one of the bases of profit projection. Finally, the ultimate adjustment leads to an analysis of the cash flows generated by the business, and to the projection of these cash flows as an indicator of economic performance and value.

Comparative data are an essential part of financial analysis as they help put judgments about a particular company or business in perspective. By implication, all judgments made about performance and value are relative to the standards and perceptions of the analyst; comparable data assist in confirming these judgments. Industry analysis involves selecting relevant groupings of companies and compiling appropriate data and ratios (sometimes available in data bases) against which to measure attributes of the company being studied. The important issue here again is the need to interpret and adjust the financial data so that they match the data used for the original company.

Competitor analysis applies the same process to individual companies that compete directly with the business. Economic conditions are brought into the analysis as a backdrop for explaining past variations, and as a guide to projecting future performance and value.

Market analysis involves the study and projection of the pattern of share prices of the company and its competitors relative to stock market trends. Here financial analysis becomes a bridge between published financial statements reporting accounting performance and market trends reflecting a firm's economic value. The analyst focuses on the value drivers behind the market value of the shares, which are basic economic variables like cash flow generated and relative cost effectiveness of the business. Market models range from simple relationships of key variables and share price to complex computer simulations, in an effort to determine current and potential shareholder value created by the business.

Managerial economics encompasses three basic objectives:

- Determining activity economics.
- Determining resource effectiveness.
- Calculating shareholder value.

All three areas are focused on economic insights that will allow management to make decisions that will enhance shareholder value. In that sense the orientation of managerial economics is closely allied to the basic purpose of financial analysis as we define it here. In fact, the third objective directly supports the ultimate question asked by financial analysis, namely, whether new value is being created by the business. Consequently, we'll address the most important areas of the second and third objectives in later chapters.

Activity economics is a summary term for analyses that define and establish economically relevant data to describe and judge the relative attractiveness of any operational aspect of a business and its subdivisions. Among these, task analysis amounts to determining the true economic cost of a task, such as the series of steps required to provide a service or the phases of a manufacturing process. This type of analytical process goes far beyond cost accounting principles which often fall short of a proper economic allocation of jointly used resources or often don't recognize all aspects of a task or an activity.

Contribution analysis refers to measuring the difference between revenues created and the economic costs involved in a given line of business or a particular product or service. Such information on economic contribution assists management in planning which combination of activities will create the most economic value. The choices always require economic trade-offs based on economic data, not accounting information. A new field of analysis called *activity-based accounting* is gaining wide acceptance as a means of gathering data relevant to this purpose.

Resource effectiveness addresses the important question of how well, from an economic standpoint, the resources employed by a business are being utilized or will be utilized in the future. The process includes measuring the returns from the existing investment base in place, gauging the justification of new capital investments or capital divestments, and measuring the returns from human resources. As we mentioned earlier, these questions will be detailed in Chapters 3 and 6, and the need to consider an economic basis for these judgments will be highlighted.

Shareholder value creation, management's ultimate goal, is measured by means of a combination of past and projected cash flow patterns, the cost of capital of the particular company, and the return expectations of investors for this type of business. In essence, shareholder value creation becomes a tangible expression of the risk/reward trade-off the investor has to judge when investing in a firm's equity. Company management must assess at all times whether its strategies, policies, and decisions are likely to serve investors' interest by creating additional shareholder value. (See Chapters 7 and 9.)

SUMMARY

In this chapter we've provided a conceptual overview of the business system as a dynamic interrelationship of funds flows activated by management decisions. We recognized three basic decision areas—investment, operations, and financing—that underlie all business activity.

The impact of decisions in any or all of these areas on the system was shown. The systems view also demonstrated how decisions in each area are affected by key strategies and policies, and how consistency in these was essential to optimize the system to achieve the ultimate goal, enhancing shareholder value. The overview also provided a first look at major areas of financial and economic analysis, and how these relate to management strategies and decisions.

A second conceptual overview introduced the major financial statements commonly prepared by companies, and their relationship both to each other and to the three decisional areas defined earlier. We also gave a first indication how the origin, rationale, and limitations of financial statements affect the potential for analyzing performance and value.

The third conceptual discussion reinforced the context within which financial analysis takes place, and provided an overview of the various objectives of analysis and data preparation. This was done to highlight the need to build a bridge between accounting-oriented data and the ultimate objective of financial analysis, judging business performance and shareholder value in economic terms. Adjustment areas were suggested as prerequisites for developing useful information. The analyst's judgmental role was emphasized.

The chapter serves as a contextual preview of the various analytical concepts explored in the remainder of this book. It's intended to reinforce the point that financial analysis isn't a free-standing activity or an end in itself, but rather an effort to understand and judge the characteristics and performance of a highly interrelated system of financial relationships.

SELECTED REFERENCES

Deschamps, B., and D. Mehta. *Chief Financial Officer: Strategy Formulation and Implementation.* New York: John Wiley & Sons, 1988.

Johnson, H. Thomas, and Robert S. Kaplan. *Relevance Lost: The Rise and Fall of Management Accounting.* Boston: Harvard Business School Press, 1987.

Porter, Michael E. *Competitive Advantage: Creating and Sustaining Superior Performance.* New York: Free Press, 1985.

Rappaport, Alfred. *Creating Shareholder Value.* New York: Free Press, 1986.

Vancil, Richard F., and Benjamin R. Makela, eds. *The CFO Handbook.* Homewood Ill.: Dow Jones-Irwin, 1986.

2 MANAGING OPERATING FUNDS

This chapter deals with key issues surrounding the flow of funds through a business, that is, how to manage in specific terms the various funds required for day-to-day operations. Having laid the foundation with a systems overview of funds flows in Chapter 1, we can begin the detailed discussion of analytical techniques with this subject.

Managers must understand the specific funds movements caused within the business system by their daily decisions on investment, operations, and financing. These decisions, in one form or another, affect the company's ability to pay its bills, obtain credit from suppliers and lenders, extend credit to its customers, and maintain a level of operations that matches the demand for the company's products or services, supported by appropriate investments.

As we've said, every decision has a monetary impact on the ongoing cycle of uses and sources of funds.

Management's job is to maintain at all times an appropriate balance between the inflows and outflows of funds, and to plan for the funds impact of any changes in operations—whether caused by their own decisions or by outside influences.

Properly managing operating funds is therefore fundamental to successful business performance. New businesses often find that balancing operating funds needs and sources is much like an ongoing struggle for plain survival. Yet, even well-established companies must devote considerable management time and effort to balance the funding of their operations as they strive for optimal economic results.

As we'll demonstrate, proper management of operating funds requires a thorough understanding of the systems impact of investment, operating, and financing decisions. Furthermore, managers must understand the effect on funds uses and sources of different basic operating patterns of the business, such as seasonal peaks and valleys, cyclical variations, rapid growth, or gradual decline. Depending on the specific pattern of a company's operations, funds flows will behave in quite different ways.

In addition, we must remember that managing short-term working capital components (such as receivables, inventories, and payables) must be carried out within the firm's longer-term financial framework. Working capital changes that arise as a matter of course during ongoing operations also affect long-term investments and long-term capital sources, as Chapter 1's systems discussion suggested.

This chapter therefore focuses on the broader issue of *operating funds* management. In addition to managing working capital (commonly defined as the difference between current assets and current liabilities), the task of balancing operating funds flows requires dealing with (1) changing cash flow patterns from periodic profits and losses and (2) the impact that current decisions on new investment and financing choices have on funds.

In Chapter 3 we'll examine a variety of performance measures drawn from financial statements, which we know to be periodic summaries of financial condition and operating results. As we'll see, these summaries often mask peaks and valleys of funds movements—a seasonal buildup causing critical near-term financing needs, for example—because these points lie within the period spanned by the statements. In fact, managing a business is an ongoing day-to-day process that must deal with peaks and valleys of funds flows at the point in time when they occur.

This chapter describes in specific terms how funds cycle through a business, these movements' implications, and how to identify the critical financial variables that must be weighed in making daily operating decisions. We'll demonstrate how widely different types of operations impact funds movements, and also discuss key accounting issues, such as inventory costing and methods of depreciation. We'll then return to the interpretation of funds flow statements, using our sample of TRW's 1991 and 1992 financial data, and examine the major types of analytical steps needed to make funds flow statements meaningful.

FUNDS FLOW CYCLES

Businesses vary widely in orientation, size, structure, and products or services, but they all experience operating funds cycles in their own specific fashion. To illustrate the simplest of circumstances, let's observe a solitary ice cream vendor who sells cones from his cart for cash. To carry on his business, he has to provide an inventory on wheels which he slowly converts into cash as the day progresses. Let's also assume that he invested his own cash at the beginning of the day to purchase ice cream from his supplier. He obviously hopes to recoup these funds as well as earn a markup for profit by the end of the day.

Our vendor's decision to commit his own cash to inventory is visualized in Figure 2–1. Note that the diagram reflects the three decision areas we discussed in Chapter 1. The initial cash investment is financed from owners' equity, and in turn the cash is used to invest in the first day's inventory.

If our vendor was short of cash, he could sign an IOU at the supplier's, promising to pay for the inventory the next morning using the day's cash receipts as funding. This assumption modifies the diagram, as shown in Figure 2–2. Here the creditor's funds effectively supplant the owners' funds, if only for a single day.

In any event, our vendor's funds cycle is very short. The initial investment in inventory, funded with his own cash or with credit from his supplier, is followed by numerous individual cash sales during the day. These receipts build up his cash balance for the following day's operations.

We've represented the first day of operations— assuming the vendor financed himself—in Figure 2–3, where cash on hand is built up by the sales receipts, where inventory is drawn down during the day, and where the difference between sales and the cost of the ice cream sold represents profit earned—which in turn increases ownership equity.

The following morning our vendor uses the accumulated cash either to replenish his inventory or to pay off the supplier so that he'll be extended credit for another day's cycle. Any profit he earned above the cost of the goods sold will of course be his to keep—or to invest in more inventory for the next day.

Figure 2–4 shows the alternative funds movements that would arise if our vendor had used supplier credit for the first day. He would find that the amount of cash left after repayment of the initial supplier credit would

FIGURE 2-1
ICE CREAM VENDOR
Initial Cash Investment to Start the Day

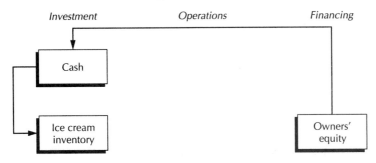

Management Decision Context

FIGURE 2-2
ICE CREAM VENDOR
Initial Use of Credit to Start the Day

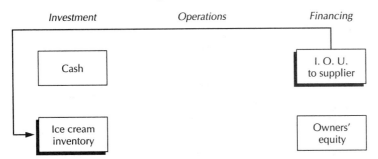

Management Decision Context

purchase only a portion of the next day's inventory; that is, his remaining cash balance would be equal to the profit he made during the first day. To continue operating on the second day he would have to decide whether to (1) ask for renewed credit from his supplier or (2) provide the additional funds required from any resources of his own that aren't yet committed to the business.

The funds cycles of larger and more structured businesses differ from this situation only in complexity, not in concept. Even for the most complex conglomerate,

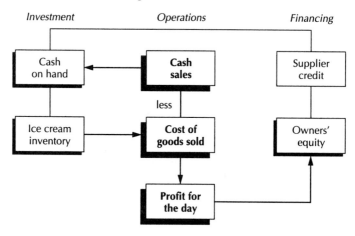

FIGURE 2–3
ICE CREAM VENDOR
Profitable Operations During the First Day

Management Decision Context

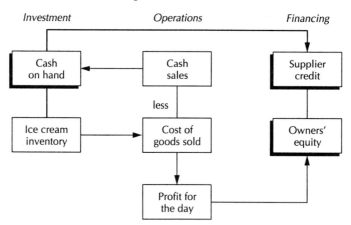

FIGURE 2–4
ICE CREAM VENDOR
Repayment of Credit After Profitable First Day

Management Decision Context

the ultimate form of settlement of any transaction is cash. Meanwhile, however, such a company's operational funds cycle usually involves a great variety of partially offsetting credit extensions, changes in inventories, transformations of assets, and so on that precede the cash collections or payments.

In essence, any funds cycle arises because of a series of lags in the timing of business transactions. Our ice cream vendor has a lag of only a few hours between the purchase of his inventory and its conversion into cash through many small transactions. In contrast, a large manufacturer may have a lag of months between the time a product is made in the factory and the ultimate collection of the selling price from customers who purchased on credit. Management must always plan for and find financing for company funds that are tied up because of these timing lags.

To illustrate the nature of the concept, we'll explore in detail two processes:

- The funds cycle of a simplified manufacturing operation.
- The funds cycle for selling the manufactured products.

We've separated these processes for purposes of illustration and discussion, even though the two funds cycles are always intertwined in any ongoing business that both produces and sells products. The sales cycle alone, of course, applies to any retail, wholesale, or trading operation that purchases goods for resale.

The Funds Cycle for Manufacturing

To keep the illustration simple, let's assume that the Widget Manufacturing Company has just begun operations, producing widgets for eventual sale. Figure 2–5 shows the company's funds flow cycle in the form of an overview, using only a minimum of detail. We've again

FIGURE 2–5
Funds Flow Cycle for Manufacturing

Management Decision Context

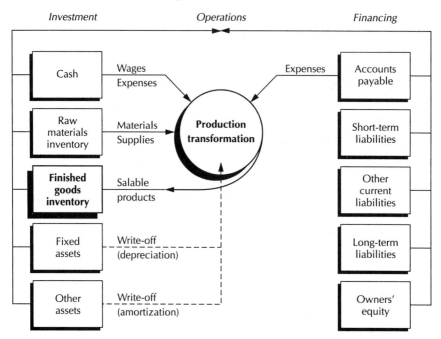

arranged the diagram to reflect the three management decision areas.

As is readily apparent, the company was initially financed through a combination of owners' equity, long-term debt, and short-term debt of three kinds:

- Accounts payable due vendors of materials and supplies.
- Some short-term loans from banks.
- Other current liabilities, such as accrued wages and taxes.

The initial investments are fixed assets (such as plant facilities), other assets (such as patents and licenses), and three kinds of current assets:

- Cash.

- Raw materials inventory.
- Finished goods inventory.

Of course, the last of these won't come about until the plant actually starts producing widgets. We can assume that long-term debt and owners' equity are the logical sources of funds for investing in plant and equipment because they match the long-term funding commitment involved. In contrast, the short-term loan most likely provided the ready cash needed to start operations. Materials and supplies were bought with short-term trade credit extended by the company's vendors.

As production begins, a basic transformation process takes place. Some of the available cash is used to pay weekly wages and various ongoing expenses. Materials and supplies are withdrawn from inventory and used in manufacturing. Some operating inputs, like power and fuel oil, are obtained on credit and are temporarily financed through accounts payable.

Depreciation from use of the plant and equipment is charged against the transformation process, and licenses are similarly amortized. As widgets are finished on the factory floor, they're moved into the warehouse and become reflected in the growing finished goods inventory account.

In the absence of any widget sales, the production process continuously transforms cash, raw materials, expense accruals, and trade credit into a growing buildup of finished goods inventory. A fraction of the original cost of fixed and other assets is also transformed into finished goods—even though no funds are moved in this case—by means of an accounting write-off which merely affects the company's books, but not the cash flows of the production process.

What are the financial implications of this transformation? In our illustration the operational funds flows occurring after the business was established only affected the working capital accounts. Cash and raw materials, which were among the initial commitments of funds, have been drawn down and thus became sources of funding for the production process. An additional source has been found in increased trade credit and in expenses accrued but not yet paid.

The major use of these funds sources was the buildup of finished goods inventory. Unless the company can eventually turn finished goods into cash through successful sales to its customers, the continued inventory buildup will drain both the cash reserves and the stores of raw material. These would have to be replenished by new infusions of credit or owners' equity—or both. Adding to the cash drain is the obligation to begin, at some point, the repayment of accounts payable for trade credit incurred, on normal terms like 30 or 45 days from the invoice date.

From a funds flow standpoint, several timing lags are significant in our example:

- A supply of raw materials sufficient for several days of operation has to be kept on hand to ensure uninterrupted manufacturing.
- A physical lag in the number of days required to produce a widget causes a buildup of an inventory of work in process, that is, widgets in various stages of completion.
- A sufficient number of widgets must be produced and kept at all times in finished goods inventory to support an ongoing sales and service effort.

The combined funds commitment caused by these lags has to be financed through resources provided by owners and creditors on a continuous basis.

Offsetting this funding requirement—but only in part—is the length of time over which credit is extended by the company's suppliers. This is a favorable lag because purchases of raw material and supplies as well as certain other expenses will be financed by vendors for 30 or 45 days or for whatever length of time is common in the industry. New credit will continue to be extended as repayments are made of the accounts coming due.

Another significant favorable lag is the temporary funding provided by company employees whose wages are paid periodically, thereby in effect extending credit to their employer for a week, two weeks, or even a month, depending on the company's payroll pattern. Such funding is recognized among current liabilities as "accrued wages." Other expense accruals, such as income taxes owed, will similarly provide temporary funds.

As we observed before, however, the buildup of finished goods in the warehouse can't go on indefinitely. At some point sales revenues become essential to replenish cash to meet the company's obligations as they become due. Thus, we must next examine the funds implications of the selling process to complete the picture.

The Funds Cycle for Sales

The funds flows caused by selling widgets can similarly be examined with our decisional framework (Figure 2–6). The operations segment in the center of the diagram now includes the main elements of an operating statement:

- Sales revenue.
- Cost of goods sold.
- Selling and other expenses.
- Net income.

The selling cycle is based on another major timing lag, which arises from the extension of credit to the company's customers. If the widgets were sold for cash, collection would, of course, be instantaneous. If the company provides normal trade credit, however, the

FIGURE 2–6
Funds Flow Cycle for Sales

Management Decision Context

collection of accounts receivable will be delayed by the terms given, such as 30, 45, or whatever number of days is common practice in the industry.

This sales lag, like the lags incurred during production, must be financed continuously because for any given sales volume, the equivalent of 30, 40, or 50 days' worth of sales will always be outstanding. As accounts becoming due are collected, new credit will be extended to customers on current sales—just as was the case with the vendors supplying materials and other items to the company itself.

Cost of goods sold represents the value of the widgets withdrawn from finished goods inventory, each of which contains a share of the labor, raw material, overhead, and other costs expended in its manufacture.

Selling expenses (which consist of the salaries of the sales force and marketing support staff plus advertising and promotional costs) will be paid partly in cash, partly with funds obtained from creditors. After these expenses have been subtracted from sales revenue, the resulting net income, subject to state and federal income taxes, will increase the owners' equity.

What are the funds flow implications of this picture? First, assuming that the company is maintaining a level volume of sales and manufacturing operations, management must plan for a continuous long-term commitment of funds to support the necessary level of working capital. This means that sufficient funds have to be provided (1) for storing raw materials and work in process to carry on production, (2) for a proper level of finished goods to support smooth sales and deliveries, and (3) for sufficient accounts receivable to permit credit extension to customers. Finally, a minimum level of cash must be maintained for punctual payment of currently due obligations.

In addition, the funds needed for any investment expenditures on fixed and other assets that support operations must be made available. Finally, arrangements have to be made for payment of declared dividends, for any scheduled repayment of debt, or for refinancing long-term obligations.

The sources of this financing will come only in part from accounts payable, which can usually support a portion of raw materials, supplies, and ongoing operating expenses in line with the normal number of days' credit extended by suppliers. The difference between the amount of funds continually tied up in inventories and receivables, and the funds provided by current accounts payable must come from sources that are relatively permanent, such as long-term debt and owners' equity— the latter augmented by aftertax profits or diminished by net losses.

The system's dynamics are such that the requirement

for operating funds will be constant as long as the business operates on a sustained level. But as we'll see, the level of this requirement will change when operating conditions themselves change.

VARIABILITY OF FUNDS FLOWS

So far we've assumed that our company, after start-up, has reached and maintained a fairly steady level of operations. Under these conditions, the funds cycle will also be stable. Unless there are significant changes in operating conditions or in the market area, the ongoing financing needed to support the operations will mainly depend on effective inventory management, sound management of customer credit, and prudent use of supplier credit as well as reliable relations with other lenders, such as banks. Also, profitable operations will generate funds that can be used as part of the funding pattern. Should there be any worsening in collections from customers, or any tightening of credit terms extended by suppliers or lenders, or a decline in profits, then the company's continuous funding needs will, of course, be increased.

Rarely does a company enjoy the steady state conditions that made financing operations so predictable in our simple example. In reality, several major external and internal factors can affect a business. Major internal forces, among others, center on management's ability to seize opportunities for growth or its inability to stem a decline in the company's volume of operations. Major external forces include seasonal variations and cyclical movements in the economy, which go beyond the impact of actions taken by the company's competitors. Each of these conditions has its own particular implications in terms of funds flow. We'll illustrate the most important of these.

Growth/Decline Variations

A pattern of ongoing growth in a business brings with it the need to fund the underlying expansion of financial requirements. Successful growth can't be achieved without providing for appropriate increases in working capital and other expenditures. Management must understand that these funds will be permanently tied up as long as growth continues or as long as operations remain at a given level. Profits from operations will normally provide only a portion of these funds needs.

Consider the following rules of thumb: If the business sells on 30-day credit, the value of each incremental layer of sales will be added to accounts receivable for 30 days and must be funded continually, because as prior sales are collected, higher current sales are added. Similarly, if the business turns over its inventory nine times per year, the value of the incremental cost of the goods sold will have to be added to inventories in the amount of 40 days' worth of inventory (360 ÷ 9), which must also be funded continually.

Offsetting this additional use of funds, but only in part, will be the incremental growth in accounts payable and other minor accruals. The credit extension by the company's vendors will amount to an equivalent value of the additional purchases for, say, 30 days, if that's the usual credit pattern. But because the required investment in accounts receivable and inventories is normally much more than twice the credit obtained from payables and accruals, it's clear that successful growth means the extensive funding of additional working capital. To this need must be added the funds required for any expansion of physical facilities to support the growth in sales.

To illustrate, let's take the simple example of a wholesaling company, which sells on average terms of 45 days, buys on terms of 40 days, and turns over its inventory every 30 days (12 times per year). Its cost of goods sold is 72 percent of sales, and its profit after taxes is 6 percent of sales. As the company grows, the funding consequences of every incremental $100 in annual sales are:

- Accounts receivable increase by $12.50 ($100 × 45/360).
- Inventories of goods purchased increase by $6.00 ($72 × 30/360).
- Accounts payable to vendors increase by $8.00 ($72 × 40/360).

The net effect is a funds increase of $10.50 in additional working capital ($12.50 + $6.00 − $8.00), assuming no other changes take place in the company's financial system. At the normal level of aftertax profits of 6 percent, the company could provide $6.00 of this funding need. Thus, a minimum of $4.50 would have to be financed for every $100 in additional sales.

The pattern of sales, operating assets (working capital plus fixed assets), and profits of the typical growing company looks something like Figure 2–7, where growth requires additional working capital every year as receivables and inventories expand, only partially offset by growing accounts payable. Periodically, new investments must be made in expanded facilities, as indicated by the jump in operating assets in 1992 and again in 1995. The asset column continues to grow as long as volume growth persists. Constant funding of this increase will be necessary through a combination of profit and other sources.

The dotted funding line indicates the total need for funds with which to finance growing operating assets, reduced by total aftertax profits in every year. An amount equal to depreciation is assumed to be spent on maintaining the facilities (a concept we used in Chapter 1's discussion of the financial system). No dividend payments have been allowed for in this line, which therefore understates the actual funding need. Note that

FIGURE 2-7
Typical Growth Pattern

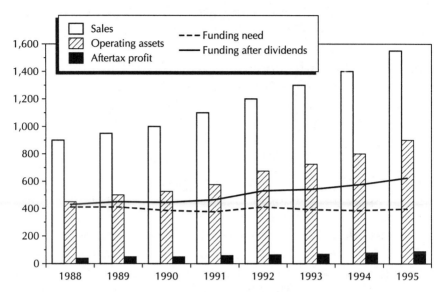

growing profits in the later years are able to gradually reduce the total requirements. But when dividend payments are provided for—in this case rising gradually from $20 in 1988 to $40 in 1995—what was essentially a level funding need becomes a growing requirement for permanent funding, as shown in the upward movement of the solid line.

What should be clear is that successful growth typically calls for a permanent and even growing funding commitment, which must likely be financed over the long term through the use of owners' equity and long-term debt. Frequently, reinvestment of profits alone isn't a sufficient source because in a high-growth business, the contribution from the profit margin may be far outweighed by the cumulative funding demands (as Chapter 5 details).

In the opposite case, when a business declines in volume and can actually be properly managed to undergo such shrinkage efficiently, the company will in fact turn into a strong generator of cash. Here the reverse of the growth situation prevails. As sales decline, management must deliberately seek to reduce operations, working capital, and other operating assets to match the decline in volume, thus releasing funds that had been tied up.

Figure 2–8 demonstrates this idealized situation. Note the dramatic decline in the basic funding needs, which turn into positive funds generation during the last two years. When dividend payments of as much as 50 percent of aftertax profits are assumed in every year, the funding requirements decline more slowly, but are still only a fraction of the level at the beginning of the period shown.

Basically, the business system's ability to release funds depends on the careful removal of layers of activity that no longer need to be supported. A proportional shrinkage of receivables and inventories, partly offset by declining payables, becomes the major potential cash source, apart from the disposal of other assets no longer needed. If the decline pattern becomes precipitous or

FIGURE 2–8
Managed Decline Pattern

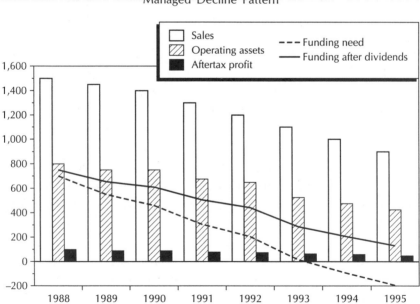

can't be managed properly, however, the specter of inventory markdowns, operating inefficiencies, and emergency actions will seriously impede the release of funds and real difficulties can arise.

Seasonal Variations

A fairly large number of industries experience distinct seasonal operating patterns (specific months or weeks of high sales followed by an often dramatic decline in demand). These ups and downs repeat themselves quite predictably. Examples are most common in retailing operations, many of which are geared to special holiday periods or specific customer segments with seasonal style or gift requirements. Producers of seasonal items (such as snowmobiles or bathing suits) will experience high fluctuations in demand. Similar patterns impact canneries that process specific crops or other seasonal foods.

Common to all seasonal businesses is a funds cycle with large short-term swings over the period of a year or less. The financial implications for management are obvious. During the low point of demand, ongoing operations have to be supported with funds from internal or external sources—unless the business can be shut down, as are some seasonal resorts. In most cases, inventories are gradually built up, either through production or through purchases from suppliers.

As was the case in our simple example earlier, funds for this buildup must come from credit, loans, and owners' equity. Once the selling activity begins, growing amounts of receivables due from customers receiving normal credit terms have to be funded by the company. Not until the first receivables are collected does cash start flowing back into the business. The financial lags are usually such that collection of the receivables from peak sales will occur well after the peak of funding requirements. Figure 2–9 demonstrates a typical seasonal pattern on a month-by-month basis, reflecting the

68

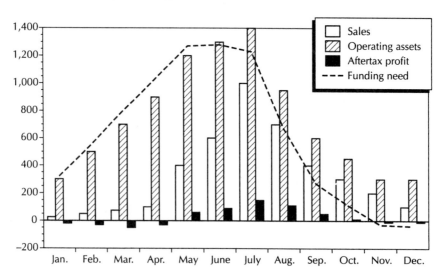

FIGURE 2–9
Typical Seasonal Pattern

dramatic rise and fall in funding needs before any dividends are considered.

As a result, management must make several critical decisions, among them the size of the buildup of inventories relative to anticipated demand, the level of operating and other expenditures during the different phases of the operating cycle, and the nature of the funding to finance the bulge in requirements. Allowances must be made for contingencies such as lower than expected demand or prices (or both), delays in collections from customers, or the time involved in arranging for short-term financing with banks and other lenders. Otherwise the business could find itself strapped because its own financial obligations must be met before collections are made.

In Chapter 3 we'll discuss applying turnover relationships and the "aging" of receivables as a means of judging the effectiveness of asset use by management. Under highly seasonal conditions, such relationships become unstable because lags and surges in the accounts within the period spanned by financial statements make ratio comparisons difficult.

A more direct evaluation of a seasonal business is possible through a month-to-month (or week-to-week) analysis of funds movements and a careful assessment of changes in the firm's funds cycle from peak to peak or trough to trough, instead of comparing quarterly or year-end financial statements.

Cyclical Variations

A variant of the seasonal cycle is the cyclical pattern of funds movements which reflects mainly external economic changes impacting the company over several years. These economic variations and specific industry cycles are generally long-term and not as regular and predictable as seasonal variations. Economic swings that affect a business or industry tend to bring many more variables to play, such as changes in raw materials prices and availability, competitive conditions in the marketplace, and capital investment needs. Nevertheless, the principles we observed in dealing with the seasonal pattern apply here as well.

Funds lags during a cyclical upturn or downturn tend to be magnified by the lag in decision making as management tries to gauge, from its day-to-day experience, whether the economy is undergoing a long-term change. For example, a sudden downturn in housing construction will leave many producers and wholesalers of building materials with inventories far in excess of slumping demand. As sales decrease and prices of lumber, plywood, and other commodities fall, management faces a funding crisis. Ongoing production operations will transform raw material into products that can't be sold; thus, production must be curtailed. Lower volume and prices will decrease the eventual cash flow from current sales, while collections from past higher sales will run out.

A cyclical downturn brings significant management

challenges. Managers must recognize—with reasonable confidence—that a turning point has indeed arrived, then proceed to manage inventories by curtailing purchases and production, and reduce ongoing costs wherever possible. Careful management of credit extended and used becomes critical as well. Meeting these challenges is easier said than done, because available data on current economic trends tend to lag significantly behind actual conditions.

Figure 2–10 demonstrates a typical cyclical pattern, where sales swing with economic conditions, but operating asset levels lag these changes due to the factors we just mentioned.

Note the steady increase in funding needs during the decline phase, brought about by a combination of rising investment (mostly working capital) and plummeting profits. If dividends are maintained at the $30 level, and if we assume that these are paid every year, the funding

FIGURE 2–10
Typical Cyclical Pattern

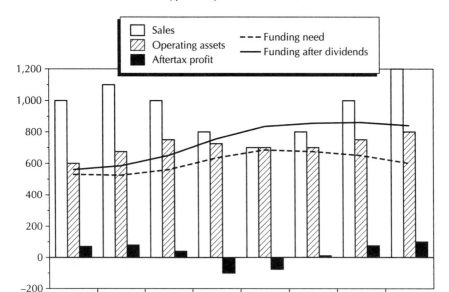

line rises to a new high, indicating that the company can't make up for the funds drain of the cyclical decline.

In the cyclical upswing, lags in decision making may result in insufficient inventory and production levels as sales volume surges. To compensate, extra shifts or outside purchases may be used, even though the costs incurred are typically higher than normal and depress profitability. Growing sales will also raise the amount of credit extended to customers. Thus, a cyclical boom will likely require the infusion of additional capital to provide the increased working capital needed and to finance increased physical operations. The latter may involve additional investment in plant and facilities.

Overall it may be said that a cyclical upswing will usually require an increase in medium-to long-term financing to support added levels of working capital and other financial requirements, while a downswing will first result in rising inventories—until management can adjust its operations—and then begin to release cash, which can be used to repay credit obligations. This condition will hold only if working capital and production levels are carefully managed downward, however.

In summary, variability in funds flows results from management actions, external conditions, or both. A business operating in a steady state has a permanent stock of working capital as well as properties, facilities, equipment, and other assets. As a general rule of thumb, the amount of funds tied up in current assets far exceeds trade credit sources and normal short-term borrowings. Thus, introducing any significant variability in the level of operations can cause major shifts in a company's financial condition from changes in working capital alone. In addition, funding for other needs (such as capital investments and major spending programs) must be superimposed on this pattern. In Chapter 4 we'll discuss these issues in the context of the techniques of forecasting funds requirements.

Generalized Funds Flow Model

At this point it's useful once again to examine the overall relationships of funds movements in a generalized framework. The diagram is applicable to any business, large or small. In Figure 2–11 we've added flow lines which show the potential funds movements and linkages between the main accounts of the balance sheet and the operating statement. A summary of sources and uses in terms of our familiar management decision context is given at the bottom of the diagram. This representation will be a useful reference when we discuss some of the more technical aspects of constructing funds flow statements in the last section of this chapter.

FIGURE 2–11
Generalized Funds Flow Diagram

Management Decision Context

Investments (increases) in all types of assets are uses of funds; reductions in assets are sources of funds.

Profitable operations are a source of funds; losses drain funds from the system. **Note:** Accounting write-offs do not affect funds and must be adjusted for (reversed).

Trade credit, new financing (increase in liabilities), and new equity are sources of funds; repayments, dividends, and returns of capital are uses of funds.

FUNDS FLOW STATEMENT REFINEMENTS

Having provided the basic concepts of how funds flow through a business, we're now ready to examine in more detail the construction of actual funds flow statements. Companies that are publicly held and publish regular financial statements are required by the SEC to provide a statement of funds flows along with balance sheets and operating statements. Where such statements aren't readily available, however, or in situations where the analyst wishes to project future funds movements, we must understand the basic principles and adjustments required to develop meaningful funds flow statements.

For the remainder of this chapter we'll therefore go through the process of developing a funds flow statement, show the major steps involved, and discuss the key accounting aspects (such as write-offs and other noncash adjustments) that have to be considered when transforming the accounting information on the financial statements into the funds flow pattern we're interested in. For this purpose, we'll again use TRW Inc.'s 1992 and 1991 balance sheets and operating statements originally shown in Chapter 1 as Figures 1–9 and 1–11. We'll work back from these statements to develop a derived funds flow statement, which we can then compare to the one published by TRW.

As we'll see, some of the adjustments must be made with our own assumptions, because we don't have the company's detailed records. Our own version of the funds flow statement will approximate, but not be identical to, the key funds figures shown in TRW's actual published statement.

We'll begin with a look at the straightforward funds movements taken directly from differences in balance sheet items between the two dates. Then we'll examine in greater detail three commonly encountered refinements in funds flow analysis:

- Adjustments to retained earnings (owners' equity).
- Adjustments to net income.
- Adjustments to net fixed assets.

TRW's consolidated balance sheets (Figure 2–12) include changes in the accounts between the two balance sheet dates. To develop a funds flow statement, we must classify these changes as funds "uses" and "sources." We do this in Figure 2–13, where increases and decreases in assets and liabilities are assigned to the appropriate categories, following rules we developed earlier.

But some balance sheet categories are too broad for our purpose. As a result, several funds flows can't be specifically delineated: (1) Net profit (or loss) from operations isn't recognized as such, but is part of the net change in retained earnings. (2) Although we know that cash *dividends* were paid, these too are immersed in the net change in retained earnings. (3) We also know that depreciation and amortization were sizable, but at this point these charges are buried in the changes in the respective accounts for accumulated depreciation and amortization. TRW's statement of earnings (Figure 2–14) covers these elements. (4) Finally, we know that there were significant investments in facilities as well as major dispositions of facilities and certain lines of business.

From Figure 2–13's simple sources and uses statement, we can observe the broad financial implications of a major restructuring begun by TRW in 1991. The major funds uses were (1) a reduction of long-term debt, which was an announced goal of the restructuring process, (2) a net reduction of retained earnings, which arose from a combination of charges for restructuring and mandated changes in accounting for future employee benefits, (3) a decrease in short-term debt, and (4) a reduction of deferred income taxes.

The key net funds sources were (1) an increase in long-term liabilities, (2) decreases in both receivables and inventories, and (3) an increase in accrued expenses

FIGURE 2-12
TRW INC. AND SUBSIDIARIES
Consolidated Balance Sheets at December 31, 1992, and 1991
($ millions)

	1992	1991	Change
Assets			
Current assets:			
Cash and cash equivalents	$ 66	$ 75	− $ 9
Accounts receivable	1,289	1,356	− 67
Inventories	422	512	− 90
Prepaid expenses	69	61	+ 8
Deferred income taxes	270	258	+ 12
Total current assets	2,116	2,262	− 146
Property, plant, and equipment at cost	5,052	5,010	+ 42
Less: Allowances for depreciation and amortization	2,741	2,686	+ 55
Total property, plant, and equipment—net	2,311	2,324	− 13
Intangible assets:			
Intangibles arising from acquisitions	552	561	− 9
Capitalized data files and other	464	420	+ 44
	1,016	981	+ 35
Less: Accumulated amortization	299	266	+ 33
Total intangible assets—net	717	715	+ 2
Other assets	314	334	− 20
Total assets	$5,458	$5,635	− 177
Liabilities and shareholders' investment			
Current liabilities:			
Short-term debt	$ 260	$ 407	− 147
Accrued compensation	286	298	− 12
Trade accounts payable	583	567	+ 16
Other accruals	752	620	+ 132
Dividends payable	30	28	+ 2
Income taxes	85	32	+ 53
Current portion of long-term debt	16	30	− 14
Total current liabilities	2,012	1,982	+ 30
Long-term liabilities	804	251	+ 553
Long-term debt	941	1,213	− 272
Deferred income taxes	222	440	− 218
Minority interests in subsidiaries	63	64	− 1
Shareholders' investment:			
Serial preference stock II	1	1	0
Common stock	39	38	+ 1
Other capital	222	184	+ 38
Retained earnings	1,105	1,377	− 272
Cumulative translation adjustments	53	98	− 45
Treasury shares—cost in excess of par	(4)	(13)	− 9
Total shareholders' investment	1,416	1,685	− 269
Total liabilities and shareholders' investment	$5,458	$5,635	− 177

Source: Adapted from 1992 TRW Inc. annual report.

FIGURE 2-13
TRW INC. AND SUBSIDIARIES
Statement of Balance Sheet Changes
For the Year Ended December 31, 1992
($ millions)

Sources:

Decrease in cash and cash equivalents	$ 9
Decrease in accounts receivable	67
Decrease in inventories	90
Increase in allowances for depreciation	55
Decrease in intangibles from acquisitions	9
Increase in accumulated amortization	33
Decrease in other assets	20
Increase in trade accounts payable	16
Increase in other accruals	132
Increase in dividends payable	2
Increase in income taxes payable	53
Increase in long-term liabilities	553
Increase in common stock	1
Increase in other capital	38
Decrease in treasury shares	9
	$1,087

Uses:

Increase in prepaid expenses	$ 8
Increase in deferred income tax assets	12
Increase in property, plant, and equipment	42
Increase in capitalized data files	44
Decrease in short-term debt	147
Decrease in accrued compensation	12
Decrease in current portion of long-term debt	14
Decrease in long-term debt	272
Decrease in deferred income taxes	218
Decrease in minority interests in subsidiaries	1
Decrease in retained earnings	272
Decrease in cumulative translation adjustments	45
	$1,087

FIGURE 2–14
TRW INC. AND SUBSIDIARIES
Statement of Earnings
For the Years Ended December 31, 1992, and 1991
($ millions)

	1992	1991
Sales	$8,311	$7,913
Cost of sales	6,617	6,307
Gross profit	1,694	1,606
Administrative and selling expenses	826	841
Research and development expenses	393	346
Restructuring expense (income)	(29)	343
Interest expense	163	190
Other expenses (income)—net	(7)	15
Total expenses	1,346	1,735
Earnings (loss) before income taxes and cumulative effect of accounting changes	348	(129)
Income taxes	154	11
Earnings (loss) before cumulative effect of accounting changes	194	(140)
Cumulative effect to January 1, 1992, of accounting changes, net of income taxes	(350)	–
Net earnings (loss)	$ (156)	$ (140)
Per share of common stock:		
Average number of shares outstanding	62.3 million	61.2 million
Fully diluted earnings		
Before cumulative effect of accounting changes	$ 3.09	$ (2.30)
Cumulative effect of accounting changes	(5.60)	–
Net earnings (loss) per share	$ (2.51)	$ (2.30)
Primary earnings		
Before cumulative effect of accounting changes	$ 3.09	$ (2.30)
Cumulative effect of accounting changes	(5.60)	–
Net earnings (loss) per share	$ (2.51)	$ (2.30)
Book value per share	$22.31	$27.12
Other data ($ millions):		
Depreciation of property, plant, and equipment	$392	$392
Amortization of intangibles, other assets	89	77
Capital expenditures	530	537
Dividends paid	114	111

and income taxes payable. The period's depreciation and amortization—which we would expect to be major sources—are so far hidden in the overall changes of the accumulated allowances shown on the balance sheet.

Although at this point we do have a broad picture of TRW's sources and uses of funds, we can further refine our analysis of the company's funds flow pattern by making a series of adjustments, using the information presently available to us.

Adjustments to Retained Earnings

The net change in retained earnings usually contains at least two elements of interest. The first is net profit or loss from operations which is, of course, reflected on the operating statement. The second is the amount of cash dividends paid to the various classes of shareholders. Both normally represent major funds movements that should be shown separately, one as a source and the other as a use. In recent years, adjustments due to restructuring and to changes in generally accepted accounting principles have also become important elements for many companies, including TRW. Such adjustments should be highlighted if they're significant.

In the case of TRW we know from the operating statement that there was a 1992 net loss of $156 million. This amount must have been subtracted from the retained earnings account. The operating statement further indicated that cash dividends paid were $114 million, which was also subtracted. The sum of these two figures is $270 million, almost the same as the $272 million shown in Figure 2–15. This suggests that no other significant adjustments were made in the account in 1992.

We can verify this by referring to the company's statement of changes in ownership equity. An abbreviated version of TRW's 1992/91 statement of changes in shareholders' investment, presented earlier (Chapter 1), appears in Figure 2–15. We see that the company

FIGURE 2–15
TRW INC. AND SUBSIDIARIES
Abbreviated Statement of Changes in Shareholders' Investment
For the Years Ended December 31, 1992, and 1991
($ millions)

	1992	1991
Serial preference stock II:	$ 1	$ 1
Common stock:	39	38
Other capital:		
Balance at January 1	184	185
Sale of stock and other	38	(1)
Balance at December 31	222	184
Retained earnings:		
Balance at January 1	1,377	1,628
Net earnings	(156)	(140)
Dividends declared:		
Preference stock	(1)	(1)
Common stock ($1.84 and $1.76 per share)	(115)	(110)
Balance at December 31	1,105	1,377
Cumulative translation adjustments:		
Balance at January 1	98	98
Translation adjustments	(45)	–
Balance at December 31	48	98
Treasure shares—cost in excess of par value:		
Balance at January 1	(13)	(43)
ESOP funding	12	26
Purchase of shares	(6)	(1)
Sold under stock options	3	5
Balance at December 31	(4)	(13)
Total shareholders' investment	$1,416	$1,685

shows dividends *declared,* in contrast to dividends paid, which gives rise to a minor difference of $1 million for common dividends. Also, $1 million dividends were declared on the small amount of preference stock outstanding. We can therefore separate the net change in retained earnings into its two main components: net loss and dividends declared (Figure 2–16).

Some additional comments are useful here. Had the company made significant bookkeeping adjustments

FIGURE 2–16
TRW INC. AND SUBSIDIARIES
Derived Funds Flow Statement
For the Year Ended December 31, 1992
($ millions)

	Sources	Uses
Funds from operations:		
Net loss		$156
Depreciation (nonfunds item)	$ 392	
Amortization (nonfunds item)	89	
Deferred income taxes (net)		230
Effect of accounting changes after taxes	350	
Increase in current liabilities (payables, accruals)	195	
Decrease in current assets (cash, receivables, inventories, less increase in prepaids)	154	–
Total operational funds flows	1,180	386
Net funds from operations	794	
Funds for investment:		
Capital investments		379
Investment in intangible assets (adjusted for amortization of $89)		91
Decrease in other assets	20	–
Total investment funds flows	20	470
Net funds used for investment		450
Funds from financing:		
Decrease in short-term debt		147
Decrease in long-term debt		286
Increase in long-term liabilities (reduced by $350 accounting change)	203	
Decrease in minority interests		1
Increase in common stock	1	
Increase in other capital	38	
Decrease in treasury shares	9	
Currency translation adjustments		45
Dividends declared	–	116
Financing funds flows	251	595
Net funds used in financing	–	344
Totals	794	794

during the period on balance sheet accounts and reflected these changes in retained earnings, the analyst
could choose to in effect cancel out the amounts
involved by adjusting both accounts to their pre-
adjustment level.

Another item is stock dividends, which some companies pay in lieu of, or in addition to, cash dividends. These can be handled similarly. Strictly speaking, stock dividends involve no change in economic value. They simply increase the number of shares outstanding slightly without affecting the stated value of the total owners' equity. Such refinements mustn't divert us from the key purpose of the analysis, which is to highlight the effect on funds of major management decisions made during the period.

Adjustments to Net Income

As we know, net income is derived after a number of bookkeeping write-offs have been taken, the largest of which normally is depreciation. Another write-off is the amortization of patents, licenses, and other intangible assets arising in the normal course of business or from acquisitions. A third write-off is used to reflect the depletion of mineral deposits and standing timber. We remember that such write-offs reflect the apportionment of past expenditures, and therefore don't involve current funds movements. Any write-offs of significance should be recognized as such and must be added back to income (thereby canceled out) in the funds flow statement.

But this practice results in a common misconception—viewing depreciation and amortization as actual sources of funds. Remember, depreciation and amortization as such don't create any funds. They're only accounting entries that reduce reported income. They do, of course, affect the amount of income taxes paid, but this positive funds effect has already been recognized in the income tax figure which was deducted before arriving at net income.

One factor to remember while adjusting for depreciation and amortization is that a corresponding adjustment must be made in the asset accounts from which they arose. Recall that depreciation charges for a period are recorded as a reduction in net fixed assets through the vehicle of accumulated depreciation. Amortization (a form of depreciation applied to intangible assets) is normally charged directly against the asset account being written off, but may also be accumulated separately like depreciation. When we now show depreciation and amortization as funds "sources," we're in effect increasing net income. But we must also restore the same amount to the relevant asset account. Otherwise our funds flows won't balance. (We'll return to the specifics of this adjustment in the next section.)

In TRW's case, depreciation and amortization were shown at the bottom of Figure 2–14's operating statement as $392 million and $89 million, respectively. These amounts should be listed in Figure 2–16 as funds sources after net income because their addition in effect restores net income to its pre–write-off level.

Deferred taxes are another major funds flow element that affects net income. As we've said, deferred taxes arise because some revenues and expenses, particularly depreciation, are timed differently for tax purposes than for financial reporting purposes. Taxes actually paid are therefore lower than taxes provided for on the income statement. The amount of the difference is shown as a liability on the balance sheet. As a result, reported net income doesn't reflect the funds benefit from the lower taxes actually remitted. We should show any increase in deferred taxes as a source in our funds flow statement, in effect adding it to reported net income.

Deferred taxes can also arise from timing differences in the recognition of revenue from installment contracts or projects that are billed on a percentage of completion basis. Also, tax effects of major accounting adjustments may be involved. Here the opposite effect can occur because a company may have to report revenue— and thus income—for tax purposes sooner than it's recognized for accounting purposes. In effect, this amounts to a prepayment of taxes, and the difference will be recorded on the balance sheet as a deferred tax asset.

As we would expect, any increase in a deferred tax asset amounts to a use of funds—the opposite of an increase in deferred tax liabilities. Over time, this asset will change, just like deferred tax liabilities, as differences between tax reporting and accounting requirements increase or decrease. Because timing differences are due to the changing requirements of the Internal Revenue Code, future modifications in tax laws may significantly affect the deferred tax concept.

For purposes of our funds flow statement, we can take changes in deferred taxes directly from the balance sheet, and there's no need to make any further adjustments. Some analysts prefer to net out the changes in deferred tax assets and deferred tax liabilities to show a single amount on the statement.

In 1992 TRW's deferred tax liabilities fell by $218 million, while deferred income tax assets rose by $12 million. Both of these changes should be reflected as uses of funds in line with our previous discussion.

For most companies, the most significant single adjustment in 1992 was a change decreed by the Financial Accounting Standards Board (FASB) in the way future employee and retiree benefits in medical coverage must be handled. Instead of continuing to charge such costs as actually incurred, the FASB required that an estimate of future expenditures be made and written off against current income. A liability for these estimated future obligations had to be established on the balance sheet. This frequently massive accounting adjustment caused many companies to report net losses for 1992, even though their operations were profitable. In TRW's case, the net aftertax effect of this accounting adjustment was $350 million, turning an operating profit of $194 million into a net loss of $156 million. The $350 million figure should be reflected as a source, just like depreciation and amortization, with an equal offset against long-term liabilities representing these future claims.

Other elements in the net income picture sometimes

result from adjustments of assets and liabilities on the balance sheet. Normally these amounts aren't significant enough to warrant special attention. If they're substantial, the analyst can again choose to reverse them to keep the funds flow analysis "pure." Any particular item's relevance to the purpose of the analysis must be the overriding factor in this decision. In TRW's case, $29 million was recognized on the income statement in the form of "restructuring income," largely due to gains from dispositions of certain automotive business segments. It would be appropriate to reflect this adjustment as a use, in effect reducing funds flows from operating activities.

Finally, net income is often affected by gains and losses from the sale of capital assets (an area detailed in the next section).

Adjustments to Net Fixed Assets

The change in net fixed assets (property, plant, and equipment) results from shifts in a variety of funds and nonfunds flow items. It's made up of changes in the gross fixed assets account and changes in accumulated depreciation. Nonrecurring asset adjustments from retirement of various fixed assets often also have an effect. In the case of a major restructuring like TRW carried out, there will have been many adjustments to fixed assets as facilities or whole lines of business were disposed of.

In most cases, funds flow analysis is more meaningful when at least the major elements of the net change in fixed assets are recognized. At the same time, the fixed assets effects are among the more difficult aspects of financial analysis for newcomers to understand. This is partly because fixed assets represent the net of an asset and a reserve account. Another part of the problem is the mystique surrounding depreciation and asset write-offs.

The easiest approach is to lay out the components of

the fixed asset account and to observe the relevance of the figures. Then we can look for additional information in other parts of the published statements. Some of this information may be available only to the insider, however. In such cases we must make do with reasonable assumptions.

In our TRW example, Figure 2–12's balance sheet provides the following information:

	12-31-92	12-31-91	Change
Property, plant, and equipment at cost	$5,052	$5,010	+ $42
Less: Accumulated depreciation and amortization	2,741	2,686	+ 55
Net property, plant, and equipment	$2,311	$2,324	− $13

Our basic task is to identify the relevant individual funds sources and uses that in combination amounted to the net source (net decrease) of $13 million shown. Obviously, there was a $42 million increase in gross property, plant, and equipment, which must have been due to new investments (a use). At the same time, accumulated depreciation rose by $55 million, which should largely be due to current write-offs (a source, as we said before).

In some cases, this coarse breakdown of sources and uses is sufficient. Many analysts would let the matter rest here. Yet we already know, for instance, that actual depreciation for the period (as shown on TRW's operating statement in Figure 2–14) was $392 million, far more than the change in accumulated depreciation. There must have been other elements affecting the picture.

As a result, depending on the depth of analysis desired, the following questions arise:

1. What are the relevant elements of funds flow in the *accumulated depreciation* account, one of which had to be the reported amount of depreciation for the year?
2. What was the *total* amount of *new investment* in

plant, equipment, and rental machines (a major aspect of the management decision process)?

3. Did any divestitures and asset retirements (i.e., reduction in gross plant and equipment) significantly affect the company's funds flow?

These questions are interrelated and can be handled at different levels of complexity. The simplest approach is to assume that normally the amount of depreciation taken for the year ($392 million in the case of TRW) will equal the amount by which accumulated depreciation has increased. If this in fact isn't the case, as we discovered in our example, then there must have been some reduction in the accumulated depreciation account which, for simplicity, we can assume to represent the abandonment of fully depreciated assets during the period.[1] We thereby imply that no proceeds at all were received.

This simple but often adequate approach also eliminates the problem of having to deal with any gains or losses on the sale of capital items. We can modify our funds flow layout as follows:

	(1) 12-31-91	(2) Additions	(3) Deductions	(4) 12-31-92	(5) Change
Gross property, etc.	$5,010	+$379††	−$337†	$5,052	+ $42
Less: Accumulated depreciation	2,686	+ 392	− 337*	2,741	+ 55
Net property, etc.	$2,324	−$ 13	−0−	$2,311	− $13

* Assumed figure in order to balance the change in the account.
† Must be same as in accumulated depreciation if fully depreciated assets were abandoned.
†† Derived figure.

Because we must reconcile the data with the net changes in the accounts on the balance sheet, our simple assumption has given us the necessary data to complete the funds flow analysis. We can recognize the actual depreciation write-off of $392 million as a source

---

[1]Fully depreciated assets, when scrapped, are removed by an accounting entry that credits (reduces) assets by the amount of the recorded value, and debits (reduces) accumulated depreciation by the same amount.

(column 2) and accept the derived amount of $379 million as the new capital investment, a use. The process relies on the *assumed* write-off of $337 million of fully depreciated assets, which under normal accounting practice equally reduces both the asset and the accumulated depreciation accounts (column 3). This practice is observed in our analysis. We're ignoring possible tax implications that would tend to confuse the issue, but would do little to improve the accuracy of our analysis.

From a funds flow point of view, we now have all the elements needed to identify and separate the sources and uses behind the decrease in the net plant and equipment account as reflected in TRW's balance sheets in Figure 2–12 (page 75):

Source: Depreciation for the period	$392
Use: New investment	379
Adjusted net source	$ 13

Obviously, our relatively simple adjustment of the net balances in the two accounts has improved our assessment of one of the most important management decisions: the amount of *new asset investment.* Our original version in Figure 2–13 (Increase in property, plant, and equipment of $42) reflected only a fraction of this sizable commitment for future growth.

We can now assemble a modified funds flow statement from the information displayed earlier in Figure 2–13 into a statement which is improved by the adjustments we've made in owners' equity, net income, and plant and equipment. Figure 2–16 (page 80) arranges the derived TRW funds flow data in terms of our three familiar areas of management decision (operations, investment, and financing) to show the effect of TRW management decisions in 1992.

We observe that operational decisions resulted in a net funds source of $794 million, which represents the reported 1992 net loss of $156 million, adjusted for depreciation ($392 million), amortization ($89 million), the reduction in deferred taxes ($230 million), and employee medical benefits ($350 million). Also involved is the decrease in working capital of $349 million (a $154 million decrease in current assets and a $195 million increase in current liabilities).

Funds required for investment amounted to $450 million, which included our derived capital investment figure of $379 million plus a similarly derived investment of $91 million in intangible assets, less a decrease in other assets of $20 million. Since we chose to show the amortization of intangibles as part of operational funds flows, an offsetting increase of $89 million had to be made to approximate the gross investment in intangibles.

Funds flows from financing decisions were most significant in debt modification, with long-term debt reduced by $286 million and short-term debt reduced by $147 million. There was also an increase in long-term liabilities of $203 million, and dividends declared amounted to $116 million. The remaining items are minor. TRW's restructuring process was targeted to further reduce long-term debt with the proceeds of divestitures once these were completed in 1993.

At this point we're still short of a fully accurate picture because we made one key assumption—that fully depreciated assets were abandoned and written off. A check of the company's annual report reveals that actual 1992 capital investment for property, plant, and equipment was $530 million, while proceeds from divestitures were $371 million. We further learn that proceeds from routine sales of property, plant, and equipment were $11 million. Thus we've understated both capital investments and divestiture proceeds because of our simplifying assumptions. In any case, however, it's generally not possible to reconstruct the exact nature of the transactions without detailed internal records.

When we compare TRW's actual statement (Figure 2–17) to our derived statement (Figure 2–16), we find

FIGURE 2–17
TRW INC. AND SUBSIDIARIES
Statement of Cash Flows
For the Years Ended December 31, 1992, and 1991
($ millions)

	1992	1991
Operating activities:		
Net earnings (loss)	$(156)	$(140)
Adjustments to reconcile net earnings (loss) to net cash provided by operating activities:		
Cumulative effect of accounting changes, net of taxes	350	–
Depreciation and amortization	481	469
Restructuring	(96)	227
Dividends received from affiliated companies	5	7
Deferred income taxes	5	27
Other—net	20	40
Changes in assets and liabilities, net of effects of businesses acquired or sold:		
Accounts receivable	(104)	(56)
Inventories and prepaid expenses	(46)	22
Accounts payable and other accruals	227	30
Other—net	(38)	(7)
Net cash provided by operating activities	648	619
Investing activities:		
Capital expenditures	(530)	(537)
Proceeds from divestitures	371	52
Acquisitions, net of cash acquired	(12)	(5)
Investments in other assets	(62)	(95)
Proceeds from sales of property, plant, and equipment	11	51
Other—net	19	(27)
Net cash used in investing activities	(203)	(561)
Financing activities:		
Increase (decrease) in short-term debt	(229)	69
Proceeds from debt in excess of 90 days	198	462
Principal repayments in excess of 90 days	(351)	(495)
Dividends paid	(114)	(111)
Other—net	18	4
Net cash provided by (used in) financing activities	(478)	(71)
Effect of exchange rate changes on cash	24	16
Increase (decrease) in cash and cash equivalents	(9)	3
Cash and cash equivalents at beginning of year	75	72
Cash and cash equivalents at end of year	$ 66	$ 75

Source: Adapted from 1992 TRW Inc. annual report.

that, apart from differences in presentation, some of the figures we've developed are reflected in TRW's statement as well. The various items on which the statements disagree all require more detailed knowledge than is normally available in published statements, especially about elements of the restructuring and various accounting adjustments.

Adjustments for the costs of restructuring, the accounting for acquisitions and dispositions, the treatment of working capital changes (shown net of the effects of businesses acquired or sold), and details in the financing section of TRW's funds flow statement (particularly debt changes by specific category and timing) reflect information that wasn't available to us. Also, a number of minor funds movements have been netted out. But in broad terms, our derived statement reasonably approaches the overall magnitude of funds movements in the three decision areas.

To summarize, in this section we constructed a funds flow statement that goes beyond simply listing the changes readily observed in a comparison of beginning and ending balance sheet accounts. We achieved this by making informed adjustments in several of the accounts. The purpose of the refinements was to highlight significant results that reflect management decisions involving investments, operations, and financing. If a company's funds flow statement isn't made available as a matter of course, the analyst can usually approximate the statement that an insider could prepare by going through the adjustment process we've demonstrated.

We must usually examine three areas in more depth: (1) the components of the change in owners' equity, (2) the elements making up net income, particularly those relating to accounting write-offs, and (3) the various components of change in the fixed asset accounts and related accumulated depreciation. Under most conditions the analyst can come close enough to the actual figures to construct a funds flow statement that's meaningful in format and content.

SUMMARY

In this chapter we demonstrated the funds flow cycle involved in any business, large or small, and its implication for management. We began with a simple illustration of basic funds movements, and then discussed operating funds cycles from a manufacturing and sales standpoint. We observed the nature and behavior of working capital, we highlighted the impact of variability of operations, and we demonstrated the effect of funds lags on the nature and duration of financing required to support a business. The insights gained included the need to consider the permanence of basic working capital requirements, the financial drain of even successful growth, and the potential funds release from decline in volume.

Several key questions arise as funds movements were analyzed. Most relate to the types of funds commitments (uses) made compared to the sources of funds available. Have enough long-term funds been provided to fund ongoing growth in working capital and fixed asset expansion? Are most sources of funds temporary loans and credit extension? Is the business counting on profits to fund peaks of need that may exceed such expectations?

In essence, funds flow analysis is a broad-brush dynamic view of the financial management of the business. It relates changes in conditions to the key financial implications by reconstructing the major funds transactions during the period. The simple techniques require only basic accounting knowledge to provide this extra dimension in assessing balance sheets and operating statements.

SELECTED REFERENCES

Anthony, Robert N., and James S. Reece. *Accounting Principles.* 6th ed. Homewood, Ill.: Richard D. Irwin, 1988.

Brealey, Richard, and Stewart Myers. *Principles of Corporate Finance.* 3d ed. New York: McGraw-Hill, 1988.

Garrison, Raymond H. *Managerial Accounting: Concepts for Planning, Control, Decision Making.* 5th ed. Homewood, Ill.: Richard D. Irwin, 1988.

Ross, Stephen; Randolph Westerfield; and Jeffrey Jaffe. *Corporate Finance.* 2d ed. Homewood, Ill.: Richard D. Irwin, 1990.

Seitz, Neil. *Financial Analysis: A Programmed Approach.* 3d ed. Reston, Va.: Reston Publishing, 1984.

Van Horne, James C. *Financial Management and Policy.* 8th ed. Englewood Cliffs, N.J.: Prentice Hall, 1989.

Vancil, Richard F., and Benjamin R. Makela, eds. *The CFO Handbook.* Homewood, Ill.: Dow Jones-Irwin, 1986.

Weston, J. Fred, and Thomas E. Copeland. *Managerial Finance.* 9th ed. Hinsdale, Ill.: Dryden Press, 1989.

SELF-STUDY EXERCISES AND PROBLEMS

(Solutions in Appendix VI)

1. Develop a funds flow statement from the balance sheets and income statements of the CBA Company for the year 1994. Make appropriate assumptions and comment on the results.

CBA COMPANY
Operating Statements for 1993 and 1994

	1993	1994
Net sales	$1,133,400	$1,147,700
Cost of goods sold*	740,500	813,300
Gross margin	392,900	334,400
Expenses:		
Selling expense	172,500	227,000
General and administrative	65,500	71,800
Other expenses	22,200	25,000
Interest on debt	9,700	14,300
Total expenses	269,900	338,100
Profit (loss) before taxes	123,000	(3,700)
Federal income tax	56,600	(1,700)
Net income (loss)†	$ 66,400	$ (2,000)

*Includes depreciation of $31,500 for 1993 and $32,200 for 1994.
†Dividends paid were $30,000 for 1993 and $15,000 for 1994.

CBA COMPANY
Balance Sheets
December 31, 1993, and 1994

Assets	1993	1994
Current assets:		
Cash	$ 39,700	$ 27,500
Marketable securities	1,000	11,000
Accounts receivable (net)	81,500	72,700
Inventories	181,300	242,000
Total current assets	303,500	353,200
Fixed assets:		
Land	112,000	112,000
Plant and equipment (net)	445,200	464,800
Total fixed assets	557,200	576,800
Other assets	13,300	21,500
Total assets	$874,000	$951,500
Liabilities and net worth		
Current liabilities:		
Accounts payable	$ 71,200	$ 83,000
Notes payable	50,000	140,000
Accrued expenses	33,400	36,300
Total current liabilities	154,600	259,300
Long-term debt:		
Mortgage payable	106,000	90,800
Net worth:		
Common stock	225,000	230,000
Retained earnings	388,400	371,400
Total net worth	613,400	601,400
Total liabilities and net worth	$874,000	$951,500

2. Work the following exercises:

   a. The following data about the ABC Company's operations and conditions for the year 1994 are available from a variety of sources:

Depreciation for 1994	$ 21,400
Net loss for 1994	14,100
Common dividends paid	12,000
Amortization of goodwill, patents	15,000
Inventory adjustment—write-down	24,000
Investments in fixed assets	57,500
Loss from abandonment of equipment	4,000
Balance of retained earnings 12-31-93	167,300

Which of the preceding items affect retained earnings during 1994 (the only surplus account of the company), and what's the balance of retained earnings as of December 31? Which of the preceding items are funds sources, and which are funds uses? Can depreciation be considered a funds flow item if the operating results are negative? What would be different if the $4,000 loss from abandonment had been a gain from sale of assets instead? Discuss.

b. The following items, among others, appear on the funds flow statement of DEF Company for the year 1994:

Outlays for properties and fixed assets	$1,250,500
Profit from operations after taxes	917,000
Funds from depreciation	1,613,000

The only other information readily available is:

Gross property and fixed assets, 12-31-93	$8,431,500
Gross property and fixed assets, 12-31-94	8,430,000
Accumulated depreciation, 12-31-94	3,874,000

Determine the change in the *net* properties and fixed assets accounts from this information, and spell out your assumptions. How significant would be the likely effect on the results if you used some possible alternative assumptions? Discuss.

c. The XYZ Company experienced the transactions and changes listed below, among many others, during 1994. These affected its balance sheet as follows:

Fixed assets recorded at $110,000 were sold for $45,000 (gain reflected in net income).

Accumulated depreciation on these specific assets was $81,000.

Accumulated depreciation for the company as a whole decreased by $5,000 during 1994.

Total depreciation charged during 1994 was $78,500.

Balance of gross fixed assets was as follows: 12-31-93, $823,700, and 12-31-94, $947,300.

From this information, determine the amount of new investment in fixed assets for 1994 that should be shown in the funds flow statement. What was the amount of change in the *net* fixed assets account during 1994? Which other items shown above or derived from these should be shown on the funds flow statement? What assumptions are necessary? Discuss.

3. Develop a funds flow statement from the balance sheets, income
    statements, and retained earnings statements of the **FED** Com-
    pany, shown below, for the year 1994. Make appropriate assump-
    tions and comment on the results. If you net out changes in
    working capital accounts into one figure, will significant informa-
    tion be obscured? Will it be helpful to assign uses and sources to
    key management decision areas? Discuss.

    Other data you may need include: (1) sold fully depreciated
    machinery for $4,000, (2) issued $20,000 of common stock ($1
    par) to reduce note payable, and (3) issued $4,000 of preferred
    stock to outsiders.

FED COMPANY
Balance Sheets, December 31, 1993, and 1994
($ thousands)

Assets	1993	1994	Change
Current assets:			
Cash	$ 12	$-0-	− $12
Marketable securities	18	-0-	− 18
Accounts receivable—net	68	73	+ 5
Notes receivable	30	50	+ 20
Inventories	131	138	+ 7
Total current assets	259	261	+ 2
Fixed assets:			
Land	25	25	-0-
Plant and equipment	268	283	+ 15
Less: Accumulated depreciation	157	160	+ 3
Net plant and equipment	111	123	+ 12
Total fixed assets	136	148	+ 12
Other assets:			
Prepaid expenses	12	14	+ 2
Patents, organization expense	30	27	− 3
Total other assets	42	41	− 1
Total assets	$437	$450	+ $13
Liabilities and net worth			
Current liabilities:			
Bank overdraft	$-0-	$ 4	+$ 4
Accounts payable	73	97	+ 24
Notes payable	100	70	− 30
Accrued expenses	13	22	+ 9
Total current liabilities	186	193	+ 7
Long-term liabilities:			
Secured notes payable	40	20	− 20
Net worth:			
Deferred income taxes	25	27	+ 2

Liabilities and net worth	1993	1994	Change
Preferred stock	35	39	+ 4
Capital surplus	90	109	+ 19
Retained earnings	51	51	–0–
Common stock	10	11	+ 1
Total net worth	211	237	+ 26
Total liabilities and net worth	$437	$450	+ $13

FED COMPANY
Operating Statement for 1993 and 1994
($ thousands)

	1993	1994
Sales	$1,115	$1,237
Cost of goods sold:		
Material	312	345
Labor	274	341
Depreciation	24	26
Overhead	158	210
Cost of goods sold	768	922
Gross profit	347	315
Expenses:		
Selling and administrative expense	268	297
Interest on debt	9	7
Total expenses	277	304
Profit before taxes	70	11
Income taxes	32	5
Net income	$ 38	$ 6

FED COMPANY
Statement of Retained Earnings for 1994
($ thousands)

Balance 12-31-93		$51
Additions:		
Net income from 1990 operations	$6	
Gain from sale of fixed assets	4	10
		61
Deductions:		
Preferred dividends	2	
Common dividends	5	
Patent, other amortization	3	10
Balance, 12-31-94		$51

4. The ZYX Company, a vegetable packing plant, operates on a highly seasonal basis, which affects its financial results during various parts of its fiscal year and forces a financial planning effort in tune with these fluctuating requirements. From the company's

nine quarterly balance sheets (covering two fiscal years of the ZYX Company and shown on page 98), develop a funds flow analysis that appropriately reflects the funds requirements and sources as balanced by company management.

Additional data you may need include (1) purchases of machinery, $48,000 in April 1994 and $50,000 in April 1995; (2) depreciation charged at $6,000 per quarter through April 1994, at $7,000 through April 1995, and at $8,000 through July 1995; and (3) dividends paid at $15,000 per quarter through October 1994 and at $18,000 per quarter through July 1995.

Comment on the various alternative ways this analysis can be developed, and state your reasons for your choices. What are your key findings?

ZYX COMPANY
Balance Sheets by Fiscal Quarters
July 31, 1993, to July 31, 1995
($ thousands)

	1993		1994				1995		
Assets	7-31	10-31	1-31	4-30	7-31	10-31	1-31	4-30	7-31
Cash	$ 21	$ 30	$ 74	$ 91	$ 7	$ 28	$ 90	$103	$ 16
Accounts receivable	114	247	319	128	141	293	388	151	103
Inventories	231	417	315	131	271	467	351	98	310
Net plant and equipment	239	233	227	269	262	255	248	291	283
Other assets	15	16	16	15	15	14	18	18	17
Total assets	$620	$943	$951	$634	$696	$1,057	$1,095	$661	$729
Liabilities and net worth									
Accounts payable	$ 68	$297	$121	$103	$ 79	$ 314	188	97	$ 84
Notes payable	35	126	294	—	63	178	342	—	80
Mortgage payable	80	80	75	75	70	70	65	65	60
Preferred stock	100	100	100	100	100	100	100	100	100
Common stock	100	100	100	100	125	125	125	125	125
Retained earnings	237	240	261	256	259	270	275	274	280
Total liabilities and net worth	$620	$943	$951	$634	$696	$1,057	$1,095	$661	$729

3 ASSESSMENT OF BUSINESS PERFORMANCE

As we established in the preceding chapters, a firm's performance results from many individual decisions made continually by its management. Assessing business performance therefore involves analyzing these decisions' cumulative financial and economic effects and judging them through the use of comparative measures. In Chapter 2 we developed a broad understanding of the nature of the funds flows that are fundamental to any business and are the consequence of various types of management decisions.

In this chapter we'll discuss the analysis of business performance on the basis of published financial data as reflected in financial statements prepared according to generally accepted accounting principles. These are the most common data available for the purpose, even though they don't necessarily represent economic results and conditions. Financial statements are the universal periodic "score cards" available to track the results of business investment, operations, and financing. Here we'll focus on key financial relationships and indicators that allow the analyst to assess past performance and also to project future results, and we'll point out their meaning as well as the limitations inherent in them.

RATIO ANALYSIS AND PERFORMANCE

Many analytical techniques, including those involving a variety of financial ratios, are available for performance assessment. But readers should be reminded that different techniques are appropriate for different purposes. Before any analysis is undertaken, the analyst must clearly define the following elements:

- The viewpoint taken.
- The objectives of the analysis.
- Potential standards of comparison.

In financial analysis there's often a temptation to "run all the numbers"—yet normally only a few selected relationships will yield the information and insights the analyst really needs. By definition a ratio can relate any magnitude to any other, such as net profit to total assets, or current liabilities to current assets. The choices are limited only by the imagination.

But the actual usefulness of any particular ratio is strictly governed by the specific objectives of the analysis. Moreover, ratios aren't absolute criteria. Meaningful ratios serve best to point out changes in financial conditions or operating performance, and help illustrate the trends and patterns of such changes which, in turn, may indicate to the analyst the risks and opportunities for the business under review.

A further caution should be noted here. Performance assessment via financial statements is based on past data and conditions from which it may be difficult to extrapolate future expectations. Yet we must remember that only the future can be affected by today's decisions made as a result of any financial analysis—the past is gone, or "sunk" as the economist calls it.

No attempt to assess business performance can provide firm answers. Any insights gained will be relative because business and operating conditions vary so much from company to company and industry to industry. Comparisons and standards based on past performance are especially difficult in large, multibusiness companies and conglomerates, where specific information by individual line of business is normally limited.

Accounting adjustments of various types present further complications. To deal with all of these aspects in detail is far beyond the scope of this book. Nevertheless, the reader must keep these cautions in mind when dealing with the available numerical data that necessarily reflect the effects of all of these conditions.

In this section we'll discuss and characterize the key ratios and measures commonly applied in financial/economic analysis of business performance. Only the most important techniques will be dealt with. Our discussion will be developed around the major viewpoints that can be taken in performing financial performance analysis, and we'll cover the usefulness of the different measures for each of these viewpoints.

Many different individuals and groups are interested in the success or failure of a given business. The most important are:

- Owners (investors).
- Managers.
- Lenders and creditors.
- Employees.
- Labor organizations.
- Government agencies.
- Society in general (the public).

These groups differ in their view of business results and performance. They'll often go beyond financial and economic data to include broader and more intangible values in their assessments.

Closest to the business from a day-to-day standpoint, but also responsible for its long-range performance, is the management of the organization—whether its members are professional managers or owner/managers. Managers are responsible and accountable for operating efficiency, current and long-term profitability, and the effective deployment of capital, human effort, and other resources.

Next are the various owners of the business, who are especially interested in the current and long-term profitability of their equity investment. They usually expect growing earnings and dividends, which will bring about growth in the economic value of their "stake."

Then there are the providers of "other people's money," lenders and creditors who extend funds to the business for various lengths of time. They're mainly concerned about the reliability of the interest payments due them, about the firm's ability to repay the principal, and about the availability of specific residual asset values that give them a margin of protection against their risk.

Other groups such as government, labor, and society have specific objectives of their own—the reliability of tax payments, the ability to pay wages, stability of employment, or the financial wherewithal to meet various social and environmental obligations, for instance.

We'll develop the ensuing discussion of business performance measures and tests around the first three viewpoints: management, owners, and lenders. These viewpoints are, of course, interdependent and differ mainly in their emphasis. Keep in mind that some measures are, of course, also applicable to the viewpoints of the other groups mentioned.

The principal areas of financial performance of interest to the three groups are shown in Figure 3–1 along with the ratios and measures relevant to these areas. We'll follow the sequence of measures shown in the table and discuss each subgroup within the three broad viewpoints.

FIGURE 3–1
Financial Performance Measures by Area and Viewpoint

Management	*Owners*	*Lenders*
Operational analysis	**Profitability**	**Liquidity**
Gross margin	Return on total net	Current ratio
Profit margin	worth	Acid test
Operating expense	Return on common	Quick sale value
analysis	equity	Cash flow patterns
Contribution analysis	Earnings per share	
Operating leverage	Cash flow per share	
Comparative analysis	Share price appreciation	
	Total shareholder return	
	Shareholder value	
	analysis	
Resource management	**Disposition of earnings**	**Financial leverage**
Asset turnover	Dividends per share	Debt to assets
Working capital	Dividend yield	Debt to capitalization
management	Payout/retention of	Debt to equity
• Inventory turnover	earnings	Risk/reward trade-off
• Accounts receivable	Dividend coverage	
patterns	Dividends to assets	
• Accounts payable		
patterns		
Human resource		
effectiveness		
Profitability	**Market indicators**	**Debt service**
Return on assets (total or	Price/earnings ratio	Interest coverage
net)	Cash flow multiples	Burden coverage
Return before interest	Market to book value	Cash flow analysis
and taxes	Relative price	
Return on current value	movements	
basis		
Investment project		
economics		
Cash flow return on		
investment		

MANAGEMENT'S POINT OF VIEW

As mentioned before, management has a dual interest in the analysis of financial performance: to assess the efficiency and profitability of operations, and to judge how effectively the firm's resources were used. Assessment of operations is largely based on an analysis of the operating (income) statement, while the effectiveness of resource use is usually measured by a review of both the balance sheet and the income statement. To make economic judgments, we must often modify the available financial data to reflect current economic values and conditions.

For purposes of illustration we'll again use appropriate information from the sample statements of TRW Inc. for 1992 and 1991, which we first introduced in Chapter 1. The same statements are shown as Figures 3–2 and 3–3. We'll use this information for the remainder of this chapter. For added convenience we've also expressed the various items on the operating statement as percentages of sales.

In addition, Figure 3–6 (at the end of this chapter) contains several selections from the "Notes to Financial Statements" as published in TRW's 1993 annual report. They are provided as explanatory background for the company's key accounting policies, recent restructuring, income tax provisions, deferred income taxes, postretirement benefits accounting change, debt, and industry segments. Because the items affect the development of many ratios in this chapter, the notes will help to understand some of the choices an analyst must make in using financial statement information.

Operational Analysis

For the business as a whole or any of its subdivisions, an initial assessment of operational effectiveness is generally performed through a "common numbers" or percentage analysis of the operating statement. Individual

FIGURE 3–2

TRW INC. AND SUBSIDIARIES

Consolidated Balance Sheets at December 31, 1992, and 1991

($ millions)

Assets	1992	1991
Current assets:		
Cash and cash equivalents	$ 66	$ 75
Accounts receivable	1,289	1,356
Inventories	422	512
Prepaid expenses	69	61
Deferred income taxes	270	258
Total current assets	2,116	2,262
Property, plant, and equipment at cost	5,052	5,010
Less: Allowances for depreciation and amortization	2,741	2,686
Total property, plant, and equipment—net	2,311	2,324
Intangible assets:		
Intangibles arising from acquisitions	552	561
Capitalized data files and other	464	420
	1,016	981
Less: Accumulated amortization	299	266
Total intangible assets—net	717	715
Other assets	314	334
Total assets	$5,458	$5,635
Liabilities and shareholders' investment		
Current liabilities:		
Short-term debt	$ 260	$ 407
Accrued compensation	286	298
Trade accounts payable	583	567
Other accruals	752	620
Dividends payable	30	28
Income taxes	85	32
Current portion of long-term debt	16	30
Total current liabilities	2,012	1,982
Long-term liabilities	804	251
Long-term debt	941	1,213
Deferred income taxes	222	440
Minority interests in subsidiaries	63	64
Shareholders' investment:		
Serial preference stock II	1	1
Common stock	39	38
Other capital	222	184
Retained earnings	1,105	1,377
Cumulative translation adjustments	53	98
Treasury shares—cost in excess of par	(4)	(13)
Total shareholders' investment	1,416	1,685
Total liabilities and shareholders' investment	$5,458	$5,635

Source: Adapted from TRW Inc. 1992 annual report.

FIGURE 3–3
TRW INC. AND SUBSIDIARIES
Statement of Earnings
For the Years Ended December 31, 1992, and 1991
($ millions)

	1992	Percent of Sales	1991	Percent of Sales
Sales	$8,311	100.0%	$7,913	100.0%
Cost of sales	6,617	79.6	6,307	79.7
Gross profit	1,694	20.4%	1,606	20.3%
Administrative and selling expenses	826	9.9	841	10.6
Research and development expenses	393	4.7	346	4.4
Restructuring expense (income)	(29)	(.3)	343	4.3
Interest expense	163	2.0	190	2.4
Other expenses (income) net	(7)	(.1)	15	.2
Total expenses	1,346	16.2%	1,735	21.9%
Earnings (loss) before income taxes and cumulative effect of accounting changes	348	4.2	(129)	(1.6)
Income taxes	154	1.9	11	.1
Earnings (loss) before cumulative effect of accounting changes	194	2.3%	(140)	(1.7)
Cumulative effect to January 1, 1992, of accounting changes, net of income taxes	(350)	(4.2)	–	–
Net earnings (loss)	$(156)	(1.9)%	$(140)	(1.7)%

Per share of common stock:

Average number of shares outstanding (millions)	62.3		61.2	
Fully diluted earnings				
Before cumulative effect of accounting changes	$3.09		$(2.30)	
Cumulative effect of accounting changes	(5.60)		–	
Net earnings (loss) per share	$(2.51)		$(2.30)	
Primary earnings (as above)	$(2.51)		$(2.30)	
Dividends paid	$1.82		$1.80	

Other data:

Depreciation of property, plant, and equipment	$392		$392	
Amortization of intangibles, other assets	89		77	
Capital expenditures	530		537	
Dividends paid	114		111	

Source: Adapted from TRW Inc. 1992 annual report.

costs and expense items are usually related to net sales, that is, gross sales revenues after any returns and allowances. Using net sales as the common denominator provides a reasonable standard for measurement, one especially useful when tracking progress over a series of past periods or when making comparisons between different companies.

Expense/sales ratios are used both to judge the relative magnitude of selected key elements and to determine any trends toward improving or declining performance. We must, however, keep in mind the type of industry involved and its particular characteristics as well as the individual trends and special conditions of the company being studied. For example, the gross margin of a jewelry store with slow turnover of merchandise and high markups will be far greater (50 percent isn't uncommon) than that of a supermarket, whose success depends on low margins and high volume (gross margins of 10 to 15 percent are typical). In fact, comparing a particular company's ratios to those of similar companies in its industry over a number of time periods will usually provide the best clues as to whether the company's performance is improving or worsening.

Many published annual overviews of company and industry performance (such as the annual Fortune 500 rankings) use such ranking approaches. Individual companies usually develop their own comparisons with the performance of comparable units within the organization or with relevant competitors on the outside. It's also often useful to graph a series of performance data over time, a process now easily achieved with the growing capabilities of computer spreadsheets and data bases.

Gross Margin and Cost of Goods Sold Analysis. One of the most common ratios in operational analysis is the calculation of cost of goods sold (cost of sales) as a percentage of net sales. This ratio indicates the magnitude of the cost of goods purchased or manufactured—or the cost of services provided—in relation to the gross margin (gross profit) left over for operating expenses and profit.

The ratios calculated from our TRW sample statements are:

$$\text{Cost of goods sold} = \frac{\$6,617}{\$8,311} = 79.6\% \quad (1991: 79.7\%)$$

and

$$\text{Gross margin} = \frac{\$1,694}{\$8,311} = 20.4\% \quad (1991: 20.3\%)$$

The cost of goods sold of 79.6 percent and the gross margin of 20.4 percent indicate the margin of "raw profit" from operations. Remember that gross margin reflects the relationship of prices, volume, and costs. A change in gross margin can result from a combination of changes in:

- The selling price of the product.
- The level of manufacturing costs for the product.
- Any volume changes in the firm's product mix.

In a trading or service organization, gross margin can be affected by a combination of changes in:

- The price charged for the products or services provided.
- The prices paid for merchandise purchased on the outside.
- The cost of services from internal or external sources.
- Any volume changes in the firm's product/service mix.

The volume of operations can also have a significant effect if, for example, a manufacturing company has high fixed costs (see Chapter 5 for a discussion of operating leverage) or a small trading company has less buying power and economies of scale than a large competitor.

In TRW's case, the cost of goods sold and the gross margin shown in its annual report represent a consolidation of the three major product lines, that is, the income statement combined Space and Defense, Automotive, and Information Systems. We note a margin improvement of one tenth of a percentage point over the prior year. For a more detailed insight, we could calculate the gross margins for the individual business areas if this information were available.

In its annual report, TRW provided a selective breakdown, by major product line, of sales, operating profit, identifiable assets, depreciation and amortization, and capital expenditures, which allows the analyst to make some overall comparisons. These data would have to be supplemented by additional internal information for a detailed ratio analysis.

There are particular complications in the analysis of manufacturing companies. The nature of manufacturing cost accounting systems governs the specific costing of products for inventory and for current sale. Significant differences can exist between the apparent cost performance of companies using standard full cost systems and those using direct costing. (In the latter case, fixed manufacturing costs aren't allocated to individual products but charged as a block against operations.) The charges against a particular period of operations can be greatly affected by the choice of accounting methods. Inflation (which affects the prices of both cost inputs and goods or services sold) and currency fluctuations (in the case of international businesses) further distort the picture. We'll discuss this later in the chapter.

Any major change in a company's cost of goods sold or gross margin over a relevant period of time calls for further analysis to identify the cause. The relevance of the time period depends on the nature of the business. For example, as we demonstrated in Chapter 2, many businesses have normal seasonal fluctuations, while others are affected by longer-term business cycles. Thus, the ratio serves as a signal rather than an absolute measure, as is the case with most of the measures discussed.

Profit Margin. The relationship of reported net profit after taxes (net income) to sales indicates management's ability to operate the business with sufficient success to recover the cost of the merchandise or services, the expenses of operating the business (including depreciation), and the cost of borrowed funds. It also shows management's ability to leave a margin of reasonable compensation to the owners for putting their capital at risk. The ratio of net profit (income) to sales (total revenue) essentially expresses the overall cost/price effectiveness of the operation. As we'll demonstrate later, a more significant ratio for this purpose is the relationship of profit to the amount of capital employed in producing it.

At this point we must take note of the $350 million charge against 1992 earnings from the mandated change in accounting for future employee medical benefits. For purposes of ratio analysis and for period-to-period comparisons, this extraordinary adjustment should be excluded, as should be any other extraordinary gains or losses a company might encounter in a particular period. In most cases such adjustments of significant size are highlighted in the company's financial statements, allowing the analyst to choose whether to include them in the analysis.

The calculation of the net profit (net earnings) ratio is simple, as the figures from our TRW example show. We've used net earnings (losses) before the cumulative effect of accounting changes in Figure 3–3:

$$\text{Profit margin*} = \frac{\$194}{\$8,311} = 2.3\% \quad (1991: -1.7\%)$$

*Before cumulative effect of accounting changes.

A variation of this ratio uses net profit *before* interest and taxes. This figure represents the operating profit before any compensation is paid to debt holders. It's also the profit before the calculation of federal and state income taxes, which are often based on modified sets of deductible expenses and accounting write-offs. The ratio is used with the assumption that it provides a "purer" view of operating effectiveness, undistorted by financing patterns and tax calculations. Called earnings before interest and taxes (EBIT), this pretax, pre-interest income ratio for TRW appears as follows:

$$\text{EBIT}^* = \frac{\$348 + \$163}{\$8,311} = 6.1\% \quad (1991: 0.7\%)$$

*Before cumulative effect of accounting changes.

A sound argument can be made, however, for considering income taxes as an ongoing expense of being in business. The formula can therefore be modified by using profit *before* interest but *after* taxes (**EBIAT**). Again, the intent is to focus on operating efficiency by leaving out any compensation to the various holders of capital.

In terms of the **TRW** figures we're using, this modified result is

$$\text{EBIAT}^* = \frac{\$194 + (1 - .442)\ 163}{\$8,311} = 3.4\% \quad (1991: -0.3\%)$$

*Before cumulative effect of accounting changes.

For convenience in making the adjustment to aftertax profit, we usually assume that the interest paid during the period was fully tax-deductible. Thus, we simply add back to the stated profit figure the aftertax cost of interest. We obtain this by multiplying pretax interest by a factor of "one minus the tax rate," employing either the effective (average) tax rate paid on earnings (44.2 percent in TRW's case) or, ideally, the marginal (highest-bracket) corporate tax rate for the firm in question.

The choice of tax rates depends on the complexity of the company's taxation pattern. TRW operates world-wide and therefore is subject to a variety of taxes which are combined in the provision for income taxes on the income statement. It's most straightforward to rely on the effective overall rate paid, which was a little higher than the marginal U.S. corporate tax rate prevailing in 1992. Chapter 7 covers the cost of debt and the nature of the necessary tax adjustments to be made to interest cost.

We note in Figure 3–3 that TRW had significant restructuring costs and income, particularly in 1991, amounting then to $343 million before taxes, or about 4.3 percent of sales. Without these costs, the company would have reported a positive 1991 operating profit. It can be argued that this item represents an extraordinary occurrence, similar to the $350 million aftertax charge for changes in the accounting for future employee medical benefits made in 1992. An analyst may choose to disregard these charges for purposes of the ratio analysis we just covered. If this were done, the year-to-year comparison would improve, as the 1991 ratios would be raised significantly by the adjustment. The reader is invited to calculate adjusted profit ratios.

As a rule, when there are unusual or nonrecurring income and expense elements not directly related to ongoing operations, the analyst should adjust the ratios by excluding such items when measuring operating effectiveness. The adjustment should be done on the same basis as we demonstrated for interest; that is, the tax effect of revenue or expense items must be calculated if aftertax comparisons are desired. For example, in TRW's case the tax adjustments to the $350 million accounting change were made by the company, putting it on an aftertax basis as stated in Figure 3–3.

Operating Expense Analysis. Various expense categories are routinely related to net sales. These comparisons include such items as administrative expense, selling and promotional expenses, and many others typical of particular businesses and industries.

The general formula used to calculate this expense ratio is

$$\text{Expense ratio} = \frac{\text{Various expense items}}{\text{Net sales}} = \text{Percent}$$

There are relatively few expense categories shown in TRW's abbreviated operating statement, but the ratio to sales was calculated for each item in Figure 3–3. In practice, a greater breakdown is generally desirable. Many trade associations collect extensive financial data from their members and compile published statistics on expense ratios as well as on most of the other ratios discussed in this chapter. These publications help provide standards of comparison and the basis for trend analysis. References to such information sources are listed at the end of the chapter and also in Appendix V.

To make such comparisons reasonable and to reduce the degree of error introduced by large-scale averaging, great care is often taken to categorize the businesses within an industry by size and other characteristics. Even without such data available, a skilled analyst will scan the revenue and expense categories on an income statement as a matter of course to see if any of them seem out of line with the particular company's experience over time.

Contribution Analysis. This type of analysis has been used mainly for internal management, although it's increasingly applied in broader financial analysis. The process involves relating net sales to the "contribution margin" of individual product groups or of the total business. Such calculations require a very selective analysis or estimate of the firm's fixed and variable costs and expenses, and they take into account the effect of operating leverage. (See Chapter 5.) Only directly variable costs are subtracted from net sales to show the operations' contribution toward fixed costs and profits for the period.

The contribution margin is calculated as follows:

$$\frac{\text{Contribution margin} = \text{Net sales} - \frac{\text{Direct costs}}{\text{(variable costs)}}}{\text{Net sales}} = \text{Percent}$$

Significant differences can exist in the contribution margins of different industries due to varying needs for capital investment and the resultant cost-volume conditions. Even within a particular company, various lines of products or services may contribute quite differently to fixed costs and profits.

In recent years much development has been expended on so-called *activity-based* accounting analysis which can be used for an economic assessment of the relative contribution of various parts of a company, thereby going beyond the limitations of existing cost accounting systems. In such an analysis a specialized financial/economic allocation is made of all resources, direct or indirect, internal or external, that support a particular activity, product line, operation, or line of business. It serves as the basis for periodic strategic assessment of the relative economic contribution of the area under study. Since the specific techniques used go beyond this book's scope, the reader is directed to the references at the end of the chapter.

Contribution margins as derived from financial statements are useful as a broad—if limited—tool in judging a business's risk characteristics. The measure suggests the amount of leeway management enjoys in pricing its products and services, and the scope of its ability to control costs and expenses under different economic conditions. Analysis of break-even conditions and of pricing strategies as they relate to volume achieved become important in this context. (See Chapter 5.)

Resource Management

Here we're interested in judging the effectiveness with which management has employed the assets entrusted to it by the firm's owners. When examining a balance sheet, an analyst will draw company-specific conclusions about the size and nature of the assets listed, looking at relative proportions and judging whether the company has a viable asset base. Clues such as high accumulated depreciation relative to recorded property, plant, and equipment may suggest that aging facilities need upgrading. Similarly, a significant jump in cash balances may suggest lagging investment and an accumulation of excess funds. Surges in working capital may signal problems with inventory management or customer credit policies.

In a more overall sense, a few ratios are used to judge broad trends in resource utilization. Such ratios essentially involve "turnover" relationships and express, in various forms, the relative amount of capital used to support the volume of business transacted.

Asset Turnover. The most commonly used ratios relate net sales to gross assets, or net sales to net assets. The measure indicates the size of the recorded asset commitment required to support a particular level of sales or, conversely, the sales dollars generated by each dollar of assets.

While simple to calculate, overall asset turnover is a crude measure at best, because most well-established companies' balance sheets list a whole variety of assets recorded at widely differing cost levels of past periods. These stated values often have little relation to current economic values, and the distortions grow with any significant change in the level of inflation, or with the appreciation of assets such as real estate. Such discrepancies in values often attract corporate raiders intent on realizing true economic values through a breakup of the

116

company and selective disposal of assets, as Chapter 9 relates.

Another distortion is caused by a company's mix of product lines. Most manufacturing activities tend to be asset-intensive, while other activities (like services or wholesaling) need fewer assets to support the volume of revenues generated. Again, wherever possible, a break-down of total financial data into major product lines should be attempted.

Basically, the turnover ratio is another of several clues that, in combination, can indicate favorable or unfavor-able performance. If gross assets are used for the pur-pose, the calculations for TRW's turnover ratios are

$$\text{Sales to assets} = \frac{\text{Net sales}}{\text{Gross assets}} = \frac{\$8,311}{\$5,458} = 1.52 \quad (1991: 1.40)$$

and

$$\text{Assets to sales} = \frac{\text{Gross assets}}{\text{Net sales}} = \frac{\$5,458}{\$8,311} = 0.66 \quad (1991: 0.71)$$

If net assets (total assets less current liabilities, repre-senting the capitalization of the business) are used, the calculations are either

$$\frac{\text{Sales to}}{\text{net assets}} = \frac{\text{Net sales}}{\text{Net assets}} = \frac{\$8,311}{\$5,458 - \$2,012} = 2.41 \quad (1991: 2.17)$$

or

$$\text{Net assets to sales} = \frac{\text{Net assets}}{\text{Net sales}} = \frac{\$3,446}{\$8,311} = 0.41 \quad (1991: 0.46)$$

The difference between the two sets of calculations lies in the choice of the asset total—that is, whether to use gross assets or net assets. Using net assets eliminates current liabilities from the ratio. The assumption is that current liabilities, which are mostly operational (accounts payable, current taxes due, current repay-ments of short-term debt, and accrued obligations), are available to the business as a matter of course. There-fore, the amount of assets employed in the business is effectively reduced by these ongoing operational credit relationships.

Such reasoning is especially important for trading firms, where the size of accounts payable to suppliers is quite significant in the total balance sheet.

Working Capital Management. Among the assets of a company, the key working capital accounts—inventories and accounts receivable—are usually given special at-tention. The ratios used to analyze these categories at-tempt to express the relative effectiveness with which inventories and receivables are managed. They aid the analyst in detecting signs of deterioration in value, or excessive accumulation of inventories and receivables. The amounts as stated on the balance sheet are gener-ally related to the single best indicator of activity levels, such as sales or cost of sales (cost of goods sold), on the assumption that a reasonably close relationship exists between assets and the indicator.

Inventories can't be judged precisely, short of an ac-tual count, verification, and appraisal of value. Because an outside analyst can rarely do this, the next best step is to relate the recorded inventory to net sales or to cost of goods sold, to see whether there's a shift in the relationship over a period of time. Normally *average* in-ventory values are used to make this calculation (the average of beginning and ending inventories). At times, it's also desirable to use only ending inventories, espe-cially in the case of rapidly growing firms where inven-tories are being built up to support steeply rising sales.

Furthermore, it's necessary to observe closely the method of inventory costing employed by the com-pany—such as last-in, first-out (LIFO), first-in, first-out (FIFO), or average costing—and any changes made dur-ing the time span covered by the analysis, as these can significantly affect the amounts recorded on the balance sheet. (We'll discuss inventory costing and other accounting issues later in this chapter.)

While the simple relationship of sales and inventories will often suffice as a broad measure of performance, it's usually more precise to relate inventories to cost of goods sold, because only then will both elements of the ratio be stated on a comparable cost basis. Using net sales causes a distortion because recorded sales include a profit markup that's not included in the stated cost of the inventories on the balance sheet.

The difference in the two methods of calculating the size of inventory relative to sales or cost of sales is reflected in the following equations:

$$\frac{\text{Inventory}}{\text{to sales}} = \frac{\text{Average inventory}}{\text{Net sales}} = \frac{.5(\$422 + \$512)}{\$8,311} = \frac{\$467}{\$8,311} = 5.6\%$$
$$(1991:\ 6.6\%)$$

and

$$\frac{\text{Inventory to}}{\text{cost of sales}} = \frac{\text{Average inventory}}{\text{Cost of sales}} = \frac{\$467}{\$6,617} = 7.1\% \quad (1991:\ 8.3\%)$$

In the sample calculations we've used total TRW sales and total cost of goods and services. The fact that TRW has three rather different major businesses and numerous product lines suggests that a more refined analysis may be desirable. Inventories essentially relate to manufactured products, which in TRW's case would be its space and defense and its automotive businesses. In contrast, the information systems and services business provides services to its customers.

If TRW's information systems and services business were more significant than its current 9 percent share of sales volume, it would be useful to develop separate ratios for the three businesses if detailed inventory information were available to the outsider. The line of business breakdown generally presented in annual reports doesn't provide this insight.

When we deal with any manufacturing company we must also be particularly aware of the problem of accounting measurements—so often encountered when using other analytical methods—because inventories' stated value can be seriously affected by the specific cost accounting system employed.

When assessing the effectiveness of a company's inventory management, it's more common to use the number of times inventory has turned over during the period of analysis, instead of the percentage approach used in the previous illustration.

The TRW inventory turnover figures are

$$\frac{\text{Inventory}}{\text{turnover (sales)}} = \frac{\text{Net sales}}{\text{Average inventory}} = \frac{\$8,311}{\$467} = 17.8 \text{ times}$$
$$(1991: 15.2 \text{ times})$$

and

$$\frac{\text{Inventory turnover}}{\text{(cost of sales)}} = \frac{\text{Cost of sales}}{\text{Average inventory}} = \frac{\$6,617}{\$467} = 14.2 \text{ times}$$
$$(1991: 12.1 \text{ times})$$

These calculations reflect the frequency with which the inventory was turned over during the operating period. In TRW's case, turnover improved due to a combination of inventory management and a change in the mix of products, partly due to its restructuring and acquisition activities. Generally speaking, the higher the turnover number, the better because low inventories often suggest efficient use of capital and minimal risk of unsalable goods.

However, inventory turnover figures that are well above industry practice may signal the potential for inventory shortages, resultant poor customer service, and thus the risk of suffering a competitive disadvantage. The final judgment about what a desirable turnover goal should be depends on the specific circumstances.

The analysis of accounts receivable again is based on net sales. Here the question is whether accounts receivable at the end of the period closely approximate the amount of credit sales we would expect to remain uncollected under prevailing credit terms. For example, a business selling under terms of net/30 would normally expect to show as accounts receivable the recorded sales of the prior month. If 40 or 50 days' sales were reflected on its balance sheet, this could mean that some customers had difficulty paying or were abusing their credit privileges, or that some sales had to be made on extended terms.

An exact analysis of accounts receivable can only be made by examining the "aging" of the individual accounts recorded on the company's books. Aging involves classifying accounts receivable into brackets of days outstanding—10 days, 20 days, 30 days, 40 days, and so on—and relating this pattern to the credit terms applicable in the business. Because this type of analysis requires access to inside information, financial analysts assessing the business from the outside must be satisfied with the relatively crude overall approach of restating accounts receivable in terms of the number of days' sales they represent.

This is done in the following two steps, using TRW's figures:

(1) Sales per day $= \dfrac{\text{Net sales}}{\text{Days in the year}} = \dfrac{\$8,311}{360} = \$23.09/\text{day}$

$$(1991: \$21.98/\text{day})$$

and

(2) Days outstanding $= \dfrac{\text{Accounts receivable}}{\text{Sales per day}} = \dfrac{\$1,289}{\$23.09} = 55.7 \text{ days}$

$$(1991: 61.7 \text{ days})$$

Again, TRW is showing a significant improvement in the management of receivables.

A complication arises when a company's sales are normally made to different types of customers under varying terms, or when the sales are made partly for cash and partly on account. If at all possible, cash and credit sales should be differentiated. If no detailed information is available on this aspect and on the terms of sale used, the rough average we just calculated must suffice to provide a broad indication of trends.

A similar process can be used to judge a company's performance regarding the management of accounts payable. The analysis is a little more complicated because accounts payable should be specifically related to the purchases made during the operating period. Normally such information isn't readily available to the outside analyst, except in the case of trading companies, where the amount of purchases can be readily deduced by adding the change from beginning to ending inventories to the cost of goods sold for the period.

In a manufacturing company, purchases of goods and services are buried in the cost-of-goods-sold account and in the inventories at the end of the operating period. A crude approximation can be made in such cases by relating accounts payable to the average daily use of raw materials if this expense element can be identified from the available information.

In most cases, we can follow the approach used for analyzing accounts receivable if we can approximate the average daily purchases for the period. The number of days of accounts payable is then directly related to the normal credit terms under which the company makes purchases, and serious deviations from that norm can be spotted.

Optimal management of accounts payable involves remitting payment within the terms, but not sooner—yet taking discounts whenever offered for early payment, such as 2 percent if paid in 10 days versus remitting the full amount due in 30 days. Credit rating agencies can be a source of information to the analyst because they'll express an opinion on the timeliness with which a company is meeting its credit obligations, including accounts payable.

Human resource effectiveness has been gaining increased attention in recent years. Ratios used in measuring this complex area go beyond purely financial relationships, and are based on carefully developed statistics on output data, such as various productivity indicators. They also focus on managing human resources, such as costs of employment, training and development, and the whole complex of compensation and benefits administration. Examples of broad measures are units of output per employee, dollars of investment per employee, costs of hiring and training per employee, and benefits costs per employee.

Profitability

Here the issue is the effectiveness with which management has employed both the total assets and the net assets as recorded on the balance sheet. This is judged by relating net profit—defined in a variety of ways—to the assets utilized in generating the profit. The relationship is one of the more telling analyses although the nature and timing of the stated values on the balance sheet will again tend to distort the results.

Return on Assets. The easiest form of profitability analysis is to relate reported net profit (net income) to the total assets on the balance sheet. Net assets (total assets less current liabilities) may also be used with the argument (mentioned earlier) that current operating liabilities are available essentially without cost to support a portion of the current assets. Net assets are also called the *capitalization* of the company or *invested capital*, representing the portion of total assets supported by equity and long-term debt. Whether total or net assets are employed, it's also appropriate to use *average* assets for the period instead of ending balances. Using average assets allows for changes due to growth, decline, or other significant influences on the business.

The calculations for both forms of return on assets—in this case using ending balances—for TRW are

$$\frac{\text{Return on}}{\text{total assets}} = \frac{\text{Net profit*}}{\text{Total assets}} = \frac{\$194}{\$5,458} = 3.6\% \quad (1991: -2.5\%)$$

*Before cumulative effect of accounting changes.

or

$$\frac{\text{Return on}}{\text{net assets}} = \frac{\text{Net profit*}}{\text{Net assets (capitalization)}} = \frac{\$194}{\$5,458 - 2,012} = 5.6\%$$
$$(1991: -3.8\%)$$

*Before cumulative effect of accounting changes.

While either ratio is an indicator of overall profitability, the results can be seriously distorted by nonrecurring gains and losses during the period, changes in the company's capital structure (the relative proportions of interest-bearing long-term debt and owners' equity), by significant restructuring and acquisitions, and by changes in federal income tax regulations applicable for the period analyzed. It's usually desirable to make further adjustments if some of these conditions prevail, as we did for TRW.

Return on Assets before Interest and Taxes. As we've stated, net profit (net income or net earnings) is the final operating result after interest and taxes have been deducted. It's therefore affected by the proportion of debt contained in the capital structure through the resultant interest charges. A somewhat more meaningful result can be obtained when we eliminate both interest and taxes from the profit figure and use **EBIT** (earnings before interest and taxes) which we demonstrated earlier. Moreover, it will again be generally useful to eliminate any significant unusual or nonrecurring income and expense items.

The revised return ratio expresses the gross earnings power of the capital employed in the business independent of the pattern of financing that provided the capital, and independent of changes in the tax laws.

We calculate TRW's return on assets before interest and taxes, based on average assets, as follows:

124

$$\begin{array}{l}\text{Return on average} \\ \text{total assets before} \\ \text{interest and taxes}\end{array} = \dfrac{\begin{array}{c}\text{Net profit*}\\\text{before interest}\\\text{and taxes (EBIT)}\end{array}}{\text{Average assets}} = \dfrac{\$348 + \$163}{\$5,546} = 9.2\%$$

(1991: 1.1%)

*Before cumulative effect of accounting changes.

or

$$\begin{array}{l}\text{Return on average} \\ \text{net assets before} \\ \text{interest and taxes}\end{array} = \dfrac{\begin{array}{c}\text{Net profit*}\\\text{before interest}\\\text{and taxes (EBIT)}\end{array}}{\begin{array}{c}\text{Average net assets}\\\text{(capitalization)}\end{array}} = \dfrac{\$511}{\$3,550} = 14.4\%$$

(1991: 1.8%)

*Before cumulative effect of accounting changes.

If we accept the argument that income taxes are a normal part of doing business, this result can be modified by using net profit before interest but after taxes. We can again employ the simple adjustment shown earlier to add back to net profit the aftertax cost of interest and the aftertax effect of any nonrecurring income and expense items.

When there's reason to believe that income taxes paid were modified for any reason and the effective tax rate doesn't reflect normal conditions, the marginal income tax rate should be used to calculate the net effect of interest and other items added back.

We calculate TRW as follows:

$$\begin{array}{l}\text{Return on average} \\ \text{total assets before} \\ \text{interest, after taxes}\end{array} = \dfrac{\begin{array}{c}\text{Net profit*}\\\text{after taxes}\\\text{before interest}\end{array}}{\text{Average assets}} = \dfrac{\$285}{\$5,546} = 5.1\%$$

(1991: −0.6%)

*Before cumulative effect of accounting changes.

or

$$\begin{array}{l}\text{Return on average} \\ \text{net assets before} \\ \text{interest, after taxes}\end{array} = \dfrac{\begin{array}{c}\text{Net profit*}\\\text{after taxes}\\\text{before interest}\end{array}}{\begin{array}{c}\text{Average net assets}\\\text{(capitalization)}\end{array}} = \dfrac{\$285}{\$3,550} = 8.0\%$$

(1991: −1.0%)

*Before cumulative effect of accounting changes.

Note that the results of our last two sets of more refined calculations show a greater improvement in TRW's overall effectiveness of asset utilization compared to the first calculation which was based on net profit alone. If we had adjusted for the restructuring elements in both years, the improvement would be less, as 1991 would be a much more profitable year. Again, it would be useful to break down these results into major product lines, but in most cases there's not enough information to make all the adjustments from published data.

Another refinement used at times is the relationship of profit, defined in the various ways we've described, to the net assets of the business restated on a *current value* basis. This requires a series of very specific assumptions about the true economic value of various assets or business segments of a company, and it's employed particularly by analysts developing a case for the takeover of a company that may be underperforming on this basis. At this writing the Financial Accounting Standards Board is developing new rules that take some changes in value into account.

As we'll discuss in Chapter 6, profitability also depends on the economic analysis and successful implementation of new *investment projects*. Here we must define and develop the relevant cash flow changes brought about by the investment decision, and judge the results through an economic appraisal process based on discounted cash flow techniques. In recent years this methodology has been expanded to measuring the *cash flow return on investment* on both existing and new investments, in effect treating the company as a whole or its major parts as if they were a series of investment projects. This calls for a number of specialized techniques—a subject we'll return to in Chapter 9's discussion of valuation concepts.

In summary, the various ratios available for judging a business from management's point of view deal with the effectiveness of operations, the effectiveness of capital deployment, and the profitability achieved on the assets deployed. These measures are all affected to some degree by uncertainties involving accounting and valuation methods, but together they can provide reasonable clues to a firm's performance, and also suggest areas for further analysis.

OWNERS' POINT OF VIEW

We now turn to the second of the three viewpoints relevant in analyzing performance, that of the owners of a business. These are the investors to whom management is responsible and accountable. So far we haven't mentioned owners directly, even though it should be clear that a firm's management must be fully cognizant of, and responsive to, the owners' viewpoint and expectations in the timing, execution, and appraisal of the results of operations. Similarly, management must be alert to the lenders' viewpoint and criteria.

The key interest of a business's owners—the shareholders in the case of a corporation—is profitability. In this context, profitability means the returns achieved, through the efforts of management, on funds invested by the owners. The owners are also interested in the disposition of earnings that belong to them, that is, how much is reinvested in the business versus how much is paid out to them as dividends. Finally, they're concerned about business results' effect on their investment's market value, especially in the case of publicly traded stock. The key concepts related to this last aspect are detailed in Chapters 7 and 9, so we'll only refer briefly to them here.

Profitability

The financial community closely watches the relationship of profits earned to shareholders' stated investment in a company. Analysts track several key measures that express the company's performance in relation to the owners' stake. Two of these—return on net worth and return on common equity—address the profitability of the total ownership investment, while the third, earnings per share, measures the proportional participation of each unit of investment in corporate earnings for the period.

Return on Net Worth.   The most common ratio used for measuring the return on the owners' investment is the relationship of net profit to net worth (equity or shareholders' investment). In performing this calculation, we don't have to make any adjustment for interest, because net profit has already been properly reduced by interest charges, if any, paid to creditors and lenders. We do have to consider the impact of nonrecurring and unusual events, such as restructuring and accounting adjustments.

For purposes of this calculation, net income is the residual result of operations and belongs totally to the holders of common or preferred equity shares. Within the shareholder group, only those holding common shares have a claim on the residual after obligatory preferred dividends have been paid.

The ratio is calculated for TRW's shareholders' investment (shown in Figure 3–2) as follows:

$$\frac{\text{Return on}}{\text{net worth}} = \frac{\text{Net profit*}}{\text{Net worth (equity)}} = \frac{\$194}{\$1,416} = 13.7\%$$

$$(1991: -8.3\%)$$

*Before cumulative effect of accounting changes.

Here we've used the ending shareholders' investment (net worth). It's quite common, however, to use the average net worth for this calculation on the assumption that profitable operations build up shareholders' equity during the year and that therefore the annual profit should be related to the midpoint of this buildup.

The ratio for TRW is calculated as follows:

$$\frac{\text{Return on average}}{\text{net worth}} = \frac{\text{Net profit*}}{\substack{\text{Average} \\ \text{net worth}}} = \frac{\$194}{.5(\$1,416+\$1,685)} = 12.5\%$$

$$(1991: -7.8\%)$$

*Before cumulative effect of accounting changes.

A possible distortion must be mentioned here. Frequently questions arise about how a particular liability account on the balance sheet, "deferred taxes," should be handled in this analysis. Less frequently there's even a deferred taxes account on the asset side of the balance sheet. As we've said, deferred taxes represent the accumulated difference between the accounting treatment and the tax treatment of a variety of revenue and expense elements. Essentially they're tax payments deferred (or advanced) due to a timing difference in recognizing tax deductions allowable under prevailing Internal Revenue Service (IRS) rules.

Such deferrals mean either (1) that a liability is recorded against the time that this accumulated tax benefit might begin to be "recaptured" by the Internal Revenue Service or (2) in the case of an asset, that advance tax payments will have to be amortized. The former would happen if the company stopped investing in depreciable assets, if future tax laws eliminated accelerated depreciation, or if recognition of income differences changed, as happened in 1989 with installment contracts under revised IRS rules, a change that particularly affects TRW's space and defense sector.

Some analysts argue that deferred income tax liabilities are, in effect, owners' equity set aside against future higher tax levels. Others argue that they represent a form of long-term debt. Because there's no consensus on the analytical treatment, deferred income taxes often aren't included in any of the ratio calculations. As this accumulation on the liability side of the balance sheet may be quite large, material differences can result from an inclusion of deferred taxes as owners' equity or long-term debt.

Return on Common Equity.   A somewhat more refined version of the calculation of return on owners' investment is necessary if there are several types of stock outstanding, such as preferred stock in different forms. The goal is to develop a return based on earnings accruing to the holders of common shares only. The net profit figure is first reduced by dividends paid to holders of preferred shares and by other obligatory payments, such as distributions to holders of minority interests. Net worth is likewise reduced by the stated amount of preferred equity and any minority elements, to arrive at the common equity figure. TRW in effect has only common stock outstanding, since its Serial Preference Stock II is reflected at the very nominal value of just $1.0 million. Thus, we'll merely show the formula for the calculation because the results will be the same:

$$\frac{\text{Return on}}{\text{common}}_{\text{equity}} = \frac{\text{Net profit to common}}{\text{Average common equity}} = \text{Percent}$$

Return on common equity is a widely published statistic. Rankings of companies and industry sectors are compiled by major business magazines and rating agencies. The ratio is closely watched by stock market analysts and, in turn, by management and the board of directors. But as we've observed, the accuracy of recorded balance sheet values and earnings calculations is an issue in this ratio as well, and adjustments may be necessary if the analyst is aware of major inconsistencies.

Earnings per Share.   The analysis of earnings from the owners' point of view centers on earnings per share in the case of a corporation. This ratio simply involves dividing the net profit to common stock by the average number of shares of common stock outstanding:

$$\frac{\text{Earnings}}{\text{per share}} = \frac{\text{Net profit to common}}{\begin{array}{c}\text{Average number of}\\\text{shares outstanding}\end{array}} = \frac{\text{Dollars}}{\text{per share}}$$

Earnings per share is a measure to which both management and shareholders pay a great deal of attention. It's widely used in the valuation of common stock, and is often the basis for setting specific corporate objectives and goals as part of strategic planning. Chapters 8 and 9 contain more background on the uses and limitations of this measure. Normally the analyst doesn't have to calculate earnings per share because the result is readily announced by large and small corporations alike.

In TRW's 1992 annual report, earnings per share were reported as $3.09 for 1992 before the cumulative effect of accounting changes, and as $(2.51) representing the net loss for 1992. For 1991, net earnings per share were also negative at $(2.30). (See Figure 3–3.) Earnings per share are available on both annual and quarterly bases, and are a matter of record whenever a company's shares are publicly traded.

A recent requirement by the Financial Accounting Standards Board and the Securities and Exchange Commission calls for the calculation of earnings per share on two bases. The first is the so-called primary earnings per share, which uses average shares actually outstanding during the period. The second basis makes the assumption that all shares potentially outstanding be counted in addition to actual shares outstanding, that is, shares that would result from the conversion of preferred and debt securities that are convertible into common shares under various provisions, or from warrants issued and outstanding.

The result, referred to as "fully diluted" earnings per share, reflects the reduction in earnings per share that would be caused by any overhang of such potential shares—putting the investment community on notice that such a dilutive effect is possible. In TRW's case, there's no potential dilution and fully diluted earnings per share are identical to primary earnings in both years.

Even though the earnings per share figure is one of the most readily available statistics reported by publicly held corporations, some complications exist nevertheless. Apart from possible unusual elements in the quarterly and annual net profit pattern, the number of shares outstanding varies during the year in many companies, either because of newly issued shares (new stock offerings, stock dividends paid, warrants and options exercised, etc.) or because outstanding old shares are retired (purchase of shares to be held by the company treasury stock). Therefore, the *average* number of shares outstanding during the year is commonly used in this calculation. Moreover, any significant change in the number of shares outstanding (such as would be caused by a stock split, for example) requires retroactive adjustments in past data to ensure comparability.

A great deal of interest among analysts is focused on past earnings per share, both quarterly and annual. Future projections are frequently made on the basis of past earnings levels. Fluctuations and trends in actual performance are compared to the projections and watched closely for indications of strength or weakness. Again, great caution is advised in interpreting these data. Allowances must be made for unusual elements both in the earnings figure and in the number of common shares outstanding.

Cash Flow per Share. A calculation to approximate the cash flow per share is frequently used as a rough measure of the company's ability to pay cash dividends. The cash flow per share ratio is used in an effort to simulate the operating funds flow on a per share basis. It's developed from the net profit figure to which operating write-offs such as depreciation, amortization, and depletion have been added back. We recall from our earlier discussion of the funds flow statement that such accounting write-offs don't represent a movement of funds. Therefore, adding back these bookkeeping entries restates the net profit in a form that roughly approximates the funds generated by operations, but leaves out other funds movements, such as changes in working capital and investments in new assets.

The calculation parallels the earnings per share ratio:

$$\frac{\text{Cash flow}}{\text{per share}} = \frac{\text{Net profit to common plus write-offs}}{\text{Average number of shares outstanding}} = \frac{\text{Dollars}}{\text{per share}}$$

In the case of TRW, we know that depreciation and amortization amounted to $392 million and $89 million, respectively. The average number of shares outstanding was given in the annual report as 62.3 million for purposes of calculating primary earnings per share. Write-offs thus amounted to $7.37 per share, which, when added to the primary earnings per share of $3.09, resulted in a cash flow per share of $10.46 in 1992.

Cash flow per share is used to indicate the potential availability of cash for dividends and various other disbursements. Because a firm's use of funds is largely at the discretion of management, however, the figure is at best only a crude indication of the potential to pay dividends. A more extensive analysis of funds flows is required to judge the pattern of sources and uses, as we showed in Chapter 2.

Share Price Appreciation. Apart from current earnings generated for the shareholders, investors expect appreciation in the value of their common shares in the stock market over time. The main driver for this appreciation is the creation of additional economic value—that is, the generation of more positive cash flows than outlays in the long run through the combined effect of investment, operating, and financing decisions.

We'll discuss shareholder value creation more fully in Chapter 9. Suffice it to say here that the analyst will look for movement in the share prices that at least matches and hopefully outperforms the stock market trend as a whole and the trend of particular business segments as expressed in relevant composites of selected companies' share price trends.

Total Shareholder Return.   The return to investors holding shares in a company will be a combination of share price appreciation (or decline) and cash dividends received over appropriate time periods selected for analysis. Since only part of the earnings belonging to shareholders are paid out in the form of dividends, the relevant positive inflow to the shareholder is the stream of dividends received, not the announced earnings per share. The full economic benefit received by the shareholder is the sum of this stream of dividends and the change in the stock's price. This concept is closely related to *shareholder value analysis* (Chapter 9).

Calculations of shareholder return for published companies are routinely available in investor services publications such as the Fortune 500 listings. (See Appendix V.)

Disposition of Earnings

The periodic separation of earnings (net profit) into dividends paid and earnings retained is closely watched by shareholders and the financial community, because the retained residual builds up the owners' equity recorded on the balance sheet and is a source of funds for management's use.

As Chapter 1 said, earnings—after payment of any interest—either are reinvested in the business to support further growth, or are paid out in part or full as dividends. Cash dividends are the most common form of payment, although stock dividends are also frequently used. In the latter case no cash is involved. Instead, additional fractional shares are issued to each holder of record. If a normal cash dividend is paid as well, stock dividends result in fractionally higher cash dividends, of course.

Dividends per Share. Dividends are generally declared publicly on a per share basis every quarter by a corporation's board of directors (the shareholders' elected representatives). Therefore, no calculation is necessary. Dividend policy is the prerogative of the board which has legal authority to set payments at any level it deems appropriate. Because the market value of common stock is in part influenced by dividends paid and anticipated, the board generally deals with this periodic decision carefully. TRW paid dividends of $1.82 per share in 1992 and $1.80 in 1991.

Dividend Yield. Annual dividends paid per share can be related to current or average share prices to derive the dividend yield:

$$\text{Dividend yield} = \frac{\text{Annual dividend per share}}{\text{Average market price per share}} = \text{Percent}$$

This is a measure of the return on the owners' investment from cash dividends. In the case of TRW, the 52-week range of stock prices from January to December 1992 was 60⅓ to 41, with an average of approximately 50⅔. The dividend yield at $1.82 per share thus amounts to 3.6 percent on the average price. The ratio falls short as a basis for comparison with other companies, however, because dividend policies differ widely. As we've said, the total economic return normally enjoyed by the shareholder is a combination of dividends and market appreciation (or decline) of the stock.

Payout/Retention. A ratio commonly used in connection with dividend policy is the so-called payout ratio, which represents the proportion of earnings paid out to shareholders in the form of cash during any given year:

$$\text{Payout ratio} = \frac{\text{Cash dividends per share}}{\text{Earnings per share*}} = \frac{\$1.82}{\$3.09} = 58.9\%$$
$$(1991: \text{negative})$$

*Before cumulative effect of accounting changes.

Because most boards of directors tend to favor paying a fairly stable dividend per share, adjusted only gradually, a firm's payout ratio may fluctuate widely in the short run in response to swings in earnings performance. Over a period of several years, however, the payout ratio can often be used to indicate directors' tendency to reinvest funds in the business versus paying out earnings to shareholders.

There are no firm standards for this ratio, but the relationship is significant in characterizing the corporation's style. High-growth companies tend to pay out relatively low proportions of earnings because they prefer to reinvest earnings to support profitable growth. Stable or moderate-growth companies tend to pay out larger proportions. Some companies pay no cash dividends at all or provide stock dividends. Many more factors must, of course, be considered in making judgments in this area. The references at the end of this chapter provide further insight into both concepts and practices.

Dividend Coverage. Owners are also interested in the degree to which their dividends are covered by earnings and cash flow. Furthermore, they're concerned about the degree to which the proportion of debt in the capital structure and its associated interest and repayment requirements will affect management's ability to achieve reasonably stable and growing earnings, and to pay dividends commensurate with the owners' expectations. A variety of coverage ratios can be calculated, but they hardly differ from the ones we'll take up in the discussion of the lenders' point of view.

Dividends to Assets. Finally, it's sometimes useful to relate the annual dividends paid by a company to the total assets or net assets involved in generating them. The rationale is similar to the dividend yield discussed earlier, except that in this case it's not the market value of the shares, but the book value of the assets they represent that's used as the denominator. It's possible to argue that the market valuation is a more current indicator for the yield relationship than the historical basis of the asset values as recorded on the balance sheet. Nevertheless, dividends to assets is often found as part of an analytical set of performance data.

Market Indicators

We'll only briefly mention two ratios that are commonly used as indicators of stock market values: the price/earnings ratio and the market to book ratio. Market valuation is detailed in Chapters 7 and 9.

Price/Earnings Ratio. The simple relationship between current or expected earnings per share and the stock's current market price is often quoted by both management and owners. The ratio is also called the *earnings multiple* and is used to indicate how the stock market is judging the company's earnings performance and prospects. The calculation is quite straightforward and relates current market prices of common shares to the most recent available earnings per share on an annual basis:

$$\frac{\text{Earnings multiple}}{\text{(price/earnings ratio)}} = \frac{\text{Market price per share}}{\text{Earnings per share}} = \text{Factor}$$

The result is a simple factor. If fully diluted earnings differ significantly from primary earnings per share, the calculation can be done on both bases. The earnings multiple is used commonly as a rough rule of thumb in valuing companies for purposes of acquisition. Earnings multiples vary widely by industry and by company, and are in effect a simple overall approximation of the market's current judgment of industry and company risk versus past and prospective earnings performance. They're tracked by various investor services and related to total market averages as well as average price earnings multiples for selected industry groups so we can assess the relative performance of a particular company.

The reverse of the earnings per share formula, the

so-called earnings yield, relates earnings per share to market price. Although it's sometimes used to express the current yield the owner enjoys, the measure can be misleading because earnings aren't normally paid out in full as dividends. Thus, the earnings yield can't be compared to, for example, the yield on a bond where interest payments are contractual cash remittances. As we already know, the economic return to the shareholder is a combination of the dividends received and the appreciation (decline) of the stock.

Cash Flow Multiple. A variant of relating current earnings performance to current market value is the use of cash flow per share, as discussed earlier. (TRW's cash flow per share in 1992 was $10.46.) Usually the definition of cash flow for this purpose is aftertax profit plus depreciation and amortization, divided by the average number of shares outstanding. We know from Chapter 2 that this represents only a limited view of the actual cash generation of the business, but the measure is widely used and quoted as a rule of thumb that relates operating cash flow to share values.

Market to Book Ratio. This indicator relates current market value on a per share basis to the stated book value of owners' equity on the balance sheet, also on a per share basis. TRW's December 31, 1992, book value per share was $22.31, while the average market value for 1992 at $50⅔ was more than twice this figure. The market to book ratio leaves much to be desired as a measure of performance for many of the reasons mentioned in earlier discussions of other ratios. It's not an economic measure of performance because it relates current share prices to historical accounting values.

In addition, while in a given company the relationship between stated balance sheet values and market values may be favorable, the ratio doesn't truly help the analyst judge what comparable expectations should be for other firms. Thus, the measure can only be a beginning step in the appraisal of long-term performance and outlook.

Relative Price Movements. While the typical investor is interested in the absolute change in the value of the shares held, the insights from the relative performance of the stock to the market as a whole and to appropriate averages for specific industries can be useful to assess the trend of a particular company. These movements can be expressed in absolute dollar terms or in several of the ratios we've mentioned. In view of the growing importance of cash flow thinking, fueled by the acquisition and leveraged buyout boom of the 1980s, services like Value Line provide cash flow multiples as an additional indicator of relative price movements. (See Appendix V.)

In summary, the ratios pertinent to the owners' view of a company's performance are measures of the return owners have earned on their stake and the cash rewards they received in the form of dividends. These results depend on the firm's earning power and on management policies and decisions regarding use of financial leverage and reinvestment. Ultimately, they affect the economic value of the owners' capital commitment as reflected in stock market prices. The concepts and issues are detailed in Chapter 9.

LENDERS' POINT OF VIEW

While the main orientation of management and owners is toward the business as a going concern, the lender—of necessity—has to be of two minds. Lenders are interested in funding the needs of a successful business that will perform as expected. At the same time, they must consider the possible negative consequences of default and liquidation. Sharing none of the rewards of success other than receiving regular payments of interest and principal, the lender must carefully assess the risk of recovering the original funds extended—particularly if they've been provided for a long period of time. Part of the assessment must be the ultimate value of the lender's claim in case of serious difficulty.

The claims of a general creditor rank behind federal tax obligations, accrued wages, and the claims of secured creditors, who lend against a specific asset, such as a building or equipment. Thus, caution dictates looking for a margin of safety in the assets held by the company—a cushion against default.

Several ratios are used to assess this protection by testing the firm's liquidity. Another set of ratios tests the relative debt exposure or leverage of the business to weigh the position of lenders versus owners. Finally, there are so-called coverage ratios relating to the company's ability to provide debt service from funds generated by ongoing operations.

Liquidity

One way to test the degree of protection afforded lenders focuses on short-term credit extended to a business for funding its operations. It involves the liquid assets of a business, that is, those current assets that can readily be converted into cash, on the assumption that these would form a ready cushion against default.

Current Ratio. The ratio most commonly used to appraise the debt exposure represented on the balance sheet is the current ratio. This relates current assets to current liabilities in an attempt to show the safety of current debt holders' claims in case of default. The calculation is shown using TRW's relevant totals from Figure 3–2:

$$\text{Current ratio} = \frac{\text{Current assets}}{\text{Current liabilities}} = \frac{\$2,116}{\$2,012} = 1.05\text{: }1$$

$$(1991\text{: }1.14\text{:}1)$$

Presumably the larger this ratio, the better the position of the debt holders. From the lenders' point of view, a higher ratio would certainly appear to provide a cushion against drastic losses of value in case of business failure. A large excess of current assets over current liabilities seems to help protect claims, should inventories have to be liquidated at a forced sale and should accounts receivable involve sizable collection problems.

Seen from another angle, however, an excessively high current ratio might signal slack management practices. It could indicate idle cash balances, inventory levels that have become excessive when compared to current needs, and poor credit management that results in over-extended accounts receivable. At the same time, the business might not be making full use of its current borrowing power.

A common rule of thumb is the belief that a current ratio of 2:1 is about right for most businesses because this ratio appears to permit a shrinkage of up to 50 percent in the value of current assets while still providing enough cushion to cover all current liabilities. The problem with this concept is that the current ratio measures an essentially static condition and assesses a business as if it were on the brink of liquidation. The ratio doesn't reflect a going concern, which should be management's top priority. The lender or creditor looking for future business with a successful client should bear this in mind. Note that TRW's year-to-year decline in the ratio was brought about by decreases in inventories and receivables, while current liabilities rose slightly. Given the temporary nature of this measure, the change should cast no negative implications on the firm's creditworthiness, especially since the restructuring activities affected both 1992 and 1991.

Acid Test. An even more stringent test, although again on a static basis, is the acid test or *quick ratio*, which is calculated using only a portion of current assets—cash, marketable securities, and accounts receivable—which are then related to current liabilities as follows:

$$\frac{\text{Acid}}{\text{test}} = \frac{\text{Cash} + \text{securities} + \text{Receivables}}{\text{Current liabilities}} = \frac{\$66 + \$1{,}289}{\$2.012} = .67{:}1$$

$$(1991{:}\ .72{:}1)$$

The key concept here is to test the collectibility of current liabilities in the case of a real crisis, on the assumption that inventories would have no value at all. As drastic tests of the ability to pay in the face of disaster, both the current ratio and acid test are helpful.

From an operational standpoint, however, it's better to analyze a business in terms of the expected total future cash flow pattern, which projects inflows and outflows over the period for which credit is extended. The proportion of current assets to current liabilities normally covers only a small part of this picture.

Quick Sale Value. Another stringent test that can be applied to the business as a whole is making a series of assumptions about what cash value the various assets of the company would bring in a hurried sale, and relating this total to the firm's liabilities. Again, this is a liquidation point of view that doesn't allow for ongoing cash flow patterns.

Financial Leverage

As Chapters 5 and 8 relate, successful use of debt enhances earnings for the firm's owners because returns earned on these funds—over and above the interest paid—belong to the owners and thus will increase owners' equity. From the lenders' viewpoint, however, when earnings don't exceed or even fall short of the interest cost, fixed interest and principal commitments must still be met. The owners must fulfill these claims, which might then severely affect owners' equity. The positive and negative effects of leverage increase with the proportion of debt in a business. The risk exposure of the providers of debt grows, as does owners' risk exposure.

From the lenders' point of view, a variety of ratios that deal with total debt, or long-term debt only, in relation to various parts of the balance sheet are more inclusive measures of risk than leverage alone. These ratios measure lenders' risk exposure in relation to the available asset values against which all claims are held.

Debt to Assets. The first and broadest test is the proportion of total debt, both current and long-term, to total assets, which we calculate as follows:

$$\text{Debt to assets} = \frac{\text{Total debt}}{\text{Total assets}} = \frac{\$3,979^*}{\$5,458} = 72.9\% \quad (1991: 69.0\%)$$

*Includes long-term liabilities and deferred income taxes.

This ratio describes the proportion of "other peoples' money" to the total claims against the firm's assets. The higher the ratio, the greater the likely risk for the lender. It's not necessarily a true test of the firm's ability to cover its debts, however, because, as we've already observed, the asset amounts recorded on the balance sheet don't necessarily indicate current economic values or even liquidation values. Nor does the ratio give any clues as to likely earnings and cash flow fluctuations that might affect current interest and principal payments.

Debt to Capitalization. A more refined version of the debt proportion analysis involves the ratio of long-term debt to capitalization (invested capital). The latter is again defined as the sum of the long-term claims against the business, both debt and owners' equity, but doesn't include short-term (current) liabilities. This total also corresponds to net assets, unless some adjustments were made, such as ignoring deferred taxes.

The calculation appears as follows, when long-term liabilities and deferred taxes are included in the debt total:

$$\text{Debt to capitalization} = \frac{\text{Long-term debt}}{\text{Capitalization (net assets)}} = \frac{\$1{,}967}{\$3{,}446} = 57.1\%$$

$$(1991): 52.1\%)$$

If deferred taxes are excluded from debt, the ratio changes to 50.6 percent and 40.1 percent, respectively.

Another definition of debt is sometimes used, which includes (1) short-term debt (other than trade credit), (2) the current portion of long-term debt, and (3) all long-term debt in the form of contractual obligations. Long-term liabilities representing potential employee benefit claims aren't counted as part of the capitalization of the company. In TRW's case the debt total thus becomes $1,217 ($260 + $16 + $941) and the capitalization becomes $2,918 ($1,217 + $222 + $63 + 1,416), resulting in a ratio of 41.7 percent for 1992 and 43.0 percent for 1991.

A great deal of emphasis is placed on the ratio of debt to capitalization, carefully defined for any particular company, because many lending agreements of both publicly held and private corporations contain covenants regulating maximum debt exposure expressed in terms of debt to capitalization proportions. There remains an issue of how to classify different liabilities and how to deal with accounting changes, such as most companies, including TRW, experienced in having to establish long-term liabilities for future employee benefits.

As we'll see later, however, there's growing emphasis on a more relevant aspect of debt exposure, namely, the ability to service the debt from ongoing funds flows, a much more dynamic view of lender relationships.

Debt to Equity. A third version of the analysis of debt proportions involves the ratio of total debt (normally the sum of current liabilities and all types of long-term debt) to total owners' equity (net worth). The debt/equity ratio is an attempt to show, in another format, the relative proportions of all lenders' claims to ownership claims, and it's used as a measure of debt exposure.

The measure is expressed as either a percentage or as a proportion. The following example's figures again were taken from TRW's balance sheet in Figure 3–2, where equity is called shareholder investment:

$$\text{Debt to equity} = \frac{\text{Total debt}}{\text{Net worth (equity)}^*} = \frac{\$3,979}{\$1,479} = 269\%$$
$$(1991: 222.6\%)$$

*Includes minority interests.

In preparing this ratio, as in some earlier instances, the question of deferred income taxes and other estimated long-term liabilities is often sidestepped by leaving these potential long-term claims out of the debt and capitalization figures altogether. We've included these elements here. One specific refinement of this formula uses only long-term debt, as related to net worth, ignoring long-term obligations and deferred taxes:

$$\begin{array}{c}\text{Debt to equity}\\ \text{(alternate)}\end{array} = \frac{\text{Long-term debt}}{\text{Net worth (equity)}^*} = \frac{\$941}{\$1,479} = 63.6\%$$
$$(1991: 69.4\%)$$

*Includes minority interests.

The various formats of these relationships imply the care with which the ground rules must be defined for any particular analysis and for the covenants governing specific lending agreements. They only hint at the risk/reward trade-off implicit in the use of debt, which we'll cover in Chapters 7 and 9.

Debt Service

Regardless of the specific choice from among the several ratios we just discussed, debt proportion analysis is in essence static and doesn't take into account the operating dynamics and economic values of the business. The analysis is totally derived from the balance sheet, which in itself is a static snapshot of the financial condition of the business at a single point in time.

Nonetheless, the relative ease with which these ratios are calculated probably accounts for their popularity.

Such ratios are useful as indicators of trends when they're applied over a series of time periods. However, they still don't get at the heart of an analysis of creditworthiness, which involves a company's ability to pay both interest and principal on schedule as contractually agreed upon (that is, to service its debt).

Interest Coverage. One frequently encountered ratio reflecting a company's debt service uses the relationship of net profit (earnings) before interest and taxes (**EBIT**) to the amount of the interest payments for the period. This ratio is developed with the expectation that annual operating earnings can be considered a basic source of funds for debt service, and that any significant change in this relationship might signal difficulties. Major earnings fluctuations are one type of risk considered.

No hard and fast standards for the ratio itself exist. Rather, prospective debt holders often require covenants in the loan agreement spelling out the number of times the business is expected to cover its debt service obligations. The ratio is simple to calculate. We can employ the **EBIT** figure developed for **TRW** earlier in the management section:

$$\frac{\text{Interest}}{\text{coverage}} = \frac{\text{Net profit before interest and taxes (EBIT)}}{\text{Interest expense}} = \frac{\$511}{\$163} = 3.1 \text{ times} \quad (1991:\text{ negative})$$

The specifics are based on judgment, often involving a detailed analysis of a company's past, current, and prospective conditions.

Burden Coverage. A somewhat more refined analysis of debt coverage relates the net profit of the business, before interest and taxes, to the sum of current interest and principal repayments, in an attempt to indicate the company's ability to service the burden of its debt in all aspects. A problem arises with this particular analysis because interest payments are tax deductible, while

146

principal repayments aren't. Thus, we must be on guard to think about these figures on a comparable basis.

One often-used correction involves converting the principal repayments into an equivalent pretax amount. This is done by dividing the principal repayment by the factor "one minus the effective tax rate." The resulting calculation appears as follows, if we take as repayments the $351 million in principal (due in over 90 days) TRW paid in 1992, as indicated in the funds flow statement in its 1992 annual report (see Chapter 2):

$$\frac{\text{Burden}}{\text{coverage}} = \frac{\text{Net profit before interest and taxes (EBIT)}}{\text{Interest} + \dfrac{\text{Principal repayments}}{(1 - \text{Tax rate})}} = \frac{\$511}{\$163 + \dfrac{\$351}{(1 - .443)}}$$

$$= \frac{\$511}{\$163 + \$630} = .74 \text{ times}$$

An alternate format uses operating cash flow (net profit after taxes plus write-offs), taken from Figure 3–3, to which aftertax interest has been added back. This is then compared to the sum of aftertax interest and principal repayment. The calculation for 1992 is

$$\frac{\text{Burden}}{\text{coverage}} = \frac{\dfrac{\text{Operating}}{\text{cash flow}} + \dfrac{\text{Interest}}{(1 - \text{Tax rate})}}{\dfrac{\text{Interest}}{(1 - \text{Tax rate})} + \dfrac{\text{Principal}}{\text{repayments}}} =$$

$$= \frac{\$194 + \$392 + \$89 + \$163(1 - .443)}{\$163(1 - .443) + \$351}$$

$$= \frac{\$675 + \$163(.557)}{\$163(.557) + \$351} = \frac{\$767}{\$442} = 1.74 \text{ times.}$$

Cash Flow Analysis. Determining a company's ability to meet its debt obligations is most meaningful when a review of past profit and cash flow patterns is made over a long enough time period to indicate the major operational and cyclical fluctuations that are normal for the company and its industry. This may involve financial statements covering several years or several seasonal swings, as appropriate, in an attempt to identify characteristic high and low points in earnings and funds needs. The pattern of past conditions must then be projected into the future to see what margin of safety remains to cover interest, principal repayments, and other fixed payments such as major lease obligations. These techniques are discussed in Chapter 4.

If a business is subject to sizable fluctuations in aftertax cash flow, lenders may be reluctant to extend credit when the debt service can't be covered several times at the low point in the operational pattern. In contrast, a very stable business would encounter less stringent coverage demands. The type of dynamic analysis involved is a form of financial modeling that can be greatly enhanced both in scope and in the number of possible alternative conditions explored by using computer spreadsheets.

RATIOS AS A SYSTEM

The ratios discussed in this chapter have many elements in common as they're derived from key components of the same financial statements. In fact, they're often interrelated and can be viewed as a system. The analyst can turn a series of ratios into a dynamic display highlighting the elements that are the most important levers used by management to affect operating performance.

In internal analysis, many companies employ systems of ratios and standards that segregate into their components the series of decisions affecting operating performance, overall returns, and shareholder expectations. Du Pont was one of the first to do so almost a century ago. Early on, the company published a chart showing the effects and interrelationships of decisions in these areas, thus representing the first "model" of its business.

We'll demonstrate the relationships between the ratios discussed by using two key parameters segregated into their elements: *return on assets,* which is of major importance for judging management performance, and *return on equity,* the key measure from the owners' viewpoint. We'll leave aside the refinements applicable to each to concentrate on the linkages. As we'll show, it's possible to model the performance of a given company by expanding and relating these ratios. Needless to say, careful attention must be paid to the exact definition of the elements entering into the ratios for a particular company to achieve internal consistency. Also, we must ensure that the ratios are interpreted in ways that foster economic trade-offs and decisions.

Elements of Return on Assets

The basic formula for return on assets (ROA) is

$$\text{Return on assets} = \frac{\text{Net profit}}{\text{Assets}}$$

We also know that net profit is related both to asset turnover and to sales. Thus, we can restate the formula as

$$\text{Return on assets} = \frac{\text{Net profit}}{\text{Sales}} \times \frac{\text{Sales}}{\text{Assets}}$$

Note that the element of sales cancels out in the second formula, resulting in the original expression. But we can further expand the relationship by substituting even more elements in the basic equation:

$$\text{ROA} = \frac{(\text{Gross margin} - \text{Expenses})(1 - \text{Tax rate})}{\text{Price} \times \text{Volume}} \times \frac{\text{Price} \times \text{Volume}}{\text{Fixed} + \text{Current} + \text{Other assets}}$$

We can see that the relationships expressed here

serve as a simple model of key decision levers management can employ to improve return on assets. For example, improvement in gross margin is important, as is control of expenses. Price/volume relationships are canceled out, but they're essential factors in arriving at gross margin, as we know. (The first bracket could have been expanded to include the price/volume relationship.)

Asset management is crucial because the return on assets will rise if fewer assets are employed and all the measures of effective management of working capital apply. Minimizing taxes within the legal options available will also improve the return.

Elements of Return on Equity

A similar approach can be taken with the basic formula for return on owners' equity:

$$\text{Return on equity} = \frac{\text{Net profit}}{\text{Equity}}$$

If we use some of the basic profit and turnover relationships to expand the expression, the following formula emerges:

$$\text{Return on equity} = \frac{\text{Net profit}}{\text{Assets}} \times \frac{\text{Assets}}{\text{Equity}}$$

Note that in effect the formula states that return on equity (ROE) consists of two elements: the net profit on assets and the degree of leverage or debt capital used in the business. *Assets to equity* is a way of describing this proportionality.

We can expand the formula even more to include components of the return on assets:

$$\text{ROE} = \frac{\text{Net profit}}{\text{Sales}} \times \frac{\text{Sales}}{\text{Assets}} \times \frac{\text{Assets}}{\text{Assets} - \text{Liabilities}}$$

Now we can again look for the key decision levers that management should use to raise the return on owners' equity. As before, improving profitability of sales (operations) comes first, combined with effective use of assets that generate sales. An added factor is the boosting effect from using debt in the capital structure. The greater the liabilities, the greater the improvement in return on equity—assuming, of course, that the business is profitable to begin with and earns more on its investments than the cost of debt.

Using other people's money can be quite helpful—until the risk of default on debt service in a down cycle becomes significant. The analyst can use this simple framework to test the impact on the return on equity from one or more changed conditions, and to test how sensitive the result is to the magnitude of change introduced.

A more inclusive format of the relationship of key ratios to each other and to the three major decision areas is displayed in Figure 3–4. We've added the major drivers behind the ratios on the left, as an indication of the levers management can use in managing the company. Note that in this diagram we've included the cost of interest on debt as part of the net contribution from leverage in the financing area, while defining operating earnings as excluding the cost of interest.

This representation can be viewed as a simple model of a business in ratio format, and can be useful in tracing through the effects from changes in any of the drivers that are caused by management decisions. Chapters 4 and 5 return to the subject of business modeling.

SELECTED ISSUES

The impact of accounting practices and decisions on the management of funds was briefly mentioned in Chapter 1, which identified accounting write-offs and deferred taxes as aspects to consider. At this point we should refine our understanding of these issues a

FIGURE 3–4
A Systems View of Key Ratios and Their Elements

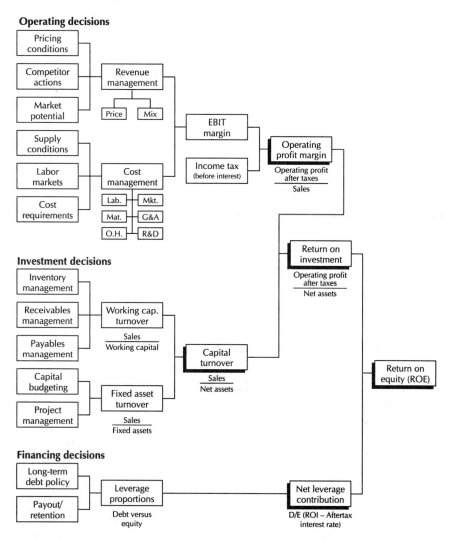

little further because possible alternative treatments of these matters at times significantly affect the assessment of operations as well as the patterns of funds flows.

A review of the key choices available to management in the areas of *inventory costing* and *depreciation methods* may help readers to form their own judgments when faced with interpreting financial statements and funds flows. We'll also briefly mention effects of *inflation,* although no satisfactory methods of dealing with that issue have been established so far.

Appendix II contains some of the more specialized issues of interpreting performance statements in an international setting, especially the problem of judging the profitability of parts of a multibusiness company operating in different countries.

Inventory Costing

One accounting challenge present at all times is the proper allocation of a portion of the costs accumulated in the inventory account to the actual goods being sold. We can visualize layers of cost built up over time in the inventory account, which correspond to the physical movement of raw materials, work in process, and finished goods into storage. The accountant wants to match revenues and expenses in keeping track of the inventory account, yet from a physical standpoint, it's just as possible to ship the oldest unit on hand as it is to ship the most recent arrival. The warehouse supervisor can even pick the goods at random.

If unit costs never changed, matching costs to revenues wouldn't be a problem because the accountant would simply track the number of units shipped and multiply them by the unchanged unit cost, regardless of the actual physical choices made by the warehouse supervisor. In real life, however, several problems arise. A manufacturing company may experience fluctuations that affect the unit cost of the products inventoried. This effectively results in different layers of cost recorded in the finished goods inventory account.

Further, the prices of raw materials and other inputs may be positively or negatively influenced by supply and demand. The materials inventory account will therefore reflect different layers of cost. Most cost accounting systems allow for variances to the extent that they're predictable, but larger swings do affect costs that are charged to periodic operating statements.

Finally, there's the impact of general inflation—or, more rarely, deflation. Inflation's impact on inventories generally is a steady rise in the cost of the more recent additions, resulting in successive layers of escalating costs.

The accountant therefore faces a real problem in the effort to match costs and revenues. If unit costs are growing significantly from period to period, deciding which costs to charge against the revenues for a period can have significant effects on the financial statements. If the more "logical" method of removing the oldest units first is used, the oldest—and presumably lowest—unit costs will be charged against current revenues. Depending on how quickly the inventory turns over, such costs may lag current conditions by months and even years. Therefore, under rising price levels, first-in, first-out inventory costing (FIFO) causes the profit on the income statement to be higher than it would be if current unit costs had been charged. At the same time, the balance sheet will reflect reasonably current inventory values because the oldest, lowest-cost units are being removed.

If we employ the opposite method—last-in, first-out costing (LIFO)—the income statement will be charged with current costs and thus reflect lower but more realistic profits. The balance sheet, however, will show inventory values that in time will be highly understated because only the oldest and lowest layers of cost remain.

We could argue that the choice of methods doesn't really matter because one of the financial statements will be distorted in either case. The question then simply becomes whether more realistic balance sheet values or more realistic reported profits are preferred.

There's a significant funds aspect involved, however. The choice of methods affects the amount of income taxes paid for the period. The higher earnings under FIFO are taxed as income from operations even though they contain a profit made from old inventories. Therefore, one criterion in making the choice is the difference in tax payments, which does affect the company's funds. LIFO is preferable from this standpoint, even though with continued inflation, inventory values stated on the balance sheet will become more and more obsolete. Yet surprisingly, FIFO has remained a common form of inventory costing despite the fact that it can lead to a funds drain from higher tax payments. Apparently the higher reported income under FIFO costing is attractive enough to many managements to outweigh the actual tax disadvantage—a trade-off between reporting and economics.

In contrast to other permissible choices of accounting methods for tax purposes, current federal tax laws don't allow the use of one inventory costing method for tax calculation and another for bookkeeping and reporting. Thus, the ideal combination of LIFO for tax purposes and FIFO for reporting earnings can't be employed. In fact, many firms employ an averaging method for inventory costing or a combination of methods.

Trading firms, retailers, and companies experiencing significant fluctuations in the current values of inventories often adjust inventory values, usually at year-end, using the conservative method of restating inventories at cost or market value, whichever is lower, and writing off the difference against current profits. Such periodic adjustments tend to reduce stated values, not raise them, and allow the company to reflect the negative effects of changed conditions so as not to overstate inventory values. Under inflationary conditions, this practice doesn't, of course, assist in resolving the inventory costing issues we've just discussed.

Depreciation Methods

Depreciation is based on the accountant's desire to reflect as a charge against current operations some appropriate fraction of the cost of assets employed in producing revenues. Because physical assets other than land deteriorate with use and eventually wear out, the accounting challenge is to establish an appropriate period of time over which portions of the cost of the asset are charged against revenues. Moreover, the accountant has to decide on the pattern of the depreciation write-off, that is, level, declining, or variable depreciation. Another issue involves estimating any salvage value that may be realized at the end of an asset's useful life. Only the difference between asset cost and such salvage value is normally depreciated.

A similar rationale is applied to intangible assets such as patents and licenses (which are amortized and charged against operations over an appropriate period of years) and to specialized assets such as mineral deposits and timber (on which depletion allowances are calculated).

In the case of physical assets, the depreciation write-off is shown as a charge in the operating statement and is accumulated on the balance sheet as an offset to the fixed assets involved, in an account called accumulated depreciation or reserve for depreciation. Thus, over time, the original asset value stated on the balance sheet is reduced as periodic charges are made against operations. For performance assessment, the significance of depreciation write-offs is in the appropriateness of the charges in light of the nature of the assets and industry conditions, and thus depreciation's impact on profits and balance sheet values. The significance for purposes of funds management is the tax impact of depreciation. Under normal circumstances, depreciation is a tax-deductible expense even though it's only an accounting allocation of past expenditures. The highest depreciation write-off legally possible will normally be taken by management to minimize the cash outlay for taxes unless operating profits are insufficient over the taxable period (including tax adjustments like operating loss carry-back and carry-forward, which permit using losses to reduce the taxes of profitable periods) to take full advantage of the deductions.

The choice of depreciation methods is made easier by current tax laws' provision allowing the use of one method for bookkeeping and reporting purposes and another method for income tax calculation. Recall that this wasn't possible for inventory valuation. Thus, a company can enjoy the best aspects of both depreciation concepts: slower depreciation for reporting higher profits, and faster depreciation for paying lower taxes.

The difference between the taxes actually paid versus what would be due had the book profit been taxed is accumulated on the balance sheet as a liability called deferred taxes, which we encountered earlier in our discussion. This liability will keep growing if a company continually adds to its depreciable assets and consistently uses faster write-offs for tax purposes. If the company stops growing or changes its depreciation policies, actual tax payments in future periods will increase and the differences will begin to reduce the deferred taxes account. There's no current consensus on how to treat this often significant amount in the calculation of performance assessment measures.

What are the most common choices for depreciation write-offs? Historically, accounting practice favored *straight-line depreciation*. This is determined by dividing the cost of the asset (less the estimated salvage value) by its expected life. For example, an asset costing $10,000, with a salvage value of $400 and a six-year life would be depreciated at the annual rate of $1,600 (one sixth, or 16⅔ percent of $9,600). A variant of this method is *unit depreciation*, in which allocation is based on the total number of units estimated to be produced over the asset's life and annual depreciation is based on the number of units produced in that year.

Because many types of assets, such as cars, lose more of their value in early years, and also because allowing faster write-offs provides an incentive to reduce current income taxes, several methods of *accelerated depreciation* were developed over time. Let's look at the two most common methods.

Double-declining balance depreciation is calculated by using twice the annual rate of straight-line depreciation (33⅓ percent for a six-year life), multiplying the full original cost of the asset for the first year with this factor, and the declining balance for each successive year. In other words, in our example one third of the remaining balance would be depreciated in each year. (See Figure 3–5.) In the last year, the remaining balance is charged as depreciation, and any salvage value is recognized by reducing this amount.

Sum-of-years-digits depreciation is calculated by adding the digits for all the years of the asset's life (1 + 2 + 3, etc.). The total is the denominator in a fraction. (For a six-year life this sum would be 21: 1 + 2 + 3 + 4 + 5

FIGURE 3–5

Comparative Annual Depreciation Patterns for a
$10,000 Asset with Six-Year Life and $400 Salvage Value

	Straight-Line Method	Double-Declining Balance Method*	150 Percent Declining Balance Method*†	Sum-of-Years Digits Method
Year 1	$1,600	$3,333	$2,500	$2,743
Year 2	1,600	2,222	1,875	2,286
Year 3	1,600	1,482	1,407	1,829
Year 4	1,600	988	1,406	1,371
Year 5	1,600	658	1,406	914
Year 6	1,600	917	1,006	457
Total:	$9,600	$9,600	$9,600	$9,600

*Year 6 is shown net of salvage value of $400.
†Switch to straight line in year 4; required for 15- and 20-year IRS asset classes.

+ 6.) The numerators represent each year of useful life, in reverse order. (In our example, the fractions are 6/21, 5/21, 4/21, 3/21, 2/21, and 1/21.) In a given year, the depreciation write-off is the asset's original cost (less salvage value) multiplied by the fraction for that year.

The depreciation methods permitted under prevailing IRS codes have changed frequently, especially during the 1980s. Under the 1986 revision of the tax code, the IRS lengthened the lives over which various classes of depreciable assets can be written off. Six asset classes were established for personal property, with lives of 3, 5, 7, 10, 15, and 20 years. For real property (e.g., buildings), the IRS defined two classes of 27.5 and 31.5 years, which must be depreciated straight-line. The IRS stipulated the double-declining balance method for assets with up to 10 years of life, and a variation of this method, the 150 percent declining balance method, for assets of 15 or 20 years.

In either case, a switch to straight-line depreciation in the latter years is permitted when this becomes advantageous. One of these methods must be used if a company chooses to use accelerated depreciation for tax purposes, while any other method can be employed for bookkeeping and reporting. The specifics of the tax regulations applicable at the time of the analysis are best examined in the detailed materials provided by the Internal Revenue Service.

Figure 3–5 shows the different patterns of depreciation resulting from the use of the various methods.

The Impact of Inflation

The extreme inflationary conditions in the United States beginning in the early 1970s resulted in significant distortions in many of the calculations we've discussed. In recent years, inflationary trends have improved greatly in the United States to the extent that inflation is now considered relatively benign. Many other countries have, of course, had to deal with far more insidious inflation levels for much longer periods of time.

In the United States, the accounting profession and the Securities and Exchange Commission have expended much effort in developing new ways to account for and disclose the impact of changes in prices of goods and services and of fluctuating exchange rates due in part to inflation. But the abundant intricacies and arguments in this difficult area are beyond this book's scope. We're only mentioning a few of the basic mechanisms commonly employed to deal with price level changes where this is necessary to understand the impact on financial analysis. Thus, Chapters 2, 4, and 9 discuss essential price level adjustments pertaining to operating funds management, projections, and valuation. Appendix III discusses the basic concepts underlying the inflation phenomenon.

In performance analysis, the main problem associated with inflation is the use of *historical costing* as a generally accepted accounting principle. The original cost of assets utilized in and charged to operations is reflected on the balance sheet. Depreciation and amortization reflect past values, which are often lower than current values. Financial statements of particularly heavily capitalized industries with long-lived depreciable assets and physical resources tend to reflect overstated profits and taxes, and understated asset values. This raises the issue of comparability of companies of different ages, and certainly of comparability of whole industries. Even short-term fluctuations in values will affect companies with high inventory turnover, such as wholesalers.

Another area of distortion affects the viewpoint of the lender. In inflationary times, currency's declining value will affect borrowing/lending relationships because eventual repayment will be made in less valuable dollars. Thus, the lender would be at a disadvantage unless the interest rate contracted for is high enough to offset this risk. The dramatic rise in the 1970s and subsequent fall in the 1980s and early 1990s of short- and long-term interest rates in response to growing and waning inflationary pressures will remain in the memories of long-term lenders in particular.

Among the many methods used to deal with price level changes are replacement cost accounting, new forms of inventory valuation, and partial or full periodic restatement of financial reports. In fact, inflation has turned the deceptively simple accounting principle of matching costs and revenues into an economic and intellectual challenge. As yet, there are no consistent ways of appraising the difference between this type of recast statement and the original accounting statements. A current proposal by the Financial Accounting Standards Board goes part way toward recasting financial statements for banks and financial institutions, asking that loans and investments be valued at current values. This raises a variety of issues that are far from resolved at the time of this writing.

SUMMARY

In this chapter, we discussed essential aspects of the main financial statements as a basis for appraising business performance. With this background, we demonstrated that the assessment of performance is made meaningful when seen from the points of view of the key groups interested in the company's success.

We concentrated on the particular viewpoints of three groups—management, owners, and lenders—that are essential to the functioning of the business. These groups' insights are used and expanded by others for their own particular needs. All three groups are concerned about the firm's success, each from its own standpoint.

Management's prime duty is to bring about stability, growth, and reliable earnings performance with the investment entrusted to it by the owners. We found that within the wide range of ratios displayed, the crucial test is the economic return on the capital employed in the business and its attendant effect on the value of the ownership stake. We also found that the ratios are linked by their common information base, and many are directly connected through the common use of certain elements. They're best interpreted when the business is viewed as a system of interdependent conditions responding to management's decisions. To this end, modeling and computer simulation are increasingly accepted and meaningful because many individual ratios are, by their nature, only static tests that can't do justice to the dynamics of a business.

Shortcomings in the analysis relate to the limitations of the accounting principles commonly used; further distortions are introduced through price level changes stemming from inflation, currency fluctuations, and economic value changes. No definitive ways of compensating for these problems have yet been found to make financial analyses comparable and economically meaningful. As a result, the analyst must use care and judgment at all times.

FIGURE 3-6
TRW INC. AND SUBSIDIARIES
Selected Notes to Financial Statements

Principles of consolidation — The financial statements include the accounts of the company and its subsidiaries except for an insurance subsidiary. The wholly-owned insurance subsidiary and the majority of investments in affiliated companies, which are not significant individually or in the aggregate, are accounted for by the equity method.

Long-term contracts — The percentage of completion (cost-to-cost) method is used to estimate sales under fixed-price and fixed-price incentive contracts. Sales under cost-reimbursement contracts are recorded as costs are incurred. Fees based on cost, award fees and incentive fees are included in sales at the time such amounts are reasonably estimable. Losses on contracts are recognized when determinable. For contracts entered into after December 31, 1990, changes in fee estimates are recognized based on costs incurred to date whereas for contracts entered into prior to such date, changes in fee estimates are recognized prospectively based on costs to be incurred.

Accounts receivable — Accounts receivable at December 31, 1992 and 1991 included $662 million and $612 million, respectively, related to long-term contracts, of which $456 million and $349 million, respectively, were unbilled. Unbilled costs, fees and claims represent revenues earned and billable in the following month as well as revenues earned but not billable under terms of the contracts. A substantial portion of such amounts are expected to be billed during the following year. Retainage receivables and receivables subject to negotiation were not significant.

Inventories — Inventories are stated at the lower of cost or market. At December 31, 1992 and 1991, inventories valued using the last-in, firstout (LIFO) method were $30 million and $87 million, respectively. Inventories not valued by the LIFO method are principally on the first-in, first-out (FIFO) method. Had the cost of all inventories been determined by the FIFO method, which approximates current cost, inventories at December 31, 1992 and 1991, would have been greater by $31 million and $61 million, respectively. Inventories applicable to long-term contracts were not significant.

Depreciation — Depreciation is computed using the straight-line method for the majority of the company's depreciable assets. The remaining assets are depreciated using accelerated methods.

Accounting changes — Effective January 1, 1992, the company adopted Statements of Financial Accounting Standards No. 106, "Employers' Accounting for Postretirement Benefits Other Than Pensions," and No. 109, "Accounting for Income Taxes." Refer to "Income taxes" and "Postretirement benefits other than pensions" notes.

Income taxes — Deferred income taxes arise from temporary differences between income tax and financial reporting and principally relate to income recognition on long-term contracts, depreciation, restructuring reserves, postretirement benefits other than pensions and certain accruals. It is the company's intention to reinvest undistributed earnings of certain of its non-U.S. subsidiaries and thereby indefinitely postpone their remittance. Accordingly, deferred income taxes have not been provided for accumulated undistributed earnings of $246 million at December 31, 1992.

Earnings(loss) per share — Fully diluted earnings(loss) per share have been computed based on the weighted average number of shares of common stock outstanding during each year, and in 1990 including common stock equivalents (stock options) and assuming the conversion of the Serial Preference Stock II, Series 1 and 3.

Primary earnings(loss) per share have been computed based on the weighted average number of shares of common stock outstanding during each year, including common stock equivalents in 1990.

Fully diluted and primary earnings(loss) per share for 1992 and 1991 are the same because the effect of including common stock equivalents and assuming the conversion of the Serial Preference Stock is anti-dilutive.

Restructuring

Restructuring expense(income) in 1992 includes gains from the sales of certain of the company's automotive businesses totaling $116 million ($67 million after tax, $1.08 per share), and net restructuring charges of $87 million ($63 million after tax, $1.01 per share) resulting from additional management decisions in 1992 related to the company's restructuring program. In addition, a charge of $5 million ($4 million after tax, 7 cents per share) for other matters is included in different captions in the statement of earnings. For balance sheet purposes, other accruals in 1992 include $184 million relating to restructuring reserves.

FIGURE 3–6

(continued)

The restructuring program announced in December 1991 resulted in a charge to 1991 earnings of $365 million ($256 million after tax, $4.18 per share). Included in that charge was $80 million of environmental costs for businesses to be or previously divested and $22 million for other matters included in different captions in the statement of earnings. For balance sheet purposes, other accruals in 1991 include $128 million relating to restructuring reserves.

Key elements of the restructuring in 1992 and 1991 include restructuring the Information Systems & Services segment to focus on core businesses; divesting nonstrategic and underperforming assets; and downsizing and streamlining certain automotive and space and defense operations.

Income taxes

Effective January 1, 1992, the company changed its method of accounting for income taxes from the deferred method to the liability method required by Statement of Financial Accounting Standards No. 109, "Accounting for Income Taxes." As permitted under the new rule, prior years' financial statements have not been restated. The cumulative effect of adopting this Statement as of January 1, 1992 was immaterial to net earnings.

The following is a summary of U.S. and non U.S. earnings(loss) before income taxes and cumulative effect of accounting changes, the components of the provisions for income taxes and deferred income taxes and a reconciliation of the U.S. statutory income tax rate to the effective income tax rate.

Earnings(loss) before income taxes and cumulative effect of accounting changes

In millions	1992	1991
U.S.	$ 213	$ (156)
Non-U.S.	135	27
	$ 348	$ (129)

Provision for income taxes	Liability method	Deferred method
In millions	1992	1991
Current		
U.S. federal	$ 60	$ 3
Non-U.S.	59	39
U.S. state and local	21	22
	140	64
Deferred	$ 13	$ (18)
U.S. federal	3	(14)
Non-U.S.	(2)	(21)
U.S. state and local	14	(53)
	$ 154	$ 11

Provision for deferred income taxes

	Liability method	Deferred method
In millions	1992	1991
Income recognition on long-term contracts	$ 40	$ 89
Difference between tax and book depreciation and amortization	(1)	(9)
Restructuring provisions	(30)	(71)
Alternative minimum tax	(10)	(22)
State and local taxes	(2)	(21)
Interest expense	(4)	(17)
Reserves for contract losses	(1)	10
Vacation accrual not currently deductible	–	(4)
ESOP contribution	–	–
Postretirement benefits other than pensions	(12)	–
Other temporary differences	7	(8)
	$ 14	$ (53)

Effective income tax rate	Liability method	Deferred method
	1992	1991
U.S. statutory income tax rate	34.0%	(34.0%)
Losses on restructuring without income tax benefit	3.6	23.1
U.S. tax rate reduction on reversing timing differences	–	2.6
U.S. state and local income taxes net of U.S. federal tax benefit	3.6	.3
Non-U.S. tax rate variances net of foreign tax credits	4.2	14.9
Translation adjustments net of monetary correction	.6	(1.9)
Other	(1.7)	3.2
Effective income tax rate	44.3%	8.2%

Deferred income taxes reflect the net tax effects of temporary differences between the carrying amounts of assets and liabilities for financial reporting purposes and the amounts used for income tax purposes. At December 31, 1992, the company had unused tax benefits of $36 million related to non-U.S. net operating loss carry-forwards for income tax purposes, of which $25 million can be carried forward indefinitely and the balance expires at various dates through 1997. A valuation allowance of $36 million has been recognized to offset the related deferred tax assets due to the uncertainty of realizing the benefit of the loss carryforwards. The following is a summary of the significant components of the company's deferred tax assets and liabilities as of December 31, 1992.

FIGURE 3–6

(continued)

In millions	Deferred tax assets	Deferred tax liabilities
Postretirement benefits other than pensions	$ 244	$ –
Completed contract method of accounting for long-term contracts	24	344
State and local taxes	89	42
Restructuring	124	27
Depreciation and amortization	–	150
Alternative mblimum tax	32	–
Non-U.S. net operating loss carryforwards	36	–
Other	177	79
	726	642
Valuation allowance for deferred tax assets	(36)	–
Total	$ 690	$ 642

Postretiremets benefits other than pensions

The company provides health care and life insurance benefits for a majority of its retired employees in the United States and Canada. The health care plans provide for cost sharing, in the form of employee contributions, deductibles, and coinsurance, between the company and its retirees. The postretirement health care plan covering a majority of employees who retired since August 1, 1988 limits the annual increase in the company's contribution toward the plan's cost to a maximum of the lesser of 50 percent of medical inflation or 4 percent. Life insurance benefits are generally noncontributory. The company's policy is to fund the cost of postretirement health care and life insurance benefits in amounts determined at the discretion of management. The plans currently are not prefunded. Retirees in certain other countries are provided similar benefits by plans sponsored by their governments.

Effective January 1, 1992, the company adopted Statement of Financial Accounting Standards No. 106, "Employers' Accounting for Postretirement Benefits Other Than Pensions," for its U.S. and Canadian plans. This Statement requires accrual of the expected cost of providing postretirement benefits during employees' active service lives. The company's previous practice was to record the cost of these benefits on a claims-incurred basis. The company elected to recognize immediately the transition obligation, measured as of January 1, 1992, as the cumulative effect of an accounting change. This resulted in a one-time charge of $350 million (after a reduction for income taxes of $225 million), which does not include amounts accrued in prior years for previously divested businesses.

The effect of this accounting change on 1992 operating results, after recording the cumulative effect for years prior to 1992, was to recognize additional pretax expense of $37 million. The pro forma effect of the change on years prior to 1992 was not determinable. Postretirement benefit costs charged to expense in 1991 and 1990 under the previous accounting practice were $22 million and $19 million, respectively.

The following table sets forth the funded status and amounts recognized in the company's balance sheet at December 31, 1992 for its postretirement benefit plans.

In millions	1992
Accumulated postretirement benefit obligation	
Retirees	$ 397
Fully eligible active participants	44
Other active participants	263
	$ 704
Plan assets at fair value	–
Accumulated postretirement benefit obligation in excess of plan assets	704
Unrecognized net (gain)loss	–
Net liability recognized in the balance sheet	$ 704

Net periodic postretirement benefit cost included the following components:

In millions	1992
Service cost	$ 15
Interest cost	57
Other	4
	$ 76

The discount rate used in determining the accumulated postretirement benefit obligation was 8-1/2 percent. For 1993, the annual rate of increase in the per capita cost of covered health care benefits was assumed to be 13 percent for participants under age 65 and 12 percent for participants age 65 or older. The rates were assumed to decrease gradually to 6 percent in the year 2021 and remain at that level thereafter. A one percent annual increase in these assumed cost trend rates would increase the accumulated postretirement benefit obligation at December 31, 1992 by approximately 8 percent, and the aggregate of the service and interest cost components of net periodic postretirement benefit cost for 1992 by 6 percent.

FIGURE 3–6
(concluded)

Debt and Credit agreements

Short-term debt

In millions	1992	1991
U.S.bank borrowings and commercial paper	$ –	$ 77
Non-U.S.borrowings	260	330
	$ 260	$ 407

Long-term debt

In millions	1992	1991
U.S.bank borrowings and commercial paper	$ 129	$ 296
Non-U.S.borrowings	725	118
7.3% ESOP obligations due 1997	95	95
8 3/4% Notes due 1996	100	100
8 1/4% Notes due 1996	150	150
8 1/8% Debentures due 2004	–	27
11 3/8% Debentures due 2015	–	34
Medium-term notes:		
9 35% Notes due 2020 (due 2000 at option of note holder)	100	100
9 3/8% Notes due 2021	100	100
Other medium-term notes	110	110
Other	101	113
Total long-term debt	957	1,243
Less current portion	16	30
	$ 947	$ 1,213

Industry segments

The company operates in the following industry segments:

Automotive — Steering systems, including power and manual rack and pinion steering, hydraulic truck and off-highway steering systems and suspension products. Occupant restraint systems, including air bag and seat belt systems; electrical and electronic controls; and engineered fasteners. Engine valves and valve train parts, pistons, stud welding systems and a service line of car and truck accessories and car care products. Products are used in cars, trucks, buses, farm machinery and off-highway vehicles and are distributed directly to original equipment manufacturers and through company and independent distributors.

Space & Defense — Spacecraft, including the design and manufacture of military and civilian spacecraft equipment, propulsion subsystems, electro-optical and instrument systems, spacecraft payloads, high-energy lasers and laser technology and other high-reliability components. Software and systems engineering support services in the fields of military command and control, earth observation, environmental monitoring and nuclear waste management, antisubmarine warfare, security and counterterrorism, undersea surveillance and other high-technology space, defense, and civil government support systems. Electronic systems, equipment and services, including the design and manufacture of space communication systems, avionics systems and other electronic technologies for tactical and strategic space and defense applications. Products and services are provided directly to defense, other government and commercial customers.

Information Systems & Services — Information systems and services, including consumer and commercial credit information and related services, direct marketing, real estate information and services, imaging systems engineering and integration, and maintenance and repair of computer systems and peripheral equipment. Information and services are provided to businesses, credit-granting organizations, financial institutions and individual consumers.

Other — On-site environmental waste reduction and clean-up services.

Source: Selected from "Notes to Financial Statements," TRW Inc. annual report, 1993.

SELECTED REFERENCES

Anthony, Robert N., and James S. Reece. *Accounting: Text and Cases.* 6th ed. Homewood, Ill.: Richard D. Irwin, 1988.

Bernstein, Leopold A. *Financial Statement Analysis: Theory, Application, and Interpretation.* 3rd ed. Homewood, Ill.: Richard D. Irwin, 1983.

Brealey, Richard, and Stewart Myers. *Principles of Corporate Finance.* 3rd ed. New York: McGraw-Hill, 1988.

Dun & Bradstreet. *Industry Norms and Key Business Ratios* (annual). New York.

Fraser, Lyn M. *Understanding Financial Statements: Through the Maze of a Corporate Annual Report.* Reston, Va.: Reston Publishing, 1985.

Robert Morris Associates. *Annual Statement Studies.* Philadelphia.

Ross, Stephen; Randolph Westerfield; and Jeffrey Jaffe. *Corporate Finance.* 2nd ed. Homewood, Ill.: Richard D. Irwin, 1990.

Standard & Poor's Analysts Handbook. New York (annual).

Troy, Leo. *Almanac of Business and Industrial Financial Ratios.* Englewood Cliffs, N.J.: Prentice Hall (annual).

Van Horne, James C. *Financial Management and Policy.* 8th ed. Englewood Cliffs, N.J.: Prentice Hall, 1989.

Weston, J. Fred, and Thomas E. Copeland. *Managerial Finance.* 9th ed. Hinsdale, Ill.: Dryden Press, 1989.

SELF-STUDY EXERCISES AND PROBLEMS

(Solutions Provided in Appendix VI)

1. Work the following exercises:

    a. A company's 1994 net profit represents 11.4 percent of net sales. What's the company's return on net worth if asset turnover is 1.34 and capitalization is 67 percent of total assets? How would faster asset turnover affect the result?

    b. A company's gross margin on 1994 sales is 31.4 percent. Total cost of goods sold amount to $4,391,300, and net profit is 9.7 percent of sales. What are the company's total assets if the ratio of sales to assets is 82.7 percent? What's the return on capitalization if current liabilities are 21 percent of total assets?

    c. What's the change in a company's current ratio of 2.2:1 (current assets are $573,100) if the following actions are taken individually? Also, how does each item affect working capital? The company:

        1. Pays $67,500 of accounts payable with cash.

        2. Collects $33,000 in notes receivable.

3. Purchases merchandise worth $41,300 on account.

4. Pays dividends of $60,000, of which $42,000 had been shown as accrued (an unpaid current liability).

5. Sells machine for $80,000, on which book value is $90,000 and accumulated depreciation is $112,000.

6. Sells merchandise on account that cost $73,500. Gross margin is 33 percent.

7. Writes off $20,000 from inventory as scrap and amortizes $15,000 of goodwill.

d. From the following data calculate the outstanding days' receivables and payables for a company, using the methods shown in the chapter. What's the inventory turnover, calculated in different ways? Discuss your assumptions.

Sales for three months	$437,500
Cost of sales	298,400
Purchases	143,500
Beginning inventory	382,200
Ending inventory	227,300
Accounts receivable	156,800
Accounts payable	69,300
Normal sales terms	2/10,n/30
Normal purchase terms	n/45

2. From the following financial statements of the ABC Company for 1993 and 1994, prepare the ratios and measures discussed in this chapter.

a. Ratios from the viewpoint of management.

b. Ratios from the viewpoint of owners.

c. Ratios from the viewpoint of lenders.

Comment on the changes shown between the two years, and discuss the results' significance from the three points of view. Indicate which additional kinds of comparison you'd like to make for this company (an electronics manufacturer) and the type of information you'd need.

ABC COMPANY
Balance Sheets
December 31, 1993, and 1994
($ millions)

Assets	1993	1994
Current assets:		
Cash	$ 82.7	$110.9
Accounts receivable—net	92.6	146.2

Assets	1993	1994
Inventories	88.8	129.5
Prepaid expenses	2.8	6.2
Advances from government	5.3	2.8
Total current assets	272.2	395.6
Property, plant, and equipment	215.2	283.4
Less: Accumulated depreciation	101.2	119.6
Net property	114.0	163.8
Other assets	3.1	4.2
Total assets	$389.3	$563.6

Liabilities and net worth

	1993	1994
Current liabilities:		
Accounts payable	$ 43.4	$ 62.9
Accrued income tax	36.7	44.0
Accrued pension and profit sharing	27.1	38.4
Other accruals	21.9	31.2
Current portion of long-term debt	2.1	—
Total current liabilities	131.2	176.5
Debentures (9% due 1997)	—	94.0
Other long-term debt	7.8	4.1
Deferred income tax	5.2	7.6
Common stock ($1 par)	10.1	10.2
Paid-in surplus	25.1	27.2
Retained earnings	209.9	244.0
Total liabilities and net worth	$389.3	$563.6

ABC COMPANY
Operating Statements for 1993 and 1994
($ millions)

Assets	1993	1994
Net sales	$655.1	$872.7
Cost of goods and services*	460.9	616.1
Gross profit	194.2	256.6
Selling, general, and administrative expenses	98.3	125.2
Employee profit sharing and retirement	26.9	38.7
	125.2	163.9
Operating profit	69.0	92.7
Other income	1.1	1.8
	70.1	94.5
Interest paid	1.0	7.4
	69.1	87.1
Provision for income taxes	31.8	40.1
Net profit†	$ 37.3	$ 47.0
*Depreciation and amortization	$28.2	$38.5
†Common dividends paid	5.5	6.0

3. Select a major manufacturing company, a retailing firm, a public utility, a bank, and a transportation firm. From an information source like Value Line, Moody's, or Standard & Poor's, develop a historical analysis of key measures you consider significant to appraise the effectiveness of management, the return to owners, and the position of the lenders. Develop significant industry comparisons and comment on the relative position of your chosen company. Also comment on some of the assumptions and choices you have to make on the selection of specific accounts and data to work the analytical techniques.

4 PROJECTION OF FINANCIAL REQUIREMENTS

Up to this point we've discussed the appraisal of performance and the management of operating funds in the context of *past* decisions involving investments, operations, and financing. This chapter shifts the emphasis to a forward look—that is, forecasting likely future conditions, a critically important task in managing any business. We'll discuss the key concepts and techniques of projecting operating performance and the expected financial requirements with which to support future operations. Such projections normally involve alternative plans developed for different conditions.

The projection of financial requirements is only part of the business planning process with which management positions the company's future activities relative to the expected economic, competitive, technical, and social environments. When business plans are developed, they're usually structured around specific goals and objectives cooperatively set by the organization and its subgroups. The plans normally spell out strategies and actions for achieving desired short-term, intermediate, and long-term results.

These plans are then quantified in financial terms in the form of projected financial statements (pro forma statements) and a variety of operational budgets. Detailed cash budgets and funds flow statements are often included to provide greater insight into the funds implications of the projected activities. Also, key ratios are usually calculated and presented as part of the material. The concepts and techniques discussed in Chapters 2 and 3 are the necessary tools for quantifying projected conditions.

The scope of this book allows us to focus only on the major methods and formats of financial projection. We can't explicitly take into account the broader strategic planning framework that is necessary for exploring the future direction of the company before any financial quantification of the plans can be made. Nor can we go into the details of statistical methods which are at times used to support the judgments involved in estimating future conditions.

Nevertheless, financial projection techniques by themselves can be useful simulations of the likely results of broad assumptions made by management about a variety of future conditions. The ease with which pro forma financial statements and cash flow projections can be developed makes them attractive as approximations from which refinements are possible with additional information and insights—especially as the number of alternatives for action is narrowed down.

The use of computer spreadsheets and planning models continues to grow rapidly, as does the selection of software packages offering financial simulation and projection capabilities. Computers' speed and multiple tracking capabilities have eliminated much of the drudgery of tracing investment, operational, and financing assumptions through the financial framework of a business. While these commercial offerings differ in their specific orientation and degree of sophistication, they're built around the very concepts we'll discuss in this chapter.

The most important requirement, however, is solid understanding of the basic financial techniques and relationships. Only then can the analyst take full advantage of the capabilities embodied within computer software and models. Therefore, this book focuses not on how to program spreadsheets or how to deal with specific software packages, but on the financial techniques themselves.

The main techniques of financial projection fall into three categories:

- Pro forma financial statements.
- Cash budgets.
- Operating budgets.

Pro forma statements, as the name implies, are projected financial statements embodying a set of assumptions about a company's future performance and funding requirements. Cash budgets are detailed projections of the specific incidence of cash moving in and out of the business. Operating budgets are detailed projections of departmental revenue and/or expense patterns; they're subsidiary to both pro forma statements and cash flow statements.

All three categories involve an organized arrangement of financial and economic data for the purpose of assessing future performance and funds requirements. As we'll see, the three methodologies are also closely interrelated. Therefore, this relationship can be exploited to achieve consistent financial forecasts.

We'll also briefly examine basic financial modeling and the use of sensitivity analysis for testing the impact of changes in critical assumptions underlying the financial projections.

PRO FORMA FINANCIAL STATEMENTS

The most comprehensive look at a firm's likely future financial performance can be obtained by developing a set of pro forma statements. These are merely an operating statement and a related balance sheet extended into the future. The pro forma operating statement represents an "operational plan" for the business as a whole, while the pro forma balance sheet reflects the anticipated cumulative impact of assumed future decisions on the financial condition of the business. Both statements are prepared by taking the most readily available estimates of future activity and projecting, account by account, the assumed results and conditions.

Many times a third statement, the pro forma funds flow statement, is prepared to add further insight by displaying the funds movements expected during the forecast period.

Pro forma projections can be done at any level of detail desired. In summarized form, these statements are one of the most widely used ways of quickly making financial estimates. They are particularly favored by bank loan officers, who must assess the client company's creditworthiness from a total financial standpoint.

Detailed plans aren't needed to construct complete pro forma statements, even though the results of a formal planning process would increase the degree of precision. Instead, selected ratios can be used to produce statements that are entirely satisfactory, particularly as a first look. As we'll demonstrate, an important aspect of pro forma analysis is the ability to find the company's funds requirements as of the date the pro forma balance sheet is prepared.

To show how pro forma statements are developed, we'll use the example of a fictitious manufacturing company called XYZ Corporation. The company makes and sells three different products, has a seasonal pattern with the low point in December, and is currently profitable. The most recent actual results available are for the third quarter of 1994. This initial set of data allows us to project ahead—but we can also ask management for additional information as needed. The pro forma projection is to be made for the last quarter of 1994. Our objective is to determine both the level of profit for the quarter and the amount of additional funds that will be needed as of the end of the year.

Pro Forma Operating Statement

We begin the process with the pro forma operating statement for XYZ Corporation. The operating statement is normally prepared first because the amount of aftertax profit developed there must also be reflected in the pro forma balance sheet as a change in retained earnings.

The starting point for the operating statement, as shown on the first two lines in Figure 4–1, is a projection of the unit and dollar volumes of *sales*. These can be estimated in a variety of ways ranging from trendline projection to detailed departmental sales forecasts by individual product, often built up from field estimates. In the absence of any other information we may, of course, make our own guesstimates based on past overall results.

In the case of XYZ Corporation, we know that a seasonal pattern exists, and that sales can be expected to decline in the last quarter. In Figure 4–1 we've shown the actual operating statement for the third quarter of 1994 as the base for our analysis. Dollar amounts are given for key revenue and cost elements, as well as a breakdown into percentage of sales, or "common numbers." The series of assumptions we must make will use the third-quarter experience as a guide, as we've been assured that the quarterly pattern over the years has been reasonably stable.

Company statistics from past years suggest that during the fourth quarter, an 18 to 20 percent drop in sales

FIGURE 4-1
XYZ CORPORATION
Pro Forma Income Statement
For the Quarter Ended December 31, 1994
($ thousands)

	Actual Quarter Ended 9–30–94		Pro Forma* Quarter Ended 12–31–94		Assumptions and Sources of Information
Units sold	137,000		111,000		Last quarter is seasonal low; past data show 18 to 20 percent decline from third quarter.
Net sales	$12,650	100.0%	$10,250	100.0%	Projected 19 percent lower volume with same price and mix.
Cost of goods sold:					
Labor	2,210		1,810		21.5% of cost of goods as before.
Materials	2,045		1,680		20.0% of cost of goods as before.
Overhead	5,685		4,660		55.5% of cost of goods as before.
Delivery	305		250		3.0% of cost of goods as before.
Cost of goods sold	10,245	81.0	8,400	82.0	Increase of 1 percentage point to simulate operating inefficiencies.

Gross margin	2,405	19.0	1,850	18.0	Assume drop of $50, to show lower activity.
Expenses:					
Selling expense	875	6.9	825	8.0	Assume slight increase for year-end costs.
General and administrative expenses	585	4.6	600	5.9	
Total expenses	1,460	11.5	1,425	13.9	
Operating profit	945	7.5	425	4.1	Shows effect of less efficient operations.
Interest	190	1.5	175	1.7	Based on outstanding debt.
Profit before taxes	755	6.0	250	2.4	
Income taxes	272	2.2	90	0.9	Projected at 36%.
Net income	483	3.8	160	1.5	
Dividends	100	0.8	-0-	-0-	No payment of dividends scheduled.
Retained earnings	383	3.0%	160	1.5%	Carried to balance sheet.
Depreciation added back	575		600		From fixed asset records. (Assume tax and book depreciation are the same.)
Cash flow after dividends	$ 958		$ 760		Rough measure of cash from operations. (We should add back any dividends to reflect operations only.)

*All projections are rounded off.

volume from the third quarter is normal. We'll take the midpoint of this range as a beginning assumption. After calculating a 19 percent drop in unit volume, we make the further assumption that both prices and product mix will remain unchanged. It's possible, of course, to make different assumptions about volume, prices, and mix in order to reflect specific insights or to test the impact of "what if" questions. In our case, an inquiry to sales management will confirm that the set of assumptions about sales matches their own forecast.

Next we turn to *cost of goods sold*. The actual third-quarter operating statement provides details on the main components—labor, materials, overhead, and delivery—contained in cost of goods sold. We can calculate the proportion of cost that each of these elements represents and assume that the same proportions will hold during the fourth quarter.

But we must also remember that the last quarter is the company's seasonal low point, and we can assume that some inefficiencies are likely to raise overall production costs as operations slow down. Without more data, we can probably assume a rise of something like one percentage point in the ratio of cost of goods sold to sales as a quick way to allow for the seasonal distortion. The dollar penalty of this assumption is a reduction in the gross margin of $10,250,000 by 1 percent ($102,500). Other levels of the cost of goods sold ratio could, of course, be tested. Note that for simplicity the cost of goods sold and gross margin can be estimated directly, without using the detailed cost breakdown (labor, materials, etc.) given in the third-quarter operating statement.

The main expense categories can be estimated by again examining the actual statement for the third quarter. The figures provided there might simply be accepted and used as our projection. *Selling expense* is shown as $875,000. Given that the fourth quarter has lower sales activity, we can probably assume a small decrease, such as $50,000. A reduction fully proportional to the 19 percent drop in volume wouldn't be realistic, however, given that many of the costs, such as salaries of marketing personnel, are essentially fixed in the near term.

General and administrative expenses should be rounded off a little higher for purposes of our projection because of expected nonrecurring year-end expenses. Note that both expense elements now represent a higher proportion of sales than was true for the actual prior quarter. If there's reason to believe that this result seems out of line, it may, of course, be modified. But we must remember that even if historical patterns were available in great detail, the projection has to deal with the future. Therefore, the purpose of the exercise is to make the most realistic assumptions possible. These estimates will, of course, remain assumptions until actual experience supersedes them.

As a result of our assumptions, the fourth-quarter *operating profit* falls by half a million dollars, and the profit ratio drops to almost half its former level. This is due mostly to the 19 percent drop in sales volume and the associated loss in profit contribution. This reduction represents $2.4 million of sales which, with a normal cost of goods sold of 81 percent, would have contributed $456,000 to profit. Moreover, we assumed certain inefficiencies in operations and expected only a partial ability to reduce what are mostly fixed expenses. As we stated before, this result can and should be examined against available experience to judge its appropriateness.

Interest expense is charged according to the provisions of the company's outstanding debt, and this information is provided to us by the financial officer. The operating statement will be completed once we calculate *income taxes* (assumed here at an effective rate of 36 percent) to arrive at net income. We note that the amount of *net income* has dropped significantly in response to the slowdown in operations.

A further assumption needs to be made about *dividends* to arrive at *retained earnings* for the period, which have to be reflected in the pro forma balance sheet. In XYZ's case, no dividends have been declared, according to the financial officer. As a last step we've added back the depreciation for the period, to approximate the *cash flow* from operations. This is a quick estimate which we'll review later in the context of all other expected funds movements.

Pro Forma Balance Sheet

Armed with data about expected operations, we can now develop the pro forma balance sheet (Figure 4–2, pages 182–83). Again we must make specific assumptions about each account, taking the actual balance sheet data at the beginning of the forecast period and using any additional information we can obtain from management. Fortunately we have relative freedom to make and vary our estimates, except that there must always be complete consistency between any assumptions affecting both the operating statement and the balance sheet. The objective isn't accounting precision, of course, but rather to develop an indication of approximate funds needs three months hence and a look at the firm's overall financial condition at that time.

We start the process with the first account, *cash*, and assume that three months hence the company needs to keep only the minimum working balance in its bank accounts. The information source for this figure ($1,250,000) again is the financial officer. In the absence of such specific data we could assume a level of cash that's common among companies of this size. As we'll see later, the desired amount of cash on hand will directly affect the amount of funds the company may have to borrow. Also, we mustn't forget that any cash balance maintained as an ongoing requirement on the balance sheet represents an investment like any other.

Next we turn to *accounts receivable*. If the company

sells its products on terms of net 30, it can expect to have at least 30 days' sales outstanding (more, if some of its customers are late in paying). Given no abnormal delays, the accounts receivable balance on the December 31 balance sheet should represent the sales of the whole month of December. However, we don't have an exact December sales estimate because our pro forma operating statement shows sales for the last three months combined. As a simple shortcut we could assume that one third of the projected quarterly sales would be outstanding at the end of the quarter.

In our case that would be one third of the sales of $10,250,000 in Figure 4–1, or $3,417,000. But we learn after some discussion with sales management that in view of the seasonal low in December, the company's sales force projects the month's sales at only $3,050,000. This amount thus represents the 30 days of sales we can assume to be outstanding in the form of accounts receivable at the end of the year, given normal collection experience.

Raw material inventory could be projected by using monthly withdrawal and purchase patterns, information that the company could provide. However, manufacturing management informs us that for reasons of continuity, they like to keep on hand $1,500,000 worth of raw materials at all times, and frequent purchases are made as needed to maintain that level.

Finished goods inventory is likely to decline in concert with lower sales and production activity, and we've calculated a 19 percent reduction. If we considered this an optimistic assumption, because of likely inefficiencies in adjusting production exactly to the seasonal low, a higher amount can, of course, be specified. The consequence would be a lesser amount of funds released from declining inventories.

When we add up all our changes in the *current asset account*, we find that the total is projected to decline by over $2 million, in effect releasing this amount for other

FIGURE 4-2

XYZ CORPORATION

Pro Forma Balance Sheet as of December 31, 1994

($ thousands)

Assets	Actual 9-30-94	Change	Pro Forma 12-31-94	Assumptions and Sources of Information
Current assets:				
Cash	$ 1,450	–$ 200	$ 1,250	Cash set at estimated minimum balance.
Accounts receivable	4,250	– 1,200	3,050	Represents 30 days' sales (from December sales projection).
Raw materials	1,500	–0–	1,500	Safety level; requirements purchased as needed.
Finished goods	4,050	– 750	3,300	Reduced production by 19 percent.
Total current assets	11,250	– 2,150	9,100	Drop reflects seasonal pattern.
Fixed assets:				
Land	2,500	–0–	2,500	No change assumed.
Plant and equipment	20,800	– 1,500	19,300	Sale of machines with original cost of $1,500 and accumulated depreciation of $950.
Less: Accumulated depreciation	8,350	– 350	8,000	Depreciation for period $600, per income statement, less reduction of $950 from sale of machines.
Net plant and equipment	12,450	– 1,150	11,300	
Total fixed assets	14,950	– 1,150	13,800	

Other assets	1,250	–0–	1,250	No change assumed.
Total assets	$27,450	–$3,300	$24,150	
Liabilities and net worth				
Current liabilities:				
Accounts payable	$ 1,120	–$ 410	$ 710	45 days' purchases (from November/December purchase estimates).
Notes payable	3,000	– 1,500	1,500	Repayment as scheduled.
Due contractor	3,400	– 2,900	500	From payment schedule.
Accruals	1,250	– 310	940	Tax payments (–$400) and tax accrual (+$90).
Total current liabilities	8,770	– 5,120	3,650	Reflects heavy current repayments of obligations.
Long-term liabilities	8,500	–0–	8,500	No change.
Common stock	4,250	+ 250	4,500	Sale of stock under option.
Retained earnings	5,930	+ 160	6,090	Retained earnings per income statement (no payment of dividends).
Total liabilities and net worth	$27,450	– 4,710	22,740	
Funds required		+ 1,410	1,410	"Plug" figure representing financing need as of 12-31-94, the same as in Figure 4-4.
		–$3,300	$24,150	

183

uses in the company. Such a pattern reflects the normal funds flow expectations from seasonal operations, as discussed in Chapter 2.

Fixed assets are affected by several events. While *land* remains unchanged, we're told that some machines will be sold during the last quarter. Their original cost was $1.5 million against which $950,000 of depreciation has been accumulated. They're to be sold for book value, which involves no taxable gain or loss. To reflect this transaction, the *plant and equipment* account on our pro forma balance sheet must be reduced by the original cost, while *accumulated depreciation* must be reduced by the $950,000 of past write-offs recorded there.

We also know from the pro forma operating statement that normal depreciation for the period will be $600,000. This amount has to be added to the accumulated depreciation account. As a net result of the two changes, accumulated depreciation will decline by $350,000. *Other assets* are assumed to be unchanged.

On the liability side, *accounts payable* are expected to decline in response to lower activity in the final quarter. We're told that payables are mostly related to purchases of raw material. We could approximate accounts payable, which have payment terms of net 45, by assuming that about one half of the 90-day raw materials use indicated on the pro forma operating statement would be outstanding ($840,000). But we have additional inside information on the actual level of *purchases* scheduled, and we can refine our assumption to show all of December's purchases ($460,000) and one-half of November's ($250,000) as total accounts payable outstanding at year end ($710,000).

Other current liabilities must be analyzed in terms of specific payment schedules. We're informed that *notes payable* carries a provision for repayment of $1.5 million during the quarter. The account *due contractor* says XYZ Corporation must make a payment of almost $3 million owed on past construction which will become due in the final quarter. *Accruals* largely involve income tax and other tax obligations. We already know from the pro forma operating statement that tax accruals projected for the quarter will be $90,000. We're also told that the company must make an estimated tax payment of $400,000 during the quarter. These two items will net out to a reduction in accruals of $310,000. Note that total current liabilities are estimated to be reduced by about $3.6 million, a significant use of funds during the forecast period.

Long-term liabilities are assumed to remain unchanged, while the recorded value of *common stock* is expected to increase by $250,000, as stock options are about to be exercised. Finally, *retained earnings* should increase by the amount of net profit (income) of $160,000 calculated on the pro forma operating statement in Figure 4–1, as no dividends are paid.

When the results are added up, we find that the pro forma balance sheet doesn't balance. This shouldn't be surprising inasmuch as we didn't use double-entry bookkeeping to balance our calculations. Instead, we made a variety of independent assumptions about many of the accounts, taking care only to be consistent with the related projections in the pro forma operating statement. Having maintained consistency, and given that we're reasonably satisfied with our assumptions, the balancing figure required to equalize assets and liabilities will represent either the *funds need* or the *excess funds* of the company on the pro forma balance sheet date.

This *plug figure*, as it's often called, serves as a quick estimate of what additional indebtedness the company will face on the date of the statement, or what uncommitted funds it will have at its disposal. But the plug won't indicate the peaks and valleys in funds requirements that may have occurred during each of the three months. These could be found by generating intermediate balance sheets more frequently than every 90 days.

In other words, we could find any major fluctuations in funds conditions by taking financial "snapshots" in more closely spaced intervals. As we'll see shortly, preparing a detailed cash budget is a more direct way of tracing the ups and downs of funds requirements within the forecast period. Before turning to the cash budget, however, we'll briefly discuss the further interpretation of balance sheet changes by means of funds flow analysis.

Pro Forma Funds Flow Statement

As we observed in Figure 4–2, some significant changes took place between the beginning and ending balance sheets of the forecast period. A pro forma funds flow statement will help us to highlight the funds movements reflected in these changes and their impact on the company's financial condition. Using the techniques discussed in Chapter 2, we can take the changes in the balance sheet and selected information from the operating statement to construct the pro forma funds flow analysis in Figure 4–3.

Under the prevailing practice we've divided the funds flows into funds from operations, funds from investments, and funds from financing. It becomes obvious that reduced operations are expected to release a significant net amount of working capital (sources of $2.15 million from cash, receivables, and finished goods less uses of $0.72 million for payables and accrued taxes for a net of $1.43 million), of which $1.2 million comes from reduced accounts receivable alone. This funds source augments the operating cash flow (net income of $0.16 million plus depreciation of $0.6 million) for a total funds from operations of $2.19 million.

The funds sources generated by operations are outweighed by significant funds needs for financing, however. To meet various financial obligations currently due, $4.4 million are scheduled for repayment. The $1.5 million notes payable represents repayment of

FIGURE 4–3
XYZ CORPORATION
Pro Forma Funds Flow Statement
For the Quarter Ended December 31, 1994
($ thousands)

	Sources	Uses
Funds from operations:		
Net income	$ 160	$ –
Depreciation (noncash charge)	600	–
Working capital changes:		
Decrease in cash	200	–
Decrease in receivables	1,200	–
Decrease in finished goods	750	–
Decrease in payables	–	410
Decrease in accrued taxes	–	310
Totals	2,910	720
Net funds from operations	2,190	
Funds from investments:		
Proceeds from sale of machinery	550	–
Funds for financing:		
Repayment of notes	–	1,500
Repayment of construction loan	–	2,900
Proceeds from stock option	250	–
Totals	250	4,400
Net funds for financing		4,150
Funding requirement as of 12/31/94	1,410	–
	$4,150	$4,150

seasonal funding, made possible by the significant release of working capital as the seasonal low approaches.

The sale of machinery and the proceeds from the exercise of stock options assist somewhat in this, but the funding gap remaining is still $1.41 million. It should be clear by now that if we make any changes in the various assumptions behind the pro forma projections, the size of the funding gap will be directly affected. In fact, it's often helpful to test the sensitivity of the projected conditions to changes in key assumptions, such as sales volume, collection patterns, and major cost deviations.

The likely funding stresses falling within the forecast

period still haven't been dealt with, however. These occur because the gradual release of operating funds caused by the seasonal slowdown during the quarter will likely lag the decline in operating volume. As a consequence, the exact scheduling of repayments within the three-month period could cause significant temporary shortfalls. For example, if all repayments came due in October, the funding gap would be much higher during that month than the pro forma statements suggest for the end of December. As we'll see, only a detailed cash budget can reveal such hidden fluctuations.

To summarize, pro forma statements are a convenient and relatively simple way of projecting expectations about a company's performance. To create these statements requires maintaining consistent assumptions between the operating statement and the balance sheet, but otherwise a great degree of subjective judgment is involved. The balancing element in the pro forma balance sheet is the funds need or funds excess resulting from the conditions assumed. This plug will vary as assumptions are changed.

Pro forma funds flow statements help highlight the funds movements implied by changes in the balance sheet. Pro forma analysis is limited by the static nature of the balance sheet which shows funds needs only at a specific point in time, and not their ebb and flow. A more dynamic intraperiod analysis requires either generating several short-term pro forma statements at key decision points, or making the detailed budgetary forecast embodied in the cash budget.

CASH BUDGETS

Cash budgets, or cash flow statements, are very specific month-by-month or even week-by-week planning vehicles normally prepared by a firm's financial staff. They focus exclusively on the specific incidence of cash receipts and payments. The financial analyst who uses a cash budget wants to observe the changing levels of the cash account, which must be maintained at a level sufficient to allow timely payments of obligations as they become due. As a consequence, the analyst must plan cash activity to reflect in very specific detail the timing of the cash inflows and outflows in response to planned operational, investment, and financing activities.

As we'll see, cash budgets again show the level of funds needs or excesses. The amount at the end of the planning period will exactly match the funding need or excess shown on the pro forma balance sheet if the cash budget was prepared using the same basic assumptions employed in generating the pro forma statements.

Cash budgeting, in principle, is quite simple. It's similar to personal budgeting, where bills due are matched with receipts from paychecks, dividend checks, bank interest payments, and so on. This matching is necessary to determine funds requirements as they affect the cash available for payment. The cash balance will probably fluctuate from day to day, week to week, or month to month. If a company's collections from credit sales tend to lag for weeks while wages and purchases must be paid currently, serious cash shortages can occur. (Recall Chapter 2's exploring the concept of lags in relation to funds flows.) Similarly, cash payments for nonrecurring items, such as outlays for capital equipment, may cause temporary funding problems that must be met. Given what it covers, the cash budget is the ultimate expression of funds flow analysis because in the end all funds movements have a cash effect.

In preparing a cash budget, a time schedule of estimated receipts and payments of cash must be laid out. This schedule shows, period by period, the net effect of projected activity on the cash balance. The selection of the time intervals covered by the cash budget depends on the nature of the business and the trade terms under which it operates. If daily fluctuations are likely to be large, as in the banking business, day-by-day projections will be necessary. In other cases weekly, monthly, or even quarterly projections will suffice.

Let's now turn to the XYZ Corporation data and prepare a monthly cash budget for the last quarter of 1994. This will increase our understanding of the funds flow picture beyond that provided by the pro forma analysis alone. Figure 4–4 (pages 192–93) presents some of the basic data of the company's operations regarding sales, production, and purchases. We show two months of actual activities prior to the forecast period because (due to the credit terms of sales and purchases) the cash lag from these past months will influence the three months being projected.

The lag effect can be clearly demonstrated in the first of the *cash receipts, collection of receivables*. On the assumption that the company's customers will continue to remit within the 30-day terms, cash receipts for any month should be the sales made in the prior month. In contrast, if there were a 60-day collection period, collections would represent the sales made two months earlier. Thus, any expected change in customer behavior or in the credit terms themselves must be reflected in a different receipts pattern.

It's often helpful to draw a scale of time periods on which the days, weeks, or months of dollar sales are first recorded when they occur. Using this scale, any assumed collection experience can be simulated by "staggering" (delaying) the dollar receipts according to the appropriate number of days. For example, a schedule of sales and collections on 30-day credit would appear as follows:

	January	February	March	April	May	June
Credit sales ...	$25,000	$30,000	$40,000	$42,000	$35,000	$30,000
Collections ...	(Dec. sales)	25,000	30,000	40,000	42,000	35,000

The proceeds from the exercise of *stock options* and from the sale of used *machinery* have been budgeted in their respective months of incidence. The total cash receipts for each month show a diminishing pattern which lags the declining sales. This reduction is moderated somewhat by the nonoperating proceeds from options and sale of used machinery.

As we turn to *cash disbursements,* we encounter another lag in payments for *purchases* made on credit. Under XYZ's normal credit terms of 45 days we can assume that the company's payments will lag by 45 days. Consequently, purchases made in the second half of August and the first half of September will be paid for in October, with a similar pattern repeating itself in November and December. In other words, one month's worth of purchases staggered by 45 days will be paid in a given month. Under these conditions a time scale with 15-day intervals will help illustrate the payment pattern.

Inasmuch as the last quarter of 1994 is projected in a declining pattern to December's seasonal low in sales and manufacturing activities, the staggered timing due to credit terms shifts somewhat higher cash receipts as well as payments into a period of low operating activity. Funds are released in the process, as we would expect when we recall Chapter 2's discussion of changes in operations and their funds impact. This funds result matches what we observed in the totals provided by the pro forma analysis.

Had there instead been a rising volume of operation, more cash would have become tied up in working capital, and additional funds would be required. In that case the cash budget would have reflected the lag effect of the lower activities of the earlier months. It should be apparent by now that there's a critical need for careful cash budgeting in any business where operating levels and payments swing widely.

Other cash disbursements *(payroll, manufacturing*

FIGURE 4–4
XYZ CORPORATION
Sample Cash Budget for the Quarter Ended December 31, 1994
($ thousands)

	August	September	October	November	December	Total for Quarter
Basic data:						
Unit sales	48,000	46,000	42,000	36,000	33,000	111,000
Unit production	50,000	50,000	35,000	34,000	31,000	100,000
Change in inventory	+2,000	+4,000	–7,000	–2,000	–2,000	–11,000
Sales volume (on credit)	$4,450	$4,250	$3,850	$3,350	$3,050	$10,250
Purchases (on credit)	760	740	520	500	460	1,480
Cash receipts:						
Collection of receivables—prior month's sales; normal terms of 30 days assumed			$4,250	$3,850	$3,350	$11,450
Proceeds from sale of stock options			–0–	250	–0–	250
Proceeds from sale of used machines at book value (original cost, $1,500)			–0–	–0–	550	550
Total cash receipts			4,250	4,100	3,900	12,250

Cash disbursements:

Payment for purchases*	750	630	510	1,890
Production payroll (from operating budget)	560	545	500	1,605
Manufacturing expenses (from operating budget)	1,265	1,260	1,235	3,760
Selling and delivery expenses (from sales budget)	350	345	335	1,030
General overhead expenses (from administrative budget)	200	200	200	600
Interest payment on debt	-0-	-0-	175	175
Principal payment on note payable	1,500	-0-	-0-	1,500
Federal tax payment	400	-0-	-0-	400
Payments on construction of new plant	-0-	2,000	900	2,900
Total cash disbursements	5,025	4,980	3,855	13,860
Net cash receipts (disbursements)	(775)	(880)	45	(1,610)
Cumulative net cash flow	$ (775)	$(1,655)	$(1,610)	$(1,610)

Analysis of cash requirements:

Beginning cash balance	$1,450	$ 675	$ (205)	$ 1,450
Net cash receipts (disbursements)	(775)	(880)	45	(1,610)
Ending cash balance	675	(205)	(160)	(160)
Minimum cash balance	1,250	1,250	1,250	1,250
Cash requirements	$ 575	$1,455	$1,410	$ 1,410

*Normal terms of 45 days assumed. Payments therefore represent one month's purchases prior to last 1.5 months (e.g., half of August and half of September paid during October).

expenses, selling and delivery expenses, and general over-head) are shown without lags on the assumption that payments for these expenses and obligations are to be made within the month they're incurred. This assumption could be slightly incorrect in the case of payroll disbursements and certain manufacturing expenses. Such items could indeed lag by one or two weeks. How precisely these lags are dealt with is a function of the relative importance of the cash flow problems they represent.

Production-related payments, such as payroll and manufacturing expenses, are based on the declining pattern of production shown in the basic data section of Figure 4–4, which also reflects a gradual inventory reduction. Yet, in the pro forma operating statement for the period, cost of goods sold is normally based on the pattern of *selling* activities for ease of projection. Thus, the pro forma statement and the more detailed cash budget may differ because the assumptions concerning sales and production are different. To ensure complete consistency, we must therefore determine carefully whether the pattern of production is projected on a different basis than the pattern of sales.

As an example of such a potential difference, it's entirely possible that the seasonal low could be used by management to build up inventories in advance of the expected resurgence of sales. If that were so, the inventory assumption for the pro forma balance sheet would have to be adjusted upward to show the buildup of inventories and the resultant additional funds need. The cash budget, in turn, would have to reflect the higher expenditures involved in producing for inventory. Recognizing differences in production and selling patterns is a key to refining the projection of company performance, and to making cash budgeting results consistent with the pro forma statements.

The final result of our cash budget is a picture of the monthly cash effect of the operating plans on which it's based, and the net funds needs or excesses each month. Note that the funds need at the end of December ($1.41 million) exactly matches the indication we received from the pro forma statements because the same assumptions were used throughout.

To summarize, cash budgets lay out in specific detail the exact timing incidence of cash receipts and disbursements. Like household budgets, they allow us to watch for peaks and valleys in cash availability and to schedule additional financing or repayments as needed. Unlike pro forma statements (which are limited to the beginning and end of a specific period), cash budgets can be drawn up for as many intervals as desired within a period to simulate the fluctuations in cash flow. Given the same assumptions in terms of the volume of production and sales, and the handling of receipts, payments, credit, and so on, the cash budget and pro forma statements will agree in terms of the funds needs or excesses at the end of the period covered.

OPERATING BUDGETS

The pro forma statements and cash budget we prepared for XYZ Corporation provide an overall view of the company's future performance. But in any sizable company, a whole hierarchy of more specific operating budgets are normally prepared. Operating budgets are essentially internal documents. As expressions of ongoing operations, such budgets are linked closely to the company's organizational structure and to the type of performance measurement used by the particular company. These budgets are part of the planning process we mentioned earlier, and are useful as a background for pro forma and cash flow projections when a higher degree of detail and accuracy is desired.

Most managements structure their companies into manageable parts, for each of which an executive or manager is held responsible. The structure may be by *functions* (sales, production, purchasing, and so on). In other cases, the organization may be composed of a set of smaller *profit centers*, each of which is expected to make a profit contribution to total company performance. Even though there are countless variations of organizational structures, the principles of budgeting and financial projection are straightforward and commonly applicable.

Projection of operating results must take a form that reflects the scope of the business unit involved. It must be related to the elements controllable by the responsible manager, and should be the basis on which the manager's performance is measured. These criteria obviously require that operating budgets be carefully designed to fit the particular unit's conditions and the management style of the company as a whole. This means that there's a great deal of difference in the approaches taken by various companies, even within the same industry, and there may be differences within the same company in terms of operating budgets for different organizational units. A growing body of literature has recognized the criteria and impact of what's called *responsibility accounting* within a given organization.

For purposes of our discussion, a few illustrations of basic operational budgeting will suffice. Among the various internal operating budgets routinely prepared by XYZ Corporation are the *annual sales budget by quarters* and a *quarterly factory budget.* The sales budget is designed to show the sales unit's projected contribution to total corporate profits, while the factory budget reflects expected output and the total costs incurred in producing the forecast volume. There are many other types of profit and expense budgets, but we'll limit our discussion to these two, showing how they're used to provide background information for the financial analyst preparing and analyzing pro forma statements and cash budgets.

Sales Budget

As Figure 4–5 shows, the sales manager must first project the level of *unit sales* expected in the market territories served. The projection is made by major product line. Most likely this forecast will be built up from the individual judgments of the persons closest to current and potential customers. Economic conditions will likely be factored in, as will the marketing strategies XYZ Corporation and its competitors are likely to follow.

Next, the *price levels* for each product must be estimated. Prices commonly are a function of three factors: industry pricing practices, the competitive environment, and the cost effectiveness of the company's manufacturing operations. Once price is established, *sales revenue* can be calculated. Then the *cost of goods sold* for the products transferred internally or possibly purchased on the outside must be determined. The difference between the revenue and cost is the *margin before delivery* achieved by the sales unit. Next are the projected *delivery costs* to the customers if these are borne by the company. Controllable *selling expenses* include *compensation* to sales personnel, *travel and entertainment*, and *sales support costs.*

The result is *gross contribution* from selling activities, which must be reduced by estimated *departmental period costs* (costs like rent, managers' salary, and other items that don't vary with short-term fluctuations in volume) to arrive at the *net contribution* provided by the department. After deducting allocated *corporate support costs* (staff support, advertising, and general overhead), the *profit contribution* for the period is established. In making all of these estimates, sales managers can use past relationships and selected ratios, tempered by their judgment concerning changes in future conditions.

In our example, both basic data and dollar elements

FIGURE 4–5

XYZ CORPORATION

Sample Quarterly Sales Budget

For the Year Ended December 31, 1994

	Quarter				
	First	Second	Third	Fourth	Total
Basic data:					
Unit sales (number of units):					
Product A	2,700	2,900	3,000	2,800	11,400
Product B	8,000	8,500	10,000	8,000	34,500
Product C	17,500	18,500	21,000	16,000	73,000
Price level (per unit):					
Product A	$ 145	$ 145	$ 150	$ 150	—
Product B	92	92	95	95	—
Product C	74	74	74	74	—
Number of salespersons	25	25	25	26	—
Operating budget ($000):					
Sales revenue	$ 2,423	$ 2,572	$ 2,954	$ 2,364	$10,313
Less: returns, allowances	25	26	28	24	103
Net sales	2,398	2,546	2,926	2,340	10,210
Cost of goods sold	1,916	2,051	2,322	1,868	8,157
Margin before delivery	482	495	604	472	2,053
Delivery expense	56	60	68	54	238
Gross margin	426	435	536	418	1,815
Selling expense (controllable):					
Salespersons' compensation	94	94	94	98	380
Travel and entertainment	32	32	32	33	129
Sales support costs	23	23	26	24	96
Total selling expenses	149	149	152	155	605
Gross contribution	277	286	384	263	1,210
Departmental period costs	18	18	18	18	72
Net contribution	259	268	366	245	1,138
Corporate support (transferred):					
Staff support	23	25	25	27	100
Advertising	50	50	75	50	225
General overhead	63	63	63	63	252
Total corporate support	136	138	163	140	577
Profit contribution (before taxes)	$ 123	$ 130	$ 203	$ 105	$ 561

have been estimated and set out by the four quarters and for the full year 1994. There's nothing unique about the format we've selected here because many different arrangements of such information are possible to suit any specific organization. Generally, a company prescribes the format for its managers to follow in preparing projected activity budgets, both to maintain a degree of uniformity and to lessen the accounting problem of consolidating the projections when preparing overall financial forecasts. From the standpoint of financial projection, the sales and contribution data in our example are the raw material that goes into the firm's total operating plan.

Factory Budget

The sales budget we just discussed is basically a projection of profit contribution. However, companies also must forecast for operations or activities that involve only costs or expenses. An example of this type of projection, a cost budget for a factory, is shown in Figure 4–6. This time data are given for each month. We've included three months and the total for the second quarter, during which sales and production are expected to increase.

Again, the amount of detail included and the presentation format are chosen to suit the particular needs and preferences of the organization. This time we selected to arrange the headings and data to show that certain cost items (both direct and period costs) are under the control of the local manager. (Other costs, like allocated general overhead, are transferred in from corporate headquarters and thus are beyond the local manager's control.) This arrangement of the data will also be useful if the operating plan serves as a control device with which to measure the unit's performance.

Both sales and cost budgets commonly include additional columns in which *actual* as opposed to *projected* figures are recorded. In addition, *variance* columns are frequently used to measure deviations from plan. We won't go into such refinements here because our examples were only meant to show the type of internal budgeting and projection used formally or informally in most organizations preparatory to developing an overall financial forecast.

FIGURE 4–6
XYZ CORPORATION
Sample Factory Budget
For the Quarter Ended June 30, 1994

	April	May	June	Total
Basic data:				
Number of shifts (5-day week) ...	3	3	3	3
Days worked	20	21	22	63
Hourly employees per shift	33	33	33	33
Number of machines	35	35	34	—
Unit production:				
Product A	1,000	1,050	1,100	3,150
Product B	2,400	2,510	2,640	7,550
Capacity utilization	94%	94%	96%	95%
Downtime for repairs (hours)	–0–	36	–0–	36
Operating budget:				
Direct costs (controllable):*				
Manufacturing labor	$ 57,600	$ 60,500	$ 63,400	$181,500
Raw materials	53,800	56,400	59,200	169,400
Operating supplies	6,500	6,900	7,300	20,700
Repair labor and parts	7,300	12,400	6,500	26,200
Power, heat, light	4,200	4,500	4,800	13,500
Total direct costs	129,400	140,700	141,200	411,300
Period costs (controllable):				
Supervision	5,500	5,500	5,500	16,500
Support labor	28,500	28,500	28,500	85,500
Insurance, taxes	8,700	8,700	8,700	26,100
Depreciation	20,500	20,500	20,500	61,500
Total period costs	63,200	63,200	63,200	189,600
Total controllable costs	192,600	203,900	204,400	600,900
General overhead				
(allocated)	72,000	72,000	72,000	216,000
Total cost	$264,600	$275,900	$276,400	$816,900

*Where appropriate, unit costs can be shown.

INTERRELATIONSHIP OF FINANCIAL PROJECTIONS

It should be obvious by now that the various types of projection presented in this chapter are closely related. If all three forecasts—pro forma statements, cash budgets, and operating budgets—are based on the same set of assumptions about receipts and collections, repayment schedules, operating rates, inventory levels, and so on, they'll all precisely fit together as Figure 4–7 shows.

The financial plans and the projected funds need or excess will differ only if different assumptions concerning funds flow are used, particularly in the pro forma statements on the one hand and the cash budget on the other. It's easy to reconcile pro forma statements and cash budgets, however, by carefully thinking through the key assumptions to be made, one by one, and by laying out formats that contain sufficient detail and background data.

The diagram shows how the various operational budgets flow into a consolidated cash budget, which in turn is reinforced by specific data from the investment and financing plans. The combined information supports the

FIGURE 4–7
Interrelationship of Financial Projections

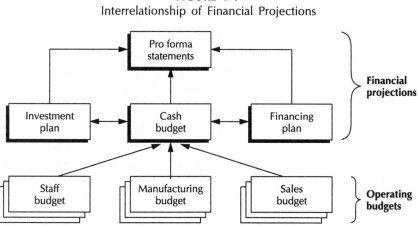

pro forma statements at the top of the diagram. Thus, pro forma statements are the all-encompassing expression of the expected conditions for the period ahead. As a consequence, if we choose to make pro forma statements direct overall estimates, as we discussed (rather than building them up from the company's budgets and plans), they in effect will imply specific assumptions about all the other elements in the diagram.

We haven't yet discussed some of the elements shown in Figure 4–7. *Staff budgets* are spending plans based on the expected cost of operating various service functions of a company. These budgets are prepared and used in the same fashion as other expense budgets.

Investment plans are projections of new outlays for land, buildings, machinery and equipment, and related incremental working capital as well as major outlays for new products and services, expanding markets, new technology, and so on. They may also contain plans to divest any of the company's assets.

We recall that XYZ Corporation made a minor reduction in its fixed assets by selling some used machines. Also, a recently constructed plant was in the final stages of payment, as evidenced by the amount that had become due and payable to the contractor. This facility investment was already reflected on the actual balance sheet of September 30, 1994, largely supported by long-term debt raised earlier. Only the current payment due the contractor was properly scheduled as a pro forma cash disbursement. The company might consider raising some additional long-term debt to fund the new facility, as operations aren't providing enough cash flow to pay off the contractor liabilities.

Financing plans are schedules of proposed future additions to or reductions in indebtedness or ownership funds during the forecast period. They may involve significant expansion or restructuring of a company's capital structure, depending on the projected capital requirements. XYZ Corporation planned no specific future financing, but provisions would have to be made to finance the sizable funds need revealed with the pro forma analysis and to avoid having to strain its current funds as the plant is paid off.

A word about projection methodology should be added here. Any form of financial projection involves both an examination of past trends and specific assumptions about future behavior of revenues, costs, expenses, and other receipts and payments. Past trend analyses range from simple "eyeballing" of obvious patterns to applying a variety of statistical methods to the available data to establish a trend line or curve as the basis for judging future conditions. The projection of key variables may start with such a trend, but the hard judgments about likely changes must override the temptation merely to extrapolate past conditions. The mathematical elegance of statistical methods shouldn't be allowed to supplant the effort to make realistic future assumptions about specific company and market conditions, industry performance, and the national and world economic outlook affecting the firm's likely financial performance. The end-of-chapter references and Appendix V are sources of information on forecasting techniques and other processes that will assist the analyst in technical and judgmental aspects of financial projection.

FINANCIAL MODELING AND SENSITIVITY ANALYSIS

In recent years computer software available or developed specially for financial modeling has vastly expanded the financial analyst's ability to explore the consequences of different assumptions, conditions, and plans. In principle, such software packages are no more than mathematical representations of key financial accounting relationships, ratios, and formats, supported by automatic subroutines that calculate, update, and display data and results in whatever form is desired. The process is based on the very same steps and reasoning discussed in this chapter.

The simplest form of financial modeling is the use of spreadsheets to represent a particular set of relationships for analysis and manipulation. A full-fledged financial model, usually developed within a company, encompasses many elements such as the company's accounting procedures, depreciation schedules, tax calculations, debt service schedules, debt covenants and restrictions, and inventory policies. In many cases the data, assumptions, and format can be custom-tailored so that the financial analyst can reflect the specific characteristics of a given company. With the help of such a model, the analyst can calculate the projected results of conditions expected by the company. The ease of using computerized models allows the analyst to examine several sets of assumptions and assess alternative outcomes.

The major difference between the projection techniques discussed in this chapter and the use of spreadsheets and computer models basically only involves the degree of automation of the process. A cash budget done by hand is essentially a model of the cash flow pattern of the company. In constructing such a budget, the analyst must take into account corporate policies regarding accounting methods, tax reporting, and other detailed operating rules. These constraints can also be incorporated into a basic financial planning software package or even a powerful spreadsheet program. The main difference is that the computer can run different options, while simultaneously tracking all important interrelationships much more easily and quickly than is possible when an analysis is done by hand, as Figure 4–8 implies.

The financial modeling software available on the market is constantly evolving, and readers should familiarize themselves with the latest offerings available. In scope, the modeling packages range all the way from

FIGURE 4–8
Financial Modeling:
An Overview of Relationships Between Inputs and Outputs

spreadsheets with which to calculate simple condensed pro forma statements to highly sophisticated representations of a company's financial accounting system. In the latter case a generalized model is extensively refined, with the help of the company's financial staff, to reflect the company's specific situation. Some companies have developed models that not only calculate the results of specific sets of assumptions, but also contain optimizing routines that select the most desirable alternative investment and financing patterns according to criteria stipulated by management. Other models include statistical projection programs that can be used for initial trending of key variables from past experience. It's clearly beyond this book's scope to detail the vast number of concepts and specialized techniques involved in the building and use of computerized financial models.

Figure 4–8 depicts a broad overview of the major relationships represented in a full-fledged model. The central element is the software program that governs the calculations and displays, with the inputs coming from various sources and the outputs grouped into our familiar categories of analysis.

Sensitivity Analysis

One of the advantages of modeling is the ability to perform sensitivity analysis with considerable ease. This type of analysis involves selecting a few key conditions and altering them to determine the sensitivity of the result to such changes. For example, one of the key assumptions in our pro forma analysis of XYZ Corporation was the usual seasonal pattern of an 18 to 20 percent decline in sales volume in the last quarter. If there were reason to believe that a more serious drop might occur, the analyst could estimate the dollar decline in contribution from each additional 1 percent decrease in volume. If all other conditions were to remain the same, that dollar decline would be the lost contribution from the units left unsold.

The impact on funds needs would be traced by adjusting aftertax profits and by recognizing that there would be a change in working capital because sales levels are lower, except in inventory where the unsold units might remain. If prices were considered unstable, a series of assumptions about the effect of lower prices for one or all of the product lines could be traced. In every case the critical test would be the sensitivity of the funds need to the changes in each of the three months. Clearly, many other tests could be made and related to the altered result brought about by the change in a given assumption.

The key to this type of reasoning is the analyst's judgment as to which elements in the operating and financial patterns being projected are most subject to variability. Then the task is to simulate how sensitive the desired result is to each change. Given such a range of results, the decision maker using the analysis can judge the risk of the proposed course and adjust operating and financial policies accordingly. A computer model isn't critical to making such sensitivity tests. Even our simple pro forma statements and cash budgets can be easily modified to answer basic questions of this sort. Nonetheless, with relevant software, the analyst can examine many more possibilities and determine the impact of a far greater number of assumptions. Sensitivity tests can be performed on more than one variable simultaneously, and whole scenarios can be developed with the financial impact reflected in the output. We'll return to sensitivity analysis in later chapters.

SUMMARY

The principles of financial projection discussed in this chapter revolve around the use of pro forma statements and various types of budgets. We observed that financial projection is only part of the broader process of business planning. Financial projection can be expressed in the familiar form of financial statements and in many specifically tailored budget formats. The process is simple in that it represents an orderly way of sorting out the financial impact of investment, operational, and financing decisions. The process is difficult in that judgments about future conditions are fraught with uncertainty, as planning of any sort must be.

Here the use of sensitivity analysis, the calculation of the impact of alternative assumptions, can narrow the range of uncertainty. Financial projection basically is modeling the future in the context of operational and policy constraints. To the extent that more detail and more options for future plans are desired, automation of the process with the help of computer-based financial modeling can yield significant benefits in terms of speed, accuracy, and insight.

SELECTED REFERENCES

Anthony, Robert N., and James S. Reece. *Accounting: Text and Cases.* 8th ed. Homewood, Ill.: Richard D. Irwin, 1988.

Murdick and Georgoff. "The Manager's Guide to Forecasting." *Harvard Business Review,* March/April 1986.

Ross, Stephen; Randolph Westerfield; and Jeffrey Jaffe. *Corporate Finance.* 2nd ed. Homewood, Ill.: Richard D. Irwin, 1990.

Seitz, Neil. *Business Forecasting on Your Personal Computer.* Reston, Va.: Reston Publishing, 1984.

Vancil, Richard F., and Benjamin R. Makela, eds. *The CFO Handbook.* Homewood, Ill.: Dow Jones-Irwin, 1986.

Van Horne, James C. *Financial Management and Policy.* 8th ed. Englewood Cliffs, N.J.: Prentice Hall, 1989.

Weston, J. Fred, and Thomas E. Copeland. *Managerial Finance.* 9th ed. Hinsdale, Ill.: Dryden Press, 1989.

SELF-STUDY EXERCISES AND PROBLEMS

(Solutions are provided in Appendix VI)

1. Complete the following exercises, based on these selected data about a company. Consider each exercise separately.

Total assets on 12-31-94	$2,750,000
Sales for the year 1994	9,137,000
Current assets on 12-31-94	1,315,000
Long-term debt on 12-31-94	210,000
Current ratio on 12-31-94	2.4:1
Cost of goods sold for 1994	83% of sales
Purchases during 1994	$5,316,000
Depreciation for 1994	174,000
Net profit after taxes for 1994	131,000
Taxes on income for 1994	112,000

   a. Currently the company's accounts receivable outstanding are

18 days' sales. To meet competitive pressures in 1995, the company must extend credit to an average of 40 days' sales to maintain operations and profits at 1994 levels. No other changes are contemplated for the next year, and sales and operations are expected to continue at 1994 rates. What's the impact of this change in credit policy on corporate funds needs? Will the company have to borrow? What if credit had to be extended to 60 days? Discuss.

b. The inventory levels maintained by the company have averaged $725,000 during 1994 with little fluctuation. If turnover were to slow to seven times (average inventory in cost of goods sold) due to a switch to a consignment policy, what would the financial impact be? Assume no change in sales levels. What other changes are likely to take place, and how would these affect the company's financial stance? What if turnover rose to 11 times? Discuss.

c. Payment for purchases has been made under normal trade terms of 2/10, n/30 with discounting done as a matter of policy. Suppliers anxious for business are beginning to offer 2/15, n/45 terms, which will become universal during the coming year. What would the financial impact of this change be if the company were to follow its policy of discounting purchases? What trade-off has to be considered? Discuss.

d. If the company is planning capital expenditures of $125,000 and simultaneously is planning to pay dividends at the rate of 60 percent of net profits, what are the financial implications, assuming all other elements are unchanged?

e. If sales are expected to grow 10 percent for the following year, with all *normal* relationships under (a) through (c) unchanged, what financial considerations arise? How would the intentions of (d) look then? Discuss.

2. In September 1995, ABC Company, a manufacturing firm, was making budget plans for the 12 months beginning November 1, 1995. Projected sales volume was $4,350,000, as compared to an estimated $3,675,000 for the fiscal year ended October 31, 1995. The best estimates of the operating results for the current year are shown in the operating statement.

The projected increase in volume of operations was expected to bring improvements in efficiency, while at the same time some of the cost factors would continue to rise absolutely, in line with past trends. Following this statement are the specific working assumptions with which to plan financial results for the next year.

ABC COMPANY
Estimated Operating Statement
For the Year Ended October 31, 1995
($ thousands)

	Amount		Percent	
Net sales		$3,675		100%
Cost of goods sold:				
Labor	$919		25.0	
Materials	522		14.2	
Overhead	743		20.2	
Depreciation	133	2,317	3.6	63.0
Gross profit		1,358		37.0
Selling expense	305		8.3	
General and administrative expenses	323	628	8.8	17.1
Profit before taxes		730		19.9
Income taxes		336		9.1
Net income		$ 394		10.8%

Assumptions for fiscal year 1996:

Manufacturing labor would drop to 24 percent of direct sales because volume efficiency would more than offset higher wage rates.

Materials cost would rise to 14.5 percent of sales because some price increases wouldn't be offset by better utilization.

Overhead costs would rise above the present level by 6 percent of the 1995 dollar amount, reflecting higher costs. Additional variable costs would be encountered at the rate of 11 percent of the incremental sales volume.

Depreciation would increase by $10,000, reflecting the addition of some production machinery.

Selling expenses would rise more proportionately, by $125,000, because additional effort would be required to increase sales volume.

General and administrative expense would drop to 8.1 percent of sales.

Income taxes (federal and state) were estimated at 46 percent of pretax profits.

Develop a pro forma operating statement for the ABC Company and discuss your findings.

3. In December 1995, the DEF Company, a distributor of stationery products, was planning its financial needs for the coming year. As a first indication, the firm's management wished to have a pro forma balance sheet as of December 31, 1995, to gauge funds

needs at that time. Estimated financial condition as of December 31, 1995, was reflected in this balance sheet:

DEF COMPANY
Estimated Balance Sheet
December 31, 1995

Assets

Current assets:

Cash	$ 217,300
Receivables	361,200
Inventories (pledged as security)	912,700
Total current assets	1,491,200

Fixed assets:

Land, buildings, trucks, and fixtures	421,500
Less: Accumulated depreciation	217,300
Total fixed assets	204,200
Other assets	21,700
Total assets	$1,717,100

Liabilities and net worth

Current liabilities:

Accounts payable	$ 612,300
Note payable—bank	425,000
Accrued expenses	63,400
Total current liabilities	1,100,700
Term loan—properties	120,000
Capital stock	200,000
Paid-in surplus	112,000
Retained earnings	184,400
Total liabilities and net worth	$1,717,100

Operations for the ensuing year were projected using the following working assumptions to plan the financial results:

Sales were forecast at $10,450,000, with a gross margin of 8.2 percent.

Purchases were expected to total $9,725,000, with some seasonal upswings in May and August.

Accounts receivable would be based on a collection period of 12 days, while 24 days' accounts payable would be outstanding.

Depreciation was expected to be $31,400 for the year.

Term loan repayments were scheduled at $10,000, while bank notes payable would be allowed to fluctuate with seasonal needs.

Capital expenditures were scheduled at $21,000 for trucks and $36,000 for warehouse improvements.

Net profits after taxes were expected at the level of 0.19 percent of sales.

Dividends for the year were scheduled at $12,500.

Cash balances were desired at no less than $150,000.

Develop a pro forma balance sheet and discuss your findings.

4. In September 1995, the **XYZ** Company, a department store, was planning for cash needs during the last quarter of 1995 and the first quarter of 1996. The Christmas buying season always meant a considerable strain on finances, and the first planning step was development of a cash budget. The following data were available for this purpose:

Projected sales (half for cash, half charged on 90-day account):

October	$ 770,000	January	$650,000
November	690,000	February	580,000
December	1,010,000	March	720,000

Projected purchases (half on n/45; 40 percent on 2/10, n/30; 10 percent for cash):

October	$610,000	January	$320,000
November	535,000	February	450,000
December	290,000	March	480,000

Projected payments on purchases as of 9-30-95:

Due by October 10 (2% discount)	$ 60,000
Due by October 31 (net 45)	257,000
Due by November 15 (net 45)	113,000
Total	$430,000

Projected collections of receivables as of 9-30-95:

Due in October	$215,000
Due in November	245,000
Due in December	265,000
Total (bad debts negligible)	$725,000

Projected financial data:

Minimum cash balance required	$75,000
Beginning cash balance (October 1)	95,000
Mortgage payments (monthly)	7,000
Cash dividend due December 31	40,000
Federal taxes due January 15	20,000

Projected operations: salaries and wages average 19 percent of sales; cash operating expenses average 14 percent of sales.

Develop a monthly cash budget to show the seasonal funds requirements. Discuss your findings.

5.   A newly formed space technology company, the ZYX Corporation, was in the early stages of planning for the first several months of operations. The initial capital put up by the founders and their associates amounted to 250,000 shares of $1 par value stock. Furthermore, patents estimated to be worth $50,000 were provided by two of the principals in exchange for 50,000 shares of common stock. Equipment costing $175,000 was purchased with the funds, and organization expenses of $15,000 were paid. Operations were to start February 1, 1995.

Orders already in hand amounted to $1,400,000 of electronic devices, which at an estimated monthly output of $400,000 (sales value) represented almost four months' sales. More orders were expected from contacts made. Monthly operating expenses and conditions were estimated as follows:

Manufacturing labor	$ 60,000
Rent for building	18,500
Overhead costs	76,000
Depreciation	6,000
Write-off of patents	500
Selling and administrative expenses	55,000
Purchases of materials, supplies	125,000
Sale terms	n/30
Collection experience expected	45 days
Purchase terms	n/30
Raw materials inventory level	$ 60,000
Finished goods inventory level	145,000
Prepaid expenses (average)	12,000
Accrued wages	1 week's
Accrued taxes (40% effective rate)	As incurred

If the company wanted to maintain a minimum cash balance of $40,000, what would the financial situation be after six months of operations? Develop pro forma statements and discuss the likely timing of any funds needs. How are the next six months likely to affect this picture? Discuss your findings.

6.   The ABC Supermarket's management expected the next six months (January 1, 1995, through June 30, 1995) to being a variety of cash requirements beyond the normal operational outflows. A monthly cash budget was to be developed to trace the specific funds needs. The following projections were available for the purpose:

a. Cash sales projected:

January	$200,000	April	$200,000
February	190,000	May	230,000
March	220,000	June	220,000

b. Cost of goods sold averages 75 percent of sales.

c. Purchases closely scheduled with sales volume. Payments average a 15-day lag behind purchases. December purchases were $168,000.

d. Operating expenses projected:

1. Salaries and wages at 12 percent of sales, paid when incurred.

2. Other expenses at an average 9 percent of sales, paid when incurred.

3. Rent of $3,500, paid monthly.

4. Income tax payments of $2,000 due in January, March, and June, and $3,500 due in April.

5. Cash receipts from sale of property at $6,000 per month due in March, April, and May.

6. Payments on note owed local bank due as follows: $3,000 in February and $5,000 in May.

7. Repayments of advances to principals of the firm due at $3,000 each in January, March, and May.

8. New store fixtures of $48,000 acquired, and four payments of $12,000 each due in February, March, April, and May.

9. Old store fixtures with a book value of $4,500 scrapped, to be written off in January.

10. Rental income from a small concession granted on the premises to begin at $300 per month in March.

Develop a cash budget as requested and show the effect of the operations and other elements described above on the beginning cash balance of $42,500. The principals of the firm would like to keep a cash balance of not less than $20,000 at any one time. Will additional funds be required? If so, when? Discuss your findings.

7. The XYZ Company, a fast-growing manufacturing operation, found its inventories in 1995 increasing faster than growth in sales. (As additional territories and customers had been developed, production schedules were stepped up in an effort to

provide excellent service levels.) Also, collections had deteriorated, and the company's receivables represented two months' sales compared to normal 30-day terms. Because both conditions caused considerable pressures on the company's finances, a change to a level production schedule was considered beginning October 1, 1995, to allow inventories to be worked off while still providing employment to the company's full-time workers. Also, more effort would be expended on collections. A six-month trial of the new policy was to be analyzed in September before implementation, and the following assumptions and data were provided:

a. Current sales and forecast:

August	$1,925,000	December	$2,450,000
September (est.)	2,050,000	January	2,625,000
October	2,175,000	February	2,750,000
November	2,300,000	March	2,850,000

b. Current purchases and forecast (terms n/45):

August	$750,000	December	$650,000
September (est.)	675,000	January	650,000
October	650,000	February	650,000
November	650,000	March	650,000

c. Collection period, current and forecast:

August 31	63 days	December 31	40 days
September 30 (est.)	60	January 31	40
October 31	50	February 28	40
November 30	50	March 31	40

d. Materials usage, beginning October: $825,000 per month.

e. Wages and salaries, beginning October: $215,000 per month, paid as incurred.

f. Other manufacturing expenses, beginning October: $420,000 per month, paid as incurred.

g. Depreciation: $43,000 per month.

h. Cost of goods sold has consistently averaged 70 percent of sales.

i. Selling and administrative expenses: October and November, 15 percent of sales; December and January, 14 percent of sales; and February and March, 12 percent of sales.

j. Payments on note payable: $750,000 each in November and February.

k. Interest due in January: $300,000.

l. Dividends payable in October and January: $25,000 each.

m. Income taxes due in January: $375,000.

n. Most recent balance sheet (estimated) is shown below.

From the data given, develop a cash budget for the six months ended March 31, 1996, and pro forma statements for the quarters ended December 31, 1995, and March 31, 1996. Assume income taxes to be 50 percent, don't detail cost of goods sold, and assume no changes in accounts not specifically analyzed or projected here. What funds needs arise, and when? What if the collection speedup effort were unsuccessful and receivables stayed at 60 days? Discuss your findings about the policy changes being considered.

XYZ COMPANY
Estimated Balance Sheet
For September 30, 1995
($ thousands)

Assets

Current assets:		
Cash		$ 740
Accounts and notes receivable		3,975
Inventories:		
Raw materials	$ 2,725	
Finished goods	6,420	9,145
Total current assets		13,860
Plant and equipment	12,525	
Less: Accumulated depreciation	5,315	7,210
Other assets		1,730
Total assets		$22,800

Liabilities and net worth

Current liabilities:	
Accounts payable	$ 1,050
Notes payable	4,120
Accrued liabilities	2,875
Total current liabilities	8,045
Long-term debt	5,250
Preferred stock	1,750
Common stock	5,000
Retained earnings	2,755
Total liabilities and net worth	$22,800

5 DYNAMICS OF THE BUSINESS SYSTEM

Having covered the basic techniques of performance analysis, funds flow analysis, and projection of financial requirements in the preceding three chapters, we need to revisit the business system as a whole and discuss the key dynamic aspects of financial management and planning. In Chapter 1 we described the interrelationship of financial yardsticks and management policies in broad terms.

Now we're equipped to demonstrate the dynamics of the business system by focusing on the concept of *leverage*, both as it affects operations and as it impacts the financing decisions of management. With these concepts more firmly established, we can then turn to describe and demonstrate integrated *financial growth plans*, in which we'll test the financial impact of policy changes in investment, operations, and financing. This integrated view of financial analysis allows us to visualize the total business system performance and to understand the concept of *sustainable growth*. The broader concept of shareholder value will be detailed in Chapter 9.

The reader is encouraged to review the first section of Chapter 1 which describes the business system and the key interrelationships within it, many of which we'll test in this discussion.

LEVERAGE

Leverage, as previously mentioned, refers to the often favorable condition of having a stable element of cost support a wide range of activity levels. *Operating leverage* means that some of the ongoing costs of the business are fixed over a broad range of operating volume. As a consequence, profits are boosted or depressed more than proportionally for changes in volume. Similarly, *financial leverage* occurs when a company's capital structure contains obligations with fixed interest rates. The effect of this condition is similar to the case of operating leverage. Again, earnings after interest are boosted or depressed more than proportionally as operating volume fluctuates. Operating and financial leverage are one and the same in principle.

However, there are differences in the specific elements involved and in the methods of calculating each type of leverage. Both operating and financial leverage can be present in any business, and their respective impact on net profit will tend to be mutually reinforcing.

Operating Leverage

Distinguishing between fixed and variable costs (those costs that vary with time and those that vary with the level of activity) is an old idea. This distinction is the basis for *break-even analysis*. The concept of breaking even essentially springs from the simple question of how many units of a product or service a business must sell to cover its fixed costs. Presumably, prices are set at a level high enough to recoup all direct (that is, variable) costs and leave a margin of contribution toward fixed costs and profit. Once sufficient units have been sold to accumulate the amount of contribution needed to offset fixed (period) costs, the margin from any additional units sold will become profit—unless a new layer of fixed costs has to be added at some future point as volume increases significantly.

An understanding of this principle will improve our insight into how the operational aspects of a business relate to financial planning and projections. But in a broader sense it will allow us to appreciate the distorting effect that significant operating leverage may exert on the measures and comparisons of financial analysis.

A word of caution must be added here. There's nothing absolute in the concept of fixed costs because in the long run every cost element becomes variable. Costs are a consequence of management decisions and can therefore be altered by management decisions. As a result the break-even concept must be handled with a degree of flexibility.

As we mentioned, introducing fixed costs to a business's operations tends to magnify profits at higher levels of operation. This is due to the incremental contribution each additional unit provides over and above the strictly variable costs incurred in producing it. Depending on the proportion of fixed and variable costs in the company's cost structure, the total incremental contribution from the added units can result in a sizable overall jump in profit.

Once all fixed costs have been recovered by the contributions from a sufficient minimum number of units, profits grow proportionately faster than volume. Unfortunately, the same effect holds for declining volumes of operations, which result in a decline in profit and accelerating losses that are disproportionate to the rate of volume reduction. Leverage is definitely a two-edged sword!

We can establish the basic definitions needed to analyze leverage as follows:

$$\text{Profit} = \text{Total revenue} - \text{Total cost}$$
$$\text{Total revenue} = \text{Volume (quantity)} \times \text{Price}$$
$$\text{Total cost} = \text{Fixed cost} + \text{Variable cost}$$

The formal way of describing leverage conditions is quite simple. We're interested in the effect on profit (I) of changes in volume (V). The elements that bear on this are the unit price (P), unit variable costs (C), and fixed costs (F). The relationship is

$$I = VP - (VC + F)$$

This formula can be rewritten as

$$I = V(P - C) - F$$

which illustrates that profit depends on the number of goods or services sold times the difference between unit price and unit variable cost—which is the contribution to the constant element, fixed costs.

As unit volume changes, the unit contribution ($P - C$) times the change in volume will equal the total change in profit. Under normal conditions, the constant, fixed costs (F) will remain just that. The relative changes in profit for a given change in volume will be magnified because of this fixed element.

Another way of stating the leverage relationships is to use profit as a percentage of sales (s), one of the ratios developed in Chapter 3. Using the previous notation,

$$s = \frac{I}{VP},$$

and defining I in terms of its components, the formula becomes

$$s = \frac{V(P - C) - F}{VP}$$

or, slightly rewritten,

$$s = \left(I - \frac{C}{P}\right) - \frac{F}{VP}$$

This indicates that the profit/sales ratio depends on the contribution per unit of sales, less fixed costs as a percentage of sales revenue. We observe that, to the extent that fixed costs are present, they cause a reduction in the profit ratio. The larger F is, the larger the reduction. Any change in volume, price, or unit cost, however, will tend to have a disproportional impact on s because F is constant.

Now let's examine how the process works using some concrete examples. We'll use the cost/profit conditions of a simple business with relatively high fixed costs of $200,000 in relation to its volume of output and variable costs per unit. Our company has a maximum level of production of 1,000 units, and for simplicity, we assume there's no lag between production and sales. Units sell for $750 each. Variable costs of materials, labor, and supplies amount to $250 per unit. As a consequence, each unit provides a contribution of $500 toward fixed costs and profit.

Figure 5–1's *break-even chart* is a simple representation of the conditions just outlined. At zero volume, fixed costs amount to $200,000, and they remain level as volume is increased until full capacity has been reached. Variable costs, on the other hand, accumulate by $250 per unit as volume is increased until a level of $250,000 has been reached at capacity, for a total cost of $450,000. Revenue rises from zero, in increments of $750, until total revenue has reached $750,000 at capacity.

Where the revenue and variable cost lines cross (at 400 units of output), a break-even condition of no profit and no loss has been reached. This means that the total cumulative revenue of $300,000 at that point is just sufficient to offset the fixed costs of $200,000 plus the total variable costs of $100,000 (400 units at $250

FIGURE 5–1
ABC CORPORATION
Simple Operating Break-Even Chart

Profits and Losses as a Function of Volume Changes of 25 Percent

Volume	Increase	Profits	Increase
400	—	–0–	—
500	25%	$ 50,000	Infinite*
625	25	112,500	125%
781	25	190,500	69
976	25	288,000	51
Volume	Decrease	Losses	Increase
400	—	–0–	—
300	25%	$ 50,000	Infinite*
225	25	87,500	75%
169	25	115,500	32
127	25	136,000	18

*Infinite because the base is zero.

each). If operations increase beyond this point, profits are generated; at volumes below 400 units, losses are incurred. The break-even point can be found numerically, of course, by simply dividing the total fixed costs of $200,000 by the unit contribution of $500, which results in 400 units, as we expected:

$$\text{Break-even point } (I = O)\text{: } \frac{F}{P - C} = V$$

$$\text{Zero profit} = \frac{\$200,000}{\$500} = 400 \text{ units}$$

The most interesting aspect of the break-even chart, however, is the clear demonstration that increases and decreases in profit aren't proportional. A series of 25 percent increases in volume above the break-even point will result in much larger percentage jumps in profit growth.

The relevant figures for the changes in our example are displayed in the table under the chart. They show a gradual decline in the growth rate of profit from infinite to 51 percent. Similarly, as volume decreases below the break-even point in 25 percent decrements, the growth rate of losses goes from infinite to a modest 18 percent, as volume approaches zero. Thus, changes in operations *close* to the break-even point, whether up or down, are likely to produce *sizable* swings in earnings. Changes in operations well above or below the break-even point cause lesser fluctuations.

We must be careful in interpreting these changes, however. As in any percentage analysis, the specific results depend on the starting point and the relative proportions of the components. In fact, operating management will generally be much more concerned about the total amount of change in profit than about percentage fluctuations. Moreover, it's easy to exaggerate the meaning of profit fluctuations unless they're carefully interpreted in the context of a company's total cost structure and its normal level of operations.

Nevertheless, the concept should be clear—the closer to its break-even point a firm operates, the more dramatic will be the profit impact of volume changes. The financial analyst assessing a company's performance or making financial projections must attempt to understand where the level of its current operations is relative to normal volume and the break-even point, and interpret the results of the analysis accordingly.

Furthermore, the greater the relative level of fixed costs, the more powerful the effect of leverage becomes. Our need to understand this aspect of the company's cost structure increases commensurably. In capital-intensive industries (such as steel, mining, forest products, and heavy manufacturing), most costs of production are fixed for a wide range of volumes. This condition tends to accentuate profit swings as such companies move away from break-even operations.

Another example is the airline industry, which from time to time substantially increases the capacity of its flight equipment (e.g., from the 727 to the 747 jumbo jet). The fixed costs associated with owning and operating these aircraft caused sharp drops in profit for most airlines. As business and private travel rose to approach the new levels of capacity, several airlines experienced dramatic improvements in profits. In contrast, service industries, such as consulting firms, can directly influence their major cost—wages and salaries—by adjusting the number of employees as demand changes. Thus, they're much less subject to the profit swings of the operating leverage phenomenon.

As we observed earlier, there are three main elements management can influence in the operating leverage relationship: (1) *fixed costs*, (2) *variable costs*, and (3) *price*, all of which are in one way or another related to *volume*. We'll demonstrate the effect of changes in all three by varying the basic conditions in our example.

Effect of Lower Fixed Costs. If management can reduce fixed costs through energetic reductions in overhead or by using facilities more intensively, the break-even point may be lowered significantly. As a consequence, the boosting effect on profits will start at a lower level of operations. Figure 5–2 shows this change.

FIGURE 5–2
ABC CORPORATION
Simple Operating Break-Even Chart: Effect of Reducing Fixed Costs
(reduction of $25,000)

Profits and Losses as a Function of Volume Changes of 25 Percent

Volume	Increase	Profits	Increase
350	—	–0–	—
438	25%	$ 44,000	Infinite*
547	25	98,500	125%
684	25	167,500	69
855	25	252,000	51

Volume	Decrease	Losses	Increase
350	—	–0–	—
262	25%	$ 44,000	Infinite*
196	25	77,000	75%
147	25	101,500	32
110	25	120,000	18

*Infinite because the base is zero.

Note that reduction of fixed costs by one eighth has led to a corresponding reduction in break-even volume. It will now take one eighth fewer units contributing $500 each to recover the lower fixed costs. From the table we can observe that successive 25 percent volume changes from the reduced break-even point lead to increases or decreases in profit that are quite similar to those in our first example in Figure 5–1. Reducing fixed costs, therefore, is a very direct and effective way of lowering the break-even point to improve the firm's profit performance.

Effect of Lower Variable Costs. If management is able to reduce the variable costs of production (direct costs)—thereby increasing the contribution per unit—the action can similarly affect profits at current levels and influence the movement of the break-even point itself. In Figure 5–3 we've shown the resulting change in the slope of the variable cost line, which in effect widens the area of profits. At the same time, loss conditions are reduced.

However, the change in break-even volume resulting from a 10 percent change in variable costs isn't as dramatic as the change experienced when fixed costs were lowered by one eighth. The reason is that the reduction applies only to a small portion of the total production cost, as variable costs are relatively low in this example. (This illustrates our earlier point about having to consider the relative proportions in this type of analysis.)

Only at full capacity (1,000 units) does the profit impact of $25,000 correspond to the effect of the reduction of $25,000 in fixed costs in the earlier example. At lower levels of operations, lower unit volumes and the lesser impact of variable costs combine to minimize the effect. Nevertheless, the result is clearly an improvement in the break-even condition, and a profit boost is achieved earlier on the volume scale. Again, 25 percent incremental changes are tabulated to show the specific results.

Effect of Lower Prices. Up to this point we've concentrated on *cost* effects which are largely under the control of management. In contrast, price changes are to a large extent dependent on the firm's competitive environment. As a result, changed prices normally affect the competitive equilibrium and directly influence the unit

FIGURE 5–3
ABC CORPORATION
Simple Operating Break-Even Chart: Effect of Reducing Variable Costs
(reduction of $25 per unit)

Profits and Losses as a Function of Volume Changes of 25 Percent

Volume	Increase	Profits	Increase
381	—	–0–	—
476	25%	$ 49,900*	Infinite†
595	25	112,375	125%
744	25	190,600	69
930	25	288,250	51
Volume	Decrease	Losses	Increase
381	—	–0–	—
286	25%	$ 50,150	Infinite†
215	25	87,125	75%
161	25	115,475	32
121	25	136,475	18

*First 25 percent change not exactly equal due to rounding.
†Infinite because the base is zero.

volume a business can sell. Thus it's not enough to trace the effect of raised or lowered prices on the break-even chart. We must also anticipate the likely change in volume resulting from the price change.

In other words, raising the price may more than proportionately affect the unit volume the company can sell competitively, and the price action may actually result in lower total profits. Conversely, lowering the price may more than compensate for the lost contribution per unit by boosting the total unit volume that can be sold against competition.

Figure 5–4 demonstrates the effect of lowering the price by $50 per unit, a 6.7 percent reduction. Note that this change raises the required break-even volume by about 11 percent, to 444 units. In other words, the company needs to sell an additional 44 units just to recoup the loss in contribution of $50 from the sale of every unit.

For example, if the current volume was 800 units, with a contribution of $400,000 and a profit of $200,000, the price drop of $50 would require the sale of enough additional units to recover 800 times $50, or $40,000. This must be done in the face of a lower per unit contribution of $450.

Consequently, 89 additional units ($40,000 ÷ $450) have to be sold at the lower price to maintain the $200,000 profit level—which represents a volume increase of 11 percent. Note that this results in a more than proportional change in unit volume (11 percent) versus the change in price (6.7 percent).

Price changes affect internal operating results, but they may have an even more pronounced and lasting impact on the competitive environment. If a more than proportional volume advantage—and therefore improved profits—can be obtained over a significant period of time after the price has been reduced, this may be a wise move. Otherwise, if price reductions can be expected to be quickly matched by other competitors, the final effect may simply be a drop in profit for everyone because little if any shift in relative market shares would result. The airline price wars of recent years are a prime example of this phenomenon.

FIGURE 5–4
ABC CORPORATION
Simple Operating Break-Even Chart: Effect of Reducing Price
(reduction of $50 per unit)

Profits and Losses as a Function of Volume Changes of 25 Percent

Volume	Increase	Profits	Increase
444	—	–0–	—
555	25%	$ 49,750*	Infinite[†]
694	25	112,300	125%
867	25	190,150	69
1084	25	287,800	51
Volume	Decrease	Losses	Increase
444	—	–0–	—
333	25%	$ 50,150*	Infinite[†]
249	25	87,950	75%
187	25	115,850	32
140	25	137,000	18

*First 25 percent change not exactly equal due to rounding.
[†]Infinite because the base is zero.

This isn't the place to discuss the many strategic issues involved in pricing policy. The intent is merely to show the effect of this important factor on the operating system and to provide a way of analyzing likely conditions.

Multiple Effects on Break-Even Conditions. In the foregoing analysis, we analyzed cost, volume, and price implications and their impact on profit separately. In practice, the many conditions and pressures encountered by a business often affect these variables simultaneously. Cost, volume, and price for a single product may all be changing at the same time in subtle and often unmeasurable ways. The analysis is further complicated when several products are involved, as is true of all major companies. In such cases, changes in the sales mix can introduce many complexities.

Moreover, our simplifying assumption that production and sales are simultaneous doesn't necessarily hold true in practice; the normal lag between production and sales has a significant effect that must be taken into account. In a manufacturing company, sales and production can be widely out of phase. Some of the implications arising from this condition were discussed in Chapter 2, when we dealt with funds flow conditions under varying levels of operations, and in Chapter 4, when we examined the relationship of cash budgets and pro forma operating statements.

Up to this point, we have assumed that operating conditions were essentially *linear*. This allowed us to simplify our analysis of leverage and break-even conditions. A more realistic framework is suggested in the chart in Figure 5–5, which shows potential changes in both fixed and variable costs over the full range of operations. Possible changes in price-revenue developments are also reflected. In other words, changes in all three factors affecting operating leverage are reflected at the same time.

Figure 5–5 further indicates that the simple straight-line relationships used in Figures 5–1 through 5–4 are normally only approximations of the "step functions" and the gradual shifts in cost and price often encountered under realistic circumstances. Inflationary distortions arising over time must also be considered. A few of the possible changes in conditions and sample reasons for them are described below the chart.

FIGURE 5–5
ABC CORPORATION
Generalized Break-Even Chart:
Allowing for Changing Cost and Revenue Conditions

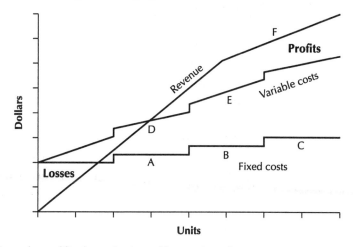

A. A new layer of fixed costs is triggered by growing volume.
B. A new shift is added, with additional requirements for overhead costs.
C. A final small increment of overhead is incurred as some operations require overtime.
D. Efficiencies in operations reduce variable unit costs.
E. The new shift causes inefficiencies and lower output, with more spoilage.
F. The last increments of output must be sold on contract at lower prices.

Target Profit Analysis. An application of operational leverage is the use of target profit analysis as part of the planning process of a company. It takes into account the relative proportions of fixed and variable costs expected to hold in the company's system. Given projections of total fixed costs (F), estimates of variable costs (C), and expected price (P), the unit volume required to achieve any desired pretax target profit (TP) can be determined with the basic break-even formula:

$$\text{Volume for target profit: } V = \frac{F + TP}{P - C}$$

Similarly, if management wishes to test the level of variable costs (C) allowable for any desired pretax target profit (TP) with an estimated unit volume (V) and price

(P) based on expected market conditions and projected fixed costs (F), the formula can be rewritten as

$$\text{Variable unit cost for target profit: } C = P - \frac{(F + TP)}{V}$$

The reader is invited to rewrite the formula for the required price to achieve a desired pretax profit and also to determine the change required to put the formula on an aftertax basis. Calculations such as these serve well to establish the dimensions of the planning process, but can't be substituted for detailed analysis and projections such as we discussed in Chapter 3. The approach helps analysts and managers recognize in broad terms the implications of the company's operating leverage.

Financial Leverage

The basic fixed/variable cost relationship can also be used to examine the effect of various proportions of debt in a firm's financial structure, that is, to analyze the company's financial leverage. A close similarity exists between operating and financial leverage in that both present an opportunity to gain from the fixed nature of certain costs in relation to increments of activity.

With financial leverage, the advantage lies in the possibility that funds borrowed at a fixed interest rate can be used for investment opportunities earning a rate of return higher than the interest paid. The difference, of course, accrues as profit to the owners of the business. Given the ability to make investments that consistently provide returns above the going rate of interest, it will be to a company's advantage to engage in "trading on equity" as the concept is sometimes called. This means borrowing as much as prudent debt management will permit, thereby boosting the return on owners' equity by the difference between the rate of return achieved and the rate of interest paid. The opposite effect will, of course, apply if the company earns returns below the rate of interest paid.

Figure 5–6 shows the leverage effect on return on equity under three conditions of return on net assets. All three curves are based on the assumption that funds can be borrowed at 4 percent per year after taxes.

If the normal return on the company's capitalization before interest and after taxes is 20 percent (curve A), growing proportions of debt cause a dramatic rise in return on equity. This return jumps to infinity as debt nears 100 percent. Curves B and C show the leverage effect under more modest earnings conditions. While somewhat lessened, the return on equity still shows sharp increases as the proportion of debt rises.

FIGURE 5–6
ABC CORPORATION
Return on Equity as Affected by Financial Leverage
(aftertax interest on debt is 4 percent)

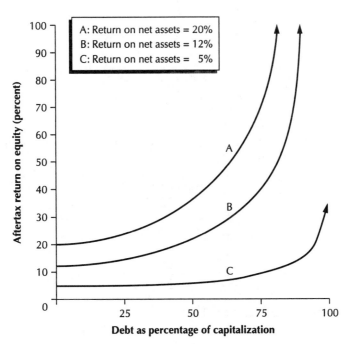

As we observed before, leverage unfortunately also works in the opposite direction. This effect is suggested by the observation that the distances between curves A, B, and C increase with higher debt levels. Should earnings drop, the plunge in return on equity can be massive.

To express the financial leverage relationships formally, we begin by defining the components, as we did in the case of operating leverage. Profit after taxes (I) now has to be related to equity (E) and long-term debt (D). We also single out the return on equity (R) and return on net assets (capitalization) before interest and after taxes. First, we define the return on equity as

$$R = \frac{I}{E}$$

and the return on capitalization (the sum of equity and debt) as

$$r = \frac{I + Di}{E + D}$$

We now restate profit (I) in terms of its components,

$$I = r(E + D) - Di$$

which represents the difference between the return on the total capitalization $(E + D)$ and the aftertax cost of interest on outstanding debt. We then find that our first formula can be rewritten as

$$R = \frac{r(E + D) - Di}{E}$$

which we can restate as

$$R = r + \frac{D}{E}(r - i)$$

This formulation highlights the leverage effect, represented by the positive expression after r (that is, the proportion of debt to equity) multiplied by the difference between the earnings power of net assets and the aftertax cost of interest. Thus, to the extent that debt is introduced into the capital structure, the return on equity is boosted as long as interest cost doesn't exceed earnings power.

When we apply the formula to one set of conditions that pertained in Figure 5–6's graph, the results can be calculated as follows. Given $i = 4\%$ and $r = 12\%$, if

(1) $D = \quad 0$ and $E = \$100$, then $R = 12.0\%$
(2) $D = \$25$ and $E = \$\ 75$, then $R = 14.7\%$
(3) $D = \$50$ and $E = \$\ 50$, then $R = 20.0\%$
(4) $D = \$75$ and $E = \$\ 25$, then $R = 36.0\%$

In this illustration, we have four different debt/equity ratios, ranging from no debt in the first case to a 3:1 debt/equity relationship in the fourth case. Given an aftertax cost of interest of 4 percent and the normal opportunity to earn 12 percent after taxes on net assets invested, the return on equity in the first case is also 12 percent after taxes—because no debt exists, and the total capitalization is represented by equity.

As increasing amounts of debt are introduced to the capital structure, however, the return on equity is boosted considerably because in each case, the return on investment far exceeds the cost of interest paid to the debt holders. This was, of course, demonstrated in Figure 5–6. The reader is invited to work through the opposite effect, that is, interest charges in excess of the ability to earn a return on the investments made with the funds.

We're also interested in the impact of leverage on the return on net assets, or capitalization (r), which we obtain first by reworking the formula

$$R = r + \frac{D}{E}\,(r - i)$$

into

$$r = \frac{RE + Di}{E + D}$$

Given $i = 4\%$ and $R = 12\%$, we can determine the minimum return on capitalization necessary to obtain a return on equity of 12% for

(1) $D = \quad 0$ and $E = \$100$, then $r = 12\%$
(2) $D = \$25$ and $E = \$\ 75$, then $r = 10\%$
(3) $D = \$50$ and $E = \$\ 50$, then $r = \quad 8\%$
(4) $D = \$75$ and $E = \$\ 25$, then $r = \quad 6\%$

This is a useful way of testing the expected return from new investments. The approach simply turns the calculation around by fixing the return on equity and letting the expected return on investment vary. The calculation is straightforward. Note that the required amount of earnings on net assets, or capitalization, drops sharply as leverage is introduced until it begins to approach the 4 percent aftertax interest cost. It will never quite reach this figure, however, because normally some small amount of equity must be maintained in the capital structure.

While it's simple to work out the mathematical relationships, the translation of these conditions into the appropriate financial strategies is much more complex. No management is completely free to vary the capital structure at will, and there are practical as well as legal and contractual constraints on any company to maintain some normalcy in the liability side of the balance sheet. While no absolute rules exist, the various tests of creditworthiness run the gamut of the ratios discussed in Chapter 2, particularly the measures oriented to the lenders' point of view.

With enlightened self-interest in mind, lenders will impose upper limits on the amount of debt capital to be utilized by a potential borrower. For manufacturing companies the amount of long-term debt will normally range between 0 and 50 percent of their capitalization, while public utilities will range between 30 and 60 percent. Trading companies with highly liquid assets may have even higher debt proportions. The vast increase in leveraged buyouts during the 1980s introduced a far higher than "normal" level of debt into many companies' capital structures. In these cases financial leverage is used to the ultimate extent, which also vastly increases the exposure to the adverse effects of cash flow falling below expectations.

As stated before, we're interested in the effects of financial leverage on the broader area of financial planning for a company. As such, it's only one of several aspects affecting performance. In the next section, we'll integrate financial leverage and the other key factors into a broader financial plan.

FINANCIAL GROWTH PLANS

Most managements aspire to successfully building ever larger businesses whenever opportunities in the marketplace permit this. Typically, common shareholders also expect growing economic benefits to accrue from share ownership. Thus, it's not surprising that one important dimension of financial planning is continual testing of the effects of growth on investment, operations, and financing. The choices of financial policy open to management have different impacts on the expected results and therefore must be tested along with the operational aspects of the plans. Management can set a variety of financial objectives and financial policies to direct and constrain the company's planning effort and the specific financial projections based on these plans. Foremost among the financial objectives is, of course, return on shareholders' equity. But this objective in turn is derived from specific objectives about

- Growth in earnings per share.
- Growth in total profits.
- Growth in dividends.
- Growth in market value.
- Growth in shareholders' equity.

None of these objectives can singly be used as an overall standard, of course.

Foremost among the financial policies is the amount of financial leverage the company considers prudent. Subsidiary to it are the various measures of creditworthiness that management will wish to observe as constraints.

To demonstrate the buildup of an integrated financial plan that enables us to observe the effect of growth and its relationship to financial objectives and policies, we'll begin by selecting just one of the objectives just named to work through a simple conceptual model of a hypothetical company. This model's format is the basic framework that will allow us later to build a more detailed integrated financial plan. It will also demonstrate the concept of sustainable growth.

Basic Financial Growth Model

A simple way of demonstrating the interrelated elements that affect growth in the business system is to use the objective of growth in owners' equity, as recorded on the balance sheet. Not only is this particular element easy to calculate, but it also indirectly encompasses the effects of profit growth and dividend payout.

Figure 5–7 represents such a simplified financial model that allows us to trace the several aspects affecting growth in a company, namely, leverage, profitability, earnings disposition, and financing. With its help we can demonstrate different financial policies' effects on the objective of growth in owners' equity.

FIGURE 5–7
Financial Growth Model: Three Different Policies
($ thousands)

	Case I	Case II	Case III
Capital structure:			
Debt as a percentage of capitalization	–0–	50%	50%
Debt	–0–	$250	$250
Equity	$500	250	250
Net assets (capitalization)	$500	$500	$500
Profitability (after taxes):			
Gross return on net assets*	10%	10%	10%
Amount of profit	$ 50	$ 50	$ 50
Interest at 4%	–0–	10	10
Profit after interest	$ 50	$ 40	$ 40
Earnings disposition:			
Dividend payout	0%	0%	50%
Dividends paid	–0–	–0–	$ 20
Reinvestment	$ 50	$ 40	$ 20
Financing:			
Additional debt	–0–	$ 40	$ 20
New investment possible (next period)	$ 50	$ 80	$ 40
Results (in percent):			
Net return on net assets (capitalization)†	10%	8%	8%
Return on equity	10	16	16
Growth in equity‡	10	16	8

*Profits *before* interest, *after* taxes related to net assets (capitalization) as a measure of operational return on assets.

†Profits *after* interest and taxes related to net assets, as often shown in financial reports.

‡The growth in recorded equity based on earnings reinvested after payment of dividends.

Three cases have been worked out. The first case shows an unleveraged company with $500,000 in equity that pays no dividends and reinvests all of its profits in operations similar to its present activities. The second case shows the same company, but in a leveraged condition with debt at 50 percent of capitalization. In the third case, we take the conditions of the second case, but assume a dividend payout of 50 percent of earnings. All other financial conditions are assumed to remain constant.

Let's trace through the data for Case I. Given a gross

return on net assets of 10 percent after taxes, the amount of net profit generated for the year is $50,000, all of which can be reinvested in the company's activities in the form of new investment for expansion, profit improvements, and so on. At the same time, we assume that the amount of annual depreciation is spent on maintaining the present facilities in sound operating condition. (Recall a similar assumption from Figure 1–4, the business system diagram in Chapter 1.)

The results of Case I are a net return (after interest, which is zero in this example) on net assets, or capitalization, of 10 percent, a return on equity of 10 percent, and therefore growth in equity of 10 percent. This condition holds because all profits are retained in the business for reinvestment. In Figure 5–8 we've calculated three additional periods of operations for this particular company without changing the assumptions. We can quickly observe that given stable policies and conditions, equity growth will indeed continue at 10 percent per year.

Case II differs only with regard to the use of debt financing. Because $250,000 has been borrowed at 4 percent after taxes, $10,000 of aftertax interest must be deducted from the amount of profit on net assets, which reduces the amount available for reinvestment to $40,000. If management wishes to maintain its policy of a 50 percent debt level, an additional $40,000 can be borrowed. This raises the funds available for new investment to $80,000.

Compared to Case I, the results have changed in several ways. Net return on capitalization has dropped to 8 percent because interest charges were introduced. As we expected, however, return on equity was boosted to 16 percent because of the leverage effect. Under these conditions, growth in equity can be similarly maintained at a level of 16 percent as long as all internally generated funds are reinvested in opportunities returning 10 percent, and matching amounts of debt funds are obtained and similarly invested.

FIGURE 5-8

Financial Growth Model: Results of Three Different Policies Held Constant Over Three Periods ($ thousands)

	Case I			Case II			Case III		
	Period 1	Period 2	Period 3	Period 1	Period 2	Period 3	Period 1	Period 2	Period 3
Capital structure:									
Debt as a percentage of capitalization	-0-	-0-	-0-	50%	50%	50%	50%	50%	50%
Debt	-0-	-0-	-0-	$250	$290	$336.4	$250	$270	$291.6
Equity	$500	$550	$605	250	290	336.4	250	270	291.6
Net assets (capitalization)	$500	$550	$605	$500	$580	$672.8	$500	$540	$583.3
Profitability (after taxes):									
Gross return on net assets*	10%	10%	10%	10%	10%	10%	10%	10%	10%
Amount of profit	$ 50	$ 55	$60.5	$ 50	$58.0	$ 67.28	$ 50	$54.0	$58.32
Interest at 4%	-0-	-0-	-0-	10	11.6	13.46	10	10.8	11.66
Profit after interest	$ 50	$ 55	$60.5	$ 40	$46.4	$ 53.82	$ 40	$43.2	$46.66
Earnings disposition:									
Dividend payout	0%	0%	0%	0%	0%	0%	50%	50%	50%
Dividends paid	-0-	-0-	-0-	-0-	-0-	-0-	$ 20	$21.6	$23.33
Reinvestment	$ 50	$ 55	$60.5	$ 40	$46.4	$ 53.82	$ 20	$21.6	$23.33
Financing:									
Additional debt	-0-	-0-	-0-	$ 40	$46.4	$ 53.82	$ 20	$21.6	$23.33
New investment possible (next period)	$ 50	$ 55	$60.5	$ 80	$92.8	$107.64	$ 40	$43.2	$46.66
Results (end of period)									
Net return on net assets (capitalization)†	10%	10%	10%	8%	8%	8%	8%	8%	8%
Return on equity	10	10	10	16	16	16	16	16	16
Growth in equity‡	10	10	10	8	16	16	8	8	8
Growth in total profit (after interest)	—	10	10	—	16	16	—	8	8

*Profits *before* interest, *after* taxes related to net assets (capitalization) as a measure of operational return on assets.
†Profits *after* interest and taxes related to net assets, as often shown in financial reports.
‡The growth in recorded equity based on earnings reinvested after payment of dividends.

In Case III, the introduction of dividends is the only change involved. A 50 percent payout reduces the internal funds available for reinvestment in period 1 to $20,000 and also reduces the available additional debt to $20,000, under a 50 percent debt ratio. Total funds for new investment have thus been reduced to $40,000. The dividend action seriously affects our assumed objective of growth in equity, which is now only half the level in Case II.

This simple model illustrates the effects of a combination of decisions about investment, operations, earnings disposition, and financing strategy. It permits easy analysis of changes. Clearly the conditions have been oversimplified, but any refinements in the assumptions about such items as return on net assets, dividend payout ratios, and increments of additional borrowing, to name but a few, will only be variations on the basic theme expressed here.

Sustainable Growth

If growth in ownership equity were indeed considered to be the chief objective in our illustration, it would be useful to express the relationships on the basis of formulas similar to those used earlier.

In Case I, when no debt was employed and no dividends were paid, the following relationship held:

$$g = r$$

where g is growth in equity and r is the aftertax rate of return on capitalization.

This formula simply expresses the fact that under these basic conditions, return on capitalization is equal to return on equity, and growth in equity is equal to return on equity.

In Case II, debt is introduced to the capital structure, and we must add the leverage effect to the formula as we did before:

$$g = r + \frac{D}{E}(r - i)$$

where D is debt, E is equity, and i is the interest rate after taxes.

Leverage, as we discussed earlier, is a direct function of (1) the proportion of debt in the total capital structure and (2) the difference between the return on investment and the interest cost of the funds, both after taxes. Because all earnings are assumed to be reinvested, the rate of growth in equity must again be equal to the return on equity—which in this case is a combination of the return on net assets and the boost from leverage.

In Case III, the introduction of dividend payments slows the growth in equity because only the earnings retained can be reinvested. We have to adjust each of the two components of the formula to reflect this change. The factor p stands for the proportion of earnings retained as a percentage of total earnings. The resulting formula is

$$g = rp + \frac{D}{E}(r - i)p$$

We now have a generalized formula for the rate of growth in equity that can be sustained by a business if stable conditions and policies hold. It's called the *sustainable growth formula*. If the business, over the long run, is able to invest its funds at the return indicated, if management maintains a stable debt/equity proportion, and if interest costs and the dividend payout ratio don't change, then the growth in equity achieved will stabilize at the rate determined by the formula.

As we stated before, growth in equity is only one of several different types of financial objectives. Figure 5–8 also shows the applicability of such modeling to other objectives, such as growth in earnings. As the last line of the "Results" section indicates, under our stable sets of policies, growth in total earnings (profit after interest) stabilizes at the same rate as growth in equity. In fact, the formula used for growth in equity applies to this objective as well, because profit growth depends on the same variables.

As changes in policies are introduced, however, the fluctuations in year-to-year profit can be severe. The reader is invited to test the formulation for other conditions.

Similar models can be developed for the variables affecting earnings per share, dividends per share, debt service, or any other financial area of the business. We won't attempt to go into detail about these. Rather, we'll let growth in equity and growth in earnings serve as examples. Computer-based spreadsheets are of great assistance in these types of analysis.

Integrated Financial Plan

We can now turn to an illustration of an integrated financial plan, which in concept and format is based on the models in Figures 5–7 and 5–8. This time we focus on taking a set of changing operating and financial assumptions and working them through this format. The XYZ company is considering a number of modifications in its financial policies so management wishes to study the impact of the combination of operating projections and policy modifications on its rate of growth and profitability over the next five years. The resulting integrated financial plan (Figure 5–9) encompasses changes in debt proportions, return on net assets, interest cost (changing as debt proportions rise), and dividend payout.

One key benefit of displaying the interrelationships in this way is that any obviously inconsistent conditions will show up in the results. As undesirable effects occur, the analyst can explore them with more tenable assumptions and calculate the impact of such changes. Planning frameworks of this kind are now easily obtainable either

FIGURE 5–9
XYZ CORPORATION
Integrated Financial Plan:
Sample Five-Year Projection of Effect of Policy Changes
($ thousands)

	Year 1	Year 2	Year 3	Year 4	Year 5
Capital structure:					
Debt as a percentage of					
capitalization	33.3%	43%	43%	50%	50%
Debt	$300.0	$ 470.7	$ 492.5	$ 688.9	$ 728.5
Equity	600.0	624.0	652.9	688.9	728.5
Net assets (capitalization)	$900.0	$1,094.7	$1,145.4	$1,377.8	$1,457.0
Profitability (after taxes):					
Return on net assets	8%	7%	8%	8%	9%
Amount of profit	$ 72.0	$ 76.6	$ 91.6	$ 110.2	$ 131.1
Interest after taxes	4%	4%	4%	4.5%	4.5%
Amount of interest	$ 12.0	$ 18.8	$ 19.7	$ 31.0	$ 32.8
Profit after interest	$ 60.0	$ 57.8	$ 71.9	$ 79.2	$ 98.3
Earnings disposition:					
Dividend payout	60%	50%	50%	50%	40%
Dividends paid	$ 36.0	$ 28.9	$ 35.9	$ 39.6	$ 39.3
Reinvestment	$ 24.0	$ 28.9	$ 36.0	$ 39.6	$ 59.0
Financing and investment (next year):					
New debt, old ratio	$ 12.0	$ 21.8	$ 27.2	$ 39.6	$ 59.0
New debt, revised ratio	158.7	–0–	169.2	–0–	–0–
New investment	$194.7	$ 50.7	$ 232.4	$ 79.2	$ 118.0
Results (end of year):					
Net return on net assets*	6.7%	5.3%	6.3%	5.8%	6.8%
Return on equity	10.0	9.3	11.0	11.5	13.5
Growth in equity	4.0	4.6	5.5	5.8	8.1
Earnings per share					
(100,000 shares)	$ 0.60	$ 0.58	$ 0.72	$ 0.79	$ 0.98
Dividends per share	0.36	0.29	0.36	0.40	0.39

*Return after taxes and interest.

in pre-set form or through readily adaptable spreadsheets for use on personal computers. Again, we stress that computing power doesn't obviate the need to understand the relationships we're demonstrating here.

XYZ Corporation has a total capitalization of $900,000 and starts with a debt proportion of 33.3 percent (i.e., every dollar of equity is matched by 50 cents of long-term debt). The current return on net assets after taxes but before interest is 8 percent, which provides a profit of $72,000. Interest after taxes requires $12,000, which leaves a net profit of $60,000. Depreciation is assumed to be automatically reinvested in maintaining existing facilities, as we did in the financial systems discussion in Chapter 1.

With an assumed dividend payout of 60 percent, cash dividends of $36,000 are required, which leaves a balance of retained earnings of $24,000 for reinvestment in new assets. If the debt proportion of 33.3 percent in year 1 were to be maintained, new debt of $12,000 could be incurred for investment in year 2, supported by the increased equity.

In anticipation of major expansion plans, XYZ management has decided to raise its debt proportion for year 2 to 43 percent. This change would allow additional borrowing of $158,700 beyond the increase of $12,000 that would be possible under the old debt proportion. The total amount of new debt is found by simply letting the increased equity of $624,000 represent 57 percent of net assets for year 2. For simplicity, we've assumed that all changes take place at year-end.

The results for the first year show a net return on capitalization of 6.7 percent, a return on equity of 10 percent, and growth in equity of 4 percent. Earnings per share are $0.60 and dividends per share are $0.36. The influx of new funds at the beginning of year 2 raises the company's capitalization to almost $1.1 million.

For year 2, the assumption about returns is lowered to reflect some normal inefficiencies as the new funds are invested; the overall return on net assets is expected to be 7 percent. After making proper allowance for interest payments, profits after taxes are $57,800. The assumed reduction in dividend payout to 50 percent requires only $28,900—which leaves $28,900 for reinvestment. Under the existing debt proportion of 43 percent, this amount is matched by $21,800 of new debt. These combined funds are added to the investment base for year 3.

The process is repetitive as changes in policies are anticipated at the end of each year's operations. For example, we find a sizable new influx of capital in year 4, as the debt proportion is again raised, this time to 50 percent. A small increase in the aftertax interest rate to 4.5 percent is assumed, because lenders will require this as the capital structure becomes more leveraged and thus more risky. At the same time, however, the effectiveness of employing capital (aftertax return on net assets) has been left at 8 percent in years 3 and 4, but was raised to 9 percent in year 5 to allow some time for the new investments to become effective.

The results at the bottom of the table indicate some fluctuations in the net return on capitalization over the years, as either profitability or interest cost is changed. The return on equity, however, after dropping in year 2, rises steadily to a sizable 13.5 percent in year 5. Growth in equity jumps, after some intermediate boosts, to about double the original 4 percent rate to 8.1 percent in year 5. Changes in total profit after interest are quite significant, as policy changes from year to year take effect. Similarly, growth in earnings per share fluctuates, as do dividends per share—showing little or no growth for most years as funds are reserved for investment.

The results obtained from using such a model raise some realistic questions. For example, it may not be prudent to change the dividend payout ratio in sizable steps as was done. We observe a drop in dividends per share of almost 20 percent in the second year. In the absence of general economic problems, the corporation's directors might be very reluctant to make this change because a consistent dividend pattern is generally considered desirable. Therefore the dividend payout rate for year 2 might be maintained near the original level to avoid a drop in dividends per share. The dividend payout percentage would be lowered only as total earnings rise sufficiently to permit paying a level or even growing dividend.

At the same time, it might be useful to refine assumptions about return on net assets. We've used an overall percentage in this example. It would be more realistic if we split the analysis into (1) return on existing assets and (2) return on incremental assets, taking into account the lag in expected returns on the new assets.

Such a refinement might be particularly useful if a company were diversifying its operations and expecting a highly different return from some of these new activities. More attention might also be paid to the assumption that depreciation will be reinvested without generating additional profits. A company that's consolidating some of its ongoing operations to free funds for redeployment in more diversified lines of business might not be willing to reinvest the equivalent of depreciation in old product lines.

The main purpose of this illustration is to show the usefulness of financial planning in the context of the overall business system. By observing the key results in response to a variety of different inputs, the analyst can arrive at a set of assumptions and recommendations that fairly reflect management's desires and capabilities. Many more refined formats are, of course, possible, and the process is greatly enhanced by the use of computer spreadsheets.

Object-Oriented Financial Analysis

A new and advanced concept of integrated financial analysis is emerging from rapid advances in computing technology and software design. *Object-oriented financial analysis*, described in some detail in Appendix IV, effectively allows a pooling of the analyst's knowledge with an extensive knowledge base inherent in the computer software to achieve a truly interactive and cooperative process of analysis and modeling. It frees the analyst to focus on creative insights rather than data input, tracking, and control.

SUMMARY

In this chapter we've attempted to integrate some key concepts discussed earlier in this book into the dynamic system framework established in Chapter 1. We added an expanded treatment of operating and financial leverage to demonstrate the important impact of fixed-cost elements on changing operating conditions. Through the use of a simplified financial modeling approach we demonstrated the need for consistency in operating and financial objectives and policies. We applied the modeling approach to the needs and policies of a sample company and developed an integrated financial plan with which we tested the impact of changes in the policies on the company's growth and performance.

In the end, the key test of financial analysis is the viability of the methods and results as predictors of future activity (a major point in the earlier chapters). Often the optimal approach requires use of quite detailed and sensitive financial models of the business. Yet the outside analyst, and even insiders, will often be well served with simplified yardsticks and models that can sufficiently approximate solutions to planning alternatives. In this sense, the chapter draws together many of the points of earlier materials and chapters to give the reader an overall, albeit simplified framework for analysis.

SELECTED REFERENCES

Anthony, Robert N., and James S. Reece. *Accounting: Text and Cases.* 8th ed. Homewood, Ill.: Richard D. Irwin, 1988.

Donaldson, Gordon. "Financial Goals and Strategic Consequences." *Harvard Business Review,* May–June 1985, p. 56.

Donaldson, Gordon. *Strategy of Financial Mobility.* Boston: Division of Research, Graduate School of Business Administration, Harvard University, 1969 (a classic).

Garrison, Raymond H., and Eric W. Noreen. *Managerial Accounting: Concepts for Planning, Control, Decision Making,* 7th ed. Homewood, Ill.: Richard D. Irwin, 1994.

Porter, Michael E. *Competitive Strategy.* New York: Free Press, 1980.

Van Horne, James C. *Financial Management and Policy.* 8th ed. Englewood Cliffs, N.J.: Prentice Hall, 1989.

Vancil, Richard F., and Benjamin R. Makela, eds. *The CFO Handbook.* Homewood, Ill.: Dow Jones-Irwin, 1986.

Weston, J. Fred, and Thomas E. Copeland. *Managerial Finance.* 9th ed. Hinsdale, Ill.: Dryden Press, 1989.

SELF-STUDY EXERCISES AND PROBLEMS

(Solutions are provided in Appendix VI.)

1. The ABC Corporation, a manufacturing company, sells a product at a price of $5.50 per unit. The variable costs involved in producing and selling the product are $3.25 per unit. Total fixed costs are $360,000. Calculate the break-even point and draw an appropriate chart.

   a. Calculate and demonstrate the effect of leverage by noting the profit impact of moving from the break-even point in 20 percent volume increments and decrements.

   b. Calculate and graph separately the impact of a 50-cent drop in price, a 25-cent increase in variable cost, and an increase of $40,000 in fixed cost.

   c. Draw a graph and discuss the implications if fixed costs increase $30,000 after 175,000 units of production, the average price drops to $5.25 per unit after 190,000 units are produced, and variable costs drop to an average of $3 after 150,000 units. How are the calculations for break-even affected?

2. Calculate the effect of financial leverage under the following two conditions:

   a. Interest rate is 5 percent after taxes; return on net assets is 8 percent after taxes.

b. Interest rate is 6 percent after taxes; return on net assets is 5 percent after taxes.

Develop the effect on return on equity in each case for debt as a percentage of capitalization at 0 percent, 25 percent, 50 percent, and 75 percent. Discuss.

3. Develop a five-year financial plan for a company based on the following assumptions:

	Year 1	Year 2	Year 3	Year 4	Year 5
Net assets (000)	$1,500	—	—	—	—
Debt/equity	0.25:1	0.25:1	0.50:1	0.50:1	0.50:1
Return on net assets					
(after taxes)	8%	9%	10%	10%	10%
Interest rate (after taxes)	4.5	4.5	5.0	5.0	5.0
Dividend payout	⅔	⅔	⅔	½	½
Number of shares	200,000	—	—	—	—

a. Calculate all relevant financial results, such as earnings per share, return on equity, growth in equity, and growth in earnings. Discuss your assumptions and findings.

b. Demonstrate the sensitivity of earnings per share, return on equity, and growth in equity by varying the conditions in Year 5 as follows: debt/equity, 0.75:1; return on net assets, 11 percent; interest rate, 4.5 percent; and dividend payout, two thirds. Discuss your findings.

6 ANALYSIS OF CAPITAL INVESTMENT DECISIONS

In earlier chapters we focused on the results and the funds implications of different types of management decisions. One of the critical aspects yet to be discussed is the economic rationale behind the primary driving force of the financial system—decisions about new capital investment. So far we've simply assumed that appropriate analytical methods were used to support business investment decisions, and that similar support existed for choosing appropriate financing alternatives to cover the funding of these investments.

In this chapter we'll examine in detail the key conceptual and practical aspects of capital investment decisions, while Chapters 7 and 8 will similarly address financing costs and the choice among financing alternatives. From time to time it will be useful to provide some of the basic conceptual background by introducing applicable portions of managerial economics and financial theory.

In keeping with the scope of this book, however, we'll

avoid the esoteric in favor of the practical and useful. At the end of each chapter we'll summarize in a list the key conceptual issues underlying the analytical approaches covered, both as a reminder and as a guide for the interested reader in exploring the references listed.

The analysis of decisions about new capital investments (as well as disinvestments) involves a particularly complex set of issues and choices that must be resolved by management. Because capital investments, in contrast to operational spending, are normally relatively long-term commitments, they should always be compatible with a firm's overall strategy. Therefore, they must first be evaluated from the strategic perspective of the business.

In addition, financial analysis underlying the decisions must be carried out within a consistent framework of accepted conceptual and practical guidelines, and methods should be employed that focus on the economic impact of the investment or disinvestment. Finally, there are several key components of analysis most capital investment projects have in common. These must be understood and made explicit—as well as comparable—for us to arrive at a proper choice among different investment alternatives.

Our emphasis will be on the latter two areas (the consistent framework and the components of analysis) as we take up the various methods of analysis used to choose among capital investments, including the important topic of risk/reward analysis. Building on these methods, we'll examine certain refinements in the analytical process. Some comments about specialized topics will follow. We'll close with a checklist of key issues affecting capital investment analysis.

STRATEGIC PERSPECTIVE

Investments in land, productive equipment, buildings, natural resources, research facilities, product development, marketing programs, and other resources deployed for future economic gain are part of a company's strategic direction which management must establish and periodically reevaluate. Investment choices should reflect the desired direction the company wishes to take, with due consideration of

- Expected economic conditions.
- Outlook for the company's specific industry or business segment.
- The competitive position of the company.

An almost infinite variety of business investments are available to most firms. A company may invest in new facilities for expansion, with the rationale that the incremental profits from additional volume will make the investment economically desirable. Investments may also be made for upgrading worn or outmoded facilities to improve cost effectiveness. Here savings in operating costs are the justification.

Some strategies call for entering new markets, which could involve entirely new facilities, or even a major repositioning of existing facilities through rebuilding or through sale and reinvestment. Other strategic proposals might involve establishing a research facility, justified on the basis of its potential for developing new products or processes. Business investment could also involve significant promotional outlays targeted on raising the company's market share over the long term and, with it, the profit contribution from higher volumes of operation.

These and other choices are conceived continuously by the organization. Typically, lists of proposals are examined during a company's strategic planning process within the context and constraints of corporate and divisional objectives and goals. Then the various alternatives are narrowed down to those options that should be given serious analysis, and periodic spending plans are prepared that contain those capital outlays that have been selected and approved.

The many steps involved in identifying, analyzing, and selecting capital investment opportunities are collectively known as *capital budgeting*. This process includes everything from broad scoping, or testing, of ideas to refined economic analyses. In the end, the company's capital budget normally contains an acceptable group of projects that individually and collectively are expected to provide economic returns that meet management's goals.

In essence, capital budgeting is like managing a personal investment portfolio. In both cases, the basic challenge is to select, within the constraint of available funds, those investments that promise to give the desired level of economic rewards in relation to the degree of risk that's acceptable. The process thus involves a conscious economic trade-off between exposure to potential adverse conditions and the expected profitability of the investment. As a general rule, the higher the profitability, the higher also will be the risk exposure. Moreover, the choice among alternatives in which to invest limited funds invariably involves opportunity costs because committing to one investment means rejecting others, thereby giving up the opportunity to earn perhaps higher but riskier returns.

In an investment portfolio, capital commitments are made in order to receive future inflows of cash in the form of dividends, interest, and eventual recovery of the principal through sale of the investment instrument—which over time may have appreciated or declined in market value. In capital budgeting, the commitment of company funds is made in exchange for future cash inflows from incremental profits and from the potential recovery of a portion of the capital invested.

However, the analogy carries only so far. In a going business, the situation is complicated by the need not only to select a portfolio of investments, but also to operate the facilities or other assets deployed. In addition, analyzing potential investments in a business context is far more complex because the outlays often involve multiple expenditures spread over a period of time. The construction and equipping of a new factory is an example.

Determining the economic benefits derived from the outlay is even more complex. An individual investor generally receives specific contractual interest payments or regular dividend checks. In contrast, a business investment typically generates additional profits from higher volume, new products, or cost reduction. The specific incremental profit from a business investment may be difficult to identify because it's intermingled in the company's financial reports with other accounting information. As we'll see, the analysis of potential capital investments involves a fair degree of economic reasoning and projection of future conditions that goes beyond merely using normal financial statements.

If we follow the analogy between a capital budget and an investment portfolio to its logical conclusion, capital budgeting would ideally amount to arraying all business investment opportunities in the order of their expected economic returns, and choosing a combination that would meet the desired portfolio return within the constraints of risk and available funding. The theoretical concepts that have been developed and refined in the past two decades rely heavily on portfolio theory, both in terms of risk evaluation and in the comparison between investment returns and the cost of capital incurred in funding the investments.

These concepts are highly structured and depend on a series of important underlying assumptions. Not easy to apply in practice, they continue to be the subject of much learned argument. In simple terms, the theory argues that business investments—arrayed in declining order of attractiveness—should be accepted up to the point at which incremental benefits equal incremental cost, given appropriate risk levels.

This theory entails several problems in practical application. First, at the time the capital budget is prepared, it's not possible to forecast all investment opportunities because management faces a continuously revolving planning horizon over which new opportunities keep appearing, while known opportunities may fade as conditions change ever more rapidly.

Second, capital budgets are prepared only once a year in most companies. As various timing lags are encountered, actual implementation may be delayed or even canceled because circumstances often change.

Third, economic criteria such as rate of return and cost of capital are mere approximations. Moreover, they aren't the sole basis for the investment decision. Instead, the broader context of strategy, the competitive environment, the ability of management to implement the investment, organizational considerations, and other factors come into play as management weighs the risk of an investment against the potential economic gain. Thus, there's nothing automatic or simple in arriving at decisions about the stream of potential investments that continuously surface within a business organization.

This chapter explores the decisional framework and the analytical techniques that support the decision process in capital budgeting. We won't delve into the broader conceptual issues of capital budgeting and portfolio theory except to point out some of the key issues. Readers with further interest in these topics should check the references at the end of the chapter. The important question of the cost of capital as related to capital budgeting is taken up in the next chapter, followed in Chapter 8 by the analytical reasoning behind the choice among types of potential funding of capital investments.

THE DECISIONAL FRAMEWORK

Effective analysis of capital investments requires that both the analyst and the decision maker be very conscious of the many dimensions involved. We need to set a series of ground rules to ensure that our results are thorough, consistent, and meaningful. These ground rules cover

- Problem definition.
- Nature of the investment.
- Estimates of future costs and benefits.
- Incremental cash flows.
- Relevant accounting data.
- Sunk costs.
- Time value of money.

Problem Definition

We should begin any evaluation by stating explicitly what the investment is supposed to accomplish. Careful definition of the problem to be solved (or the opportunity presented) by the investment, and identification of any potential alternatives to the proposed action are critical to proper analysis. Unfortunately, this elementary point is often overlooked—at times deliberately.

In most cases at least two or three alternatives are available for achieving the purpose of an investment, and careful examination of the specific circumstances may reveal an even greater number. For example, the decision of whether to replace a machine nearing the end of its useful life at first appears to be a relatively straightforward either/or problem.

The most obvious alternative, as in any case, is to do nothing (that is, to continue patching up the machine until it falls apart). The ongoing, rising costs likely to be incurred with that option are compared with the expected cost pattern of a new machine when we decide whether or not to replace it.

Yet there are some not-so-obvious alternatives. Perhaps the company should stop making the product altogether! This "go out of business" option should at least be considered—painful as it may be to think about—before new resources are committed.

The reasoning behind this seemingly radical notion is straightforward. While the improved efficiency of a new machine or a whole new facility may raise the product's profit performance from poor to average, there may indeed be alternatives elsewhere in the company that would yield greater profit from the funds committed. By going ahead with the replacement, an opportunity cost from losing a higher profit option might be incurred.

Moreover, even if the decision is to continue making the product, there still are several more alternatives open to management. Among these, for example, are replacement with the same machine or with a larger, more automated model, or with equipment using an altogether different technology and manufacturing process.

Figure 6–1's simple diagram can help us to visualize the key options for deciding on a capital investment, such as replacing a facility. It's crucial to select the appropriate alternatives for analysis and to structure the

FIGURE 6–1
Alternatives for An Investment Decision

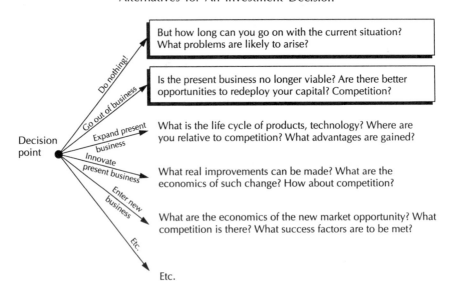

But how long can you go on with the current situation? What problems are likely to arise?

Is the present business no longer viable? Are there better opportunities to redeploy your capital? Competition?

What is the life cycle of products, technology? Where are you relative to competition? What advantages are gained?

What real improvements can be made? What are the economics of such change? How about competition?

What are the economics of the new market opportunity? What competition is there? What success factors are to be met?

Etc.

problem in such a way that the analytical tools are applied to the real issue to be decided. No significant investment should be undertaken unless the best analytical judgment allows it to clear the hurdles implied in the first two branches of the decision tree.

Nature of the Investment

Most capital investments tend to be independent of each other, that is, the choice of any one of them doesn't preclude also choosing any other unless there are insufficient funds available. In that sense they can be viewed as a portfolio of choices. The analysis and reasoning behind every decision will be relatively unaffected by past and future choices.

There are, however, circumstances in which investments compete with each other in their purpose to the extent that choosing one will preclude the other. Typically, this arises when two alternative ways of solving the same problem are being considered. Such investment projects are called *mutually exclusive.* The significance of this condition will become apparent when we discuss the measures used to judge economic desirability. Of course, a similar condition can also arise when management sets a strict limit on the amount of spending, often called *capital rationing,* which will preclude investing in some worthy projects once others have been accepted.

Another type of investment involves *sequential outlays* beyond the initial expenditure. Any major capital outlay for plant and equipment usually also entails additional future outlays for major maintenance, upgrading, and partial replacement some years hence. These future outlays—to which the company is committing itself— should be considered when the initial decision is made. The most logical evaluation of such investments comes from taking into account all major consequences recognizable at the time of analysis. If this isn't done, such a project may be viewed more favorably than a more straightforward one. Moreover, management may become trapped into approving unanticipated future outlays on the argument that these incremental funds are justifiable because the project is already in place.

Estimates of Future Costs and Benefits

It's essential to recognize that the economic calculations used to justify any capital investment must be based on projections and forecasts of *future revenues and costs*. It's simply not enough to assume that past conditions and experience (such as operating costs or product prices) will continue unchanged and be applicable to a new venture. While this may seem obvious, there's a practical temptation to extrapolate past conditions instead of carefully forecasting likely developments. The past is at best a rough guide, and at worst irrelevant for analysis.

The success of investments with time horizons of 2, 5, 10, and even 25 years rests entirely on future events and the uncertainty surrounding them. It therefore behooves the analyst to explore as much as possible the likely changes from present conditions in all of the variables relevant to the analysis. If potential deviations are great, it may be useful to run the analysis under different assumptions, thus testing the sensitivity of the quantitative result to changes in particular variables, such as product volumes, prices, and key raw material costs. (Recall our references to this type of analysis in earlier chapters.)

The uncertainty of future conditions affecting an investment is the *risk* of not meeting expectations and suffering an insufficient economic return or even an economic loss—the degree of risk being a function of the relative uncertainty of the key variables of the project. Careful estimates and research are often warranted to narrow the margin of error in the predicted conditions on which the analysis is based. Since the basic rationale of making investments relies on a conscious economic trade-off of risk versus reward, as we established earlier, the importance of explicitly addressing key areas of uncertainty should be obvious.

Incremental Cash Flows

The economic reasoning behind any capital outlay is based strictly on the incremental changes resulting directly from the decision to make the investment. Moreover, the analysis recognizes only *cash flows* (the cash effect of positive or negative funds movements caused by the investment). Any accounting transactions related to the decision but not involving cash flows are irrelevant for the purpose.

Thus, the first basic question to be asked is: What additional funds will be required to carry out the chosen alternative? For example, the investment proposal may, in addition to the outlay for new equipment, entail the sale or other disposal of assets that will no longer be used. Therefore, the decision may actually free some previously committed funds. In such a case, it's the *net outlay* that counts, after any applicable incremental tax effects have been factored in.

Similarly, the next question is: What additional revenues will be created over and above any existing ones? If an investment results in new revenues, but at the same time causes the loss of some existing revenues, only the *net impact,* after applicable taxes, is relevant for economic analysis.

The third question concerns the costs that will be added or removed as a result of the investment. The only relevant items here are those costs, including applicable taxes, that will go up or down as a consequence of the investment decision. Any cost or expense that's expected to remain the same before and after the investment has been made isn't relevant for the analysis.

These three questions illustrate why we refer to the economic analysis of investments as an *incremental* process. The approach is relative rather than absolute, and is tied closely to carefully defined alternatives and the differences among them. The only data relevant and applicable in any investment analysis are the *differential* funds commitments as well as *differential* revenues and costs caused by the decision, all viewed in terms of *aftertax cash flows.*

Relevant Accounting Data

Investment analysis in large part involves the use of data derived from accounting records, not all of which are relevant for the purpose. Accounting conventions not involving cash flows must be viewed with extreme caution. This is true particularly with investments that cause changes in operating costs. There a clear distinction must be drawn between those cost elements that in fact vary with the operation of the new investment and those that only *appear* to vary. The latter are often *accounting allocations* which may change in magnitude but don't necessarily represent a true change in costs incurred.

For example, for accounting purposes, general overhead costs (administrative costs, insurance, etc.) may be allocated on the basis of operating volume expressed in units produced. At other times direct labor hours are the basis for allocation. In the former case, a new machine with higher output will be charged by the accounting system with a higher share of overhead than the machine it replaces was charged.

Yet there has likely been no actual change in general overhead that can be attributed to the substitution of one machine for the other. Therefore, the reported change in the allocation isn't relevant for purposes of economic analysis. The analyst must constantly judge whether there has been a change in the true cash outlays and revenues—not whether the accounting system is redistributing existing costs differently. A sound rule that helps avoid being trapped by allocations is to avoid unit costs whenever possible and to perform the analysis on the basis of annual changes in costs expected to be caused by the investment decision.

Sunk Costs

It's a common temptation to include in the analysis of a new investment all outlays or portions of outlays that occurred in the past, perhaps preparatory to making the new commitment. There's nothing in economic analysis that justifies such backtracking to expenditures that have already been made and recorded on the books, and that aren't recoverable in part or as a whole. Past decisions simply don't count in the economic trade-off underlying a current investment decision. The basic reason for this is that such *sunk costs*, even if they're connected in some way to the decision at hand, can't be altered by making the investment now.

If, for example, significant amounts had been spent on research and development (R&D) of a new product, the current decision about whether to invest in facilities to produce the product should in no way be affected by those sunk costs. Perhaps in retrospect, the earlier decision to do R&D was less rewarding than expected so it shouldn't have been undertaken. But the point is that a current investment to exploit the results of such past research appears economically justified on its own merits at the present time.

Economic decisions are always forward-looking and must involve only those things that can be changed by the action being decided. This is the essential test of relevance for any element to be included in the analysis.

The Time Value of Money

Given the future orientation of investment analysis, the proper application of economic reasoning requires us to recognize the intimate connection between the *timing* of incremental cash inflows and outflows and the *value* of such cash flows relative to the point of decision. It's a simple axiom that a dollar received today is worth more than a dollar received one year hence because we forgo the opportunity of investing today the future dollar we have to wait for. Thus, the time value of money is related both to the *timing* of receipt or expenditure, and the *opportunity* to earn a return on any funds invested.

Since economic analysis of capital investments involves projecting a whole series and pattern of incremental cash flows (both positive and negative), we need a consistent method that will translate the respective values of these future flows into today's terms. Figure 6–2 shows the pattern of cash flows connected with a typical investment, consisting of an initial outlay, a series of positive benefits, an intermediate additional outlay, and ultimate recovery of part of the resources committed.

All of these future cash flows have to be "brought back" in time to the present point of decision by an appropriate methodology. The process of expressing future dollars in the form of *equivalent* present dollars is called *discounting*. It's the basis for all the modern techniques of investment analysis that we'll discuss later in this chapter. We'll say more about key technical aspects of the time value of money shortly.

COMPONENTS OF ANALYSIS

Bearing in mind the strategic perspective and the ground rules just enumerated, we can now turn to the basic components common to all business investment proposals. In essence, capital is invested for one basic reason: to obtain sufficient future economic returns to warrant the original outlay, that is, sufficient cash receipts over the life of the project to justify the cash spent. This basic trade-off of current cash outflow against expected future cash inflow must be recognized by the analytical methods in one way or another.

To judge the attractiveness of any investment, we must consider the following four elements:

FIGURE 6-2

Typical Cash Flow Pattern for Capital Investment

- The amount expended—the *net investment.*
- The potential benefits—the *net operating cash inflows.*
- The time period over which the investment is expected to provide those benefits—the *economic life* of the investment.
- Any recovery of capital at the end of the investment's life—the *terminal value.*

A proper economic analysis must relate these four elements to provide an indication of whether the investment is worthy of consideration.

We can use a simple example to show how this is done. A $100,000 outlay for equipment needed to manufacture a new product is expected to provide aftertax cash flow benefits of $25,000 per year over a six-year period, without significant annual fluctuations. Although the equipment won't be fully worn out after six years, it's unlikely that more than scrap value will be realized at that time due to technological obsolescence. The cost of removal is expected to offset this scrap value. Straight-line depreciation over the six years ($16,667 per year) has been correctly adjusted for in the final cash flow figure of $25,000 by having been added back to the net aftertax improvement in profits of $8,333.

Net Investment

The first element in the analysis, *net investment,* normally consists of the gross capital requirements for the new assets reduced by any funds recovered from the trade or sale of existing assets resulting from the decision. Such recoveries must be adjusted for any change in income taxes arising from a recognized gain or loss on the disposal of existing assets.

The basic rule for finding the investment amount committed to the decision is to calculate the *net amount* of outlays and recoveries caused by the decision to invest. In our simple case no funds were recovered and therefore the net investment is the full outlay of $100,000.

When an investment is made to support a new product or to provide an increased volume of existing products, any additions to working capital that are required by the increased level of sales must be included in the analysis. Normally, such incremental working capital is added to net investment. For our first example this refinement is ignored. Later in the chapter we'll demonstrate how working capital increments are handled.

Further capital outlays may also become necessary during the life of the investment project, and may be foreseeable enough to be estimated at the time of analysis. Such potential consequences of the initial decision must also be considered as part of the investment proposal. We'll also demonstrate the method of dealing with such sequential elements later on.

Net Operating Cash Inflows

The operational basis for economic benefits over the life of the investment is the period-by-period *net change* in revenues and expenses caused by the investment, after adjusting for applicable income taxes. These incremental changes include such elements as operating savings caused by a machine replacement, the additional profits from a new product line, the increased profits from plant expansion, or the profits created by developing land or other natural resources. Generally they'll be reflected as increased profit reported in periodic operating statements, once the investment is in place and functioning. Our main focus, however, has to be on finding the estimated net impact on cash flow, adjusted for all applicable taxes. We'll later give numerous examples of how such project cash flows are derived.

For our simplified case we'll assume that the net annual operating aftertax cash inflow will be a level $25,000 over the project's life. This represents the sum of estimated net aftertax profits of $8,333 and depreciation of $16,667. As we'll see, introducing a variable pattern of periodic cash flows can significantly influence the analytical results. Level periodic flows are easiest to deal with, but are quite rare in practice. Uneven cash flows are more common and make the analysis more complex—but they can be handled readily, as we'll demonstrate.

Economic Life

The third element, the time period selected for the analysis, is commonly referred to as the *economic life* of the investment project. For purposes of investment analysis, the only relevant time period is the economic life, as distinguished from the *physical* life of equipment and *technological* life of a particular process.

Even though a building or piece of equipment may be perfectly usable from a physical standpoint, the economic life of the investment is finished if the market for the product or service has disappeared. Similarly, the economic life of any given technology is bound up with the economics of the marketplace—the best process is useless if the resulting product can no longer be sold. At that point, any usable resources must be repositioned—which requires another investment decision—or they may be disposed of for their recovery value. When redeploying such resources into another project, the net investment for that decision would, of course, be the estimated recovery value after taxes.

In our simple example, we've assumed a six-year economic life, the period over which the product manufactured with the equipment will be sold. The *depreciation life* used for accounting or tax purposes doesn't normally reflect an investment's true life span. As we discussed earlier, such write-offs are based on standard accounting and tax guidelines, and don't necessarily represent the investment's economic usefulness.

Terminal Value

Normally, if one expects a substantial *recovery of capital* from eventual disposal of remaining assets at the end of the economic life, these estimated amounts must be made part of the analysis. Such recoveries can be proceeds from facilities and equipment (beyond the minor scrap value assumed in our example) as well as the release of any working capital associated with the investment. Again, we'll demonstrate the handling of these elements later on.

METHODS OF ANALYSIS

Up to this point in the chapter we've laid the groundwork for analyzing any capital investment by describing the *strategic perspective*, the *decisional framework*, and the four essential *components* of the analysis. This was necessary because the analyst or manager must be aware that analyzing a capital investment isn't the simple matter it may appear to be.

Therefore our focus was on *what* must be analyzed. We now turn to the question of *how* this is done—the methods and criteria of analysis that will help us judge the economics of the decision.

How do we relate the four basic components (net

investment, operating cash flow, economic life, and terminal value) to determine the project's attractiveness? We'll first dispose quickly of some simple methods of analysis, which are mere rules of thumb that intuitively grapple with the trade-off between investment and operating cash flows. These methods are the *payback* and the *simple rate of return,* both of which occasionally are still used in practice despite their demonstrable shortcomings.

Discussing the shortcomings of these simplistic tools, however, will provide important insights into economic reasoning and provide a natural transition to modern investment analysis. Our major emphasis in this section will be on measures employing the *time value of money,* enabling the analyst to deal with relevant cash flows in equivalent terms, that is, regardless of the timing of their incidence. Those key measures are *net present value,* the *profitability index,* and the *internal rate of return (yield).*

Thereafter we'll turn to basic *risk analysis* and discuss the *present value payback, annualized net present value, ranges of estimates, probabilistic simulation,* and *risk-adjusted return standards.*

Simple Measures

Payback. This crude rule of thumb directly relates assumed level annual cash inflows from a project to the net investment required:

$$\text{Payback} = \frac{\text{Net investment}}{\text{Average annual operating cash inflow}} = \frac{\$100,000}{\$25,000} = 4 \text{ years}$$

The result is the number of years required for the original outlay to be "repaid." It's a rough test of whether the investment will be recovered within its economic life span. For our simple example this is true, as payback is achieved in only four years versus the estimated economic life of six years.

The measure tests the recovery of the original investment on, so to speak, the installment basis. The implied query is "How long will it be until I get my money back?" Recovering the capital isn't enough, of course, because from an economic standpoint, one would hope to earn a profit on the funds while they're invested.

To illustrate, we can picture a savings account in which $100 is deposited and from which $25 is withdrawn at the end of each year. After four years, the principal will have been repaid in full. The saver would be very upset, however, if the bank statement showed that the account was now depleted. The investment was made with the expectation of earning 5 or 6 percent every year on the declining balance in the account. The saver would certainly demand payment of the accumulated interest.

In the case of our machine investment, the simple payback period of four years also implies that no economic return has been earned on the funds committed. Four years is just sufficient to recover the original outlay. Thus, we must look to the years beyond the payback point to provide an economic return. In fact, if the economic life and payback period were to coincide precisely, an opportunity loss would have been suffered because the same funds invested elsewhere would probably have earned some return every year—at least at the level of savings account interest! This point is demonstrated in Figure 6–3.

Here we assume that a $100,000 capital investment provides an annual operating cash inflow after taxes of $25,000. If our hypothetical company typically earned 10 percent after taxes on its investments, part of every year's cash inflow would have to be considered as normal return, while the remainder would be applied to reducing the outstanding balance.

The first column shows the beginning balance of the investment in every year. In the second column, normal earnings of 10 percent are calculated on these balances.

FIGURE 6–3
Amortization of $100,000 Investment at 10 Percent

Year	(1) Beginning Balance	(2) Normal Earnings at 10 Percent	(3) Operating Cash Inflow	(4) Ending Balance to Be Recovered
1	$100,000	$10,000	$25,000	$ 85,000
2	85,000	8,500	25,000	68,500
3	68,500	6,850	25,000	50,350
4	50,350	5,035	25,000	30,385*
5	30,385	3,039	25,000	8,424
6	8,424	842	25,000	(15,734)

*Payback.

In the third column, annual operating cash inflows are shown. In the fourth column, these inflows, reduced by the normal earnings, are applied against the beginning balances of the investment to calculate every year's ending balance. The result is an amortization schedule for our simple investment that extends to the sixth year—requiring two more years of annual benefits than the payback measure would suggest.

Strictly for simplicity we've assumed that earnings are calculated on the beginning balance of the investment, and operating cash inflows are received at the end of the period. A more precise simulation wouldn't materially affect the result. From the figures in the table it's obvious that a payback of four years would mean an opportunity loss of about $30,400 if the project ended at this point. By extending the economic life to five years, the opportunity loss would be reduced to about $8,400, while at six years there would be a sizable economic advantage of $15,700.

This brief illustration points up a critical shortcoming of the payback measure: It's insensitive to the economic life span and thus not a meaningful criterion of earnings power. All we can say about our example in payback terms is that the project pays out in four years, with two "extra" years for profit. Moreover, the payback measure would also give the same "four years plus something extra" reading on other projects with similar cash inflows but with 8- or 10-year economic lives even though those projects are clearly superior to our example. Thus, the basic economic trade-off between all inflows and all outflows isn't recognized.

Another shortcoming is that the payback measure implicitly assumes level annual operating cash inflows. Projects with rising or declining cash flow patterns—although very common—can't properly be evaluated. An investment in a new product, for example, may yield cash inflows that slowly rise during the early years, eventually level out, and decline sharply in the later stages of the product's economic life. A machine replacement, in contrast, will generate ever growing improvements in operating costs as the existing machine deteriorates. Moreover, any additional investments made during the period or capital recoveries at the end of the economic life are ignored by this simple measure. Figure 6–4 illustrates the insensitivity of payback to variations in cash flow.

If we assume similar risks for each of the three projects, we would chose Project 2 over Project 1 because over its economic life Project 2 will return $50,000 more than Project 1. But the payback ranking is the same for both projects. Project 3, on the other hand, appears to be the most favorable one if judged only on its payback period of three years. Yet Project 3 obviously involves an opportunity loss because the operating cash inflows during its three-year economic life are just sufficient to recover the original outlay without providing any economic return at all.

The difference in the cash flow patterns of Projects 1 and 2 is also masked by the payout criterion. Although both projects recover the initial investment in four years, the cumulative operating cash inflows are higher for Project 2 than for Project 1. Average annual cash flows are $35,000 versus $25,000 during the first four

FIGURE 6–4
Payback Results under Varying Conditions

	Project 1	Project 2	Project 3
Net investment	$100,000	$100,000	$100,000
Average annual operating cash inflow	$ 25,000	$ 25,000	$ 33,333
Economic life	6 years	8 years	3 years
Payback	4 years	4 years	3 years
Cash flow pattern (years):			
1	$ 25,000	$ 20,000	$ 16,667
2	25,000	30,000	33,333
3	25,000	50,000	50,000
4	25,000	40,000	-0-
5	25,000	30,000	-0-
6	25,000	15,000	-0-
7	-0-	10,000	-0-
8	-0-	5,000	-0-
Total	$150,000	$200,000	$100,000
Cumulative first four years	$100,000	$140,000	n.a.
Average first four years	$ 25,000	$ 35,000	n.a.

n.a. = Not applicable.

years. Thus, Project 2 clearly provides significantly higher operating cash inflows early on and is more desirable when the time value of money is considered.

A modification of the payback measure substitutes *average annual accounting profit after taxes* as the denominator in the formula to replace aftertax cash inflow. The rationale is that the net income improvement (in accounting terms) attributable to the investment, calculated *after* the annual depreciation allowance, implicitly provides for both the return of principal and a periodic profit. The amount of depreciation charged against net income is assumed to roughly simulate the recovery of principal—something we'd done more precisely in Figure 6–3—while the net profit improvement is thought to represent earnings on the original investment.

In our simple example the average aftertax cash inflow is composed of an average accounting profit improvement of $8,333, after depreciation of $16,667

($100,000 depreciated straight-line over six years). In the revised formula the payback jumps to 12 years:

$$\frac{\text{Net investment}}{\substack{\text{Average annual} \\ \text{aftertax profit}}} = \frac{\$100,000}{\$8,333} = 12 \text{ years}$$

This crude form of investment amortization simply can't be substituted for the "cash-in, cash-out" reasoning that underlies economic investment analysis. We mustn't let changes in accounting profits and associated depreciation write-offs take the place of the economic cash flows because each is designed for a valid but different purpose. Figure 6–3 demonstrated that the project was desirable if its economic life was only five years or better. The degree of distortion introduced by the use of accounting profits will, of course, vary with the circumstances, particularly with different economic lives and earnings rates.

Simple Rate of Return. Only passing comments are warranted about this rule of thumb, which in fact is the inverse of the payback formula. It states the desirability of an investment in terms of a percentage return on the original outlay. The method shares all of the shortcomings of the payback because it again relates only two of the four critical aspects of any project (net investment and operating cash flows) and ignores the economic life and any terminal value:

$$\frac{\text{Return on}}{\text{investment}} = \frac{\substack{\text{Average annual} \\ \text{operating cash inflow}}}{\text{Net investment}} = \frac{\$25,000}{\$100,000} = 25\%$$

All this result indicates is that $25,000 happens to be 25 percent of $100,000. It's the only conclusion we can draw because there's no reference to economic life and no recognition that, as is true with a savings account, regular cash benefits will draw down the balance of the principal. Note that the calculation will give the same answer whether the economic life were 1 year, 10 years, or 100 years. The return indicated would be valid in an economic sense only if the investment provided $25,000 per year in perpetuity. It would take this unrealistic condition to be able to say that the return was truly 25 percent.

A slightly more meaningful version of the simple rate of return uses aftertax accounting profit as the numerator. A much more credible result seems to emerge for our example, but not necessarily for others:

$$\frac{\text{Return on}}{\text{investment}} = \frac{\text{Average annual aftertax profit}}{\text{Net investment}} = \frac{\$8,333}{\$100,000} = 8.3\%$$

This version of the simple rate of return happens to simulate the impact the project will have on corporate financial statements. It approximates the resulting changes in the operating statement and the balance sheet (at least for the early part of the project's life) and is consistent with the basic rate of return measures applied to investments in place, as discussed in Chapter 2. But as a decisional criterion, it's still subject to all the other shortcomings we've pointed out.

Economic Investment Analysis

Earlier we described capital investment analysis as the process of weighing the economic trade-off between current dollar outlays and future net cash flow benefits that are expected to be obtained over a relevant period of time. This concept applies to all types of investments, whether made by individuals or businesses. The time value of money is used as the underlying methodology.

We'll begin this section by discussing in detail how the basic principles of *compounding and discounting* can be used to translate cash flows into equivalent monetary values irrespective of their timing. Then we'll explain and demonstrate the major measures of investment analysis that utilize these principles to calculate the quantitative basis for making economic choices among investment propositions.

Compounding, Discounting, and Equivalence. We said earlier that common sense tells us a person won't be indifferent between two investment propositions that are exactly alike in all aspects except for a difference in timing of the future benefits. An investor will obviously prefer the one providing more immediate benefits. The reason, of course, is that more immediately available funds offer an individual or a company the opportunity to invest these funds at a profit—be it in a savings account, a government bond, a loan, a new facility, or any of countless other economic possibilities. Having to wait for a period of time until funds become available entails an opportunity cost in the form of lost earnings potential.

Conversely, common sense also dictates that, given a choice between making an expenditure now versus making the same expenditure some time in the future, it's advantageous to defer the outlay. Again, the reason is the opportunity to earn a profit on the funds in the meantime. Stated another way, the value of money is affected directly by the specific *timing* of its receipt or disbursement, and this in turn is related to the *opportunity* of earning a profit during the timing interval.

A simple example illustrates this point. If a person normally uses a savings account to earn interest of 5 percent per year, a deposit of $1,000 made today will grow to $1,050 in one year. (For simplicity we ignore the practice of daily or monthly compounding commonly used by banks and savings institutions.) If for some reason the person had to wait one year to receive the $1,000, the opportunity to earn $50 in interest would be lost. Without question, a sum of $1,000 offered to the person one year hence has to be worth less today than the same amount offered immediately. Specifically, today's value of the delayed $1,000 must be related to the person's opportunity to earn 5 percent.

Given this earnings goal, we can calculate the *present value* of the $1,000 to be received in one year's time:

$$\text{Present value} = \frac{\$1,000}{1 + 0.05} = \$952.38$$

The equation shows that with an assumed rate of return of 5 percent, $1,000 received one year from now is the equivalent of $952.38 today. This is because $952.38 invested at 5 percent today will grow into $1,000 by the end of one year. This calculation clearly reflects the economic trade-off between dollars received today versus those received at a future date, based on the length of time involved and the available earnings opportunity. If we ignore risk for the moment, it also follows that our investor should be willing to pay $952.38 today for a financial contract that will pay $1,000 one year hence.

The longer the waiting period, the lower becomes the present value of a sum of money to be received because for each additional period of delay, the opportunity to earn a return during that period is forgone. Principal and interest left in place would have compounded by earning an annual return on the growing balance. As we already pointed out, it will also be advantageous to defer an expenditure as long as possible because this allows the individual to earn a return during every period on the amount not spent plus the earnings left in place.

The process of calculating this change in the value of receipts or expenditures is quite simple when we know the time period and the earnings opportunity rate. For example, a sum of $1,000 to be received at the end of five years will be worth only $783.53 today because that amount invested today at 5 percent compounded annually would grow to $1,000 five years hence if the earnings are left to accumulate and interest is earned on the growing balance each year.

The formula for this calculation is

$$\text{Present value} = \frac{\$1,000}{(1+0.05)^5} = \frac{\$1,000}{1.27628} = \$783.53$$

The result of $783.53 was obtained by relating the *future value* of $1,000 to the *compound earnings factor* at 5 percent over five years, shown in the denominator as 1.27628—which is simply 1.05 raised to the fifth power. When we divide the future value by the compound earnings factor, we have in effect *discounted* the future value into a lower *equivalent present value.*

Note that the mathematics are straightforward in achieving what we described in concept earlier: The value of a future sum is lowered in precise relationship to the earnings opportunity and the timing incidence. The earnings opportunity is our assumed 5 percent compound interest, while the timing incidence of five years is reflected in the number of times the interest is compounded to express the number of years during which earnings were forgone.

We refer to the calculation of present values as *discounting,* while the reverse (the calculation of future values) is called *compounding.* These basic mathematical relationships allow us to derive the equivalent value of any sum to be received or paid at any point in time, either at the present moment or at any specified future date.

The process of compounding and discounting is as old as money lending and has been used by financial institutions from time immemorial. Though the application of this methodology to business investments is of more recent vintage, the techniques have become commonplace. Hand-held electronic calculators and ubiquitous computer software with compounding and discounting capability have made deriving equivalent values and time-adjusted investment measures a routine matter.

The discount factors are also published in so-called

present value tables, which analysts used to calculate present values before computer-assisted methods were available. Two of these tables appear at the end of this chapter. Even though they're no longer necessary for making the actual calculations, they provide a visual demonstration of the effect of discounting.

We can clarify a few points with the help of these tables. Table I near the end of this chapter (p. 332) contains the factors that translate into equivalent present values a single sum of $1 received or disbursed at the end of any period under different assumptions about the rate of earnings. It's based on this general formula:

$$\text{Present value} = \frac{1}{(1 + i)^n}$$

where i is the applicable earnings rate (discount rate) and n the number of periods over which discounting takes place. The table covers a range from 1 to 60 periods and discount rates from 1 to 50 percent. The rates are related to periods, however defined. For example, if the periods represent years, the rates are annual, while if months are used, the rates are monthly. The present value of a sum of money therefore can be found by simply multiplying the amount involved by the appropriate factor in the table:

$$\text{Present value} = \text{Factor} \times \text{Amount}$$

Note that the results from our recent savings account example can be found in Table II (p. 334) in the 5 percent column, lines 1 and 5, for the 1-year and 5-year illustrations respectively.

Table II, a variation of Table I, allows the user to directly calculate the present value of a *series* of equal receipts or payments occurring over a number of periods. Such series are called *annuities*. The same result could, of course, be obtained by using Table I and repetitively multiplying the periodic amount with the appropriate series of successive factors and adding all of the results. Table II directly provides a set of such additive factors, however, which allows the analyst to obtain the present value of an annuity in the single step of multiplying the periodic receipt or payment by the appropriate factor:

$$\text{Present value} = \text{Factor} \times \text{Annuity}$$

These basic tables can be used for practically all investment problems normally encountered. There are many possible variations and refinements in timing, such as more frequent discounting (monthly, weekly) or an assumption that the annuity is received or disbursed in weekly or monthly increments rather than at the end of the period. The assumption of a continuous flow of receipts or disbursements more closely approximates the cash incidence from such changes in operations as labor and materials savings and other daily, weekly, or monthly changes.

The use of the continuous flow option introduces a forward shift in timing that leads to slightly higher present values for both single sums and annuities. Many discounting refinements also relate to financial instruments, such as mortgages, bonds, and charge accounts, which involve specific practices, such as daily discounting or compounding.

For the practical purpose of analyzing business capital investments, such refinements aren't critical because the imprecision of many of the economic estimates easily outweighs any incremental numerical precision that might be obtained. The periodic discounting embodied in the formula of the two tables at the end of the chapter is quite adequate for most analytical needs and matches the internal programs of most calculators and computer spreadsheets.

We'll now turn to the discussion of the measures that employ these compounding and discounting principles. We'll cover the basic rationale on which these measures are based, their applicability to economic investment analysis, and their shortcomings.

Net Present Value. The net present value measure weighs the cash flow trade-off between investment outlays, future benefits, and terminal values in *equivalent* present value terms, and allows the analyst to determine whether the net balance of these amounts is favorable or unfavorable. To use the tool, we must first specify a rate of discount representing normal earnings opportunities. Appropriate present value factors are then applied to both inflows and outflows over the economic life of the investment proposal. Finally, the present values of all inflows (positive amounts) and outflows (negative amounts) are summed, and the net amount represents the net present value. It can be positive or negative, depending on whether there's a net inflow or net outflow over the project's economic life.

As a standard of comparison the measure indicates whether an investment, over its economic life, will achieve the earnings rate applied in the calculation. Inasmuch as present value results depend on both timing and earnings opportunity, a positive net present value indicates that the cash flows generated by the investment over its economic life will

- Recover the original outlay (as well as any future capital outlays or recoveries considered in the analysis).
- Earn the desired return standard on the outstanding balance.
- Provide a cushion of excess economic value.

Conversely, a negative result indicates that the project isn't achieving the earnings standard and thus will cause an opportunity loss if implemented. Obviously, the result will be affected by the level of earnings assumed, the specific timing pattern of the cash flows, and the relative magnitudes of the amounts involved.

A word should be said at this point about the rate of discount employed. From an economic standpoint, it should be the rate of return an investor normally enjoys from investments of similar nature and risk. In effect, this is an opportunity rate of return. In the corporate setting the choice of a discount rate is complicated both by the variety of investment possibilities and by the types of financing provided by both owners and lenders. The corporate earnings standard normally used to discount capital investment cash flows should reflect the minimum return requirement that will provide the level of shareholder returns normally expected, while taking advantage of financial leverage.

The standard most commonly employed is based on the overall corporate *cost of capital*, which takes into account shareholder expectations, business risk, and leverage. As we'll discuss in Chapter 7, shareholder value can be created only by making investments that exceed the cost of capital. Therefore, the actual level of the standard established by a company will often reflect a specific management objective to achieve returns higher than the cost of capital. Sometimes a corporate earnings standard is separated into a set of multiple discount rates for different lines of business within a company in order to recognize specific risk differentials. We'll deal with these concepts in greater depth in the next chapter.

For purposes of this discussion we'll assume that management has chosen an appropriate earnings standard with which to discount investment cash flows, and we'll focus on how present value measures are used to assess potential investments on an economic basis.

To illustrate, let's return to the simple investment example we used earlier in the chapter. As a first step, it's generally helpful to lay out the pertinent information period by period to give us a time perspective. A horizontal time scale can be used, on which the periods are marked off. Positive and negative cash flows are then inserted at the appropriate positions, as Figure 6–5 shows. The information can also be shown in the tabular format, as is done in Figure 6–6.

When we represent the timing of cash flows on a scale, the present time is normally considered the zero point, with periods marked off in positive increments into the future, and in negative increments into the past. Figure 6–6 demonstrates that our sample net investment of $100,000 at point zero and the six annual benefit inflows of $25,000 each result in a net present value of almost $16,000, on the assumption that our

FIGURE 6–5
Generalized Time Scale for Investment Analysis

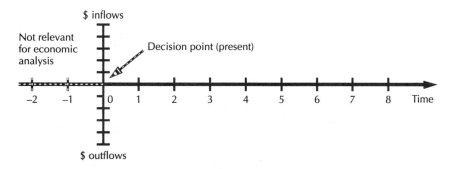

FIGURE 6–6
Net Present Value Analysis by Period at 8 Percent

Time Period	Investment (Outlays)	Benefits (Inflows)	Present Value Factor at 8 Percent*	Present Value	Cumulative Net Present Value
0	$100,000	—	1.000	−$100,000	−$100,000
1	—	$ 25,000	0.926	+ 23,150	− 76,850
2	—	25,000	0.857	+ 21,425	− 55,425
3	—	25,000	0.794	+ 19,850	− 35,575
4	—	25,000	0.735	+ 18,375	− 17,200
5	—	25,000	0.681	+ 17,025	− 175
6	—	25,000	0.630	+ 15,750	+ 15,575
	$100,000	$150,000		+$ 15,575	

*To illustrate the use of Table I, assuming that benefits occur at year-end. We could instead use a factor from Table II: 4.623 times $25,000, because the annual inflows are equal. The result for the total present value of the inflows is identical. (The factors for years 1 through 6 total 4.623.)

company considers 8 percent after taxes a normal earnings standard.

All of the initial outflow will have been recovered over the six year period, while 8 percent after taxes will have been earned all along on the declining investment balance outstanding during the project life. An additional cushion of $15,575 in equivalent present value dollars can be expected if the cash flow estimates are correct and if the project lives out its full economic life.

Note the similarity of this approach with the payback concept we discussed earlier, where we found the recovery of the original investment and something extra. The critical difference between simple payback and net present value, however, is the fact that net present value has a built-in earnings requirement in addition to the recovery of the investment. Thus, the cushion implicit in a positive net present value is truly a calculated economic value gain that goes beyond satisfying the required earnings standard.

If a higher earnings standard had been required (say, 12 percent), the results would be those shown in Figure 6–7. The net present value remains positive, but the size of the cushion has dramatically decreased to only $2,800. We would expect such a decrease because at

FIGURE 6–7
Net Present Value Analysis by Period at 12 Percent

Time Period	Investment (Outlays)	Benefits (Inflows)	Present Value Factor at 12 Percent*	Present Value	Cumulative Net Present Value
0	$100,000	—	1.000	−$100,000	−$100,000
1	—	$ 25,000	0.893	+ 22,325	− 77,675
2	—	25,000	0.797	+ 19,925	− 57,750
3	—	25,000	0.712	+ 17,800	− 39,950
4	—	25,000	0.636	+ 15,900	− 24,050
5	—	25,000	0.567	+ 14,175	− 9,875
6	—	25,000	0.507	+ 12,675	+ 2,800
	$100,000	$150,000		+$ 2,800	

*As in Figure 6–6, we could use 4.112 times $25,000 from Table II.

the higher discount rate, the present value of the cash inflows must decline, with all other circumstances unchanged.

At an assumed earnings standard of 14 percent, the net present value shrinks even further. In fact, it's transformed into a negative result ($25,000 × 3.889 − $100,000 = −$2,775). These results illustrate the high sensitivity of net present value to the choice of earnings standards.

The importance of the length of the economic life of the investment is demonstrated in the last column of Figures 6–6 and 6–7. There we can observe that the time required for the cumulative present value to turn positive was lengthened as the earnings standard was raised. At 8 percent the economic life had to be about five years for the switch to occur (the net present value after the benefits of year 5 is just about zero), while at 12 percent most of the sixth year of economic life was necessary for a positive turnaround (about $10,000 of negative present value remaining at the end of year 5 has to be recovered from the benefits of year 6).

In our example, we assumed a level operating cash inflow of $25,000. Uneven cash flow patterns will have a notable impact on the results, although the method of calculation remains the same. The net present value approach can accommodate any combination of cash flow patterns without difficulty. The reader is invited to test this, using a cash inflow pattern that rises from, say, $15,000 to $40,000, and one that falls from $40,000 to $15,000, each totaling $150,000 over six years.

The best use of net present value is as a screening device that indicates whether a stipulated minimum earnings standard can be met over an investment proposal's economic life. When net present value is positive, there's potential for earnings in excess of the standard and therefore economic value creation. When net present value is negative, the minimum earnings standard and capital recovery can't be achieved with the

288

FIGURE 6–8
A Representation of Net Present Value

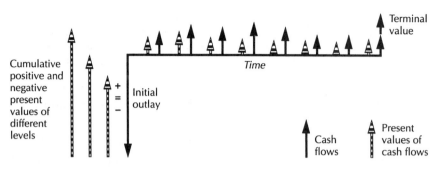

projected cash flows. When net present value is close to or exactly zero, the earnings standard has just been met, on the assumption that the earnings estimates and the projected life are quite certain. Figure 6–8 demonstrates the various conditions.

While net present value is a useful tool in evaluating investment alternatives, it doesn't answer all our questions about the economic attractiveness of capital outlays. For example, when comparing different projects, how do we evaluate the respective size of the "cushion" calculated with a given return standard, particularly if the investment amounts differ significantly? Also, to what extent is achieving the expected economic life a factor in such comparisons?

Furthermore, how do we quantify the potential errors and uncertainties inherent in the cash flow estimates, and how does the measure assist in investment choices if such deviations are significant? Finally, we can ask what specific return the project will yield if all estimates are in fact realized? Further measures and analytical methods are necessary to answer these questions, and we'll show how a combination of techniques helps to narrow the choices to be made.

Profitability Index. After calculating the net present values of a series of projects, we may be faced with a choice that involves several alternative investments of different sizes. In such a case we can't ignore the fact that even though the net present values of the alternatives may be close or even equal, they involve initial funds commitments of widely varying amounts.

In other words, it does make a difference whether an investment proposal promises a net present value of $1,000 for an outlay of $10,000, or whether in another case a net present value of $1,000 requires an investment of $25,000—even if we can assume equivalent economic lives and equivalent risk. In the first case, the cushion (excess benefit) is a much larger fraction of the net investment than it is in the second, which makes the first investment clearly more attractive, given that all other conditions are comparable.

The profitability index (PI) is a formal way of expressing this *cost/benefit* relationship:

$$\text{Profitability index} = \frac{\text{Present value of operating inflows (benefit)}}{\text{Present value of net investment (cost)}}$$

The present values in this formula are the same amounts we used earlier to derive the net present value, although then we subtracted inflows from outflows. In the case of the profitability index, the question is simply: How much in present value benefits is being created for each dollar of net investment?

The two cases we just cited yield these results:

$$\text{1. Profitability index} = \frac{\$11,000}{\$10,000} = 1.10$$

$$\text{2. Profitability index} = \frac{\$26,000}{\$25,000} = 1.04$$

The higher the index, the better the project. As we expected, the first project is much more favorable, given the assumption that all other aspects of the investment are reasonably comparable. If the index is 1.0 or lower, the project is just meeting or is even below the minimum earnings standard used to derive the present values. An index of exactly 1.0 corresponds to a zero net present value.

Our simple machine example has a profitability index of 1.16 at 8 percent in Figure 6–6 ($115,575 ÷ $100,000) and 1.03 at 12 percent in Figure 6–7 ($102,800 ÷ $100,000).

The profitability index provides additional insight for the analyst or manager. As already mentioned, it allows us to choose between investment alternatives of differing size. But it still leaves several points unanswered, and there are some theoretical issues involved that we'll point out later in the chapter.

Internal Rate of Return (Yield). The concept of a "true" return yielded by an investment over its economic life—also referred to as the *discounted cash flow return, (DCF)*—was mentioned in our earlier discussion of net present value. The internal rate of return is simply the unique discount rate that, when applied to both cash inflows and cash outflows over the investment's economic life, provides a zero net present value—that is, the present value of the inflows exactly equals the present value of the outflows. Figure 6–9 visually presents this measure.

Stated another way, the principal can be amortized

FIGURE 6–9
A Representation of Internal Rate of Return (DCF)

over the economic life, while earning the exact return implied by the underlying discount rate. Thus, the project may yield the earnings standard desired, but only if the underlying rate happens to coincide with the standard.

Naturally, the result will vary with changes in the economic life and the pattern of cash flows. In fact, the internal rate of return is found by letting it become a variable that's dependent on cash flows and economic life. In the case of net present value and the profitability index, we had employed a specified earnings standard to discount the investment's cash flows. For the internal rate of return, we turn the problem around to find the discount rate that makes cash inflows and outflows equal.

We can again employ our simple formula (Present value = Factor × Annuity) if the project is simple enough to involve a single investment outlay and only level annual cash inflows. The relationship can then be expressed as

$$\text{Factor} = \frac{\text{Present value (investment)}}{\text{Annuity}}$$

The factor can be located in the present value table for annuities (Table II). Because the economic life is a given, we can find the rate of return by moving along the proper period row to the column containing a factor that approximates the formula result.

To illustrate, our earlier investment example has a factor of 4.0 ($100,000 ÷ $25,000). On the line for period 6 in Table II, we find that 4.0 lies almost exactly between 12 percent (4.112) and 14 percent (3.889). Approximate interpolation suggests that the result is about 13 percent. Again, using electronic calculators or computer software with discounting capability will eliminate the need for using the table.

When a project has a more complex cash flow pattern, a trial-and-error approach is needed if the analysis is done with the help of present value tables. Successive application of different discount rates to all cash flows over the investment's economic life must be made until a reasonably close approximation of a zero net present value has been found.

With some experience, an analyst will find that usually no more than two trials are necessary because the first result will show the direction of any refinement needed. A positive net present value calls for applying a higher discount rate, while a negative one requires a lower rate. We observed this effect in our earlier example, when the net present value declined as the discount rate was raised from 8 to 12 percent (Figures 6–6 and 6–7). Again, programmed calculators and computers will arrive at the result directly.

The internal rate of return is much superior for ranking investments compared to the simple methods we discussed earlier. The method isn't without problems, however. First, there's the mathematical possibility that a complex project with many varied cash inflows and outflows over its economic life may in fact yield two different internal rates of return. This is caused by the specific pattern and timing of the various cash inflows and outflows. While relatively rare, such a result can be an inconvenience.

More important, however, is the practical issue of choosing among alternative projects that involve widely differing net investments and have internal rates of return inverse to the size of the project. (The smaller investment has the higher return.) A $10,000 investment with an internal rate of return of 50 percent can't be directly compared to an outlay of $100,000 with a 30 percent internal rate of return, particularly if the risks are similar and the company normally requires a 15 percent earnings standard. While both projects exceed the desired return, it may indeed be better to employ the larger sum at 30 percent than the smaller sum at 50 percent unless both projects can be undertaken. If the economic life of alternative projects differs widely, it may similarly be advantageous to employ funds at a lower rate for a longer period of time than to opt for a brief period of higher return. This will be true if a choice must be made between two investments, both of which exceed the corporate standard.

It should be apparent that the internal rate of return, like all other measures, must be used with caution. Inasmuch as it provides the analyst with a unique ("true") rate of return inherent to each project, the yield of an investment permits a ranking of potential alternatives by a single "number." We recall from our earlier discussion of the net present value method that a specified earnings standard reflecting the company's expectations from such investments was used there.

In contrast, the internal rate of return approach solves for an earnings rate unique to each project. When the internal rates of return of different projects are compared, there's the implied assumption that the cash flows thrown off during each project's economic life can in fact be reinvested at their unique rates.

We know, however, that the company's earnings standard usually is an expression of the long-run earnings power of the company, even if only approximate. Thus, a management applying a 15 or 20 percent return standard to investments must realize that a project with its own internal rate of return of, say, 30 percent can't be assumed to have its cash flows reinvested at this unique higher rate. Unless the general earnings standard is quite unrealistic, funds thrown off by capital investments can only be expected to be reemployed over time at this lower average rate.

But this apparent dilemma doesn't invalidate the internal rate of return measure because any project will certainly yield its calculated return if all conditions hold over its economic life. Therefore, it's appropriate to rank projects by their respective yields.

Later in this chapter we'll return to a comparative overview of all measures and develop basic rules for their application. The references at the end of the chapter cover the many theoretical and practical arguments surrounding the use of present value, particularly in the case of the internal rate of return.

Risk Analysis. The estimates used to analyze capital investments are inevitably uncertain because of their future orientation. As we stated before, capital investments involve risk because of the uncertainties surrounding the key variables used. Consequently, the analyst who prepares the investment calculations and managers who use these results for decision making must allow for a whole range of possible outcomes. Even the best estimates can go wrong as events unfold, yet the decisions have to be made in advance of the actual experience.

As a result, the risk inherent in the variations must be ascertained. Such risk analysis can take many forms. In Chapter 4 we mentioned sensitivity analysis as a formal means of testing the impact of changes in key assumptions. This process can be very informal, such as back-of-the-envelope reasoning, or it can involve systematically working through the impact of assumed changes in revenues, operating savings, costs, size of outlays, recovery of capital, and so on, either singly or in combination, and testing the impact on the results.

We also mentioned using ranges of estimates, either for the total result or for individual key variables. This approach allows management to examine the most optimistic and pessimistic cases as well as the most likely figures, and it's quite superior to single-point estimating, especially when significant funds are involved.

In this section we'll discuss two time-adjusted measures that help management ascertain how much risk is possible for a project to still meet return standards. These measures, *present value payback* and *annualized net present value,* are technically related to the net present value criterion. We'll also discuss the use of *ranges of estimates* and their refined application in *probabilistic simulation.* Finally we'll touch on the subject of *risk-adjusted return standards.* Only the first two measures will be taken up in detail, while the other areas will be covered just enough to show you the potential value of further studying these concepts.

Present Value Payback. This measure establishes the *minimum life* necessary for an investment to operate as expected, and still meet the earnings standard of the present value analysis. In other words, present value payback is achieved at the specific point in time when the cumulative amount of the positive present values equals the negative present value of all the outlays. It's the point in the project's economic life when the original investment has been fully amortized and a return equal to the earnings standard has been achieved on the declining balance—the point at which the project becomes economically attractive. Figure 6–10 visually presents this concept.

Figures 6–6 and 6–7 included a column for the project's cumulative net present value. It served as a visual check for determining the point at which net present value turned positive. The present value payback for our example with a discount rate of 8 percent was about five years, while a 12 percent standard required almost

FIGURE 6–10
A Representation of Present Value Payback

six years, just about the full economic life of the investment.

The minimum time needed to recover the investment and earn the return standard on the declining balance, when compared to the economic life, is a way of expressing the project's potential risk. The measure doesn't specifically address the nature of the risk, but rather serves to identify any remaining part of the economic life as a risk allowance. Management can then judge whether the risk entailed in the combined elements of the project—or any one key variable in particular—are likely to outweigh the cushion of safety implied in the additional time the project may operate once it has passed the present value payback point. We must remember, however, that the measure focuses only on the life of the project, with the implicit assumption that the estimated operating conditions will continue to be achieved.

If uneven and more complicated cash flows are projected (a condition we'll examine later), the minimum life test of the present value payback requires a year-by-year accumulation of the negative and positive present values, as was done in simplified form in Figures 6–6, 6–7, and 6–10.

If a project is a straightforward combination of a single outlay at point zero and level annual operating cash inflows, we can make use of the annuity factors of Table II to quickly identify the present value payback. To illustrate, the following relationship is utilized:

$$\text{Present value} = \text{Factor} \times \text{Annuity}$$

We're looking for the condition under which the present value of the outflows exactly equals the present value of the inflows. Inasmuch as net investment (outflow) must be recovered by the inflows, we can change the formula to

$$\text{Net investment} = \text{Factor} \times \text{Annuity}$$

Because we know the level of the annuity (which is represented by the annual operating cash inflows), we can find the factor that satisfies the condition

$$\text{Factor} = \frac{\text{Net investment}}{\text{Annuity}}$$

For our machine example we can calculate the following results: $100,000 ÷ $25,000 = 4.0. We can look for the closest factor in the 8 percent column of Table II. The answer lies almost exactly on the line for period 5 (3.993), which indicates that the project's minimum life under the assumed operating conditions must be five years to achieve the standard 8 percent return. If the standard were 12 percent, the minimum life has to be approximately 5⅔ years, which is an interpolation between 3.605 and 4.112.

The test for present value payout or minimum life at any given return standard thus becomes one more factor in assessing the margin for error in the project estimates. It sharpens the analyst's understanding of the relationship of economic life and acceptable performance, and it's a much improved version of the simple payback rule of thumb. The measure is a useful companion to the net present value criterion. But it doesn't address specific risk elements and, in fact, leaves the assessment of any favorable difference between minimum and economic life to the decision maker's judgment.

Annualized Net Present Value. Another approach to testing for risk involves an estimate of how much of an annual shortfall in operating cash inflows is permissible over the project's full economic life while still meeting the minimum return standard. We know that the net present value calculation normally results in either a cumulative excess or a cumulative deficiency of present value benefits vis-à-vis the net investment. We also know that if the net present value is positive, the amount can be viewed as a cushion against any estimating error contained in future cash inflows.

Unless a project has highly irregular annual flows, it's often useful to transform this net present value cushion into an *equivalent annuity* over the project's economic life. Such an annual equivalent, representing the allowable margin of error, can then be directly compared to the original estimates of annual operating cash inflow.

This is possible because the present value cushion has in effect been reconstituted into level cash flows on the same basis as the estimates themselves, that is, in terms of annual flows unadjusted for time value. To illustrate, we can transform the net present value shown in Figure 6–6, $15,575, into an annuity over the six-year life by simply using the familiar present value relationship:

$$\text{Present value} = \text{Factor} \times \text{Annuity}$$

Because we're interested in finding the annuity represented by the net present value, and wish to do so over a known economic life and at a specified discount rate—which is the earnings standard employed in the net present value calculation in the first place—we can transform the annuity formula as follows:

$$\text{Annuity} = \frac{\text{Net present value}}{\text{Factor}}$$

Our example has the following result:

$$\text{Annuity} = \frac{\$15,575}{4.623} = \$3,369$$

The annual operating cash inflows were originally estimated to be $25,000. Given the preceding result, the actual cash flow experienced could be lower by about $3,400 per year and the project would still meet the minimum standard of 8 percent. Note, however, that the investment has to operate over its full economic life for this to be true.

In this case, the risk allowance directly translates into a permissible downward adjustment of estimated operating cash inflows by 13 percent. More important, however, is that we know cash flow consists of aftertax operating profit to which depreciation has been added back. In view of the sizable depreciation allowance of $16,667 contained in our cash flow figure—which isn't subject to uncertainty—the permissible reduction in the aftertax profit alone (from $8,333 to $4,964) amounts to a hefty 40 percent! As we can see, this type of analysis represents a more direct approach to judging the allowable risk in the key variables than did the present value payback.

Annualization can be more generally applied as a practical, quick preliminary test of the attractiveness of an investment project that hasn't yet been fleshed out in detail. In effect, this method reverses the normal investment analysis by finding the approximate annual operating cash inflow necessary to justify an estimated capital outlay when specific operating benefits have yet to be estimated. Given an estimate of the economic life and an earnings standard, we can employ the formula

$$\text{Operating cash inflow} = \frac{\text{Net investment}}{\text{Factor}}$$

to find the annual cash flow equivalent that, on average, will be the minimum target benefit.

The analyst must be careful, however, to interpret this figure properly. Because it's an aftertax cash flow by definition, the result has to be properly adjusted for the assumed annual depreciation in order to transform it into the minimum pretax operating improvement necessary to justify the outlay. The process simply involves working backward through the analysis, using the knowledge that cash flow consists of the sum of aftertax operating profit and annual depreciation. We can apply this to our example from Figure 6–6 as follows:

First, we find the target cash flow benefits over six years at 8 percent, using the appropriate factor from Table II:

$$\frac{\$100,000}{4.623} = \$21,631$$

Next, we transform this aftertax cash flow into its equivalent pretax operating improvement:

Aftertax cash flow	$21,631
Less: Depreciation	16,667
Aftertax profit	4,964
Tax at 34% of *pretax* profit	2,557
Pretax profit	7,521
Add back depreciation	16,667
Minimum pretax operating improvement	$24,188

Thus, our investment has to provide a minimum of about $24,200 in direct operating improvements such as lower costs and incremental revenues. Clearly, this method results in a quick estimate of the magnitude of pretax profit improvement required and the potential of the investment to bring it about. Annualization applied in this way is a useful tool for making a first assessment of the chances that an investment will be in the ballpark.

Needless to say, annualization is quickly performed on a programmed calculator or computer, and present value tables are unnecessary. Yet, even though electronic assists make the process almost automatic, working the calculation as we've just done will give the reader a more secure feeling for the rationale.

Ranges of Estimates. Risk can be defined as the degree of variation in the actual versus estimated cash benefit levels of an investment. The wider the possible deviations, the greater the risk. Therefore, using a range of estimates is a more direct approach to investment risk analysis. It may not be necessary to do this for all types of investments, however, because degrees of risk vary widely among business and financial investments, as do the relative importance and magnitude of the investments themselves.

The risk involved in holding a U.S. government bond, for example, is very small indeed, because default on the interest payments is extremely unlikely. Therefore, the range of possible benefits from the bond investment is narrowly focused on the contractual payments. In effect, there's no range at all.

In contrast, the risk of a business investment for a product or service is a function of the whole range of possible benefit levels that may go from very positive cash flows to negative loss conditions. The uncertainty surrounding these outcomes poses a challenge to the analyst and the decision maker.

The "single-point" estimates of annual cash flow projections we've used so far are the expected results based on the analyst's best judgment and the information available. In effect, they amount to the average of the possible outcomes, implicitly weighed by their respective probabilities. By introducing a range of high, low, and expected levels of annual cash inflows and outflows, the analyst can employ a form of sensitivity analysis to indicate the consequences of expected fluctuations in the annual results—and thus the degree of risk. At times, past experience can provide clues to the range of future outcomes, but essentially the projection of future conditions has to be judgmental and based on specific forward-looking estimates.

The decision maker must assess the likelihood that the range of estimated outcomes fairly expresses the characteristics of the project, and decide whether the expected outcome is sufficiently attractive to compensate for the possibility that the actual results may vary as defined. Risk assessment in essence comes down to how comfortable the decision maker is with the possibility of experiencing adverse results—that is, a very personal risk preference or risk aversion. Stipulating a range helps the responsible person or group visualize the possible extremes in the expected results.

Probabilistic Simulation. A more refined approach to risk assessment consists of estimating ranges not only for the total annual cash flows, but also for the individual key variables that make up these cash flows. Probability distributions are then assigned to the likelihood of the outcomes for each of the variables. Any interdependencies between variables are defined, and the outcomes of the project can then be simulated by running many iterations on the computer. The method is an extension of sensitivity analysis in that the potential changes in many variables are evaluated both simultaneously and in relation to each other.

The result is a range of possible annual cash inflows in the form of a probability distribution, or even a range of net present values or internal rates of return arrayed by probability. Such a *risk profile* allows the decision maker to think about the relative attractiveness of a project in terms of statements such as "Chances are 9 out of 10 that the project will meet the minimum standard of 10 percent" or "There's a probability of 60 percent that the net present value of the project will be $1.0 million or better." Cumulative probability distributions such as those in Figure 6–11 can be drawn up as an aid.

The relative ease with which such computer simulations can be carried out doesn't eliminate the many practical issues involved in assigning specific probability distributions to the individual variables in the first place, or ease the problem of interpreting the final results. As we said before, judging both the likelihood of an event and one's own attitude toward the risk expressed in this fashion is a highly personal response that often defies precise quantification. The amount of risk a decision maker will accept is largely a matter of personal experience and preference. In addition, investment decisions in a business setting are as much a function of complex personal and group dynamics as

FIGURE 6–11
Cumulative Probability Distribution for Two Projects

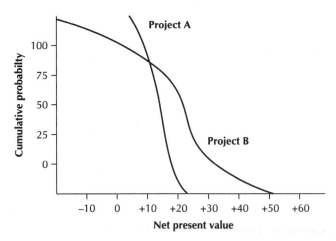

they are dependent on the pure analytical results, the quality of presentation, and examination of specific economic data.

Risk-Adjusted Return Standards. Another way of adjusting for risk is to modify the return standard itself to include a risk premium where warranted. In a sense, the concept is quite simple—the greater the risk, the higher the return desired from the investment. Also, this reasoning is intuitively attractive to business decision makers because the process parallels the way we think about personal investments.

Investments in businesses subject to wide profit swings and competitive pressures would command a premium above the return standard, while fairly predictable businesses might find a less-than-average return acceptable. When multiple return standards are employed, it's done on the assumption that a diversified company can use different standards that, in combination, will ensure an appropriate return to the shareholders and also fairly reflect the risk exposure of the individual lines of business. We'll return to the basis for earnings standards in the next chapter, where we'll discuss both the conceptual and practical issues involved in deriving them.

REFINEMENTS OF INVESTMENT ANALYSIS

We'll now turn to more realistic and complex examples in order to refine various aspects of both the components of analysis and the methodology itself. No new concepts or techniques will be introduced; instead, two expanded practical examples will help us work through the implications of many of the points we've so far only mentioned in passing. As we go through the projects step by step, the essentials of economic investment analysis should become firmly implanted in your mind.

At this point we stress again the need to carefully define the problem in all of its aspects as well as to clearly understand the rationale for deriving the net investment, operating cash flows, economic life, and any terminal values. Once these have been properly established, the actual calculation of the appropriate yardsticks becomes almost automatic.

Example 1: A Machine Replacement

A company is analyzing whether to replace an existing five-year-old machine with a more automatic, faster model. Acquiring a new machine of some sort is considered to be the only reasonable alternative under the circumstances because the product fabricated on the equipment is expected to continue to be profitable for at least 10 years. Moreover, the markets served could absorb additional output beyond the current capacity, as much as one third more than the present volume.

The old machine is estimated to have at most five years' life left before it becomes physically worn out, while the new machine will operate acceptably for 10 years before it has to be scrapped. The old machine originally cost $25,000 and has a current book value of $12,500, having been depreciated straight-line at $2,500 per year. It can be sold for $15,000 in cash to a ready buyer.

The new machine will cost $40,000 installed. Also to be depreciated straight-line over 10 years, it will likely be salable at book value if disposed of before the end of its physical life. It has an annual capacity of 125,000 units (compared to the present equipment's 100,000-unit ceiling) and it will produce at lower unit costs for both labor and materials. In fact, the new machine will involve lower total labor costs because it will require fewer setups, releasing the time of the skilled mechanics performing the setups for other productive tasks in the plant. Two operators will be required as before. Materials usage will be more efficient due to a lower level of rejects. The company expects no difficulty in selling the additional volume at the current price of $1.50, and will only incur modest incremental selling and promotional expense in the process.

Such a set of conditions is both common and realistic, with the possible exception of the stable long-term market conditions assumed. As we analyze this project, we'll expand on several aspects of economic capital investment analysis and draw generalized conclusions where appropriate.

Net Investment Refined. We recall that net investment was defined as the net change in funds committed to a project as a result of the investment decision. Two specific changes in funds must be considered in this case.

First, there's the initial outlay of $40,000 for the new machine, which is a straightforward cash commitment.

Second, there's the recovery of cash from the sale of the old machine. Since it's a direct consequence of the decision to replace, the release of these funds is relevant to the analysis. The amount received for the old machine will be less than its $15,000 cash value, however, because the gain realized on the sale is a taxable event. We recall that the book value was only $12,500;

thus, the company will be taxed on the difference of $2,500. For simplicity we'll assume that the applicable tax rate is the top corporate income tax rate of 34 percent, resulting in an incremental tax outlay of $850.

We now have all the components of the initial net investment figure relevant for this example:

Cost of the new machine	$40,000
Cash from sale of old machine	(15,000)
Tax payable on capital gain	850
Net investment	$25,850

In this economic analysis we don't recognize the remaining book value on the old machine except for its impact on income taxes. As we observed before, any funds expended in the past are irrelevant because they represent a sunk cost. We're interested only in the changes that are caused by the current decision. Therefore, the proceeds from the equipment sale and the incremental tax due on the capital gain are the only relevant elements.

Had the old machine been unsalable despite its stated book value of $12,500, the only item of relevance would be the tax savings on the capital loss incurred with this condition. Yet some analysts are tempted to confuse accounting practice with economic analysis and will include book values even though they're irrelevant.

The net investment shown represents a net balance of cash movements, both in and out, that are direct consequences of the investment decision. Were we to assume that the decision might also cause working capital (incremental receivables and inventories less incremental payables) to rise in order to support the expected higher product sales volume, any funds committed for this purpose would also become relevant for our analysis. Similarly, if the decision were expected to directly cause further capital outlays in later years, such amounts would have to be recognized in the analysis. Later on in our second example, we'll demonstrate how incremental working capital and sequential investments are handled.

Operating Cash Inflows Refined.   As we established before, operating cash inflows are the net aftertax cash changes in revenue and cost elements resulting from the investment decision. In our replacement example, we must first carefully sort out the relevant conditions to identify relevant *differential revenues and costs.* Each element should be tested to determine whether the decision to replace will make a cash difference in operating conditions.

The decision to replace has three significant effects. First, the new machine will bring about greater efficiency which should result in operating savings vis-à-vis the old machine. Second, the additional volume of product produced will provide an incremental profit contribution if we assume the sales efforts are successful. Third, we must allow for the tax impact of the change in the level of depreciation charged against operations. The calculations in Figure 6–12 illustrate how to deal with these elements in clearly labeled successive stages.

Stage 1: Operating Savings.   Operating savings for the existing level of output (100,000 units) are determined by simply comparing the annual costs of operating the two machines at that rate. Each requires two operators, but the new machine will incur $1,000 less in setup costs because the time of the skilled mechanics involved can be employed elsewhere in the plant. We were also told earlier that the new machine uses materials more efficiently, and this attribute will save about $2,000.

Overhead changes, in contrast, aren't relevant for this comparison because overhead costs are represented by allocations at the rate of 120 percent of direct labor. The fact that direct labor cost has declined doesn't mean that spending on overhead has changed. The only change is in the basis of allocation, which in this case happens to be a lower labor cost against which an

FIGURE 6–12
Differential Cost and Revenue Analysis

	Old Machine	New Machine	Relevant Annual Differences
1. Operating savings from current volume of 100,000 units:			
Labor (2 operators plus setup)	$ 31,000	$ 30,000	$ 1,000
Material	38,000	36,000	2,000
Overhead (120% of direct labor)	37,200	36,000	—*
	$106,200	$102,000	$ 3,000
2. Contribution from additional volume of 25,000 units:			
25,000 units sold at $1.50 per unit		$ 37,500	
Less:			
Labor (no additional operators)		—	
Material cost at 36¢/unit		(9,000)	
Additional selling expense		(11,500)	
Additional promotional expense		(13,000)	$ 4,000
Total savings and additional contribution			$ 7,000
3. Differential depreciation (additional) expense; for tax purposes only)	$ 2,500	$ 4,000	$ (1,500)
Taxable operating improvements			5,500
Income tax at 34%			1,870
Aftertax profit improvement			3,630
Add back depreciation			1,500
Aftertax operating cash flow			$ 5,130

*Not relevant, because it represents an allocation only.

unvarying percentage rate is applied. Clearly, the plant manager and the office staff still receive the same salaries, and other overhead costs aren't affected.

Only if the decision to replace *directly* caused an actual change in overhead spending (such as higher property taxes, insurance premiums, or maintenance or technical support costs) would a change have to be reflected in the calculation. Under those conditions, we'd estimate the annual overhead expenditures before and after the installation of the new machine, and develop the differential cost to be included in the analysis, just as we did for the other differential operating cash inflows.

Whenever we're comparing operating costs, it's usually more appropriate to use annual costs or revenues than to rely on per unit figures. The latter may cause the analyst to inadvertently apply accounting allocations, which as a rule are irrelevant for economic analysis—even though they're necessary and appropriate for cost accounting (determining cost of goods sold, inventory values, price estimating, etc.) in line with generally accepted accounting principles.

Stage 2: Contribution from Additional Volume. Now we're ready to determine the incremental contribution from the increased output. This change must be counted as an additional benefit from the decision to replace because the old machine had a ceiling of 100,000 units of production. The additional sales revenue from the extra 25,000 units available for sale at $1.50 each is relevant, as are any additional costs that can be attributed to the higher sales volume.

We know that the two existing operators are able to produce the higher output, so there will be no additional labor cost. But the higher volume will require additional materials, which are charged at the usage rate of the more efficient machine (36 cents per unit). We've also been told that additional selling and promotional expenses of $24,500 will be incurred to move the higher volume, and these are relevant as well. The combination of operating savings and incremental product profit totals $7,000.

Stage 3: Differential Depreciation. The only remaining relevant item is the tax impact of differential depreciation. As we discussed in Chapters 1 and 2, depreciation as such isn't relevant to funds flows. For purposes of our analysis it merits attention only because depreciation is tax deductible. Because depreciation charges normally reduce income tax payments, they're called a *tax shield*. If an investment decision causes higher or lower depreciation charges, such a difference must be reflected as a change in the tax shield.

For our replacement example, the differential depreciation for the next five years will be $1,500 per year, an increase due to the higher cost basis of the new machine. We're assuming that straight-line depreciation is also used for tax purposes, to keep the calculations simple.

As shown in Figure 6–12 (p. 308), the analysis results in taxable operating improvements of $7,000, an incremental tax of $1,870, and a change in aftertax profit of $3,630. The applicable tax rate is normally the rate a company would be paying on any incremental profit. As the final step, the differential depreciation is added back to arrive at the aftertax operating cash flow of $5,130.

In following these steps, we've correctly reflected a tax reduction due to the differential depreciation, but then removed depreciation itself from the picture to leave us with the economic cash effect of the investment.

We could have obtained the same result by doing the analysis in two steps: (1) determining the tax on the operating improvement before depreciation and (2) directly determining the tax shield effect of the differential depreciation. This would appear as shown below, and as we might expect, the result is exactly the same.

Taxable operating improvement	$7,000
Tax at 34 percent	2,380
Aftertax operating improvement	$4,620
Tax shield at 34%* of depreciation of $1,500	510
Aftertax operating cash flow	$5,130

*Each dollar of depreciation provides a tax shield of $1 times the applicable tax rate.

Economic Life Refined. Earlier we defined economic life as the length of time over which an investment yields economic benefits. Now we find that a complication has been introduced because of the expected difference in the two machines' physical lives. Inasmuch as the old machine is assumed to wear out in 5 years while the new one will last for 10, the two investments are comparable only over the next five years. After that, the original alternative no longer exists, and a decision would have to be made at that point in any case. The situation is illustrated in Figure 6–13.

Differential revenues and costs can be defined only as long as both alternatives exist together. After five years the old machine would be gone, which means that we can't analyze the situation beyond five years without making some assumptions about the remaining life of the new machine. While we have estimates that the product is likely to be salable for at least the total 10-year life of the new machine, the economic comparison for the replacement decision can be made only over five years.

There are two ways of handling this problem. First, we can cut off the analysis at the end of year 5 and assign an assumed recovery value to the new machine at that point because it should be able to operate well for another five years. This *terminal value estimate* must be counted as a capital recovery in year 5, that is, its present value should be counted as a benefit. This approach is widely used in practice, and usually the amount of terminal value is estimated as at least the book value.

FIGURE 6–13
Overlapping Economic Life Spans

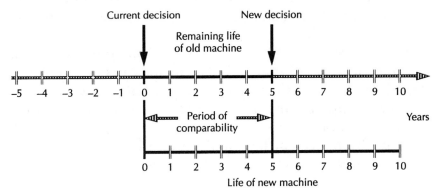

312

But if the asset's value is quite predictable (as is the case with cars or trucks), the estimated sales value is entered in the present value analysis as a benefit.

An alternative way of dealing with the problem is to assume that the old machine would be replaced by a new one in year 5, and that a similar replacement would be made in year 10 when the current new machine wears out. This approach involves a great deal of sequential guessing about possible replacement options 5 and 10 years hence. Moreover, in spite of such analytical effort, the two machines' economic lives still wouldn't be the same. Admittedly, the power of discounting would make the later years' estimates almost immaterial. On balance, unless there are compelling reasons to develop such a series of replacement assumptions, the cutoff analysis described earlier is far more straightforward and less fraught with judgmental traps.

Capital Additions and Recoveries. The treatment of terminal values deserves a few more comments here. It's quite common for larger projects to require a series of additional capital outlays and, later on, to provide likely recoveries of at least part of these funds. As a practical matter, any increments of capital committed or recovered should be entered as cash outflows or cash inflows in the present value framework at the point in time when they occur. This also applies to incremental working capital commitments, which should be shown as outflows as incurred, and which can be assumed to be recovered in total or in part at the end of the economic life of the project.

In our replacement example we've made no provision for additional working capital in order to keep the problem focused on other basic refinements. The assumed terminal value of the new machine after five years, however, would be treated as a capital recovery and entered as a positive cash inflow at the end of year 5. For simplicity we'll assume that its economic value (realizable through sale or trade) will equal its book value. This would amount to $20,000 ($40,000 less five years' depreciation at $4,000 per year), with no taxable capital gain or loss expected.

We would have to modify this amount, of course, if circumstances indicated a higher or lower value due to changes in technology or other conditions. Book value is frequently used because (1) it's easy to do, (2) it causes no taxable gains or losses, and (3) the need for precision in terminal values is diminished by the exponential impact of discounting in later years.

Analytical Framework for Example 1.   With all the basic data at hand, we can now lay out the framework for a present value analysis. We'll assume a 10 percent return standard and again set up the figures in a tabular format. The result in Figure 6–14 indicates a sizable net present value of $6,013—that is, of course, if all of our assumptions are borne out in fact! It would suggest that the replacement is desirable, at least on a numerical basis.

Note that the analysis is significantly affected by the assumed recovery of the book value of $20,000 in year 5, which amounts to a present value inflow of $12,420. In effect, this inflow reduces the net investment to only

FIGURE 6–14
Present Value Analysis of Machine Replacement

Time Period	Investment	Operating Cash Inflow	Present Value Factor at 10 Percent*	Present Value of Net Investment	Present Value of Operating Inflows
0	−$25,850	—	1.000	−$25,850	—
1	—	+$ 5,130	0.909	—	+$ 4,663
2	—	+ 5,130	0.826	—	+ 4,237
3	—	+ 5,130	0.751	—	+ 3,853
4	—	+ 5,130	0.683	—	+ 3,504
5	—	+ 5,130	0.621	—	+ 3,186
5 (end)	+ 20,000	—	0.621	$ 12,420	—
	−$ 5,850	+$25,650		−$13,430	+$19,443
				Net present value	+$ 6,013

*For years 1 to 5, we could use 3.791 from Table II.

$13,430 in present value terms. For purposes of economic analysis, this value has to be considered an inflow at the end of year 5, even though there's no intention of actually selling the machine at that point.

The relevance for today's decision is that the company would have the option of selling at the end of year 5 and thereby realizing this economic value. After the five years are over, the alternative of selling could, of course, be compared with the alternative of recommitting the realizable value of $20,000 in order to preserve the profitable business at the level of 125,000 units. But these latter considerations deal with a future set of decisions and therefore are not relevant today.

The profitability index of the project is positive, as we might expect from the sizable net present value of about $6,000. Dividing $13,430 (net investment less recovery) into the operating benefits of $19,443 results in an index of 1.45, which should give the project a favorable ranking if the average return from the company's investment opportunities is only 10 percent. Some analysts prefer to express the profitability index by relating the original net investment to the total of all inflows, including capital recoveries. In our example the result would be $31,863 ÷ $25,850 = 1.23, again a very favorable showing when this more stringent test is applied. While we could argue for and against either method, consistent application of one of them will be satisfactory.

The internal rate of return has to be found by trial and error using the present value tables because the capital recovery at the end of year 5 complicates an otherwise straightforward annuity. The problem can be handled as shown in Figure 6–15. The trial at 15 percent indicates a positive net present value of $1,286, but at 16 percent it's reduced to $466. Thus, the precise result is somewhat over 16 percent.

A risk analysis can be carried out by calculating the

FIGURE 6–15
Present Value Analysis to Find Internal Rate of Return

Time Period	Cash Flow	Present Value Factor at 15 Percent	Present Value at 15 Percent	Present Value Factor at 16 Percent	Present Value at 16 Percent
0	−$25,850	1.000	−$25,850	1.000	−$26,510
1					
2					
3	+ 5,130/yr.	3.352*	+ 17,196	3.274*	+ 16,796
4					
5					
5 (end)	+ 20,000	0.497	+ 9,940	0.476	+ 9,520
	+$19,800		+$ 1,286		−$ 466

*From Table II.

present value payback (minimum life) and the annualized net present value. For the former we must cumulate the present values of the operating cash inflows until they approximate the net investment of $13,430 (Figure 6–14). A quick addition shows that this will happen after slightly more than three years, leaving a cushion of almost two years of economic life against risk.

A technical question arises here as to whether we should bring the assumed recovery at the end of year 5 forward in time to obtain a more precise calculation of minimum life. This would involve a process of iteration because not only would the present value of the recovery rise, but the machine's sales value would also be higher in earlier years. Such a refinement normally isn't called for even though it can be handled through computer simulation.

The annualized net present value can be found when we divide the net present value in Figure 6–14 by the 10 percent annuity factor in year 5 from Table II, or $6,013 ÷ 3.791, which is $1,586 per year. All other aspects being equal, the project would still be acceptable if the annual operating cash inflows over the five years dropped from $5,130 to only $3,544, a possible shrinkage of over 30 percent. If we remove the depreciation tax shield of $510 from this test, the allowable drop in the pure aftertax operating improvement could be better than 34 percent ($1,586 against $4,620).

Another way of looking at the net present value cushion would be to ask how sensitive the result would be to a reduction in the expected capital recovery at the end of year 5. This answer can be readily found by reconstituting at the end of year 5 a dollar amount that has the equivalent present value of the cushion of $6,013. To find this future dollar amount we simply divide the net present value of $6,013 by the single sum factor given in Table I for 10 percent in period 5, which is 0.621, to get an amount of $9,683. We can see that if the expected recovery of $20,000 were reduced by about $9,700, the project would still be acceptable, given that all other conditions hold.

While perhaps a little complex, the step-by-step process we've just completed has exposed most of the practical issues encountered in investment analysis. Let's turn to one more illustration which additionally shows the handling of working capital and successive investments.

Example 2: Business Expansion

The cash flow patterns in Figure 6–16 show the kinds of commitments and recoveries normally associated with a major business expansion. In the early life of the project, we find not only an outlay for facilities, but also a buildup of working capital during the first and second years. Additional equipment outlays are required at the end of years 4 and 6, while recoveries of equipment and working capital are made as the economic life comes to an end. All cash flows are assumed to have been adjusted for tax consequences along the lines we discussed in our first example. The operating cash flows show a growth stage, peak in the middle years, and decline toward the end.

No new concepts are required for us to deal with this investment example. Working capital (incremental inventories and receivables less new trade obligations)

FIGURE 6-16

Present Value Analysis of a Complex Expansion Project
($ thousands)

Time Period	Investments	Operating Cash Inflow (All Tax Adjustments Made)	Present Value Factor at 12%	Present Value of Investments	Present Value of Operating Inflows
0	−$130,000 (facilities)	—	1.000	−$130,000	—
1	— 25,000 (working capital)	+$ 20,000	0.893*	— 22,325	+$ 17,860
2	— 20,000 (working capital)	+ 40,000	0.797*	— 15,940	—
3	—	+ 40,000	} 2.144†	—	+ 85,760
4	—	+ 40,000	}	—	
4 (end)	— 15,000 (additional equipment)‡	—	0.636*	— 9,540	
5	—	+ 50,000	} 1.075†	—	+ 53,750
6	—	+ 50,000	}	—	
6 (end)	— 10,000 (equipment overhaul)‡	—	0.507*	— 5,070	
7	—	+ 20,000	0.452*	—	+ 9,040
8	—	+ 10,000	} 0.404*	—	+ 4,040
8 (end)	+ 25,000 (equipment recovery)	—	0.404*	+ 24,240	
	+ 35,000 (working capital recovery)§	—	—		
	−$140,000	+$270,000		−$158,635	+$170,450
				Net present value	+$ 11,815

*From Table I.

†From Table II, representing the difference between the annuity factors applicable: 3.037 − 0.893 = 2.144 and 4.112 − 3.037 = 1.075, respectively.

‡Additional depreciation has been reflected in cash inflows.

§Assume loss in liquidation of $10,000.

317

represents a commitment of capital just as definite as an expenditure for buildings and equipment, except that no depreciation write-off is involved. If all inventories and receivables can be expected to be successfully liquidated at the end of the economic life, these funds (net of payables) will be an inflow at that point, a capital recovery. If we assume some fraction of this investment to be unsalable or uncollectible, the figure must be lowered.

Additional capital expenditures for equipment during the life of the project are simply recognized as cash outflows when incurred. Care must be taken, however, to reflect the additional depreciation pattern in each case as a tax shield during future operating periods. Uneven cash flows present no problems when programmed calculators or spreadsheets are used to find the present value of each period's flows. But to demonstrate how the calculations are made, we've again employed the present value tables to find the factors, including those for partial annuities.

As Figure 6–16 showed, the expected result of the project is a positive net present value of almost $12 million. We can calculate the profitability index at 1.07, while the internal rate of return is approximately 13 percent. This finding leaves little margin for error, indeed. The annualized net present value suggests that the annual operating cash inflows can be reduced by $11,815 ÷ 4.968, or at most by about $2.4 million per year. The minimum life (present value payback) is about six years when all capital recoveries are included.

This is as far as we can carry the analysis with the data at hand. The various judgments leading to the final decision call for much more insight into the nature of the product, the technology, the requirements and outlook of the marketplace, the competitive setting, and so on, as we outlined in the first section of this chapter.

Mutually Exclusive Alternatives

So far we've dealt with individual investment projects without regard to the broader question of how these projects fit into the whole range of possibilities open to a company. We assumed that our examples were independent investment projects that could be evaluated and ranked against other independent projects. At times, however, managements face the issue of evaluating projects that aren't independent of each other. Such is the case when sets of alternatives are available to achieve the same purpose. These are called mutually exclusive alternatives because if one is chosen, the others are eliminated by that very decision.

Dealing with such a situation is merely a special case of economic analysis that uses the same underlying concepts as before but emphasizes incremental reasoning. To illustrate, let's assume that a company has developed three alternatives to investing in facilities and working capital to produce and sell a modified product over the next seven years. The company's return standard is 14 percent. The first alternative represents existing technology, the second a more costly but advanced process, while the third provides higher capacity as well as the advanced process. Let's assume further that both the quality of the estimates and the uncertainty about the outcomes are the same in all three cases.

The key dimensions of the three alternatives are:

Alternative	Net Investment	Annual Inflow	Terminal Value
(1) Standard	$500,000	$112,000	$150,000
(2) Advanced	600,000	128,000	150,000
(3) Expanded	750,000	169,000	200,000

The major investment measures were calculated as:

Alternative	Net Present Value (NPV)	Internal Rate of Return (IRR)	Present Value Index (PVI)
(1) Standard	$40,256	16.3%	1.08
(2) Advanced	8,864	14.4	1.01
(3) Expanded	54,672	16.1	1.07

The first observation is that all three alternatives meet the company standard by every measure, although to different degrees. The issue is to select the best of the three alternatives, however, and we have somewhat different signals to contend with. From a net present value standpoint, alternative 3 is clearly best, while the IRR and PVI results favor alternative 1.

We must remember that the objective of successful investment is to create an economic trade-off that will increase shareholder value. If only one alternative can be chosen, this would argue for number 3 with the highest net present value. But alternative 3 is also the most expensive, and its creation of value per dollar invested (PVI) is somewhat less than alternative 1.

A useful way of thinking through mutually exclusive alternatives is to examine the incremental benefits obtained as we move from the least expensive to the most expensive one. In our example, the incremental investment for alternative 2 is $100,000, but it reduces net present value from $40,256 to $8,864. This is clearly not desirable, and the lower IRR and PVI measures for alternative 2 confirm this. Going from alternative 1 to alternative 3, however, results in an incremental investment of $250,000, which improves net present value by $14,416.

The incremental investment certainly exceeds the company standard of 14 percent because its IRR can be calculated at 15.4 percent (incremental investment of $250,000; incremental annual inflows of $57,000; and incremental terminal value of $50,000). This result isn't quite as attractive as alternative 1 with an IRR of 16.3 percent—but then the question becomes whether the company has any other projects that might give a better return than 15.4 percent. If not, alternative 3 should be favored, assuming that all other judgmental aspects are comparable among the three alternatives—especially that the higher volume of business can be secured.

Actual Results below Estimates

Throughout this discussion we've dealt with estimates of future costs and benefits as givens. In practice, estimates are more often than not proven wrong by actual experience—in either direction. When projects are performing better than expected, all is well. But when actual results are disappointing, economic analysis becomes important if decisions can be taken to terminate the project in midstream. This is particularly important if a project contains another decision point for additional investment.

Figure 6–17 illustrates such a situation, where the first four years of the project's life have passed with disappointing results, and management is faced with deciding whether to fund the second investment phase.

The cardinal rule of economics to remember here is that past investments and cash flows are *sunk,* and that only *present* and *future cash flows* affect the decision to continue or quit. The economic trade-off, therefore, is between the net present value of the additional investment and the revised future cash flows on the one hand, and any recovery value of the investment in place on the other. If no additional investment were required, the trade-off is between the present value of expected

FIGURE 6–17
Actual Results Lower—New Decision

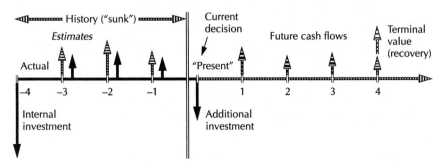

future cash flows and the recovery value. In either case, the view taken must be from the decision point onward into the future.

The same argument can be made when a company is faced with the decision to produce a product or service after having spent much more than planned on research and product development. With hindsight, the decision made at some point in the past to invest in the total project was a poor one. But the current decision to fund production may very well remain a sound economic choice if the estimates about future price, volume, and cost continue to be favorable.

The weight of past mistakes must not be allowed to suppress sound judgment based on the only relevant factors: present and future conditions that can be affected by a decision now. At the same time, it should be obvious that any management must be careful not to make a series of such investments that as a whole are unsatisfactory. Remember, sunk costs were future costs at one time and should have been properly taken into account when they were relevant to the initial decision.

When to Use the Investment Measures

During our discussion of the different investment analysis measures, we cautioned the reader about various shortcomings and issues of interpretation. We'll now review and expand some of these caveats.

Basically, investment analysis measures exist to help analysts and managers determine whether a project meets the earnings standard established for the business. Also, they assist them in ranking the relative desirability of a group of proposals during the capital budgeting process. If the projects being considered are independent of each other, the time-adjusted measures of net present value, profitability index, discounted payback, and internal rate of return will singly or in combination properly reflect the projects' relative economic attractiveness and result in an appropriate ranking sequence. As we observed before, the simplistic measures (payback and simple rate of return) are quite limited in their use as indicators of economic desirability. They'll give a proper ranking only if the projects' cash flow patterns and economic lives are quite similar, a very restrictive assumption.

Figure 6–18 shows a comparative view of the consistent readings of net present value, internal rate of return, and present value payback as applied to three types of independent projects. Project A exceeds the company standard, Project B falls short, and Project C just meets the standard.

Uneven lives of capital investments pose complications that are handled by adjusting the analysis to equalize the time spans for purposes of comparison. This can be achieved by truncating the life of a project with an assumed recovery of funds from disposal at an earlier point, as we did in the replacement example, or by extending the shorter alternative by assuming repeated investment. Mutually exclusive projects with different lives can also be compared by annualizing their net

FIGURE 6–18
Investment Measures Applied to Three Projects

present values over their respective economic lives to determine their respective annual equivalent benefits or cost. This process simply calls for dividing the net present value by the relevant annuity factor, or using an appropriate computer program.

For mutually exclusive projects the profitability index will normally give a fair assessment, but the choice has to be considered in terms of the relative size and length of the commitment as well—the risk/reward trade-off. As we discussed earlier, a larger investment with a somewhat lower profitability index and yield may be preferable to a smaller investment if both alternatives show benefits well above normal.

If a company's identified projects exceed the limits of its funding potential—a fairly common condition—management has to apply what's called *capital rationing.* This involves spending the company's limited funds on the best selection of projects from the larger list of acceptable projects. The investment measures used here have to provide an economic ranking, that is, optimize the benefits obtained from the investment dollars spent. Essentially, the company should choose that group of projects within the budget limit that will generate the highest aggregate net present value.

To do this, projects can be ranked in declining order of their profitability index until the budgeted amount has been exhausted. This amounts to maximizing the present value benefits achieved per dollar of investment because investment funds are the limiting factor. This concept ties closely to the principles of shareholder value, as we'll discuss in Chapter 9. In practice, capital budgets are rarely so precise that truly attractive projects initially rejected for lack of funds couldn't at least be reconsidered at another point in time.

Let's also remember that there should be nothing automatic about the use of any of the investment measures. The seemingly precise results achieved with present value calculations can tempt us to "let the numbers decide." Many more elements have to be weighed in even fairly straightforward projects, as we observed at the beginning of the chapter. Besides the obvious constraints imposed by uncertainty in the economic estimates, management must also consider competitive, technical, human, societal, and other constraints within the company's strategic context before significant investment or divestment decisions are made.

SOME FURTHER CONSIDERATIONS

Several specialized aspects of capital investment analysis have been mentioned only briefly so far. A detailed treatment would go beyond the scope of this book. Yet, for completeness, we'll add some further comments on the topics of *leasing*, the impact of *accelerated depreciation* on present value analysis, and the consequences of *inflation*. Finally, we'll once more put into perspective the degree of *accuracy* warranted in the calculations.

Leasing

Leasing is a popular means of obtaining a wide variety of capital assets for businesses as well as individuals. For our purposes, the most important point to consider is that leasing represents merely one form of financing. Alternative ways of financing should be considered only *after* economic investment analysis has shown that a project is acceptable. This principle is consistent with the business systems approach we've taken, where we're separating decisions on investment, operations, and financing. The funding for capital investments should come from appropriate sources, of course, matching their long-term nature. But the specific alternatives of financing, including leasing, are independent from the economic justification of the investment itself.

When leasing is used to fund an investment, the periodic charges incurred by the lessee compensate the lessor for elements such as interest on the capital advanced, risk, obsolescence, maintenance costs, and profit to the legal owner of the asset. The pattern of the lease payments can vary widely among competing offerings. Lease payments are generally tax-deductible outlays for the lessee, but they differ from the economic cash flows we've discussed in this chapter because they do include elements of compensation to the lessor.

All along we've viewed investment analysis as a cash flow trade-off that's independent of the compensation paid for the funds that finance the asset. Therefore, the economic desirability of an investment is tested purely on the basis of the benefits expected. If the analysis is favorable, a separate economic test can then be made to determine whether the company is better off leasing or owning the assets involved. In essence this involves comparing various funding methods. Here the question clearly becomes "lease versus buy," not "invest versus not invest." A number of specialized software applications permit analysts and managers to make the necessary calculations and tests for comparing financing alternatives. Because of the special complexities involved in these analytical methods, the reader is directed to the references at the end of the chapter for detained discussion and illustration.

Accelerated Depreciation

For simplicity, we've used straight-line depreciation in this chapter to derive the tax shield effect of depreciation charges as they affect economic analysis. However, we also referred to the accelerated write-offs allowed under the Internal Revenue Code (see Chapter 3) which are periodically modified by Congress. Rather than focus on any one of the several methods permitted, we'll make only a few generally applicable comments.

We're interested in depreciation, whatever pattern it may take, only insofar as it changes the tax expenditures of the company undertaking the investment analysis.

From a present value standpoint, accelerated depreciation provides an advantage because it moves the tax impact of the write-offs forward in time. In other words, in the early years of a project the tax shield effect will be greater than under straight-line conditions.

Similarly, shorter lives permitted by the ever-changing Internal Revenue Code will also place more tax benefits into the early stages of a project. Project benefits will be increased in the present value context, assuming, of course, that the company has sufficient taxable profits to take advantage of higher early write-offs. The calculations required to take account of accelerated depreciation in economic investment analysis can be easily handled with computer spreadsheets, just as any other uneven cash flow pattern can be accommodated.

The reader is encouraged to seek out the most current information published by the IRS to ascertain the proper depreciation class and write-off patterns for the assets being analyzed, and also to be aware of the particular tax management circumstances of the company that may affect its election of write-off patterns for tax purposes.

Inflation and Investment Analysis

The most important point to remember about the impact of inflation on investment analysis is the need for consistency between the measures used and the data being analyzed. As we'll see in the next chapter, company return standards are commonly based on the weighted cost of capital. This cost embodies inflation expectations both in the interest rate ascribed to debt, and in the investors' return expectations on which the cost of shareholder equity is based.

The analysis of capital investment projects should therefore be carried out with revenue and cost estimates that contain the same inflation expectations as the return standard employed. In other words, reasonable assumptions about price level changes affecting every part of the investment cash flow analysis should be built in to make the discounting process meaningful. For example, using a return standard that contains an inflation allowance in discounting constant dollar projections would give a result biased against the project. Similarly, using a constant dollar return standard to discount inflated cash flows would unduly improve the project's measures. Appendix III on inflation discusses the underlying concepts.

Accuracy

At all times we must remember that the precision implied by the mathematical basis of capital investment tools should be viewed with extreme caution. As we've pointed out before, the very nature of cash flow estimates is uncertain because they're based on expectations, forecasts, projections, and sometimes plain guesses. Only rarely does the analyst deal with contractual sums, such as interest or lease payments—and even these are subject to a degree of uncertainty. It therefore makes no sense to generate deceptively precise results or to allow highly specific numerical rankings to take on undue importance.

In our examples we have been more precise than we needed to be. The main intention was to give enough specific details to be able to follow the various methods step by step. In practice, liberal rounding of calculations and certainly of the final results is highly advisable to prevent the mathematical process from overwhelming the realistic business judgments required.

Keeping accuracy in proper perspective is even more important when we realize that the power of discounting is such that even widely different estimates for distant time periods can be so severely reduced in present value terms that they have relatively minor effects on the final result. A glance at the present value tables will confirm the rapid shrinkage of factors as discount rates rise and periods are more remote.

KEY ISSUES

The following is a recap of the key issues raised directly or indirectly in this chapter. They're enumerated here to help the reader keep the analysis techniques within the perspective of financial theory and business practice.

1. Business investment decisions are made continuously in the larger context of business strategy. This context evolves over time, and the portfolio of potential investments never remains constant.

2. The trade-off between outlays and benefits must be made with the objective of increasing shareholder wealth; that is, the return standards employed in measuring this trade-off must reflect the earnings potential and risks expected from a given business.

3. Shareholder expectations are incorporated into relevant earnings yardsticks through the concept of a weighted cost of capital, which reflects the appropriate level of future compensation to all providers of capital.

4. For an economic judgment, investment measures must take into account the timing of inflows and outflows of an investment and relate economic attractiveness to defined return expectations.

5. Economic analysis of investment decisions must be based on differential revenues and costs in the form of cash flows, and not on changes merely due to accounting conventions.

6. Risk is inherent in all estimates of future conditions because of the uncertainty about most variables affecting an investment project. It must be

expressed consistently in cash flows and investment measures alike.

7. Inflation and specific price changes in revenues
and costs can complicate both the estimating process and the use of investment measures, and they
must be handled consistently in both.

8. Capital budgets in practice aren't absolute ceilings
on the amount of investments for a company, nor
are they automatically affected by purely quantitative project ranking.

9. Financing patterns affect the capability to invest
and management's risk tolerance because of the
impact of leverage and the need to cover fixed
obligations.

10. Analytical techniques can provide ranges of results
and quantitative insights of considerable sophistication, but can't supplant qualitative business
judgments that reflect the broader context of
strategy and risk assessment.

SUMMARY

This chapter presented the basic analytical framework
for investment analysis in the broad context of capital
budgeting. The strategic backdrop of this activity was
highlighted before the techniques themselves were discussed. We emphasized time-adjusted concepts and
measures because they reflect the economic nature of
the analysis and decisions, and we relegated simple
rules of thumb to the limited situations where they can
be useful.

All along we stressed that the critical aspect of the
process was thoughtful analysis before the techniques
themselves are applied. We emphasized the need to define the problem, including development of relevant alternatives, and the careful preparation of relevant data

about the investment, operating differentials, and capital recoveries in an economic cash flow context. We found conceptual problems in all of these aspects, particularly in the use and meaning of the investment measures themselves. Working through increasingly complex examples, we provided the reader with a basic ability to perform investment analysis. But we cautioned that numerical results are only inputs to the broader management task of strategic positioning of the business—the selection and matching of appropriate long-term capital commitments with appropriate funding sources, in the framework of defined corporate objectives and goals, and with the ultimate aim of increasing shareholder value.

SELECTED REFERENCES

Analytical Process

Anthony, Robert N., and James S. Reece. *Accounting: Text and Cases.* 8th ed. Homewood, Ill.: Richard D. Irwin, 1988.

Garrison, Raymond H., and Erick W. Noreen. *Managerial Accounting: Concepts for Planning, Control, Decision Making.* 7th ed. Homewood, Ill.: Richard D. Irwin, 1994.

Grant, Eugene L., et al. *Principles of Engineering Economy.* 8th ed. New York: John Wiley & Sons, 1990. A classic.

Rosen, Lawrence R. *Dow Jones-Irwin Guide to Interest: What You Should Know about the Time Value of Money.* Rev. ed. Homewood, Ill.: Dow Jones-Irwin, 1981.

Broader Framework of Capital Budgeting

Bierman, Harold, Jr., and Seymour Smidt. *The Capital Budgeting Decision.* 6th ed. New York: Macmillan, 1984.

Hull, J. C. *The Evaluation of Risk in Business Investment.* Elmsford, N.Y.: Pergamon Press, 1980.

Kaufman, Mike, ed. *The Capital Budgeting Handbook.* Homewood, Ill.: Dow Jones-Irwin, 1985.

TABLE 6-9
Present Value of Single Sum of $1.00 Received or Paid at End of Period

Period of Receipt or Payment	1%	2%	4%	5%	6%	8%	10%	12%	14%	15%	16%	18%	20%	22%	24%	25%	26%	28%	30%	35%	40%	45%	50%
1	0.990	0.980	0.962	0.952	0.943	0.926	0.909	0.893	0.877	0.870	0.862	0.847	0.833	0.820	0.806	0.800	0.794	0.781	0.769	0.741	0.714	0.690	0.667
2	0.980	0.961	0.925	0.907	0.890	0.857	0.826	0.797	0.769	0.756	0.743	0.718	0.694	0.672	0.650	0.640	0.630	0.610	0.592	0.549	0.510	0.476	0.444
3	0.971	0.942	0.889	0.863	0.840	0.794	0.751	0.712	0.675	0.658	0.641	0.609	0.579	0.551	0.524	0.512	0.500	0.477	0.455	0.406	0.364	0.328	0.296
4	0.961	0.924	0.855	0.823	0.792	0.735	0.683	0.636	0.592	0.572	0.552	0.516	0.482	0.451	0.423	0.410	0.397	0.373	0.350	0.301	0.260	0.226	0.198
5	0.951	0.906	0.822	0.784	0.747	0.681	0.621	0.567	0.519	0.497	0.476	0.437	0.402	0.370	0.341	0.328	0.315	0.291	0.269	0.223	0.186	0.156	0.132
6	0.942	0.888	0.790	0.746	0.705	0.630	0.564	0.507	0.456	0.432	0.410	0.370	0.335	0.303	0.275	0.262	0.250	0.227	0.207	0.165	0.133	0.108	0.088
7	0.933	0.871	0.760	0.711	0.665	0.583	0.513	0.452	0.400	0.376	0.354	0.314	0.279	0.249	0.222	0.210	0.198	0.178	0.159	0.122	0.095	0.074	0.059
8	0.923	0.853	0.731	0.677	0.627	0.540	0.467	0.404	0.351	0.327	0.305	0.266	0.233	0.204	0.179	0.168	0.157	0.139	0.123	0.091	0.068	0.051	0.039
9	0.914	0.837	0.703	0.645	0.592	0.500	0.424	0.361	0.308	0.284	0.263	0.225	0.194	0.167	0.144	0.134	0.125	0.108	0.094	0.067	0.048	0.035	0.026
10	0.905	0.820	0.676	0.614	0.558	0.463	0.386	0.322	0.270	0.247	0.227	0.191	0.162	0.137	0.116	0.107	0.099	0.085	0.073	0.050	0.035	0.024	0.017
11	0.896	0.804	0.650	0.585	0.527	0.429	0.350	0.287	0.237	0.215	0.195	0.162	0.135	0.112	0.094	0.086	0.079	0.066	0.056	0.037	0.025	0.017	0.012
12	0.887	0.788	0.625	0.557	0.497	0.397	0.319	0.257	0.208	0.187	0.168	0.137	0.112	0.092	0.076	0.069	0.062	0.052	0.043	0.027	0.018	0.012	0.008
13	0.879	0.773	0.601	0.530	0.469	0.368	0.290	0.229	0.182	0.163	0.145	0.116	0.093	0.075	0.061	0.055	0.050	0.040	0.033	0.020	0.013	0.008	0.005
14	0.870	0.758	0.577	0.505	0.442	0.340	0.263	0.205	0.160	0.141	0.125	0.099	0.078	0.062	0.049	0.044	0.039	0.032	0.025	0.015	0.009	0.006	0.003
15	0.861	0.743	0.555	0.481	0.417	0.315	0.239	0.183	0.140	0.123	0.108	0.084	0.065	0.051	0.040	0.035	0.031	0.025	0.020	0.011	0.006	0.004	0.002

16	0.853	0.728	0.534	0.458	0.394	0.292	0.218	0.163	0.123	0.107	0.093	0.071	0.054	0.042	0.032	0.028	0.025	0.019	0.015	0.008	0.005	0.003	0.002
17	0.844	0.714	0.513	0.436	0.371	0.270	0.198	0.146	0.108	0.093	0.080	0.060	0.045	0.034	0.026	0.023	0.020	0.015	0.012	0.006	0.003	0.002	0.001
18	0.836	0.700	0.494	0.416	0.350	0.250	0.180	0.130	0.095	0.081	0.069	0.051	0.038	0.028	0.021	0.018	0.016	0.012	0.009	0.005	0.002	0.001	0.001
19	0.828	0.686	0.475	0.396	0.331	0.232	0.164	0.116	0.083	0.070	0.060	0.043	0.031	0.023	0.017	0.014	0.012	0.009	0.007	0.003	0.001	0.001	
20	0.820	0.673	0.456	0.377	0.312	0.215	0.149	0.104	0.073	0.061	0.051	0.037	0.026	0.019	0.014	0.012	0.010	0.007	0.005	0.002	0.001		
21	0.811	0.660	0.439	0.359	0.294	0.199	0.135	0.093	0.064	0.053	0.044	0.031	0.022	0.015	0.011	0.009	0.008	0.006	0.004	0.002	0.001		
22	0.803	0.647	0.422	0.342	0.278	0.184	0.123	0.083	0.056	0.046	0.038	0.026	0.018	0.013	0.009	0.007	0.006	0.004	0.003	0.001	0.001		
23	0.795	0.634	0.406	0.326	0.262	0.170	0.112	0.074	0.049	0.040	0.033	0.022	0.015	0.010	0.007	0.006	0.005	0.003	0.002	0.001			
24	0.788	0.622	0.390	0.310	0.247	0.158	0.102	0.066	0.043	0.035	0.028	0.019	0.013	0.008	0.006	0.005	0.004	0.003	0.002	0.001			
25	0.780	0.610	0.375	0.295	0.233	0.146	0.092	0.059	0.038	0.030	0.024	0.016	0.010	0.007	0.005	0.004	0.003	0.002	0.001	0.001			
26	0.772	0.598	0.361	0.281	0.220	0.135	0.084	0.053	0.033	0.026	0.021	0.014	0.009	0.006	0.004	0.003	0.002	0.002	0.001				
27	0.764	0.586	0.347	0.268	0.207	0.125	0.076	0.047	0.029	0.023	0.018	0.011	0.007	0.005	0.003	0.002	0.002	0.001	0.001				
28	0.757	0.574	0.333	0.255	0.196	0.116	0.069	0.042	0.026	0.020	0.016	0.010	0.006	0.004	0.002	0.002	0.002	0.001	0.001				
29	0.749	0.563	0.321	0.243	0.185	0.107	0.063	0.037	0.022	0.017	0.014	0.008	0.005	0.003	0.002	0.001	0.001	0.001					
30	0.742	0.552	0.308	0.231	0.174	0.099	0.057	0.033	0.020	0.015	0.012	0.007	0.004	0.003	0.002	0.001	0.001						
35	0.706	0.500	0.253	0.181	0.130	0.066	0.036	0.019	0.010	0.008	0.006	0.003	0.002	0.001	0.001								
40	0.672	0.453	0.208	0.142	0.097	0.046	0.022	0.011	0.005	0.004	0.003	0.001	0.001										
45	0.639	0.410	0.171	0.111	0.073	0.031	0.014	0.006	0.003	0.002	0.001	0.001											
50	0.608	0.372	0.141	0.087	0.054	0.021	0.009	0.003	0.001	0.001	0.001												
60	0.550	0.305	0.095	0.054	0.030	0.010	0.002	0.001	0.001	0.001													

1. To find present value (PV) of future amount:
   PV = Factor × Amount
2. To find future amount representing given PV:
   Amount = PV/Factor
3. To find period given future amount, PV and yield:
   Factor = PV/Amount; locate in column
4. To find yield given future amount, PV and period:
   Factor = PV/Amount; locate in row

TABLE 6–10

Present Value of $1.00 per Period Received or Paid at End of Period (Annuity)

Number of Periods	1%	2%	4%	5%	6%	8%	10%	12%	14%	15%	16%	18%	20%	22%	24%	25%	26%	28%	30%	35%	40%	45%	50%
1	0.990	0.980	0.962	0.952	0.943	0.926	0.909	0.893	0.877	0.870	0.862	0.847	0.833	0.820	0.806	0.800	0.794	0.781	0.769	0.741	0.714	0.690	0.667
2	1.970	1.942	1.886	1.859	1.833	1.783	1.736	1.690	1.647	1.626	1.605	1.566	1.528	1.492	1.457	1.440	1.424	1.392	1.361	1.289	1.224	1.165	1.111
3	2.941	2.884	2.775	2.722	2.673	2.577	2.487	2.402	2.322	2.283	2.246	2.174	2.106	2.042	1.981	1.952	1.923	1.868	1.816	1.696	1.589	1.493	1.407
4	3.902	3.808	3.630	3.545	3.465	3.312	3.170	3.037	2.914	2.855	2.798	2.690	2.589	2.494	2.404	2.362	2.320	2.241	2.166	1.997	1.849	1.720	1.605
5	4.853	4.713	4.452	4.329	4.212	3.993	3.791	3.605	3.433	3.352	3.274	3.127	2.991	2.864	2.745	2.689	2.635	2.532	2.436	2.220	2.035	1.876	1.737
6	5.795	5.601	5.242	5.075	4.917	4.623	4.355	4.112	3.889	3.784	3.685	3.498	3.326	3.167	3.020	2.951	2.885	2.759	2.643	2.385	2.168	1.983	1.824
7	6.728	6.472	6.002	5.786	5.582	5.206	4.868	4.564	4.288	4.160	4.039	3.812	3.605	3.416	3.242	3.161	3.083	2.937	2.802	2.508	2.263	2.057	1.883
8	7.652	7.325	6.733	6.463	6.210	5.747	5.335	4.968	4.639	4.487	4.344	4.078	3.837	3.619	3.421	3.329	3.241	3.076	2.925	2.598	2.331	2.108	1.922
9	8.566	8.162	7.435	7.108	6.802	6.247	5.759	5.328	4.946	4.772	4.607	4.303	4.031	3.786	3.566	3.463	3.366	3.184	3.019	2.665	2.379	2.144	1.948
10	9.471	8.983	8.111	7.722	7.360	6.710	6.145	5.650	5.216	5.019	4.833	4.494	4.192	3.923	3.682	3.571	3.465	3.269	3.092	2.715	2.414	2.168	1.965
11	10.368	9.787	8.760	8.307	7.887	7.139	6.495	5.937	5.453	5.234	5.029	4.656	4.327	4.035	3.776	3.656	3.544	3.335	3.147	2.752	2.438	2.185	1.977
12	11.255	10.575	9.385	8.863	8.384	7.536	6.814	6.194	5.660	5.421	5.197	4.793	4.439	4.127	3.851	3.725	3.606	3.387	3.190	2.779	2.456	2.196	1.985
13	12.134	11.343	9.986	9.393	8.853	7.904	7.103	6.424	5.842	5.583	5.342	4.910	4.533	4.203	3.912	3.780	3.656	3.427	3.223	2.799	2.468	2.204	1.990
14	13.004	12.106	10.563	9.898	9.295	8.244	7.367	6.628	6.002	5.724	5.468	5.008	4.611	4.265	3.962	3.824	3.695	3.459	3.249	2.814	2.477	2.210	1.993
15	13.865	12.849	11.118	10.379	9.712	8.559	7.606	6.811	6.142	5.847	5.575	5.092	4.675	4.315	4.001	3.859	3.726	3.483	3.268	2.825	2.484	2.214	1.995

Period																							
16	14.718	13.578	11.652	10.838	10.106	8.851	7.824	6.974	6.265	5.954	5.669	5.162	4.730	4.357	4.033	3.887	3.751	3.503	3.283	2.834	2.489	2.216	1.997
17	15.562	14.292	12.116	11.274	10.477	9.122	8.022	7.120	6.373	6.047	5.749	5.222	4.775	4.391	4.059	3.910	3.771	3.518	3.295	2.840	2.492	2.218	1.998
18	16.398	14.992	12.659	11.690	10.828	9.372	8.201	7.250	6.467	6.128	5.818	5.273	4.812	4.419	4.080	3.928	3.786	3.529	3.304	2.844	2.494	2.219	1.999
19	17.226	15.678	13.134	12.086	11.158	9.604	8.365	7.366	6.550	6.198	5.877	5.316	4.844	4.442	4.097	3.942	3.799	3.539	3.311	2.848	2.496	2.220	1.999
20	18.046	16.351	13.590	12.463	11.470	9.818	8.514	7.469	6.623	6.259	5.929	5.353	4.870	4.460	4.110	3.954	3.808	3.546	3.316	2.850	2.497	2.221	1.999
21	18.857	17.011	14.029	12.821	11.764	10.017	8.649	7.562	6.687	6.312	5.973	5.384	4.891	4.476	4.121	3.963	3.816	3.551	3.320	2.852	2.498	2.221	2.000
22	19.660	17.658	14.451	13.163	12.042	10.201	8.772	7.645	6.743	6.359	6.011	5.410	4.909	4.488	4.130	3.970	3.822	3.556	3.323	2.853	2.498	2.222	2.000
23	20.456	18.292	14.857	13.489	12.303	10.371	8.883	7.718	6.792	6.399	6.044	5.432	4.925	4.499	4.137	3.976	3.827	3.559	3.325	2.854	2.499	2.222	2.000
24	21.243	18.914	15.247	13.799	12.550	10.529	8.985	7.784	6.835	6.434	6.073	5.451	4.937	4.507	4.143	3.981	3.831	3.562	3.327	2.855	2.499	2.222	2.000
25	22.023	19.523	15.622	14.094	12.783	10.675	9.077	7.843	6.873	6.464	6.097	5.467	4.948	4.514	4.147	3.985	3.834	3.564	3.329	2.856	2.499	2.222	2.000
26	22.795	20.121	15.983	14.375	13.003	10.810	9.161	7.896	6.906	6.491	6.118	5.480	4.956	4.520	4.151	3.988	3.837	3.566	3.330	2.856	2.500	2.222	2.000
27	23.560	20.707	16.330	14.643	13.211	10.935	9.237	7.943	6.935	6.514	6.136	5.492	4.964	4.524	4.154	3.990	3.839	3.567	3.331	2.856	2.500	2.222	2.000
28	24.316	21.281	16.663	14.898	13.406	11.051	9.307	7.984	6.961	6.534	6.152	5.502	4.970	4.528	4.157	3.992	3.840	3.568	3.331	2.857	2.500	2.222	2.000
29	25.066	21.844	16.984	15.141	13.591	11.158	9.370	8.022	6.983	6.551	6.166	5.510	4.975	4.531	4.159	3.994	3.841	3.569	3.332	2.857	2.500	2.222	2.000
30	25.808	22.396	17.292	15.372	13.765	11.258	9.427	8.055	7.003	6.566	6.177	5.517	4.979	4.534	4.160	3.995	3.842	3.569	3.332	2.857	2.500	2.222	2.000
35	29.408	24.999	18.665	16.374	14.498	11.654	9.664	8.176	7.070	6.617	6.215	5.539	4.992	4.541	4.164	3.998	3.845	3.571	3.333	2.857	2.500	2.222	2.000
40	32.835	27.355	19.793	17.159	15.046	11.925	9.779	8.244	7.105	6.642	6.234	5.548	4.997	4.544	4.166	3.999	3.846	3.571	3.333	2.857	2.500	2.222	2.000
45	36.094	29.490	20.720	17.774	15.456	12.108	9.863	8.282	7.123	6.654	6.242	5.552	4.998	4.545	4.166	4.000	3.846	3.571	3.333	1.857	2.500	2.222	2.000
50	39.196	31.424	21.482	18.256	15.762	12.234	9.915	8.304	7.133	6.661	6.246	5.554	4.999	4.545	4.167	4.000	3.846	3.571	3.333	2.857	2.500	2.222	2.000
60	44.955	34.761	22.623	18.929	16.161	12.376	9.967	8.324	7.140	6.665	6.249	5.555	5.000	4.545	4.167	4.000	3.846	3.571	3.333	2.857	2.500	2.222	2.000

1. To find present value (PV) of series of equal receipts or payments:
   PV = Factor × Annuity

2. To find annuity representing given P.V.:
   Annuity = PV/Factor

3. To find number of periods to recover investment:
   Factor = Investment/Annuity; locate in column

4. To find yield of annuity given investment:
   Factor = Investment/Annuity; locate in row

Van Horne, James C. *Financial Management and Policy.* 8th ed. Englewood Cliffs, N.J.: Prentice Hall, 1989.

Weston, J. Fred, and Thomas E. Copeland. *Managerial Finance.* 9th ed. Hinsdale, Ill.: Dryden Press, 1989.

Specialized Areas

Present Value Tables

Gushee, Charles II, ed. *Financial Compound Interest and Annuity Tables.* 6th ed. Boston: Financial Publishing, 1980.

Thorndike, David. *The Thorndike Encyclopedia of Banking and Financial Tables, 1993 Yearbook.* Boston: Warren, Gorham & Lamont.

Risk Analysis

Hertz, David B. "Risk Analysis in Capital Investment." *Harvard Business Review,* September–December 1979, pp. 42–49. (A classic.)

Holder, James E., and Henry E. Riggs. "Pitfalls in Evaluating Risk Projects." *Harvard Business Review,* January–February 1985, pp. 128–35.

Levy, Haim, and Marshall Sarnat. *Capital Investment and Financial Decisions.* 4th ed. Englewood Cliffs, N.J.: Prentice Hall, 1990.

NcNamee, Peter, and John Celona. *Decision Analysis with Supertree.* 2nd ed. South San Francisco, CA.: The Scientific Press, 1990.

Ross, Stephen A.; Randolph W. Westerfield; and Jeffrey F. Jaffe. *Corporate Finance.* 3rd ed. Homewood, Ill.: Richard D. Irwin, 1993.

Leasing

Prichard, Robert E., and Thomas J. Hindelang. *The Lease/Buy Decision.* New York: AMACOM, 1980.

SELF-STUDY EXERCISES AND PROBLEMS

(Solutions are provided in Appendix VI)

1. An investment proposition costing $60,000 is expected to result in the following aftertax cash inflows over seven years:

Year	
1	$10,000
2	15,000
3	15,000

4	20,000
5	15,000
6	10,000
7	5,000

a. Calculate the net present value at 10 percent and at 16 percent.

b. Determine the internal rate of return (yield) of the proposition.

c. If the annual cash flows were an even $13,000 per year for seven years, what would be the net present value at 10 percent?

d. What level of annual cash flows would be required to yield a 16 percent return?

e. How would the results of (a) and (b) change if there were a capital recovery of $10,000 at the end of year 7?

f. How would the result of (d) change if there were a capital recovery of $10,000 at the end of year 7?

2. After having spent and written off against expenses of past periods an estimated $1,150,000 of R&D funds on a new product, the ABC Company must decide whether to invest a total of $1,500,000 in a large-scale initial promotional and advertising campaign to bring the product to market. The campaign will be conducted over a six-month period, and all costs will be charged off as expenses in the current year. The effect of the campaign is an estimated average incremental profit of $400,000 per year for at least the next five years, before taxes and without the initial promotional costs. The likely pattern of profits is estimated to be $200,000 in the first year, $300,000 in the second, $600,000 in the third, $500,000 in the fourth, and $400,000 in the fifth year.

Assume that income taxes on incremental profits are paid at the rate of 36 percent and that the company normally has the opportunity to earn 14 percent after taxes. Calculate the various measures of investment desirability, first on the average profit and then on the annual pattern expected. Determine the simple payback and return on investment, average return, net present value, present value index, present value payback, annualized net present value, and internal rate of return (yield).

What's the effect of the R&D expenditures on these results? Discuss your findings.

3. After careful analysis of a number of possible investments, a trustee of a major estate is weighing the choice between two

$100,000 investments considered to be of equal risk. The first (a) will provide a series of eight year-end payments to the estate of $16,500 each, while the second (b) will provide a single lump sum of $233,000 at the end of 11 years. Which proposition provides the higher yield? If the normal return experienced by the estate for investments of this risk category is 6 percent, which investment is preferable? Should the pattern of cash flows be a consideration here, and how would this affect the choice? Ignore taxes and discuss your findings.

4. In an effort to replace a manual operation with a more efficient and reliable automatic process, the DEF Company is considering the purchase of a machine that will cost $52,800 installed and has an expected economic life of eight years. It will be depreciated over this period on a straight-line basis for both book and tax purposes, with no salvage value foreseen. The main benefit expected is a true reduction in costs due to the elimination of two operator positions and less materials spoilage. There will be some additional costs such as power, supplies, and repairs. The net annual savings are estimated to be $12,100, and the machine will be scrapped at the end of its life.

Assume that income taxes on incremental profits are paid at the rate of 36 percent and that normal opportunities return 12 percent after taxes. Calculate the simple payback and return on investment, average return, net present value, present value index, present value payback, annualized net present value, and internal rate of return (yield). Discuss your findings.

5. The XYZ Corporation's strategy includes the periodic introduction of a new product line, which involves investments in R&D, promotion, plant, equipment, and working capital. Now the company has readied a new product after an expenditure of $3.75 million on R&D during the past 12 months. The decision to be made is whether to invest $6.3 million for the production of the new line. The economic life of the product is estimated at 12 years, while straight-line depreciation will be taken over 15 years. At the end of 12 years, the equipment's book value is expected to be recovered through sale of the machinery. Working capital of $1.5 million must be committed to the project during the first year, and $1.25 million of this amount is expected to be recovered at the end of the 12 years. An expenditure of $1 million for promotion must be made and expensed in the first year as well.

The best estimate of profits before depreciation, promotion expenses, and income taxes is $1.9 million per year for the first three years, $2.2 million per year for the fourth through eighth years, and $1.3 million per year for years 9 through 12. Assume that income taxes on incremental profits are paid at the rate of 36 percent and that the company normally earns 12 percent after taxes on its investments. Calculate the various measures of investment desirability. Which of these best indicates the project's attractiveness? Should the company plan to develop similar opportunities by spending research and development funds? How much margin for error exists in this project? Discuss your findings.

6. The ZYX Company has found that after only two years of using a new machine for a semiautomatic production process, a more advanced and faster model has arrived on the market, which not only will turn out the current volume of products more efficiently but will allow an increased output of the item. The original machine had cost $32,000 and was being depreciated straight-line over a 10-year period, at the end of which time it would be scrapped. This machine's market value currently is $15,000, and a buyer is interested in acquiring it.

The advanced model now available costs $55,500 installed, and because of its more complex mechanism is expected to last eight years. A scrap value of $1,500 is considered reasonable.

The current level of output of the old machine, now running at capacity, is 200,000 units per year, which the new machine would boost by 15 percent. There's no question in the minds of the sales management that this additional output could be sold. The current machine produces the product at a unit cost of 12 cents for labor, 48 cents for materials, and 24 cents for allocated overhead (at the rate of 200 percent of direct labor). At the higher level of output, the new machine would turn out the product at a unit cost of 8 cents for labor (because one less operator is needed), 46 cents for materials (because of less spoilage), and 16 cents for allocated overhead. Differences in other operating costs, such as power, repairs, and supplies, are negligible at both volume levels.

If the new machine were run at the old 200,000-unit level, the operators would be freed for a proportionate period of time for reassignment in other operations of the company.

The additional output is expected to be sold at the normal price of $0.95 per unit, but additional selling and promotional costs are expected to amount to $5,500 per year.

Assume that income taxes are paid at the rate of 36 percent and that the company normally earns 16 percent after taxes on its investments. Calculate the various measures of investment desirability and select those that are most meaningful for this analysis.

What major considerations should be taken into account in this decision? Discuss your findings.

7. The UVW Company, a small but growing oil company, was about to invest $275,000 in drilling development wells on a lease near a major oil field with proven reserves. Since other companies were also drilling in the vicinity, the volume of the flow of oil expected couldn't be predicted except within wide limits. Nevertheless, some oil would be obtained for a period of 12 years, in the best judgment of the geologists. After careful evaluation of the market and distribution aspects, company management decided that the major uncertainty lay in the physical yield, with lesser risk in the other areas. Consequently, an assessment was made of the range of aftertax cash flows (after considering depletion, depreciation, etc.) at various levels of production, and the likelihood of occurrence of these levels was estimated. There was believed to be a 5 percent chance that the cash flow would be $15,000 yearly over the life of the project, a 15 percent chance that it would be $35,000 yearly, a 40 percent chance that it would be $45,000 yearly, a 25 percent chance that it would be $50,000, and a 15 percent chance that it would be $60,000 per year. It was expected that oil would flow at any given level for the full life of the project, although there was the risk that the wells could run dry sooner. Would this be a worthwhile project if the company normally earned 10 percent after taxes? What considerations are critical? Discuss your findings.

7 ASSESSMENT OF THE COST OF CAPITAL

As we've pointed out repeatedly, the economic nature of business decisions amounts to a cost/benefit trade-off. Up to this point we've focused mainly on the economic benefits from investing in and operating a business. Yet there are also economic costs incurred with every business decision.

For example, in Chapter 5, during our discussion of financial leverage, we encountered the special profit impact caused by the cost of long-term debt funds. We demonstrated how such fixed obligations introduce magnified earnings fluctuations at different levels of profitability. Later, in Chapter 6, we referred to the overall cost of long-term capital as a criterion by which to judge the desirability of business investments because projects that provide a time-adjusted cash flow return at or above the cost of capital will leave shareholders at least as well off as before.

In this chapter we'll discuss in greater detail the cost of various types of capital employed in a business. We'll examine how this cost is measured and in what ways this economic reality affects business decision making. We'll begin by sketching out the *types of decisions* for which cost of capital considerations are important. Then we'll discuss the cost of the different types of capital, including *operating funds, long-term debt,* and *owners' equity* (*preferred stock* and *common equity*).

Given the specific costs of each of these types of capital, we'll derive an approach to determining the overall corporate *weighted cost of capital,* and discuss the use of this cost of capital in relation to the various *return standards* for business investments. The chapter will end with a list of key issues.

COST OF CAPITAL AND FINANCIAL DECISIONS

The decisional context we used in the first five chapters stressed the interrelationship of investment, operations, and financing. We observed that, over time, most management decisions cause funds movements. However, we didn't deal directly with the sources of these funds and their respective costs.

The dynamics of the business system are such that at any time there must be temporary and/or permanent utilization of funds from a variety of sources, either external (e.g., borrowing or raising new equity) or internal (e.g., retained earnings from profitable operations or shifts in existing uses of funds). Because the basic purpose of investing in, operating, and funding a business is to increase the economic value of the owners' stake over time, management decisions should create economic value for the shareholders that is higher than the cost of the inputs. Among these inputs is the cost of capital obtained from various long-term sources.

Investment Decisions

Chapter 6 discussed the various measures used to judge an investment's desirability. Most of these incorporated the basic requirement that the project provide an economic return. This implies that all costs must be recovered, including compensation to the providers of all types of funds. We also said that minimum standards for investments had to be set high enough to compensate both for the project's specific risk and for the opportunity cost of forgoing the returns from alternative uses of the funds invested. Such alternative investments in the company's normal activities were assumed to adequately compensate both shareholders and lenders for providing their capital. We then suggested that the company's overall cost of capital, when used as a minimum standard for the economic desirability of investments, implicitly embodied all of these requirements.

The analytic methods in Chapter 5 didn't directly include any financing costs. Rather, the cash outflows and inflows as defined represented only capital outlays on the one hand, and incremental aftertax operating benefits and capital recoveries on the other. These cash flows were then discounted at a return standard that *implicitly* allowed for recovery of all actual costs and opportunity costs combined. Very importantly, we didn't take into account the cost of the *specific* funds to be used for financing the project. Instead, we let a broad overall standard represent the *combined* cost of all types of funding used by the company.

The economic results from an investment have to be sufficiently attractive to justify allocation of part of the various long-term funds available to the company. Here we must recognize an important principle, based on our systems discussion in Chapter 1: Normally, funds for investment come from a pool of different sources, none of which can or should be specifically identified with the particular project under review. Instead, funds for investment should carry the overall cost of the company's pool of funds, as Figure 7–1 suggests.

Given the long-term nature of capital expenditures for working capital, facilities, technology, and so on, these funds commitments are normally backed by the long-term capital structure of a company. This structure may include different degrees of leverage and a whole range of financial instruments. Thus the *weighted* cost of capital measure, which we'll discuss shortly, is an important criterion in the capital budgeting context.

Operational Decisions

The time horizon for operational decisions is generally shorter than that of the typical capital investment. Nonetheless, operational funds movements (such as increases or decreases in trade credit—both used and extended) and swings in cash balances and accruals do involve costs in the form of both out-of-pocket charges and opportunity costs. For example, a near-term decision to take purchase discounts may involve significant economic benefits when weighed against any incremental borrowing necessary to take advantage of the

FIGURE 7–1
Long-Term Funds Commitments versus Long-Term Sources

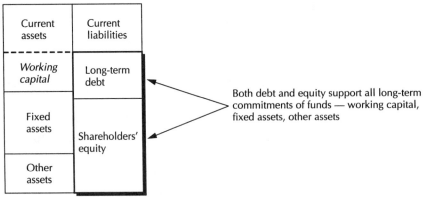

discount. Cash management decisions to minimize bank balances can eliminate the opportunity costs of tying up idle funds. In fact, there are myriad circumstances in which near-term decisions cause or eliminate the cost of employing funds, as these decisions are often directly connected with incremental sources that entail specific costs. We'll discuss some of these shortly.

Financing Decisions

There are costs connected with obtaining and compensating providers for various sources of funds, both short-term and long-term, which must be considered by management in making any financing decisions. Clearly, the use of any type of funds entails an economic cost to the company in one form or another. One of management's obligations is to develop a pattern of funding that both matches the business's risk/reward profile and is sufficiently adaptable to meeting the firm's evolving needs. We'll discuss financing choices and the framework of analyzing them in the next chapter.

COST OF OPERATING FUNDS

In the course of its operations, a business commonly employs many types of debt, including trade obligations (in the form of accounts and notes payable), intermediate-term credit, notes payable to banks or individuals, tax accruals owed various government agencies, wages due employees, payments due on installment purchases, and lease obligations. For all types of debt, including long-term obligations in the company's capital structure, the *specific cost* of borrowing can be determined rather easily. Normally, debt arrangements carry stated interest provisions that call for interest payments during the debt period, at its end, or as an advance deduction from principal. The last of these provisions is called discounting. In all of the cases the specific cost of debt is simply the direct cost of this interest commitment.

We must also remember that under current IRS guidelines, interest payments of all kinds are tax deductible for corporations. Because of this feature, the net cost of interest to corporations (at least for those with sufficient profits to be liable for taxes or able to apply tax-averaging provisions) is the annual interest multiplied by a factor (f) of one minus the applicable tax rate.

For example, if a corporation pays 9 percent per year on the principal of a note and its effective tax rate (t) for any incremental revenue or cost is 34 percent, the net annual effective interest cost (i) of this note will be

$$f = 1 - t$$
$$f = 1 - 0.34 = 0.66$$
$$i = 9\% \times 0.66 = 5.94\% \text{ (after taxes)}$$

Tax deductibility effectively reduces the cost of debt to a net amount after the prevailing tax rate is applied if the company is in a position where changes in net income affect the amount of taxes due. This tax advantage may also be enjoyed by individuals in some circumstances, as in the case of home mortgage interest deductions. Deductibility of the specific cost *doesn't* apply to other forms of capital at this time, however, as we'll see later.

We can define operating debt as short- or intermediate-term revolving obligations incurred in the ordinary daily operations of most businesses. Some of these debt funds are provided by creditors free of charge for short periods, under trade terms generally accepted in the industry or service in which the company operates.

Foremost in this category are accounts payable, which are the amounts owed vendors for goods or services purchased. Depending on the terms of the purchase agreement, the company being billed for goods and services can hold off payment for 10 or 15 days, or as long as 45 or even 60 days. In the interim, it can make use of the funds without incurring any specific cost. Recall from Chapter 2 that such trade credit is in fact a significant funds source that's rolled over continuously, and that grows or declines with the volume of operations.

In most cases suppliers offer a discount for early payment. For example, the terms may provide for a 2 percent reduction in the invoice amount if payment is received within 10 days (2/10), or 3 percent within 15 days (3/15) of the date of the invoice. This practice, common in many business sectors, allows the customer effectively to reduce the original cost of the goods or service by the specified discount. This incentive is intended to speed up the vendor's collections and thus to reduce the level of the vendor's funds tied up in credit extended.

If the buyer lets the discount period lapse, however, the invoice amount becomes due and payable in full at the end of the period specified (n/30, n/45, etc.). Failure to take advantage of the trade discount (thereby prolonging the time during which the buyer can make alternative use of the funds) results in a definite opportunity cost. While often ignored, this cost can be sizable.

For instance, if the credit terms are 2/10, n/30, the cost of using the funds for the extra 20 days amounts to 2 percent of lost cash discount, or an annual rate of 36 percent! The calculation is simple:

$$\frac{360 \text{ days}}{20 \text{ days}} \times 2\% = 36\% \text{ (before taxes)}$$

In effect, the company loses, as taxable income, the cash discount it would otherwise have earned. To arrive at the net cost, the cash discount must be reduced by the taxes that would have been paid on the lost income. If we assume taxes to be 34 percent, the net cost for using the creditor's funds for the extra 20 days amounts to

$$1 - 0.34 = 0.66$$
$$2\% \times 0.66 = 1.32\% \text{ (after taxes)}$$

On an annualized basis this cost is still sizable, especially when compared to the prime interest rate, which is the rate normally charged large corporations of impeccable credit rating—or even to the higher interest rates smaller companies pay to borrow operating funds. The annualization is calculated as

$$\frac{360 \text{ days}}{20 \text{ days}} \times 1.32\% = 23.76\% \text{ (after taxes)}$$

Some companies, especially small and rapidly growing enterprises, make it a practice to use accounts payable as a convenient source of credit, often unilaterally exceeding the outside limits of credit terms by significant periods. The longer the funds are kept, of course, the lower the specific cost of accounts payable becomes, as trade creditors normally don't charge interest unless the receivable has to be renegotiated. In extreme cases, unpaid accounts may be converted into notes payable due on specific dates, with or without interest. This is usually done at the request of a trade creditor who wishes to establish a somewhat stronger claim against the debtor's resources.

It's clearly a poor practice for any borrower to violate stipulated trade credit agreements, from the standpoint of both business reputation and continuing creditworthiness. Prospective creditors will take such tardy performance into account when evaluating the customer's credit history, as such information is readily available from the data bases of credit rating agencies. This *implicit* economic cost must be considered in addition to the specific monetary cost incurred with trade credit.

Another form of operating debt includes short-term notes and installment contracts, where interest is either charged ahead of time or is added to the amount of principal stated in the contract. For example, a one-year, $1,000 note that carries an interest rate of 9 percent will provide the debtor with only $910 in ready cash if the note is "discounted" by deducting the interest in advance. The effective cost before taxes now becomes higher than the stated interest because the company is in effect paying $90 for the privilege of borrowing $910 for one year:

$$\frac{\$90}{\$910} = 9.89\% \text{ (before taxes)}$$

The adjustment for income taxes is handled exactly as shown in the previous example.

In the case of an installment contract for, say, $1,000 payable in four equal quarterly installments, with annual interest of 10 percent on the original balance, the effective cost of interest is far higher than stated because decreasing amounts of principal will be outstanding over the term of the contract as the quarterly payments amortize the principal while providing interest on the declining balance. The precise cost of 15.7 percent can be easily calculated with a preprogrammed calculator using the present value approach discussed in Chapter 6.

We can employ an averaging process as a quick method of determining the approximate effective cost. Over the term of the contract the amount of principal will decline from $1,000 to zero, with the average outstanding balance of roughly one half of this range, or $500. The contractual interest was 10 percent on $1,000, or $100, one quarter of which was added to each of the four payments. When we relate the total interest paid to the average amount of funds used by the borrowing company during the term of the contract, the approximate cost doubles:

$$\frac{\$100}{\$500} = 20\% \text{ (before taxes)}$$

The actual result of 15.7 percent was lower because in our example, the interest in effect is also paid on the installment basis. (The adjustment for income taxes is the same as before.) If the contract ran for more than one year, the interest cost must be annualized; that is, the amount of interest must be allocated to the specific time period involved to derive the true cost per year, which is the normal period of comparison.

More complex financial arrangements are normally handled using present value techniques. Banks and other lending institutions use computers to precisely calculate the payments and charges, and are legally bound to disclose the effective cost of the arrangement on an annualized basis. The simple averaging technique shown earlier is useful as a quick check in many circumstances, including personal finance, for approximating the effective cost of credit with which to make initial comparisons.

The discussion so far has focused on the specific cost of operational debt, which can range from zero to substantial annual rates of interest. This specific cost isn't the only aspect of debt, however. As earlier chapters said, repayment of principal has to be made, which commits part of the company's future cash flows. The obligation to repay the principal in a timely fashion forces the financial manager to forecast and plan cash receipts and disbursements with care. The outlook could be such that a refinancing may be desirable when the principal becomes due. The basic techniques of making cash flow projections as discussed in Chapter 4 are applicable here.

Another element of the debt burden, as already mentioned, is the impact of various forms of debt obligations on a firm's creditworthiness regarding current and future funding requirements. In other words, the balance between owners' equity and other peoples' money may become precarious and forestall borrowing of any kind for some time until the company has worked itself out from under its debt obligations. "Closing off the top," as debt-heavy operations are often described, can be costly in terms of (1) the risk of not meeting obligations as they fall due and (2) having to turn to much more expensive sources of credit or equity funds as additional needs arise.

COST OF LONG-TERM DEBT

Most companies employ at least some type of long-term debt obligations to support part of their permanent financing needs arising from major capital outlays, growth of operations, or replacement of other types of capital. This type of debt becomes integral to the long-term capital structure of the company. Examples are bonds of various types issued by a company and traded in the financial markets, or long-term borrowing arrangements with banks and other financial institutions. When determining an appropriate level of debt in the capital structure, management must make well-planned decisions, weighing the cost, risk, and debt service involved relative to the prospective uses of the funds. Commitments to long-term debt by their very nature have a much more lasting impact on a company's situation than do short-term working capital financing or intermediate-term loans.

The *specific cost* of long-term debt is expressed in the stated annual interest rate of the financial instrument involved. For example, a 12 percent debenture bond, which is an unsecured (no specific assets are pledged) general debt obligation of the company, has a specific aftertax cost of

$$12\% \times (1 - .34) = 7.92\%$$

if we assume that the company is able to take advantage of the interest deduction. An incremental tax rate of 34 percent was used here.

In addition, we'll assume that the bond had been sold at a price that nets the company its *par value* (face value). A bond's stated annual interest rate (coupon rate) is based on the par value, that is, 100 percent of the principal due at a specified future date—regardless of the actual proceeds received by the issuing company. These proceeds often vary because marketable debt securities are generally sold at the best possible price obtainable in the market through underwriters who take some or all of the risk of marketing the issue for a small percentage of the gross receipts. Legal and registration expenses are also borne by the company. Therefore, depending on the issue price (which is related to prevailing interest yields and to the quality of the company's credit rating), the company may actually receive net proceeds at a *discount* (below par value), or it may receive a small *premium* over par.

In either case, the specific cost has to be adjusted to take the actual proceeds into account. The effect is similar to the short-term loan discussed earlier, on which the interest was due in advance and which therefore entailed a specific cost somewhat higher than the stated rate. If we assume that instead of 100 percent of par value, the company received 95 percent for its debentures after all expenses and commissions, the effective aftertax cost with a 12 percent coupon rate is

$$0.12 \ (1 - .34) \times \frac{1}{.95} = 8.34\%$$

Apart from the specific cost of interest, long-term debt also involves repayment of the principal. There are many types of repayment provisions, generally structured to fit the nature of the company and the type of risks the debt holder visualizes. Periodic repayment requirements may be met through a *sinking fund* set aside for that purpose and held in trust by a depository institution. Partial or full principal payments due at the end of the lending period are called *balloon payments.*

The basic point to remember is that debt instruments, even if long-term, must be repaid in some form and at some time. The cost of this repayment is implicit in the need to carefully plan future cash flows, and also to consider the company's ability to achieve future refinancing if the funds needs are likely to continue or even grow. Recall Chapter 4's discussion of funds projections.

Another implicit cost of long-term debt involves the nature and degree of restrictions normally embodied in the debt agreement (*indenture*). Such provisions may limit management's ability to use other forms of credit (e.g., leasing), they may specify minimum levels of some financial ratios (e.g., working capital proportions or burden coverage), or they may limit the amount of dividends that can be paid to shareholders. At times, specific assets may have to be pledged as security. Any set of such provisions carries an implicit cost in that they limit management's freedom of choice in making decisions. The greater the perceived risk of the indebtedness, the greater the restrictions are likely to be.

The rationale for these restrictions was presented in the discussion of financial ratios from the lenders' point of view (Chapter 3). Not to be overlooked is the introduction of *financial leverage* into the capital structure, as discussed in Chapter 5. The implicit cost of this condition again depends on the degree of risk exposure caused by specific company and industry conditions.

COST OF OWNERS' EQUITY

Preferred Stock

This form of equity ownership is conceptually at the midway point between debt and common stock. Although subordinated to the various creditors of the corporation, the preferred shareholder has a claim on corporate earnings that ranks ahead of the common shareholders' position up to the amount of the stated preferred dividend. In liquidation the preferred shareholders' claims are satisfied prior to the residual claims of the holders of common stock.

The *specific cost* of preferred stock is normally higher than that of debt with a similar quality rating. Because of the near-equity status of preferred stock, preferred dividends at this writing aren't tax deductible for the issuing corporation and are therefore an outflow of aftertax funds. For instance, a 14 percent preferred stock issued at par (net of expenses) costs the corporation 14 percent after taxes. For each dollar of dividends to be paid on this preferred stock, the corporation must therefore earn, before taxes,

$$\$1.00 \times \frac{1}{1 - .34} = \$1.52$$

as compared to $1.00 for every dollar of interest paid on a long-term debt obligation. Where the 12 percent bond in the previous section had an aftertax cost of 7.92 percent, the 14 percent preferred bond has an aftertax cost of 14 percent. The stated dividend rate of a preferred stock is therefore directly comparable to the tax-adjusted interest rate of a bond.

We can easily compare the cost to the company of long-term debt and preferred stock if we assume that they were issued at prices that result in proceeds exactly equal to the par (face) value. When the proceeds don't equal par value, as often happens because of market conditions, the cost must be based on the proceeds to obtain the effective cost as we've discussed.

The additional *implicit* cost of preferred stock lies in the fact that it's a security senior to common stock, and its holders' dividend claims rank ahead of common dividends. In addition, the essentially fixed nature of preferred dividends (they can be omitted only under serious circumstances) introduces a degree of financial leverage with varying earnings levels. Preferred stock being closer in concept to owners' equity than to debt, however, makes the implicit costs of its encumbrances far less serious than those of debt.

Common Equity

The holder of common shares is the residual owner of the corporation, as the claims of common stock extend to all assets and earnings not subject to prior claims. Common shareholders provide long-term funds with the expectation of being rewarded with an increase in the economic value of their shares. This value accretion consists of the interlocking impact of (hopefully) growing earnings and growing dividends on the market value of the shares. In turn, the market value is impacted by general economic conditions and by risks specific to the industry and to the individual company.

In other words, in the case of common stock we're dealing with more variables, while contractual provisions for compensation (such as coupon interest or the stated preferred dividend rate) are absent. As a result, the *specific cost* of common equity calls for a more complex evaluation than we encountered with either debt or preferred stock.

The cost of common equity has to be viewed in an opportunity framework. The investor has provided funds to the corporation and so expects to receive the combined economic return of dividends declared by the board of directors and future appreciation in market value. The investment was made—presumably on a logical basis—because the type of risk embodied in the company and its business reasonably matched the investor's own risk preference. In addition, the investor's expectations about earnings, dividends, and market appreciation were considered satisfactory.

The investor made this choice, however, by forgoing other investment opportunities. The commitment was made under conditions of uncertainty about future results, because the only hard data available to any investor are *past* performance statistics. The challenge of measuring the cost of the shareholder's funds to the corporation arises from the need to meet investor expectations about the risk/reward trade-off involved in investing in this opportunity. In other words, the company must compensate the shareholder with the economic return implicit in its *future* outlook, which may be different from its past performance.

Several approaches to measuring the cost of common equity are used in practice; all involve many assumptions and a great deal of judgment. The greatest difficulty lies in finding a specific link with the risk versus value judgments in the security markets that affect the market value of the common shares. We'll discuss three major methods: (1) an *earnings* approach, (2) a *dividend* approach, and (3) a *risk assessment* approach based on the *capital asset pricing model.* Both the earnings and dividend approaches are fairly straightforward; in effect they directly value future streams of earnings or dividends. But they also use highly simplifying assumptions and thus are very limited in effectiveness.

The third method, in contrast, approximates shareholder return expectations by adding to a "normalized" (broadly based) rate of return on securities in general a calculated numerical *risk premium* that's *company-specific.* As we'll see, it's the only approach that arrives at an economic return for the specific security relative to average yields experienced in the securities markets.

Earnings Approach to Cost of Common Equity. In Chapter 3 we discussed the price/earnings ratio as a rough indicator of market valuation. This relationship is the simplest way of approximating the cost of common equity. Because we're interested in a measure of the opportunity cost of common equity (k_e), we'll use projected earnings per share as related to the current market price of the stock:

$$\text{Cost of equity} \;=\; \frac{\text{Projected earnings per share}}{\text{Current market price per share}}$$

$$k_e \;=\; \frac{eps}{p}$$

or

$$\text{Cost of equity} \;=\; \frac{1}{\text{Price/earnings ratio}}$$

$$k_e \;=\; \frac{1}{P/E}$$

This result is based on the implicit assumption that all of the firm's earnings will be paid out to the shareholders, which isn't realistic. At the same time, the measure doesn't allow for the effect of any reinvested earnings creating further value for the shareholders. Finally, the result is static in that future growth in earnings is ignored.

If the first assumption about a 100 percent dividend payout holds, an alternative way of estimating the cost of equity would be to project, year by year, the expected earnings pattern and to find the discount rate that would equate these aftertax earnings with the current market value, adjusted for a terminal value at the time the analysis is cut off. Clearly, the number of assumptions we must make for the analysis to be valid multiplies rapidly under these conditions. This simple measure therefore is at best a rough approximation.

Dividend Approach to Cost of Common Equity. A more direct way of dealing with at least one of the measurable benefits obtained by the shareholder is to use annual dividends to estimate the cost of common equity. Yet the approach also suffers from serious oversimplification because companies vary greatly in their rate of dividend payout, and the effect of reinvestment of retained earnings is again ignored. In its simplest form, the dividend approach is the same as the dividend yield we discussed as one of the market indicators in Chapter 3:

$$\text{Cost of common equity} = \frac{\text{Projected dividend per share}}{\text{Current market price per share}}$$

$$k_e = \frac{dps}{P}$$

Introducing growth in dividends into the formula is an improvement that partially accounts for the reinvestment portion of the value received by shareholders. The assumption here is that successful reinvestment of retained earnings will lead to growing earnings and thus growing dividends. The mathematics of the formula allow us simply to add the assumed rate of growth in dividends to the preceding equation. We again begin with the dividend yield and add a stable percentage rate of dividend growth (g) to simulate the economic expectations of the shareholders:

$$k_e = \frac{dps}{P} + g$$

The difficulty, however, lies in determining the dividend growth rate, which must be based on our best assumptions about future performance, tempered by past experience. Many estimating processes can be used. In Chapter 5 we discussed the concept of sustainable growth, given stable policies on investment, payout, and financing. This may yield clues to the growth rate that can be applied with the dividend approach, but again a great deal of judgment must be exercised in projecting expected future dividend policies set by the company's directors. If significant changes in policies are forecast, the analyst may want to modify the approach, making a series of year-by-year assumptions and in effect calculating a composite of future dividend growth patterns from these yearly forecasts.

A word about taxes is necessary here. In both the earnings and the dividend approaches, we're dealing with aftertax values from the company's point of view. Earnings per share are stated after taxes, while common dividends, like preferred dividends, aren't deductible and paid out of aftertax earnings. No adjustment is therefore necessary in the results to make them comparable with the aftertax cost of debt and preferred stock.

The investor likewise is judging the opportunity to earn an economic return in these terms. However, interest and dividends are taxable income to the recipient. Therefore, because personal tax conditions vary greatly, one more adjustment is necessary from the investor's point of view to assess investment options objectively. Yet the business analyst can't perform the precise calculation without knowing the individual's tax status. Consequently, the only working assumption we can make in this context is that most investors are subject to some taxation; we can arrive at financial results that are consistent up to the point that the individual investor must calculate the personal tax impact.

Risk Assessment Approach to Cost of Common Equity. As we said earlier, the risk assessment method doesn't rely on specific estimations of present and future earnings or dividends. Instead, a *normal market return* is developed from published data on financial returns and yields, which is adjusted by a *company-specific risk premium or discount.* The rationale is the assumption that a company's cost of equity in terms of shareholder return expectations is related to the *relative risk* of its common stock. The greater this relative risk, the greater the premium—in the form of an additional economic return over and above a normalized return—that should be expected by an investor. This approach makes intuitive sense and can also be demonstrated statistically.

At any time the securities markets yield a spread of rates of return ranging from those on essentially risk-free government securities at the low end of the scale to the sizable returns from highly speculative securities, including high-yield but risky junk bonds. The risk/return trade-off inherent in the many classes of security investments is reflected in this spread. Risk is defined as the *variability* of returns inherent in the type of security, while return is defined as the total *economic* return obtained from the security, including both interest or dividends and changes in market value.

The Capital Asset Pricing Model (CAPM). A number of specific methods have been developed over the years to express the risk premium concept of return on common equity—which reflects the cost of common equity to the corporation—as a methodology that's both theoretically acceptable and practically usable. While no individual method is totally satisfactory in these terms, the most widely accepted is the *capital asset pricing model (CAPM)*. We'll discuss some of its salient features here, but its extensive conceptual and theoretical underpinnings are far beyond the scope of this book. The references at the end of this chapter cover the evolution, theory, and validation of the CAPM.

Three elements are required in applying the capital asset pricing model approach, and each must be carefully estimated.

The first element is an estimate of the level of return from a risk-free security. The purpose is to find the lowest part of the range of yields currently experienced in the security markets as the starting point from which to build up the higher, risk-adjusted return specific to the particular common stock. Long-term U.S. government obligations are commonly used as a surrogate for such a risk-free return. The yields on U.S. government obligations are widely quoted and accessible, both for the present and for historical periods. For purposes of analysis, current yields can be used, possibly adjusted for expected changes, such as the inflation outlook during the next several years. Precision isn't possible here, and reasonable approximations supported by the analyst's judgment are quite workable.

The second element is an estimate of the return from a comparable type of security of average risk. This is needed because the CAPM method develops a specific adjustment for the *relative* riskiness of the particular security as compared to an average or base line. For our common equity problem we can use an estimate of the total expected return for the Standard & Poor's 500 Index, a broad-based measure of the price levels of 500 widely traded companies' common stocks. Security analysts often project the total return—both dividends and market appreciation—expected from the companies represented in the index. Their projections are published in financial services and newsletters (see Appendix V). While the S&P 500 Index provides a broad-based estimate of return, more specific indexes could be chosen. Again, the analyst must exercise judgment in using projections of future economic returns. The main point is to obtain a reasonable approximation of the average return from average investments of the type being evaluated.

The third element required is an expression of relative risk, which is based on the *variability of returns* of the particular security being analyzed. The definition of risk is very specific in the CAPM method, which has caused some controversy. Risk isn't defined as total variability of returns, but rather, as the *covariance* of the particular stock's returns with those of assets of average risk. The assumption here is that an investor doesn't focus on the total variability of return experienced with each individual security, but rather on how each security affects the variability of the total return from the investor's portfolio.

Risk, therefore, is a very relative concept in the CAPM, and its specific definition may not be acceptable to everyone. We'll ignore the arguments pro and con this risk definition in our discussion and concentrate instead on how it's used in the CAPM to arrive at a company-specific return. The risk measure, in the form of the covariance of an individual stock's returns with that of the portfolio of stocks of average risk, is called *beta* (β). It's found by linear regression of past monthly total returns of the particular security against a base line such as the S&P 500 Index. Services like Value Line provide the current β for publicly traded securities as a matter of course.

How are these three elements combined to arrive at an expected return and, thus, the company's cost for a particular equity security? As we've said, the CAPM method defines the cost of common equity as the combination of the risk-free return and a risk premium that has been adjusted for the specific company risk.

The CAPM formula is

$$k_e = R_f + \beta(R_m - R_f)$$

where

k_e is the cost of capital.

R_f is the risk-free return.

β is the company's covariance of returns against the portfolio.

R_m is the average returns on common stocks.

β is expressed as a simple factor that's used to multiply the difference between the expected return on the average portfolio and the expected risk-free return. This difference, of course, equals the risk premium inherent in the portfolio. The β factor adjusts this average risk premium to reflect the *individual* stock's higher or lower relative riskiness. β goes above 1.0 as the relative risk of the stock exceeds the average, and drops below 1.0 when the relative risk is below average.

The calculation itself is quite simple, while deriving the inputs isn't, as we already observed. To illustrate, let's arbitrarily choose a risk-free rate of return of 9 percent, an S&P 500 return estimate of 13.5 percent, and a company with a fairly risky β of 1.4. The cost of equity in this hypothetical example would be

$$k_e = 9.0 + 1.4(13.5 - 9.0) = 15.3\%$$

composed of the risk-free return of 9 percent plus the calculated company-specific risk premium of 6.3 percent, for a total of 15.3 percent.

A large number of issues surface when the CAPM or related measures are used to derive the cost of securities. One of these, already mentioned, is the quality of the estimate of both the risk-free return and the average return on a portfolio of common stocks. While the return on long-term U.S. government securities is a reasonable surrogate for the former, estimating an average portfolio return is fraught with conceptual problems. If β is the sole indicator of relative risk, the nature of the portfolio against which covariance is measured is clearly important. Broad averages such as the S&P 500 may or may not be appropriate under the circumstances. Also, there's the problem of using past data, particularly for variability of returns, in estimating the future relationships that indicate shareholder expectations.

Consequently, the results of the CAPM calculations, as with most types of financial analysis, should be used with caution and a great deal of commonsense judgment.

Inflation.   So far we've been talking about the cost of capital without specific reference to the impact of inflation. We could do this because *no* adjustment is in fact needed. The risk-free return on a government bond does implicitly allow for the expected level of inflation inasmuch as expectations about future inflationary conditions affect the yield from such securities. When inflation abates, the yields decline—as dramatically occurred in the mid-1980s and early 1990s. When inflation expectations rise, so do bond yields. The same is true of yields from other financial instruments.

If no inflation existed, risk-free returns would probably be in the range of 3 to 4 percent. In fact, not just the CAPM, but all of the measures of cost of capital we've been discussing include expected inflationary effects in that estimates of future returns take these expectations into account. The spectrum of returns ranging from risk-free bonds to those on speculative securities is also consistent in reflecting the effects of inflation.

To summarize, it should be obvious by now that the cost of common equity, apart from the specific method of calculation, is generally higher than the cost of interest-bearing securities or preferred stocks. As we said at the beginning of this section, the residual claim represented by common shares involves the highest risk/reward trade-off. Thus, returns expected of common shares are higher, which in turn must translate into the highest cost of capital from the corporation's standpoint. This fact will become even more important when we examine the alternative choices of financing new funds requirements, the subject of the next chapter.

WEIGHTED COST OF CAPITAL

Having determined the specific costs of the various types of capital individually, we now have all the specific cost inputs needed to make some of the funding decisions listed earlier. But because most companies use more than one form of long-term capital in funding investments and operations, and because over time the mix of sources used for long-term financing may change, we must examine the cost of the company's capital structure as a whole. The result we're looking for is a cost of capital figure that's weighted to reflect the differences in the various sources used. It encompasses the cost of compensating long-term creditors and preferred shareholders in terms of the specific provisions applicable to them, and rewarding the holders of common stock in terms of the expected risk-adjusted return.

Several issues have to be resolved in determining an overall corporate cost of capital. The first is generating appropriate costs for the different types of long-term capital employed, which we've already done conceptually. The second is a decision about the weights, or proportions of each type of capital in the structure to be analyzed. The third is the question of whether to apply market values versus book values of the various categories of capital in arriving at the weighting. Only then can we calculate a weighted cost of capital that's meaningful for the intended purpose.

Cost

First to be resolved is the question of whether it's relevant to consider the *past* costs of existing securities in a company's capital structure or, alternatively, the *incremental* costs involved in adding newly issued securities. Often the debt and preferred stock section of the balance sheet lists a whole array of past issues, many of which carry interest or dividend rates that differ significantly from current experience. Obligations that are 10, 15, or 20 years old likely carry stated costs that are no longer relevant today. Moreover, the various methods of arriving at the cost of common equity were based on future expectations, which aren't necessarily consistent with past debt or preferred costs. To solve this dilemma we must remember the principle established early in this book: The purpose of the analysis always determines the choice of data and methodology.

Normally, the key purpose of calculating a weighted cost of capital is for use in making decisions about new capital investments which are judged against a standard of return that will adequately compensate all providers of capital. Unless a company undergoes significant restructuring, the funds for new capital commitments are likely to come from current internal cash flow, augmented by new debt, new equity, or both. This is an *incremental* condition in that the choices for adding new investments are still being made. As we already know, past decisions on investments and financing are *sunk costs*. Consequently, the cost of capital measure most appropriate here is based on the incremental costs of the various forms of capital employed by the company.

Weighting

As we mentioned, we are deriving a weighted cost that reflects the proportions of the different types of capital in a company's capital structure. Again, significant issues arise. The current capital structure as reflected on the balance sheet is the result of past management decisions on funding both investments and operations. The question to be asked here is whether the types and proportions of capital in this capital structure are likely to hold in the future (i.e., whether they match the strategic plans of management). The intended capital budget supporting the company's future strategy, particularly when calling for sizable outlays, may indeed cause significant changes in a firm's long-term financing pattern. Also, management may choose to make gradual modifications to its financial policies that, over time, can cause sizable shifts in the capital structure. (Recall Chapter 5's discussion of the impact of policy changes.)

In other cases, management may well be satisfied with the current proportions of the company's capital structure as a long-term objective. Yet raising the incremental capital required from time to time is normally done in blocks limited to one form of security, that is, debt, preferred stock, or common equity. Therefore, in the near term any one type of capital may be emphasized more than the long-term proportions desired would suggest. Capital must be raised in response to market conditions, and the choice of which type is appropriate at any given point is based on a series of considerations that we'll explore in the next chapter.

The analyst has to resolve the dilemma caused by such divergences through judgment. Given the fact that a company never remains static in the long run, the choice of proportions has to be a compromise intended to approximate the conditions relevant for purposes of analysis, and precision becomes secondary to common sense. Current proportions are a good starting point, but should normally be modified by specific assumptions about the future direction of the company's long-term financing. It may also be useful to generate a range of assumptions to bracket the findings, which is a form of sensitivity analysis.

Market Value versus Book Value

The weights to be assigned to different types of capital are clearly going to be different if we choose to apply current market values as contrasted with the stated values on the right-hand side of the balance sheet. Again we must be guided by the purpose of the analysis to decide which value is relevant. If we're deriving a criterion against which to judge expected returns from future investments, we should use the current market values of the various types of capital of the company because these values reflect the expectations of both creditors and shareholders. The latter certainly didn't invest in the book value of common equity, which may differ significantly from the current share value as traded in the market. Further, management's obligation is to meet shareholders' expectations in terms of the future economic value to be created by investments and operations, and to compensate creditors out of future earnings. Stated book values, as we've observed, are static and not responsive to changing performance.

The choice of market values also complements the use of incremental funding in that both are expressed in current market terms. The market value of common equity automatically (and implicitly) includes retained earnings as reported on the balance sheet. Although many people feel that retained earnings bear no cost, this is a misconception. In fact, retained earnings represent part of the residual claim of the shareholders even if they're imperfectly valued on the balance sheet because of accounting conventions.

In this area there are again conceptual issues and arguments that can be raised for and against market value weights. One of these concerns a company experiencing financing requirements rather different from the historical pattern reflected in its capital structure. There it can be argued that a book value approach may be more suitable. Again we must leave the in-depth exploration of these concepts to the reader, as they go beyond the scope of this book.

Calculation of Weighted Cost of Capital

Now let's turn to a simplified example of calculating a weighted cost of capital for a hypothetical company. This will allow us to demonstrate the basic mechanics of what we now understand to be a process that involves a great deal of judgment. We'll use the condensed balance sheet of ABC Corporation in Figure 7–2, augmented by some additional data and assumptions.

The company has three types of long-term capital: debt, preferred stock, and common equity. We assume that it could issue new bonds at an effective cost of 12 percent, and new preferred stock at an effective cost of

FIGURE 7–2
ABC CORPORATION
Condensed Balance Sheet
($ thousands)

Assets		Liabilities and Net Worth	
Current assets	$27,500	Current liabilities	$ 9,500
Fixed assets (net)	35,000	Bonds (10%)	12,000
Other assets	1,500	Preferred stock (12%)	6,000
Total assets	$64,000	Common stock (1.0 million shares)	10,000
		Retained earnings	26,500
		Total liabilities and net worth	$64,000

13 percent, based on proceeds from expected pricing in the market and after applicable underwriting and legal expenses. Note that these current costs are above the rates the company has been paying on its long-term capital as stated in the balance sheet. ABC's common stock is currently trading between $63 and $67, and the most recent earnings per share were $4.72. Dividends per share last year were $2.50. The company's β, as calculated by security analysts, is 1.1, a fairly average risk. We further assume that the estimated risk-free return is 8.5 percent, and the best available forecast for the total return from the S&P 500 is 15 percent.

Overall company prospects are assumed to be satisfactory, and security analysts are forecasting normal growth in earnings at about 6 percent. Given this background, we can calculate a weighted cost of capital. As we proceed, the choices to be made will be highlighted.

The respective costs of the three types of capital employed can be derived as shown next. Note that we're employing the *incremental* cost of funds in each case, rather than the *past* costs as reflected in the balance sheet, where outstanding bonds carry a rate of 10 percent and preferred stock has a dividend rate of 12 percent. Using the methods discussed earlier, the calculations for each type of capital are

Long-term debt: k_d = 12.0 × (1 − .34) = 7.92% after taxes
Preferred stock: k_p = 13.0% after taxes
Common equity: k_e = 8.5 + 1.1 (15.0−8.5) = 15.65% after taxes

The cost of debt was based on the effective cost of 12 percent, adjusted for taxes, while the effective cost of preferred stock provided required no tax adjustment. The CAPM was used for the common equity calculation. The result for common equity should be compared to the less satisfactory answers obtained using the earnings or dividend approaches.

If we use the earnings approach, employing the average current market price of $65—or ($\frac{1}{2}$) ($63 + $67) —the following cost of common equity results:

$$\text{Common equity: } k_e = \frac{1}{\$65/\$4.72} = 7.31\% \text{ after taxes}$$

If we were to modify the formula to include expected growth in earnings (g), in this case where $g = 6$ percent, the result would come closer to the 15.65 percent cost derived using the CAPM:

$$\text{Common equity: } k_e = 7.31\% + 6.0\% = 13.31\% \text{ after taxes}$$

The dividend approach provides another alternative result, which is a function of the dividend rate and the expected growth rate:

$$\text{Common equity: } k_e = \frac{\$2.50}{\$65} + 6.0\% = 9.85\% \text{ after taxes}$$

It's not uncommon to find that the three approaches to determining the cost of equity provide rather different results, as the data and assumptions going into the calculations aren't comparable. Our earlier discussion of each measure highlighted the most significant issues.

The weights to be used in calculating the corporate cost of capital depend both on the relative stability of the current capital structure and the relevance of market values to the results. Let's assume that management is satisfied with the current capital structure and is likely to raise funds in the same proportions over time. Let's further assume that the company's existing bonds are currently trading at 83⅜ (a $1,000 bond with a coupon rate of 10 percent is worth a discounted price of about $837.50 in view of the increase in bond yields), while the existing preferred stock with a $12 dividend rate is trading at 92¼ because of the increase in yields (each share with a nominal value of $100 is currently worth about $92.25).

FIGURE 7-3
Capital Structure of ABC Corporation

	Book Value	Proportion	Market Value	Proportion
Bonds	$12,000	22.0%	$10,050	12.5%
Preferred stock	6,000	11.0	5,535	6.9
Common equity	36,500	67.0	65,000	80.6
Totals	$54,500	100.0%	$80,585	100.0%

FIGURE 7-4
Weighted Cost of Capital for ABC Corporation

	Book Value Weighting			Market Value Weighting		
	Cost	Weight	Composite	Cost	Weight	Composite
Bonds	7.92%	.22	1.74%	7.92%	.12	0.95%
Preferred stock	13.00	.11	1.43	13.00	.07	0.91
Common equity	15.65	.67	10.48	15.65	.81	12.68
Totals		1.00	13.65%		1.00	14.54%

As Figure 7–3 shows, the following proportions result when we list both book value and market value for each type of capital. Depending on the way management assesses its future needs, the proportions could remain as shown in the table, or they could be altogether different.

Assuming that no significant change is foreseen, we can calculate the weighted cost of capital for both the market and book value (Figure 7–4). The results don't differ materially in this case. Differences would become significant only after more than one percentage point.

Given that the assumptions and choices needed to make the calculations all involved a margin of error, the results should be liberally rounded off in all cases before the measure is used as a decision criterion. We can say that for ABC Corporation, under the stipulated conditions, the weighted cost of incremental capital is approximately 14 percent.

If the measure is used to judge the expected return from new investments, it would represent a minimum standard of return from investments with comparable risk characteristics. Under these conditions, the weighted cost of capital could be used as the discount rate to determine net present values as discussed in Chapter 6.

COST OF CAPITAL AND RETURN STANDARDS

We've stated all along that the basic purpose of deriving a weighted cost of capital was to find a reasonable criterion for measuring new investments. This amounts to establishing a level of return high enough to compensate all providers of funds according to their expectations. By implication, projects considered acceptable when their cash flows are discounted at this return standard would create economic value for the shareholder in the form of growing dividends and market appreciation.

However, using a weighted cost of capital for this purpose warrants further discussion. This section examines more closely the notion of this measure as a *cutoff rate* and then discusses the question of projects in different *risk categories.* It also reviews the problem of the *multi-business firm* in which a variety of *business risks* are combined. Finally, it touches on the issue of modified standards using *multiple discount rates.* In all of these areas a balance has to be found between the theoretically desirable and the practically doable.

Cost of Capital as a Cutoff Rate

In a *single-business company* with fairly definable risk characteristics, the weighted cost of capital as we've calculated it here can well serve as a cutoff rate in assessing capital investment projects ranked in declining order of economic desirability. If consistent analytical methods and judgments are applied to projecting the project cash flows, and if the risks inherent in the projects are similar and have been consistently estimated and tested through sensitivity analysis, then acceptance or rejection can be decided with this minimum return standard. We're assuming that the company can finance all of the projects being considered at the same incremental cost of capital and without significantly changing the capital structure.

The weighted cost of capital works well in this idealized condition because the risk premium built into the measure, the proportions of the sources of new funds, and the range of risks embodied in the projects are all consistent with each other and with the business risk inherent in the company. When some of these conditions change, however, managerial judgment must be exercised to modify the cost of capital and its application.

One common problem even in the single-business firm is the real possibility that the amount of potential capital spending will exceed the readily available financing to some degree. If the list of projects contains many that more than meet the standard, they may be attractive enough for management to modify the company's capital structure to accommodate them. Then the weighted cost of capital will likely change.

Increasing leverage may introduce additional risk, thus exerting upward pressure on the cost of both debt and equity. Increasing the equity base significantly will result in near-term dilution of earnings per share, thus affecting the stock's market value and possibly the β of the company's common stock as judged by security analysts. While the changes may be manageable, the point is that the process of business investment and the selection of appropriate standards is never a static exercise.

Another practical issue is management's attitude toward taking business risks. Knowing that the analyses underlying capital investment projects contain many uncertainties, management may wish to set the cutoff rate arbitrarily higher than the weighted cost of capital to allow for estimating error—and even for deliberate bias in preparation of the estimates, which isn't at all uncommon in most organizations as managers compete for funds. There may also be a desire to play it a little safer in view of the limited reliability of the return standard itself.

From a theoretical standpoint, using higher cutoff rates may cause opportunity losses in that potentially worthwhile projects are likely to be rejected. But from a practical standpoint, it may be deemed prudent to leave a margin for error. It's still possible, of course, at any time to reach below the higher standard if a project has many other strategic or operational advantages that mitigate the effects of its marginal economic performance.

Finally, we must reiterate that capital budgeting and project selection aren't merely numerical processes. Even in the most tightly focused single-product company, where all levels of management have first-hand knowledge about the business setting, the decision process is always a combination of judgments affected by personal preferences, group dynamics, and the pressures of organizational realities.

Risk Categories

By definition, the weighted cost of capital represents a company's unique relative risk and particular capital structure. Yet in a sense this is misleading because even in the single-business company, different capital investment projects will involve different degrees of risk. Normally, a company encounters a variety of classes of investments ranging from replacement of equipment and facilities to expansion in existing markets, and beyond that to ventures into new products or services and new markets.

The degrees of risk inherent in these classes of investments will differ, sometimes materially, even though the products and services involved are within the scope of a single industry with a definable overall risk. Replacement of physical assets to continue serving a proven market where the company holds a strong position clearly is far less risky and permits more reliable estimates of cash flow benefits than entering a new domestic or even international market.

A common way of handling such divergences is to set a higher discount standard for projects that are perceived to be riskier. A hierarchy of minimum rates of return can be established, somewhat arbitrarily, that ranges upward from the weighted cost of capital cutoff point. For example, if the weighted cost of capital is, say, 15 percent, that standard may be applied to ordinary replacements and expansion in markets where the company has a position. A standard of 16 or 17 percent may be applied to entering related markets, while a new venture may be measured at a premium standard of even 20 percent or higher.

As we demonstrated earlier in discussing the power of discounting, particularly at the higher rates, the chances of riskier projects being acceptable will be severely tested under such conditions. Yet such a demanding risk/reward trade-off standard may be appropriate if management's risk preferences are modest.

On the other hand, it's often argued—particularly with single-business companies—that the weighted cost of capital implicitly embodies the whole range of risks normally encountered while participating and growing in that business. Consequently, the argument is advanced that the range of discount standards should be grouped around the weighted cost of capital. In effect, this allows the less risky projects to be discounted at a return standard below the weighted cost of capital, while riskier ones would be tested at or above that level. When all projects are combined, the result should be an average return at or above the weighted cost of capital.

This approach would require, however, that the proportions of projects being approved in the various risk classes be carefully monitored to ensure that the overall average will achieve the desired result over time. Otherwise, the company could encounter significant deviations from expected performance. Moreover, we must remember that shareholder value can grow only if investment returns exceed the cost of capital in the long run.

An additional practical issue tends to support raising the return standards for the different classes of capital projects. Every company faces a certain percentage of capital expenditures that yield no definable cash flow benefits. Among these are mandated outlays for environmental protection, investments for improved infrastructure of facilities, and expenditures for office space and equipment.

A strong argument can be made that funds required for these purposes must in fact be economically carried along by the expected cash flow benefits obtained from all other productive investments. By definition, therefore, the total amount of capital invested should provide a return sufficient to meet or exceed the weighted cost of capital. If some part of the capital budget is economically neutral, the returns from the economically positive projects must be higher to make up for such "nonproductive" investments. If management chooses to adjust its return standards for this condition, the modification will likely involve a fair degree of judgment about the mix and characteristics of the expected project portfolio.

Our discussion has gone beyond the purely analytical aspects of the subject and we've pointed out many practical issues involved in choosing and using economic measures for business decisions, of which discount standards are only one form. Remember that the actual procedures employed by a company are likely to allow for a fair degree of judgmental override of the quantitative results of any financial analysis. This includes the specific return standards for capital investments, which are likely to be modified from time to time, to assist not only in project-specific economic assessment, but also in shifting the strategic emphasis between classes of investments. Senior management must, of course, continuously monitor and guide the pattern of investments they wish to undertake so that shareholder expectations are met. The pattern of investments suggested by the economic analyses and the return standards can and should be modified to fit a firm's changing strategic direction.

Cost of Capital in Multibusiness Companies

The issues involved in setting appropriate return standards become even more complex when a company has several divisions or subsidiaries engaged in rather different businesses and markets that vary greatly in their risk characteristics. While we can calculate a company's overall cost of capital with the help of a β that reflects the company's covariance of consolidated returns with the market return, it's far harder to derive the equivalent cost of capital standards for the individual operating divisions. Most commonly a multibusiness company has a single capital structure that supplies funds for the various businesses. Therefore, capital can't be apportioned to the different risk categories on the basis of individual cost of capital standards that employ specific βs and debt ratings. These would be available only if the divisions were autonomous companies whose shares are traded in the securities markets.

The approach often used under such conditions is to estimate a series of surrogate costs of capital based on costs for comparable independent companies, if this is at all possible. In this way a group of individual standards can be developed for the multibusiness company—modified with a great deal of judgment—that are similar to the array of risk categories in a single-business company.

Obviously, the apportionment of capital in a multibusiness setting is also complicated by the practical issue of divisional management competing for limited funds while having to meet different standards. Corporate management must be very careful first to establish broad allocations of funds to the various operating divisions that match the desired corporate strategic emphasis. Then projects can be ranked within those individual blocks of allocated funds according to the different discount rates, and decisions can be made to accept or reject specific investments.

A predictable consequence of such an approach, however, is the dilemma of having to refuse specific higher return (and higher risk) opportunities in one division, whose overall allocation is exhausted, in favor of lower return (and lower risk) opportunities in another division. This dilemma has to be resolved at the corporate management level where the total company's strategic direction is developed and monitored. The main point to remember is that top management needs to shape the company's overall capital investment portfolio in line with shareholder expectations, so that the sum of the parts can be expected to meet or exceed the corporate weighted cost of capital standard.

As we'll discuss in Chapter 9, the cost of capital is also used to determine whether individual lines of business in a diversified company are contributing to or detracting from shareholder value. The point in this application is to test past and prospective overall cash flows from each business unit as a whole in relation to a minimum cash flow return standard based on the cost of capital.

Multiple Rate Analysis

One additional technical observation should be made here. Some practitioners argue for applying different discount rates to different portions of the cash flow pattern of a single project when calculating the measures of economic desirability to reflect the relative risk of the various elements of the project. In effect, this is one more risk adjustment beyond the risk premium already inherent in a particular discount standard. There are many variations of this approach, although it's not widely used in practice.

It should be apparent that the uncertainties inherent in project analysis and complexities of establishing the standards for multiple rate analysis may not be warranted in most normal business investment situations. At the same time, they may indeed be necessary in assessing specialized projects, such as real estate investments, complex leasing proposals, and other uniquely structured cash flow proposals. Such special conditions may involve financial contracts integral to the projects themselves.

In those cases it's warranted to discount portions of project cash flows at rates that reflect their contractual nature, as compared with other portions of the cash flow pattern that are subject to the uncertainties of operating in the business environment. These analytical refinements are too specific to be covered here, but are dealt with in the references listed at the end of the chapter.

KEY ISSUES

The following is a recap of the key issues raised directly or indirectly in this chapter. We enumerate them here to help you keep the techniques discussed within the perspective of financial theory and business practice.

1. The specific costs to a company of various types of indebtedness and preferred securities are readily apparent in the tax-adjusted cash obligations involved, but it's difficult to measure the secondary costs implicit in debt service, credit rating, and market assessment.

2. Determining the cost of equity capital is intricately linked to the risk/reward expectations of the financial markets because the cost must be expressed in terms of an expected economic return for the company's shareholders.

3. Simple surrogates for the cost of equity capital, such as earnings and dividend models, suffer both from variability of underlying conditions (which can distort their results) and from conceptual shortcomings.

4. The conceptual link established by modern financial theory between general financial market expectations and the value of an individual company's equity securities remains an approximation based on a series of simplifying assumptions.

5. The use of a company-specific risk factor (β) to adjust average return expectations is a valid theoretical concept, but both definition and measurement of this factor remain open to disagreement and continue to pose practical problems.

6. The development of a weighted cost of capital raises significant questions not only regarding the elements comprising the various costs, but also regarding the weights to be used and the concept of measuring incremental funding.

7. The use of a weighted cost of capital in setting capital investment return standards is conceptually useful for projects within a company's normal range of risk, but the measure may need modification for business investments of dissimilar risk.

8. The theory of finance continues to evolve, but as concepts generated are introduced and refined in the decision making process, careful linkages to both data sources and to the organization have to be established to make practical application both understandable and feasible.

9. Objective analytical approaches to capital investment assessment are only one important input in the choices management must make. Individual and group attitudes, preferences, and judgments exert significant influences over interpretation and decision processes in the areas of investment, operations, and financing.

10. The precision implied in the calculations of economic measures like cost of capital or net present value must be tempered by the knowledge that the data and assumptions underlying them are potentially subject to a wide range of error.

SUMMARY

In this chapter we've sketched out the rationale for determining the costs of various forms of financing as an input in making different types of financial decisions. We found that the specific cost of debt, both short-term and long-term, was relatively easy to calculate, given the nature of the contracts underlying it in most cases. The same was true for preferred stock. We also found that the fixed nature of the obligations incurred with debt and preferred stock raised a host of secondary considerations that exact an economic cost from the company in terms of debt service and restrictive covenants. Establishing the cost of common equity was particularly challenging because of the residual claim common shareholders have on the company, and because of their risk/reward expectations which are reflected in the market's valuation of the shares.

Once we discussed techniques for calculating the respective costs of the three basic types of financing, and pointed out the theoretical and practical caveats, we developed the weighted cost of capital as an input in investment analysis. Here we found that the application of the weighted cost of capital as a minimum standard for discounting investment cash flows is affected by the way project and business risks are interpreted within the corporate portfolio, and by the attitudes of corporate decision makers. At the same time, we found the approximate weighted cost of capital to be a conceptually appropriate target around which to build a series of return standards befitting a particular company's range of businesses and the investments and risks connected with them.

SELECTED REFERENCES

Brealey, Richard, and Stewart Myers. *Principles of Corporate Finance.* 3rd ed. New York: McGraw-Hill, 1988.

Harrington, Diana R. *Modern Portfolio Theory. The Capital Asset Pricing Model and Arbitrage Pricing Theory: A Users' Guide.* 2nd ed. Englewood Cliffs, N.J.: Prentice Hall, 1986.

Mullins, David W., Jr. "Does the Capital Asset Pricing Model Work?" *Harvard Business Review,* January-February 1982, pp. 105–14.

Solomon, Ezra, and John J. Pringle. *An Introduction to Financial Management.* 2nd ed. Santa Monica, Calif.: Goodyear, 1980.

Van Horne, James C. *Financial Management and Policy.* 7th ed. Englewood Cliffs, N.J.: Prentice Hall, 1986.

Weston, J. Fred, and Thomas E. Copeland. *Managerial Finance.* 8th ed. Hinsdale, Ill.: Dryden Press, 1986.

SELF-STUDY EXERCISES AND PROBLEMS

(Solutions are provided in Appendix VI)

1. The GHI company has three types of capital in its capital structure:

   Long-term debt at 12%. (Current yield is 10%.)
   14% preferred stock. (Current yield is 12%.)
   Common stock with a book value of $67.50 per share.

   Currently, the company's common stock is trading in the range of $75 to $82; the most recent closing price was $77. The most recent annual earnings per share were $9.50, while dividends paid over the past year were at the rate of $4.50 per share. The company's earnings have been growing on average about 7 percent per year. *Value Line* lists the company's β at 1.25, while the risk-free return is estimated to be 9%. Forecasts for returns from the S&P 500 are currently about 15%. Calculate the specific cost of capital for each type of capital of GHI Company. Assume a tax rate of 34 percent. Discuss your findings.

2. The KLN Company has the following capital structure:

	Proportion	Existing Conditions	Current (Incremental)
Long-term debt	$250	7% average rate	11% yield
Preferred stock	50	6% stated rate	9% yield
Common equity	400	—	Price range $45–$60
(10 million shares) ...			(Recent price $50)
Total capitalization	$700		

The company's β is currently estimated at 1.2, while the risk-free return in considered to be 7.5 percent. The most recent estimate of the return from the S&P 500 is 13.5 percent. Develop the weighted corporate cost of capital for KLN Company for both the existing conditions (original costs) and incremental conditions. Also use both a book value and a market value weighting for each case. Assume a tax rate of 34 percent. Discuss your findings and the range of results achieved.

8 ANALYSIS OF FINANCING CHOICES

It's now time to turn to the analysis of the final portion of the three-part decisional systems context introduced in Chapter 1—investment, operations, and *financing*. We'll concentrate on analyzing the choices available in long-term financing, setting aside the incremental operational funds sources that are used fairly routinely by companies in accordance with the customs of a particular industry or service. This focus is chosen because, as we observed in earlier chapters, the nature and pattern of long-term funding sources is intricately connected with the types of investments made, and is critical to the growth, stability, or decline of operations. As we've said, management must fund its strategic design with an appropriate mix of capital sources that will assist in bringing about the desired increase in shareholder value.

This chapter will deal with the main considerations in

assessing the basic financing options open to management. Even though the choice among debt, preferred, and common equity is blurred by the bewildering array of modifications and specialized instruments in each category, we'll only focus on the main characteristics of the three basic types of securities. While the emphasis is on quantitative analysis, you must realize that many other considerations enter into these choices. For example, the specific types of business and the industry in which it operates will affect the long-term capital structure chosen at various stages of a company's development, as will the preferences and experiences of senior management and the board of directors. These aspects can't be adequately covered within the scope of this book.

We'll begin with a framework for analysis that defines the key areas to be analyzed and weighed in choosing sources of long-term financing. Next we'll look at the techniques of calculating the impact on a company's financial performance brought about by introducing new capital from each of the three basic sources. Then we'll turn to a commonly used form of graphic representation, the *EBIT break-even chart*, to demonstrate the dynamic impact funds choices have on changing company conditions. After touching on leasing as a special source, we'll list the key issues involved in funds choices.

FRAMEWORK FOR ANALYSIS

Several key elements must be considered and weighed when a company is faced with raising additional (incremental) long-term funds. We'll take up five of these in some detail: *cost, risk exposure, flexibility, timing,* and *control.* The analyst can use this framework as a conceptual checklist to ensure that the most important considerations have been covered.

Cost of Incremental Funds

One of the main criteria for choosing from among alternative sources of additional long-term capital is the cost involved in obtaining and servicing the funds. Chapter 7 detailed the specific and implicit costs a company incurs in using debt, preferred stock, or common equity.

As a general rule we found that funds raised through various forms of debt are least costly in specific terms, in part because the interest paid by the borrowing company is tax deductible under current laws. The actual rate of interest charged on incremental debt will depend, of course, on the credit rating of the company and on the degree of change introduced into the capital structure by the new debt. In other words, the specific cost will be affected not only by current market conditions for all long-term debt instruments, but also by the company-specific risk as perceived by the underwriters and investors. As mentioned earlier, other costs are also implicit in raising long-term debt, including legal and underwriting expenses at the time of issue, and the nature and severity of any restrictions imposed by creditors.

The stated cost of preferred stock is generally higher than debt, partly because preferred dividends paid aren't tax deductible, and partly because preferred stock has a somewhat weaker position on the risk/reward hierarchy, so that holders of these shares expect a higher return. The comparative specific cost of preferred stock is relatively easy to calculate. The dividend level is clearly defined, and legal and underwriting costs incurred at the time of the issue are reflected in the net proceeds to the company. However, a variety of specific provisions could involve implicit costs to the company.

Determining the cost of common equity turned out to be a fairly complex task. It involved constructing a theoretical framework within which to assess the risk/reward expectations of the shareholder. Direct approaches (shortcuts) to measuring the specific cost of common equity were found wanting because they didn't address the company's relative risk as reflected in common share values. Therefore, we had to use a more complex framework involving some surrogates and approximations to arrive at a practical result based on the theoretical model.

The approximate cost of common equity based on the CAPM approach could be directly compared to the specific costs of debt and preferred stock, and it could also be used to arrive at a weighted overall cost of the company's capital structure. But as we'll see shortly, increasing common equity in the capital structure by issuing new shares involves additional considerations. The incremental shares dilute earnings per share, require additional and even growing dividends where these are paid, and also change the capital structure proportions. Such effects amount to implicit economic costs or advantages in the funding picture.

Risk Exposure

If we use *variability of earnings* as a working definition of risk, we find that a company's risk is affected by the specific cost commitments—such as interest on debt, or dividends on preferred shares—that each funding source entails. These commitments introduce financial leverage effects in the company's earnings performance, or heighten any financial leverage already existing. As we discussed in Chapter 5, use of instruments involving fixed financial charges will widen the swings in earnings as economic and operating conditions change.

Being responsible for providing holders of common shares with growing economic value, management must therefore expend much thought and care in determining the appropriate mix of debt and equity in their company's capital structure. This balance involves providing enough lower-cost debt to boost the shareholders' returns, but not so much debt as to endanger share-holder value creation during periods of low earnings.

The ultimate risk, of course, is that a company won't be able to fulfill its debt service obligations. The proportion of debt in the capital structure and, similarly, the proportion of preferred stock affects the degree of risk of partial or total default. The analysis of risk exposure is based on establishing a historical pattern of earnings variability and cash flows from which future conditions are projected. These must take into account the extent to which a company's strategy is changing, any shifts in exposure to the business cycle, shifting competitive pressures, and potential operating inefficiencies.

Clearly, company-specific risk (earnings variability) and the company's ability to service its debt burden are intimately related to the particular characteristics of the business or businesses in which the company operates. Moreover, they're affected by general economic conditions—apart from management's ability to generate satisfactory operating performance.

The degree of financial leverage advisable and prudent will therefore differ greatly for different industries and services, and will also depend on the firm's relative competitive position and maturity stage. A business just starting up entails a far different risk exposure for the creditor than does the established industry leader, apart from the specific industry situation.

Flexibility

The third area that must be considered is flexibility, defined here as the range of future funding options remaining once a specific alternative has been chosen. As each increment of financing is completed, the choice among future alternatives may be more limited on the next round. For example, if long-term debt obligations are chosen as a funding source, restrictive covenants, encumbered assets, and other constraints that impose minimum financial ratios may mean that the company can only use common equity as a future source of capital for some time.

Flexibility essentially involves forward planning. Consideration must be given to strategic plans and to matching corporate financial policies. Potential acquisitions, expansion, and diversification all are affected by the degree of flexibility management has in choosing proper funding, and by the funds drain resulting from servicing debt commitments. To the extent possible, management must match its planned future funds flows and investment patterns to the pattern of successive rounds of financing that will support them. Having future funds sources limited to one option because of present commitments poses an additional problem. Changing conditions in the financial markets for different types of securities may make this single option less appealing or even infeasible when funds needs are critical.

Timing

The fourth element in choosing long-term funding is timing of the transaction. Timing is important in relation to the movement of prices and yields in the securities markets. Shifting conditions in these markets affect the specific cost a company will incur with each option in terms of (1) the stated interest or the preferred dividend rate carried by the new debt or preferred stock and (2) the proceeds to be received from each of the alternatives. Timing of the issue will therefore affect the cost spread between the several funding alternatives. At times, market conditions may in fact either preclude or distinctly favor particular choices.

For instance, in times of depressed stock prices, bonds may prove to be the most suitable alternative from the standpoint of both cost and market demand. Inasmuch as the proceeds from any issue depend on the success of the placement—public or private—of the securities, the conditions in the stock or bond markets at the moment may seriously affect the choice. Uncertainty in financial markets is therefore a strong argument for always maintaining some degree of flexibility in the capital structure.

Control

Finally, from a funding standpoint, the degree of control over the company exerted by existing shareholders is an important factor. As should be obvious, when new shares of common stock are issued to others, the effect is dilution of both earnings per share and the proportion of ownership of the existing shareholders. In the past decade, the issue of control has been raised to new heights in the many battles over control during the corporate takeover boom.

Even if debt or preferred stock is used as the source of long-term funding, existing shareholders may be indirectly affected because restrictive provisions and covenants are necessary to obtain bond financing, or because concessions must be made to protect the rights of the more senior preferred shareholders.

Dilution of ownership is an important issue in closely held corporations, particularly new ventures. In such situations, founders of the company or majority shareholders may exercise full effective control over the company. Issuing new shares will dilute both control over the direction of the company and the key shareholders' ability to enjoy the major share of the appreciation of economic value from successful performance. The dilution of earnings and the possible retardation of growth in earnings per share brought about by diluting common equity ownership is, of course, not limited to closely held companies. Rather, it's a general phenomenon that we'll discuss shortly.

Finally, dilution of control and earnings is a major consideration in *convertibility*, a common feature found in certain bonds and preferred stocks. This provision allows conversion of the security into common stock under specified conditions of timing and price. In effect, such instruments are hybrid securities as they represent delayed issues of common stock at a price higher than the market value of the common stock at the time the convertible bond or preferred stock is issued. We mentioned this feature in earlier chapters in terms of its effect on financial ratios, particularly the concept of fully diluted earnings per share, and we'll return to it later in this chapter.

Control becomes an issue in convertible financing options because the eventual conversion of the bond or preferred stock will add new common shares to the capital structure and thus cause dilution. The effect is just like a direct issue of common stock.

The Choice

It should be clear from this brief résumé of the considerations involved that any decision about alternative sources of long-term funding can't be based on cost alone even though cost is a very important factor and must be analyzed early in the decision-making process. Unfortunately, there are no hard and fast rules spelling out precisely how the final decision should be made because the choice depends so much on the circumstances prevailing in the company and in the securities markets at the time. The best approach is to consider carefully the five areas we've just presented and to examine the pros and cons of each as an input to the decision. Needless to say, a very significant consideration is the effect of each funding source on a company's future earnings performance. In the section that follows, we'll examine methods of calculating this effect.

TECHNIQUES OF CALCULATION

For purposes of illustration, we'll employ the basic statements of a hypothetical company, ABC Corporation. The company is weighing alternative ways of

FIGURE 8–1
ABC CORPORATION
Balance Sheet
($ millions)

Assets		Liabilities and Net Worth	
Current assets	$15	Current liabilities	$ 7
Fixed assets (net)	29	Common stock	10
Other assets	1	Retained earnings	28
Total assets	$45	Total liabilities and net worth	$45

raising $10 million to support the introduction of a new product. After analyzing the corporation's current performance, we'll successively discuss the impact on that performance level caused by introducing long-term debt, preferred stock, and common equity in equal amounts of $10 million each.

ABC's abbreviated balance sheet is shown in Figure 8–1. The company currently has 1 million shares of common stock outstanding with a par value of $10 per share. From the company's operating statement (not shown), we learned that ABC Corporation has earned $9 million before taxes on sales of $115 million in the most recent year. Income taxes paid amounted to $3.06 million, an effective rate of 34 percent.

Current Performance

We begin our appraisal of the current performance of ABC Corporation by calculating the earnings per share (EPS) of common stock. Throughout the chapter, this format of calculating EPS and related measures will be used. It's a step-by-step analysis of the earnings impact of each type of long-term capital.

First, we state the earnings before interest and taxes (EBIT), a measure discussed in Chapter 3. From that figure we must subtract a variety of charges applicable to different long-term funds. The first of these is interest charges on long-term debt. Normally short-term

FIGURE 8–2
ABC CORPORATION
Earnings per Share Calculation
($ thousands, except per share figures)

Earnings before interest and taxes (EBIT)	$9,000
Less: Interest charges on long-term debt	–0–
Earnings before income taxes	9,000
Less: Federal income taxes at 34%	3,060
Earnings after income taxes	5,940
Less: Preferred dividends	–0–
Earnings available for common stock	$5,940
Common shares outstanding (number)	1 million
Earnings per share (EPS)	$ 5.94
Less: Common dividends per share	2.50
Retained earnings per share	$ 3.44
Retained earnings in total	$3,440

interest can be ignored unless it's a significant amount because we assume, given the temporary nature of short-term obligations that arise from ongoing operations, that the related interest charges have been properly deducted from income before arriving at the EBIT figure.

The calculations of earnings per share are shown in Figure 8–2. Provision is made for both long-term interest and preferred dividends. No amounts are shown for these as yet, however, because our hypothetical company at this point has neither long-term debt nor preferred stock outstanding. The calculations result in earnings available to common stock of $5.94 per share. From that figure $2.50 has been subtracted, which represents a cash dividend voted by the board of directors. We assume that this level of dividend payout (between 40 and 50 percent of earnings) has been maintained for many years. We further assume that earnings have steadily grown by about 4 percent on average over the past decade.

The stock is widely held and traded, and currently commands a market price ranging from about $38 to

$47, which means it's trading at roughly seven to eight times earnings. The latest security analyst's report suggests a β of 0.9, while the risk-free rate of return is judged to be 6.5 percent, and the average expected return from the S&P 500 is forecast at 14.0 percent.

Long-Term Debt in the Capital Structure

As debt is introduced into this structure, both the financial condition and the earnings performance of ABC Corporation are significantly affected. To raise the $10 million needed to fund the new product, management has found that it's possible, as one alternative, to issue debenture bonds. Debentures are unsecured by any specific assets of the company; instead they're issued against the company's general credit standing. These bonds, under current market conditions, carry an interest (coupon) rate of 11.5 percent, become due 20 years from date of issue, and entail a sinking fund provision of $400,000 per year beginning with the fifth year. The balance outstanding at the end of 20 years will be repaid as a balloon payment of $4 million. The company expects to raise the full $10 million from the bond issue after all underwriting expenses, in effect receiving the par value.

Once the new product financed with the proceeds has been successfully introduced, the company projects incremental earnings of at least $2.0 million before taxes. Little risk of product obsolescence or major competitive inroads are expected by management for the next 5 to 10 years because the company has developed a unique process protected by careful patent coverage.

We can now trace the impact of long-term debt on the company's performance, observing both the change in earnings and dividends, and the specific cost of the newly created debt itself. We'll analyze two contrasting conditions, (1) the immediate impact of the $10 million debt without any offsetting benefits from the new product, and (2) the improved conditions expected once the investment has become operative and the new product has begun to generate earnings, probably after one year.

The results of the two calculations are shown in Figure 8–3. The instantaneous effect of adding debt is a reduction of the earnings available for common stock. This is caused by the stated interest cost of 11.5 percent on $10 million of bonds, or $1,150,000 before taxes. Earnings after interest and taxes drop by $759,000 as compared to the initial conditions in Figure 8–2. This reduction represents, of course, the aftertax cost of the bond interest, or $1,150,000 times (1 − .34).

As a consequence, earnings per share are reduced to $5.18, a drop of 76 cents, or an immediate dilution of 12.8 percent from the prior level. This change is purely due to the incremental interest cost, which on a per

FIGURE 8–3
ABC CORPORATION
Earnings per Share with New Bond Issue
($ thousands, except per share figures)

	Before New Product	With New Product
Earnings before interest and taxes (EBIT)	$9,000	$11,000
Less: Interest charges on long-term debt	1,150	1,150
Earnings before income taxes	7,850	9,850
Less: Federal income taxes at 34%	2,669	3,349
Earnings after income taxes	5,181	6,501
Less: Preferred dividends	–0–	–0–
Earnings available for common stock	$5,181	$ 6,501
Common shares outstanding (number)	1 million	1 million
Earnings per share (EPS)	$ 5.18	$ 6.50
Less: Common dividends per share	2.50	2.50
Retained earnings per share	$ 2.68	$ 4.00
Retained earnings in total	$2,681	$ 4,001
Original EPS (Figure 8–2)	$ 5.94	$ 5.94
Change in EPS	−0.76	+0.56
Percent change in EPS	−12.8%	+9.4%

share basis amounts to the same 76 cents, that is, the aftertax interest of $759,000 divided by 1 million shares.

In Chapter 7 we discussed the stated annual cost of debt funds, defined as the tax-adjusted rate of interest carried by the debt instrument. Assuming an effective tax rate of 34 percent in our example, the stated cost of debt for ABC Corporation is therefore 7.59 percent. We also explained in Chapter 7 that the specific annual cost of debt is found by relating the stated annual cost to the actual proceeds received. If these proceeds differed from the par value of the debt instrument, the specific annual cost of the debt will, of course, be higher or lower than the stated rate.

In the case of ABC Corporation we assumed that net proceeds were effectively at par, and therefore the specific cost of ABC's new debt is also 7.59 percent, a figure that we'll compare with the specific cost of the other alternatives for raising capital.

Turning to the second column of Figure 8–3, we find that the assumed successful introduction of the new product will more than compensate ABC Company for the earnings impact of the interest paid on the bonds. In other words, the investment project is earning more than the specific cost of the debt employed to fund it. Aftertax earnings have risen to $6,501,000, a net increase of $561,000 over the original $5,940,000 in Figure 8–2. As a consequence, earnings per share rose 56 cents above the original $5.94, an increase of almost 10 percent.

By more than offsetting the total aftertax interest cost of the debentures of $759,000, the successful new investment is expected to boost the common shares' earnings. Incremental earnings of $1,320,000 ($2,000,000 pretax earnings less tax at 34 percent) significantly exceed the incremental cost of $759,000. Therefore, the investment—if ABC's earnings assumptions prove realistic—has made possible an increment of economic value. In effect, the financial leverage introduced with the debt alternative is positive.

Yet, several questions might be asked. For example, suppose the investment earned just $759,000 after taxes, exactly covering the cost of the debt supporting it and maintaining the shareholders' position just as before in terms of earnings per share. Would the investment still be justified? Would this mean that the investment was made at no cost to the shareholders?

At first glance, we might believe this, but a number of issues must be considered here. First of all, no mention has been made of the sinking fund obligations that will begin five years hence and that represent a cash outlay of $400,000 per year. Such principal payments aren't tax deductible and must be paid out of the aftertax cash flow generated by the company. Thus, debt service (burden coverage) will require 40 cents per share over and above the interest cost of 76 cents per share, for a total of $1.16 per share. The $400,000 will no longer be available for dividends or other corporate purposes because it's committed to the repayment of principal. If we suppose that earnings from the investment exactly equaled the interest cost of the debt, how would the company repay the principal? At what point are the shareholders better off than they were before?

There's an obvious fallacy in this line of discussion. It stems from the use of accounting earnings to represent the project's benefits and comparing these to the aftertax cost of the debt capital used to finance it. This isn't a proper economic comparison, as we pointed out in Chapters 6 and 7. Only a time-adjusted cash flow analysis can determine the economic cost/benefit trade-off. We could say that the project was exactly yielding the specific cost of the debt capital associated with it only if the net present value of the project were exactly zero when we discount the incremental annual cash flows at 7.59 percent.

This result would then represent an internal rate of return of 7.59 percent, a level of economic performance that would scarcely be acceptable to management. Yet even under that condition the project's cash flows (as contrasted to the accounting profit recorded in the operating statement) would have to be higher than the $759,000 aftertax earnings required to pay only the interest on the bonds. This must be so because under the present value framework of investment analysis, the incremental cash flows associated with a project must be sufficient not only to provide the specified return but also to amortize the investment itself. We demonstrated this basic concept earlier in Chapter 6.

Let's now return to the purpose of the framework we're using here. The objective of the analysis isn't to judge the desirability of the investment—we must assume that this has been adequately done by management. Instead, we're interested only in which alternative form of financing is most advantageous for the company under the circumstances presented. In this context, the impact of each alternative on the company's earnings is only one aspect in deciding on new funding.

In the case of debt, which under normal conditions is the lowest-cost alternative, we would indeed expect a financial leverage effect in favor of the shareholder. When the project was chosen, it must have met a return standard based approximately on the weighted cost of capital—a return that far exceeds the cost of debt capital alone.

The introduction of debt, in summary, immediately dilutes earnings per share, but this is followed by a boost in earnings per share as the project's reported accounting earnings exceed the interest cost reflected in the company's income statement. The company must allow for the future sinking fund payments from a cash planning standpoint because beginning with the fifth year, 40 cents per share of the company's cash flow will be committed annually to repayment of principal.

It's generally useful to examine the implications of these facts under a variety of conditions, that is, the risk posed by earnings fluctuations both in the basic business and in the incremental profit contribution of the new product, which all along we've assumed to be successful. We'll take such variations into account later.

Preferred Stock in the Capital Structure

ABC Corporation could also meet its long-term financing needs with an alternative issue of $10 million of preferred stock, at $100 per share, which carries a stated dividend rate of 12.5 percent. For simplicity we'll again assume that the net proceeds to the company will be equivalent to the nominal price of $100, after legal and underwriting expenses. Figure 8–4 analyzes the conditions before and after the introduction of the new product project.

FIGURE 8–4
ABC CORPORATION
Earnings per Share with New Preferred Stock Issue
($ thousands, except per share figures)

	Before New Product	With New Product
Earnings before interest and taxes (EBIT)	$9,000	$11,000
Less: Interest charges on long-term debt	–0–	–0–
Earnings before income taxes	9,000	11,000
Less: Federal income taxes at 34%	3,060	3,740
Earnings after income taxes	5,940	7,260
Less: Preferred dividends	1,250	1,250
Earnings available for common stock	$4,690	$ 6,010
Common shares outstanding (number)	1 million	1 million
Earnings per share (EPS)	$ 4.69	$ 6.01
Less: Common dividends per share	2.50	2.50
Retained earnings per share	$ 2.19	$ 3.51
Retained earnings in total	$2,190	$ 3,510
Original EPS (Figure 8–2)	$ 5.94	$ 5.94
Change in EPS	–1.25	+0.07
Percent change in EPS	–21.0%	+1.2%

This time we find a more severe initial drop in the earnings available for common stock due to the impact of the preferred dividends of $1.25 million per year. Not only is the stated cost (as well as the specific cost, given that the net proceeds were again at par) of the preferred stock higher by one full percentage point than the stated 11.5 percent cost of the bonds, but also the dividends paid on the preferred stock aren't tax deductible under current laws. In fact, we're dealing with an alternative that costs, in comparable terms, 12.5 percent after taxes versus 7.59 percent after taxes for the bonds.

Therefore, the immediate dilution in earnings with the preferred issue is $1.25 per share, or 21 percent, when compared to the initial situation. Over time, as the earnings from the new product are realized, the eventual increase in earnings per share amounts to only 7 cents, a slight improvement of 1.2 percent. The $1.25 million annual commitment of aftertax funds for dividends leaves little room for any net gain in reported profit from the earnings generated by the investment— which we know are estimated as $2.0 million before taxes and $1,320,000 after taxes.

In this situation, the assumed conditions allow for very limited financial leverage. Only little more than a 1 percent rise in earnings per share is achieved over the starting level, inasmuch as the fixed aftertax financing costs introduced have nearly doubled when compared to the bond alternative. Earnings per share would be unchanged if the product were to achieve minimum earnings that represent the pretax cost of the preferred dividends:

$$\frac{\$1,250,000}{(1 - .34)} = \$1,894,000$$

At that level, the incremental earnings from the new product would just offset the incremental financing cost—a break-even situation. Note that the sizable earnings requirement of almost $1.9 million is two thirds larger than the $1,150,000 pretax interest cost with the bond alternative.

Common Stock in the Capital Structure

When ABC considers a new issue of common stock as the third alternative for raising $10 million, the impact on earnings is even more severe. Let's assume that ABC Corporation will issue 275,000 new shares at a net price to the company of $36.36 after underwriters' fees and legal expenses are met. Such a discount from the current market price of $40 should ensure successful placement of the issue. The number of shares outstanding thus increases by 27.5 percent over the current 1.0 million shares. Figure 8–5 shows the impact on earnings in the same way as we showed it for the other two alternatives.

FIGURE 8–5
ABC CORPORATION
Earnings per Share with New Common Stock Issue
($ thousands, except per share figures)

	Before New Product	With New Product
Earnings before interest and taxes (EBIT)	$9,000	$11,000
Less: Interest charges on long-term debt	–0–	–0–
Earnings before income taxes	9,000	11,000
Less: Federal income taxes at 34%	3,060	3,740
Earnings after income taxes	5,940	7,260
Less: Preferred dividends	–0–	–0–
Earnings available for common stock	$5,940	$ 7,260
Common shares outstanding (number)	1.275 million	1.275 million
Earnings per share (EPS)	$ 4.66	$ 5.69
Less: Common dividends per share	2.50	2.50
Retained earnings per share	$ 2.16	$ 3.19
Retained earnings in total	$2,752	$ 4,072
Original EPS (Figure 8–2)	$ 5.94	$ 5.94
Change in EPS	–1.28	–0.25
Percent change in EPS	–21.5%	–4.2%

We observe that immediate dilution is a full $1.28 per share, a drop of 21.5 percent, which is the highest impact of the three choices analyzed. Common stock, in terms of this comparison, is the costliest form of capital—if only because it results in the greatest immediate dilution in the earnings of current shareholders.

Moreover, there will also be an annual cash drain of at least $687,500 in aftertax earnings from the 275,000 new shares if the current $2.50 annual dividend on common stock is maintained.

Further, we can project that this cash drain could grow at the historical earnings growth rate of 4 percent per year. This assumption will hold if the directors continue their policy of declaring regular cash dividends at a fairly constant payout rate from future earnings that continue growing.

For the present, the pretax earnings required to cover the $2.50 per share dividend is

$$\$2.50 \times 275,000 \text{ shares} = \$687,500 \text{ (after taxes)}$$
$$\frac{\$687,500}{(1 - .34)} = \$1,042,000 \text{ (before taxes)}$$

We can directly compare this earnings requirement of about $1.0 million to the alternative bond requirement of $1,150 million and the preferred stock requirement of $1.894 million. From both an earnings and a cash planning standpoint these amounts are clearly significant.

The effect of immediate dilution of earnings is only part of the consideration. There will be the second-stage effect of *continuing dilution* because in contrast to the other two types of capital, the new common shares created represent an ongoing claim on corporate earnings on a par with that of the existing shares. Thus, the rate of growth in earnings per share experienced to date will be slowed in the future merely because more shares will be outstanding—unless, of course, the earnings provided by the investment of the proceeds are superior in level and potential growth to the existing earnings performance.

When we turn to the second column of Figure 8–5, it's apparent that despite the incremental earnings from the new product, the net dilution of earnings per share in the amount of 25 cents (4.2 percent) will in fact continue. The new product's contribution to reported earnings wasn't sufficient to meet the earnings claims of the new shareholders and maintain the old per share earnings level. The impact on earnings of the common stock alternative thus is greater than the earnings generated by the new capital raised.

Up to this point we've dealt with the earnings impact of common stock financing. To find a first rough approximation of the specific cost of this alternative, we can establish as a minimum condition the maintenance of the old earnings per share level, and relate this to the proceeds from each new share of common stock. The current EPS of $5.94 (Figure 8–2) and the proceeds of $36.36 result in a cost of about 16 percent:

$$\frac{\$5.94}{\$36.36} = 16.34\% \text{ (after taxes)}$$

We know from Chapter 7, however, that the earnings approach to measuring the cost of common equity for many reasons has very limited usefulness even if an allowance is made in the formula for expected growth in earnings.

If we employ the dividend approach to find the specific cost of the incremental common stock, as discussed in Chapter 7, we must relate the current dividend per share to the net price received, and add prospective dividend growth. We know that the company has experienced fairly consistent growth in earnings of 4 percent per year, and we'll assume that, given a constant rate of dividend payout, common dividends will continue to grow at the same rate. The result is a cost of about 11 percent:

$$\frac{\$2.50}{\$36.36} + 4.0 = 10.9\%$$

As we stated in Chapter 7, however, the dividend approach is similarly lacking both in concept and in practical usefulness. Therefore, let's now use the background data provided to test the specific cost of capital for ABC's common equity with the CAPM approach explained in Chapter 7.

The resulting cost of common equity, k_e, is approximately 13.25 percent when we put into the CAPM formula the risk-free return, R_f, of 6.5 percent, the β of 0.9, and the expected average return, R_m, represented by the S&P 500 estimate of 14 percent:

$$\begin{aligned} k_e &= R_f + \beta(R_m - R_f) \\ &= 6.5 + 0.9(14.0 - 6.5) \\ &= 13.25\% \end{aligned}$$

This result is the most credible one for judging the specific cost of the common stock. It can be compared to the specific cost of the bonds (7.59 percent) and specific cost of the preferred stock (12.5 percent).

Clearly, the common equity alternative is the most expensive source of financing, and we've already established that the dilution effect is also serious. In addition, the cash flow requirements for paying the current dividend of $2.50 per share plus any future increases in the common dividend have to be planned for. Because it's difficult to keep all of these quantitative aspects visible in our deliberations, let's now turn to a graphic representation of the various earnings and dilution effects to compare the relative position of the three alternatives.

EBIT BREAK-EVEN CHART

We've referred several times to changes in a company's earnings performance and the different impact the three basic financing alternatives have under varying conditions. The static format of analysis we've used so far doesn't readily allow us to explore the range of possibilities as earnings change, or to visualize the sensitivity of the alternative funding sources to these changes. It would be quite laborious to calculate earnings per share and other data for a great number of earnings levels and assumptions. Instead, we can exploit the direct linear relationships that exist between the quantitative factors analyzed.

A graphic break-even approach can be used to compare the alternative sources of financing. In this section, we'll show how such a model, keyed to fluctuations in EBIT and resulting EPS levels, can be employed to display for us the most important quantitative aspects of the relative desirability of the options available. As we'll see, the break-even model allows us to perform a variety of analytical tests with ease.

To begin with, we've summarized the data for ABC Corporation in Figure 8–6. Variations in these data can then be displayed graphically in a simple break-even chart showing earnings per share on the vertical axis and EBIT on the horizontal axis. This EBIT chart allows us to plot on straight lines the EPS for each alternative under varying conditions, and to find the break-even points between them.

Commonly we use as one of the reference points the intersection of each line with the horizontal axis, that is, the exact point where EPS are zero. These points can easily be found by working the EPS calculations backward, that is, starting with an assumed EPS of zero and deriving an EBIT that just provides for this condition. This calculation is shown in Figure 8–7 for the original situation and for each of the three alternatives. The calculations in Figures 8–6 and 8–7 give us sufficient points with which to draw the linear functions of EPS and EBIT for the various alternatives (Figure 8–8).

We can quickly observe that the conclusions about the earnings impact of the alternatives we drew from

FIGURE 8–6
ABC CORPORATION
Recap of EPS Analyses with New Product
($ thousands, except per share figures)

	Original	Debt	Preferred	Common
EBIT	$9,000	$11,000	$11,000	$11,000
Less: Interest	–0–	1,150	–0–	–0–
Earnings before taxes	9,000	9,850	11,000	11,000
Less: Taxes at 34%	3,060	3,349	3,740	3,740
Earnings after taxes	5,940	6,501	7,260	7,260
Less: Preferred dividends	–0–	–0–	1,250	–0–
Earnings available for common stock	$5,940	$ 6,501	$ 6,010	$ 7,260
Common shares outstanding (number)	1 million	1 million	1 million	1.275 million
EPS	$ 5.94	$ 6.50	$ 6.01	$ 5.69
Less: Common dividends	2.50	2.50	2.50	2.50
Retained earnings	$ 3.44	$ 4.00	$ 3.51	$ 3.19
Retained earnings in total	$3,440	$ 4,001	$ 3,510	$ 4,072
Original EPS change		–12.8%	–21.0%	–21.5%
Final EPS change		+9.4%	+1.2%	–4.2%
Specific cost		7.59%	12.5%	13.25%

FIGURE 8–7
ABC CORPORATION
Zero EPS Calculation
($ thousands, except per share figures)

	Original	Debt	Preferred	Common
EPS	–0–	–0–	–0–	–0–
Common shares	1 million	1 million	1 million	1.275 million
Earnings to common	–0–	–0–	–0–	–0–
Preferred dividends	–0–	–0–	$1,250	–0–
Earnings after taxes	–0–	–0–	1,250	–0–
Taxes at 34%	–0–	–0–	644	–0–
Earnings before taxes	–0–	–0–	1,894	–0–
Interest	–0–	$1,150	–0–	–0–
EBIT or zero EPS	–0–	$1,150	$1,894	–0–

408

FIGURE 8–8

ABC CORPORATION: Range of EBIT and EPS Chart

the two **EBIT** levels previously analyzed, $9 million and
$11 million, hold true over the fairly wide range of
earnings presented; that is, every alternative considered
causes a significant reduction in earnings per share relative to the original condition.

There's a major new observation, however. Under the
common stock alternative, the slope of the **EPS** line is
different. In fact, the line for common stock intersects
both the debt and the preferred stock lines. The latter
two lines are parallel with each other and also with the
line representing the original situation, both appearing
to the right of that line. The lesser slope of the common
stock line is easily explained. Introducing new shares of
common stock results in a proportional dilution of earnings per share at all **EBIT** levels. As a consequence, the
incremental shares cause earnings per share to rise less
rapidly with growth in **EBIT.**

In contrast, the parallel shift by the debt and preferred stock lines to the right of the original line is

caused by the introduction of fixed interest or dividend charges, while at the same time the number of common shares outstanding remains constant over the EBIT range studied.

The significance of the intersections should now become apparent. These are break-even points at which, for a given EBIT level, the EPS for the common stock alternative and one of the other two alternatives are the same. Note that the break-even point of the common stock line with the bond alternative occurs at about $5.3 million EBIT, while the break-even point of common stock with preferred stock occurs at about $8.8 million EBIT.

Below $5.0 million EBIT, therefore, the common stock alternative causes the least EPS dilution, while above $9 million EBIT it causes the worst relative dilution in EPS. Recall that ABC's current EBIT level is $9.0 million and is expected to be at least $11 million once the new product is fully contributing its projected earnings. Both break-even points thus lie below the likely future EBIT performance, which makes the common stock alternative the costliest in terms of earnings dilution.

Therefore, given that the relative earnings effects of the three alternatives are different over the wide range of EBIT shown, it's not possible to assess the three alternatives without defining a "normal" range of EBIT for the company's expected performance. If future EBIT levels could in fact be expected to move fairly well within the two break-even points, common stock looks more attractive than preferred stock from the standpoint of EPS dilution, but worse than debt. If EBIT can be expected to grow and move significantly to the right of the second break-even point, as is almost certain in the case of ABC Corporation, new common stock not only is least attractive from the standpoint of EPS dilution, but will remain so.

All of these considerations are based, of course, on

unchanging assumptions about the terms under which the three forms of incremental capital could be issued. If we can expect significant change in any of these terms (such as the common stock's offering price or the terms of the bond), an entirely new chart must be drawn up, or we must at least reflect any possible discontinuities in cost or proportions of the alternatives as EBIT levels change.

The intersections between the EPS lines that represent the EBIT break-even points for the common stock alternative with the other two choices can be easily calculated. For this purpose we formulate simple equations for the conditions underlying any intersecting pair of lines. EPS are then set as equal for the two alternatives, and the equations are solved for the specific EBIT level at which this condition holds. To illustrate, let's first establish the following definitions:

E = EBIT level for any break-even point with common stock alternative.
i = Annual interest on bonds in dollars (before taxes).
t = Tax rate applicable to the company.
d = Annual preferred dividends in dollars.
s = Number of common shares outstanding.

The equation for any of the EPS lines can be found by substituting known facts for the symbols in the following generalized equation:

$$\text{EPS} = \frac{(E - i)\,(i - t)\, -d}{s}$$

We can now find the EBIT break-even levels for bonds and common stock at the point of EPS equality. For this purpose, we fill in the data for the two expressions and set them as equal:

$$\underset{\text{Bonds}}{\frac{(E - \$1{,}150{,}000)\ .66 - 0}{1{,}000{,}000}} = \underset{\text{Common}}{\frac{(E - 0)\ .66 - 0}{1{,}275{,}000}}$$

When we solve for E, we obtain the following result:

$$0.66 \ E - \$759,000 = \frac{0.66E}{1.275}$$

$$0.842 \ E - \$967,725 = 0.66E$$

$$E = \$5,317,200$$

This break-even level of $5.32 million can easily be verified graphically in Figure 8–8.

When the same approach is applied to the preferred and common stock alternatives, the following result emerges:

$$\underset{Preferred}{\frac{(E - 0) \ .66 - \$1,250,000}{1,000,000}} = \underset{Common}{\frac{(E - 0) \ .66 - 0}{1,275,000}}$$

$$0.66 \ E - \$1,250,000 = \frac{0.66E}{1.275}$$

$$0.842E - \$1,593,750 = 0.66E$$

$$E = \$8,756,900$$

Again, the chart can be used to verify the break-even level of $8.76 million.

We can also use the **EBIT** chart to show the impact of any common dividend assumption on the three alternatives. The horizontal line at $2.50 in the chart represents the current annual common dividend. Where this line intersects any alternative EPS line, we can read off the minimum level of **EBIT** required to supply this dividend. Similarly, the chart can reflect the earnings requirements for sinking funds or other regular repayment provisions. In effect, such annual provisions commit a portion of future earnings for this purpose.

We can develop the effect of these requirements by carrying the calculations one step further and arriving at the so-called *uncommitted earnings per share (UEPS)* for each alternative after provision for any repayments. We simply subtract the per share cost of such repayments (which require aftertax dollars) from the respective **EPS** of the alternative thus affected, and redraw the lines in the chart. The result will be a parallel shift of the affected line to the right of its prior position.

For example, the sinking fund requirement of $400,000 per year in the bond alternative would represent 40 cents per share, and the new line for bonds would move to the right by this amount over its whole range. Similarly, the intersection at the zero EPS point, currently $1,150,000 EBIT, would move right to a zero UEPS point of $1,756,060. This shift reflects the sinking fund requirement of $400,000 per year, which translates into an incremental pretax earnings requirement of $400,000 ÷ (1 − 0.34), or $606,060. As it turns out in this case, the UEPS line for bonds would move very close to the EPS line for preferred stock in Figure 8–8.

By now the usefulness of this framework for a dynamic analysis of the various financing alternatives should be clear. The reader is invited to think through the implications of the variety of tests that can be applied. For example, we can determine the minimum EBIT level under each alternative that would cover the current common dividend of $2.50 per share, while assuming a variety of different payout ratios, such as 50 percent or 40 percent. This means that with an assumed 50 percent payout, EPS would have to be $5.00. A horizontal line would be drawn at the $5.00 EPS level, and its intersection with the lines of the various alternatives would represent the minimum EBIT levels for the $2.50 dividend. The analyst would have to assess the likelihood of EBIT declining to this level, and judge whether this endangers the current dividend payout.

Other tests can be applied, of course, depending on the particular circumstances of the company. The framework can also be used to work through the cash flow implications of each of the results by translating the respective EBIT levels into equivalent cash flow from operations, as discussed in Chapter 3. This extra step would require determining the tax shield effect of depreciation and depletion write-offs. Computer spreadsheet analysis can be used to make the multiple calculations required.

But again it must be emphasized that any one specific EBIT chart works only under fixed assumptions about proceeds received and about stable interest and preferred dividend rates. If there's reason to believe that any of the key assumptions might change, the positions of the EPS lines on the graph must be adjusted.

Obviously, any changes in the relative cost of the various alternatives will also have an effect. As the spread between the alternatives increases, for example, the differences in earnings impact will widen, and thus the distance between the parallel lines will increase. This simply reflects that the imposition of higher fixed obligations depresses EPS.

Enlarging the amount of capital issued also has an effect because the slope of the line is determined by the amount of leverage already present in the existing capital structure. In other words, if there's already some debt and preferred stock in the capital structure, the basic EPS would rise and fall much more sharply with changes in EBIT. Any increases in the fixed financing cost alternatives would simply magnify this leverage. At the same time, the slope of the EPS line for common equity is governed by the relative number of shares issued, which in turn is related to the degree of earnings dilution, as demonstrated in the example.

Financial planning models and computer spreadsheets can be used to enhance the basic analysis demonstrated here. The point to remember, however, is that the analysis in essence quantifies the relative impact of the alternatives on reported earnings only. This effect is but one of the many factors that have to be weighed in making funding choices. As we mentioned in the chapter's beginning, the conceptual and practical setting for the eventual decision is far more inclusive than this graphic expression of respective break-even conditions suggests. Strategic plans for the future, risk expectations, market factors, the specific criteria we listed, and current company conditions all have to enter the final judgment.

SOME SPECIAL FORMS OF FINANCING

Our earlier discussion focused on the very basic choice between debt, preferred stock, and common stock, setting aside the many variations often found in these instruments as well as in other specialized forms of financing. We'll now cover briefly several more specialized areas of financing choices, namely *convertible bonds and preferred stocks, rights offerings, warrants,* and *leasing.*

Convertible Securities

As we stated earlier, convertibility into common shares is a feature sometimes added to issues of bonds or preferred stocks for reasons of marketability and timing. The essence of convertibility is the issuing company's ability in effect to sell common shares at prices higher than those prevailing at the time the bond or preferred stock is issued. This is due to the fact that the *conversion price* for the common stock it represents is set at an expected future level based on the company's value growth experience and expectation.

The conversion price underlies the *conversion ratio* set for the bond or preferred issue. For example, a new $100 convertible preferred may have a conversion ratio of 3, that is, each share of preferred is convertible into three shares of common stock. This represents a conversion price of $33.33 per common share, while the company's shares may currently be trading in the $25.00 to $27.00 range. The difference between current prices and the conversion price is called the *conversion premium*. The same approach applies to bonds, which are usually denominated in thousand-dollar units.

Given the expectation that the company's common stock will in time exceed the conversion price, the bond or preferred stock will trade at values that represent both the underlying interest or dividend yield, and the *conversion value* itself. Initially the stated yield will predominate, but when common share prices begin to exceed the conversion price, the price of the bond or preferred stock will be boosted to reflect the current market value or the underlying common shares. This is the point at which conversion becomes increasingly attractive to the investor. If share prices remain below the conversion price, however, the conversion value will always be the floor value for the bond or preferred—while the actual price will depend on the yield provided by the stated interest rate or the preferred dividend.

Given the potential attraction of conversion to the investor, the issuing company usually pays a somewhat lower rate of interest or preferred dividend on these instruments. To limit the time period over which these securities are outstanding, the company can usually force conversion once the market price of common stock has reached the conversion price by exercising the *call provision* (the right of the company to redeem all or part of the issue) included in most convertible issues. This is usually based on a predetermined price close to the conversion price.

Convertibility adds a number of considerations to the basic choices we discussed earlier. Because successful convertible issues eventually result in an increase in common shares, the delayed impact on control, earnings per share, and the amount of future common dividends must be taken into account in the analysis. The graphic display we used earlier can be applied by showing this situation in two steps: (1) the convertible bond or preferred as a straight bond or preferred and (2) the additional common shares from eventual conversion. As long as significant convertible issues remain outstanding, companies are required to calculate fully diluted earnings per share, as discussed in Chapter 3.

Rights Offerings

A so-called *rights offering* is a form of common stock financing that minimizes the dilution of existing shareholders' proportional holdings. Also referred to as a *privileged subscription,* such an offering provides to each existing shareholder the right to purchase a specified number of new common shares from the company at a specified price during a limited time period, after which the rights expire. The number of rights issued normally is equal to the number of shares of common stock outstanding. A specified number of rights are necessary to purchase each share of new stock. Rights are issued as special certificates and are often traded on securities exchanges or in the over-the-counter market.

To illustrate, if the XYZ company has 1,000,000 common shares outstanding and wishes to sell 250,000 new shares, 1,000,000 rights will be issued to existing shareholders with the provision that four rights are required to purchase a new share of stock at the subscription price. If the subscription price is $30, while the current market price is $40, a shareholder has to surrender 4 rights and $30 to the company to receive another share currently worth $40.

To a company, the attraction of this course of action apart from limiting the potential for dilution of control —is a direct appeal for funds to a group of investors already familiar with its history and outlook. If shareholders are so inclined, they'll exercise the right by purchasing directly from the company the number of shares specified in the rights at the set subscription price. If a shareholder isn't interested, the rights can be sold as such because they'll reflect the value differential between the stock offer and the market price of the stock. We'll return to determining the value of rights to the investor in Chapter 9.

The implications of this alternative for analysis are quite similar to those of a public offering, which we assumed to be the case earlier in the chapter. The subscription price may differ somewhat from the price the underwriters provide in a public offering, but otherwise the analysis will be parallel to the common stock alternative we explored.

Warrants

Warrants are a form of corporate security that entitle the holder to purchase a specified number of common shares at a fixed *exercise price* over a stated period of time. Some warrants even have no expiration date. They're issued as an added incentive for investors to purchase a new public issue of bonds or a private placement of loans or bonds. Sometimes warrants are even issued as part of an offering of common stock. The proportion of warrants issued with the new offering varies depending on the exercise price and the degree of incentive desired to move the new debt issue into the hands of investors. Warrants are attached to these new securities as part of the offering, but in most cases they can be detached by the holder and sold separately if desired. Numerous warrants are traded at any time in the securities markets.

In effect, a warrant gives the holder the option to buy common stock if there's an advantage to do so (i.e., if the exercise price is below the market price). Just as in the case of rights, when a warrant is exercised, the funds go directly to the company. Since warrants, in contrast to rights, are valid for relatively long time periods, there's the potential for earnings dilution from unexpired warrants. Companies with significant numbers of warrants outstanding must calculate fully diluted earnings per share, just as in the case of convertible issues outstanding.

The implications for analysis of a new debt offering with attached warrants are mainly in the need to recognize the potential funds inflow from new shares as warrants are exercised, and the earnings dilution from these shares. Our graphic analysis has to be modified to allow for the combination of these effects. We'll return to the value of warrants in Chapter 9.

Leasing

We've referred to leasing at several points in this book. Leasing is a special form of financing that gives a company access to a whole range of assets, from buildings to automobiles, without having to acquire these items outright. The lessee pays an agreed upon periodic fee that covers the lessor's ownership costs and financing and tax expenses, and also provides an economic return. The lessee can use the asset for a specified period, assumes none of the risks of ownership or technical obsolescence, and can replace or upgrade the asset while the lessor assumes the task of disposing of the old items. The latter provision is particularly appealing in the case of computers or technical equipment. The lessee, in effect, only incurs a tax-deductible periodic expense.

Long-term lease contracts, particularly for buildings, can extend over many years and thus become, in fact, part of a company's financial structure. Current accounting practice requires the disclosure of lease obligations in a company's published financial statements if such leases represent a commitment of material size. While leases aren't normally included as liabilities in the balance sheet itself (they are called "off-balance-sheet debt"), footnotes to the balance sheet must disclose the amount of periodic payments and an estimated capitalized value of the lease obligations.

Such disclosure recognizes the fact that lease obligations represent a financial burden that must be serviced just like any other form of financing. Any company that leases a significant portion of its assets has less flexibility in its financing choices. The effect is the same as that of a large outstanding long-term debt. Fixed leasing charges introduce a degree of leverage into the company's operations that's quite comparable to leverage resulting from other sources.

There are many considerations involved in the choice of leasing versus ownership. We won't deal with the techniques of analyzing the cash flow implications of the many types of leasing arrangements because they're too specialized and complex to be covered here. But we must emphasize that there's an economic cost in leasing because the lessor must be compensated for providing, financing, servicing, and replacing the asset. By definition, leasing charges must be high enough to make leasing attractive for the lessor. At the same time, the lessor is often able to use economies of scale that may favorably affect the cost of leasing, as is the case with major equipment leasing companies, for example.

The comparative analysis necessary to make the final choice between leasing and ownership has to weigh such elements as the cost to the lessee, the technological advantages, service, the flexibility of not owning, and the impact on the company's financial position. As in all financial analyses, the choice is based on both quantifiable data and management judgment. In some industries, leasing is part of the normal way of doing business. For example, in wholesaling, warehouses are commonly leased, not purchased, while in the transportation industry, leasing of rolling stock, trucks, and aircraft prevails. In other areas the choice of leasing is wide open and depends on what financing alternative is considered advantageous at the time.

KEY ISSUES

The following is a recap of the key issues raised directly or indirectly in this chapter. They're enumerated here to help the reader use the analysis techniques discussed within the perspective of financial theory and business practice:

1. The choice among different types of long-term financing is inextricably connected with a firm's business strategy. The choice must match the risk/reward characteristics inherent in both strategy and financing.

2. The cost of different types of capital is only one element on which a decision about new funding is based. While debt is generally the lowest-cost alternative and common equity the highest-cost alternative, the need to build and maintain an appropriate balance in the capital structure often overrides the cost criterion.

3. Noncost elements (such as risk, flexibility, timing, and shareholder control) as well as management preferences have to be weighed in relation to both changing market conditions and the company's future policies.

4. New financing at times may represent a significant proportion of the existing capital structure. How these funds are raised can cause shifts away from a firm's ideal target capital structure. Because a block of one form of long-term capital was chosen at one point in time, management may be limited in the choices for the next round of financing. To compensate for this imbalance, a compromise mix of funds may have to be used.

5. The specific provisions of a new issue of securities are generally tailor-made for the situation. Investment bankers, underwriters, and management collaborate to negotiate the design and price of a financial instrument that reflects market conditions, the company's credit rating and reputation, risk assessment, the company's strategic plans, and current financial practices.

6. As a company's capital structure changes, so does its weighted cost of capital. However, temporary

shifts resulting from adding blocks of new capital shouldn't affect the return standards based on cost of capital unless there's a deliberate and permanent change in the company's policies.

7. New common equity has the long-term effect of diluting both ownership and earnings per share. This is true whether the new shares are directly issued or brought about by conversion of other securities or by exercise of warrants. The decision of whether to issue new common shares thus must be closely tied to the expected results from the strategic plans in place. It also involves weighing the advantages of introducing new permanent equity capital into the capital structure.

8. Leasing as a form of financing is based on a series of trade-offs that must be weighed in relation to both the company's capital structure and its business direction.

SUMMARY

This chapter reviewed both the decisional framework and some of the techniques used to analyze the different types of long-term funds. We focused on the three basic alternatives open to management (long-term debt, preferred stock, and common equity), leaving discussion of the many specialized aspects of funding instruments to be pursued in the references at the end of the chapter. We found that the choice of financing alternatives is a complex mixture of analysis and judgment. Several areas of consideration were highlighted. We reviewed the cost to the company, the relative risks, and the issues of flexibility, timing, and control with respect to the various funding sources. We found that many of the aspects of the choice of types of capital involve more than quantifiable data.

422

We also focused on the impact of each financing alternative on the reported earnings of a company, and then developed a break-even graph relating **EPS** and **EBIT**, which allowed us to test visually the earnings impact of the alternatives over the whole dynamic range of potential earnings levels. This simple model suggested the potential use of broader financial models or computer spreadsheets with which to simulate more fully the impact of alternative financing packages or changing conditions. Last, we briefly examined the key aspects of some more specialized forms of financing (convertible securities, rights, warrants, and leasing) and suggested the kind of analytical considerations applicable to these modified conditions.

SELECTED REFERENCES

Brealey, Richard, and Stewart Myers. *Principles of Corporate Finance.* 3d ed. New York: McGraw-Hill, 1988.

Myers, Stewart C. "The Search for Optimal Capital Structures." *Midland Corporate Finance Journal,* Spring 1983, pp. 6–16.

Piper, Thomas R., and Wolf A. Weinhold. "How Much Debt Is Right for Your Company?" *Harvard Business Review,* July–August 1982, pp. 106–14.

Ross, Stephen A.; Randolph W. Westerfield; and Bradford D. Jordan. *Fundamentals of Corporate Finance.* Homewood, Ill.: Richard D. Irwin, 1991.

Van Horne, James C. *Financial Management and Policy.* 7th ed. Englewood Cliffs, N.J.: Prentice Hall, 1986.

Weston, J. Fred, and Thomas E. Copeland. *Managerial Finance.* 8th ed. Hinsdale, Ill.: Dryden Press, 1986.

SELF-STUDY EXERCISES AND PROBLEMS

(Solutions are provided in Appendix VI)

1. The ABC Corporation is planning the financing of a major expansion program for late 1994. Common stock has been chosen as the vehicle, and the 50,000 shares to be issued in addition to the

300,000 shares outstanding are to bring estimated proceeds of $5
million. The current price range of common stock is $120 to
$140 per share. The new program is expected to raise current
operating profits of $14.7 million by 18 percent. The company's
capital structure contains long-term debt of $10 million, with an
annual sinking fund provision of $900,000 to begin in 1995 and
interest charges of 11 percent. The most recent estimated operating statement of the company, which includes the additional
profit, appears as follows:

ABC CORPORATION
Pro Forma Operating Statement
For the Year Ended December 31, 1995
($ thousands)

Net sales	$66,000
Cost of goods sold*	42,000
Gross profit	24,000
Selling and administrative expenses	9,300
Operating profit	14,700
Interest on debt	1,100
Profit before taxes	13,600
Federal income tax (34%)	4,600
Net income	$ 9,000

*Includes depreciation of $2,250.

The company's β was calculated at 1.4, while the risk-free return
was estimated to be 8 percent, and the expected return from the
stock market 14.5 percent.

a. Develop an analysis of earnings per share, uncommitted earnings per share, and cash flow per share, and show the effects
of dilution in earnings.

b. Develop the same analysis for an alternative issue of $5 mil-
lion of 10 percent preferred stock, and an alternative issue of
$5 million of 9 percent debentures due in full after 15 years.

c. Develop the specific comparative cost of capital for all three
alternatives and discuss your findings.

2. XYZ Corporation is planning to raise an additional $30 million in
capital, either via 240,000 shares of common at $125 per share
net proceeds, or via 300,000 shares of 9 percent preferred stock.
Current earnings are $12.50 per share on 1 million shares out-
standing, $2.5 million in interest is paid annually on existing long-
term debt, and dividends on existing preferred stock amount to
$1.5 million per year. The current market price is $140 per share,

the β is 1.2, and risk-free return is 8 percent. The expected return from the stock market is 13 percent.

a. Develop the specific cost of capital for each alternative and show calculations (long form). Assume income taxes are 46 percent.

b. Develop the point of earnings per share equivalence between the common and preferred alternatives. Assuming a common dividend of $8 per share, calculate the EPS/dividends per share break-even point for the common stock alternative.

c. Assuming EBIT levels of $10 million, $15 million, $22.5 million, and $33.75 million, demonstrate the effect of leverage with the preferred stock alternative, by graph and calculation. Discuss your findings.

3. The DEF Company was weighing three financing options for a diversification program that would require $50 million and provide greater stability in sales and profits. The options were as follows:

a. One million common shares at $50 net to the company.

b. 500,000 shares of 9.5 percent preferred stock.

c. $50 million of 8.5 percent bonds (entailing a sinking fund provision of $2 million per year).

The current capital structure contained debt on which $1 million per year was paid into a sinking fund and on which interest of $1.2 million was currently paid. Preferred stock obligations were dividends of $1.8 million per year. Common shares outstanding were 2 million, on which $2 per share was paid in dividends. The current market price range was $55 to $60, and the company's β was 1.2. The risk-free rate of return was 7.5 percent, while expectations about the returns from a portfolio of stocks were 14 percent. EBIT levels had fluctuated between $22 million and $57 million, and earnings before interest and taxes from diversification were expected to be about $8 million. The most recent EBIT level of the company had been $34 million.

Assume that proceeds to the company after expenses would equal the par value of the securities in the second and third alternatives; also, disregard the obvious exaggerations in the relationships that were made for better contrast. Income taxes are 36 percent.

Develop a graphic analysis of the data given and establish by calculation the earnings per share, uncommitted earnings per share, dilution, specific costs of capital, break-even points, dividend coverage, and zero earnings per share. Discuss your findings.

9 VALUATION AND BUSINESS PERFORMANCE

We will now examine in greater detail the concept of value in its various forms and relate it to business performance. Earlier we discussed such value categories as the stated values reflected in a company's financial statements, the economic values represented by the cash flows generated through capital investments, and the market value of common equity. In each case, value was examined in a specific context of analysis and assessment, but not necessarily against the full dynamics of management decisions about investment, operating, and financing that underlie the performance of any business.

We'll discuss the meaning of value as it applies to a variety of common situations in which the issue of valuation arises. In the process we'll not only define the several concepts of value in more precise terms, but also once again we'll use some of the now familiar analytical approaches that can be applied to the process of valuation. Among these, of course, is present value analysis (the main subject of Chapter 6).

We'll begin with some basic definitions of value in the business setting. Then we'll take the point of view of the investor assessing the value of the main forms of securities issued by a company. Finally, we'll discuss the main issues involved in valuing an ongoing business, as the basis for determining shareholder value, which we described earlier as the principal objective of modern management. As we've emphasized throughout this book, the linkage between cash flows and the creation of economic value is the ultimate expression of success or failure of business decisions on investment, operating, and financing. Recognition of this linkage spurred the wave of takeovers and restructuring activities of the 1980s—essentially a reassessment of the effectiveness with which resources were employed by target companies—leading to redeployment of those resources in alternative ways that were expected to generate higher cash flows.

DEFINITIONS OF VALUE

It will be useful briefly to refresh our memory about the different types of value we've encountered so far, and to state as clearly as possible what they represent and for what purposes they may be appropriate.

Economic Value

This concept relates to the basic ability of an asset—or a claim—to provide a stream of aftertax cash flows to the holder. These cash flows may be generated through earnings, or contractual payments, or partial or total liquidation at a future point. As earlier chapters said, economic value is essentially a trade-off concept. The value of any good is defined as the amount of cash a buyer is willing to give up now—its present value—in exchange for a pattern of future expected cash flows. Therefore, economic value is also a future-oriented concept. Economic value is determined by assessing potential future cash flows, including proceeds from ultimate disposal of the good itself. We remember that costs and expenditures incurred by past decisions are sunk costs and thus irrelevant from an economic standpoint.

As we'll see, economic value underlies some of the other common concepts of value because it's based on a trade-off logic that's quite natural to the process of investing funds. Calculating economic value isn't without practical difficulties, however. Recall that a representative discount rate (return standard) has to be selected and applied to the expected positive and negative cash flows over a defined period of time. These cash flows also include the terminal value assumption. The process in effect determines the equivalence of the cash flow amounts occurring in different parts of the time spectrum.

We also recall the need for risk assessment, both of the cash flow pattern itself and in setting the appropriate return standard. In other words, economic value isn't absolute; rather, it's a criterion based on the relative risk assessment of future expectations. In fact, economic value is closely tied to individual risk preferences. Yet, economic value lies at the core of all business decisions on investment, operating, and financing, whether or not these aspects are recognized.

Market Value

Also referred to as *fair market value*, this is the value of any asset, or collection of assets, when traded in an organized market or between private parties in an unencumbered transaction without duress. The securities and commodity exchanges are examples of organized markets, as are literally thousands of regional and local markets and exchanges that enable buyers and sellers to find mutually acceptable values for all kinds of tangible and intangible assets. Market value is, of course, also established through individual transactions when no convenient organized market is available.

Again, there's nothing absolute in market value. Instead, it represents a momentary consensus of two or more parties. In a sense, the parties to a transaction adjust their respective individual assessments of the asset's economic value sufficiently to arrive at the consensus. The market value at any one time can therefore be subject to the preferences and even whims of the individuals involved, the psychological climate prevalent in an organized exchange, the heat of a takeover battle, economic variations, industry developments, political conditions, and so forth. Moreover, the current volume of trading in the asset or security will influence the value placed on it by buyers and sellers.

Despite its potential variability, market value is generally regarded as a reasonable criterion to use for estimating the value of individual balance sheet assets and liabilities. It's frequently used in inventory valuation and in capital investment analysis in the form of future recovery values. Mergers and purchases of going concerns are also based on market values established by the parties.

As was the case with economic value, there are practical problems associated with calculating market value. A true market value can be found only by actually engaging in a transaction. Thus, unless the item is in fact traded, any market value assigned to it remains merely an estimate, which will tend to shift as conditions change and the perceptions of the parties are altered.

But even if market quotations are readily available, certain judgments apply. For example, popular common stocks traded on the major exchanges have widely quoted market prices, yet there frequently are significant price fluctuations even within a day's trading. Thus, market value based on many similar transactions can be fixed only within a given range, which in turn, is tied to the trading conditions of the day, week, or month. For items that are traded infrequently, estimating a realistic transaction value can become even more difficult.

Book Value

Recall from Chapter 1 that the book value of an asset or liability is the stated value on the balance sheet, which has been recorded according to generally accepted accounting principles. While book value is generally handled consistently for accounting purposes, it usually has little relationship to current economic value. It's a historical value that, at one time, may have represented economic value to the company, but the passage of time and changes in economic conditions increasingly distort it. This is especially true of the frequently quoted book value of common shares, which represents the shareholder's claim on the composite residual of all recorded past transactions in assets, liabilities, and operations. Its usefulness for financial analysis is therefore questionable under most circumstances.

Liquidation Value

This value relates to the special condition when a company has to liquidate part or all of its assets and claims. In essence, this represents an abnormal situation where time pressures and even duress distort the value assessments made by buyers and sellers. Under the cloud of impending business failure or intense pressure from creditors, management will find that liquidation values are generally considerably below potential market values. The economic setting is adversely affected by the known disadvantage under which the selling party must act in the transaction. As a consequence, liquidation value is really applicable only for the limited purpose intended. Nevertheless, it's sometimes used in valuing assets of unproven companies to perform ratio analysis in credit assessment.

Breakup Value

A variation of liquidation value, breakup value is related to corporate takeover and restructuring activities, as discussed later in this chapter. On the assumption that the combined economic values of the individual segments of a multibusiness company exceed the company's value as a whole, because of inadequate past management or current opportunities not recognized earlier, the company is broken up into salable components for disposal to other buyers. Any redundant assets, such as excess real estate, are also sold for their current values.

Note that breakup value is usually realized on business segments with ongoing operations, and less frequently through forced liquidation of individual assets supporting these business segments, as would be the case in a bankruptcy sale, for example. Redundant assets may, of course, be liquidated as such. Estimates of breakup value are a critical element in the analysis preceding takeover bids.

Reproduction Value

This is the amount that would be required to replace an existing fixed asset in kind. In other words, it's the like-for-like replacement cost of a machine, facility, or other similar asset. Reproduction value is, in fact, one of several yardsticks used in judging the worth of an ongoing business. Determining reproduction value is an estimate largely based on engineering judgments.

There are several practical problems involved. The most important is whether the fixed asset in question could—or would—in fact be reproduced exactly as it was constructed originally. Most physical assets are subject to some technological obsolescence with the passage of time, in addition to physical wear and tear. There's also the problem of estimating the currently applicable cost of actually reproducing the item in kind.

For purposes of analysis, reproduction value often becomes just one checkpoint in assessing the market value of the assets of a going business.

Collateral Value

This is the value of an asset used as security for a loan or other type of credit. The collateral value is generally considered the maximum amount of credit that can be extended against a pledge of the asset. With their own position in mind, creditors usually set the collateral value lower than the market value of an asset. This is done to provide a cushion of safety in case of default, and the individual risk preference of the individual creditor will determine the size of the often arbitrary downward adjustment. Where no market value can be readily estimated, the collateral value is set on a purely judgmental basis, the creditor being in a position to allow for as much of a margin of safety as deemed advisable in the particular circumstances.

Assessed Value

This value concept is established in local legal statutes as the basis for property taxation. The rules governing assessment vary widely, and may or may not take market values into account. The use of assessed values is limited to raising tax revenues, and thus such values bear little relationship to the other value concepts.

Appraised Value

Appraised value is subjectively determined and used when the asset involved has no clearly definable market value. An effort is usually made to find evidence of transactions that are reasonably comparable to the asset being appraised. Often used in transactions of considerable size—especially in the case of commercial or residential real estate—appraised value is determined by an impartial expert accepted by both parties to the transaction, whose knowledge of the type of asset involved can narrow the gap that may exist between buyer and seller, or at least establish a bargaining range. The quality of the estimate depends on the expertise of the appraiser solicited and on the availability of comparable situations. Again, individual ability and preference enter into the value equation. Only rarely will different appraisals yield exactly the same results.

Going Concern Value

This is an application of the economic value concept because a business viewed as a going concern is expected to produce a series of future cash flows that the potential buyer must value to arrive at a price for the business as a whole. Note that the same concept applies to ongoing business segments in finding breakup value, as discussed earlier. Apart from the specific valuation technique applied here, the concept requires that the business be viewed as an ongoing "living system" of operating parts rather than as a collection of assets and liabilities.

Recall this book's earlier emphasis on the fact that business value is created by a positive trade-off of future cash flows for present commitments and outlays. As we'll see later in the chapter, the going concern value is useful when comparative cash flow analyses, singly and in combination, are considered for acquisitions and mergers. The continuing challenge to the analyst is to properly weigh this pattern of cash flows.

In summary, we've discussed a number of value definitions. Some were specialized yardsticks designed for specific situations. Many are directly or indirectly related to economic value. We defined economic value as the present value of future cash flows, discounted at the investor's risk-adjusted standard. This value concept is broadly applicable and we'll exploit it as we examine various decision areas where measures of value are necessary.

VALUE TO THE INVESTOR

As in Chapters 5, 7, and 8, we'll concentrate only on the three main types of corporate securities—bonds, preferred stock, and common stock—in discussing the techniques involved to assess *value* and *yield*. As used here, value is defined as the current value of the investment to the investor in present value terms, while yield represents the internal rate of return (IRR) earned by the investor on the price paid for the investment. We'll discuss major provisions in the basic securities types only insofar as they may affect their value and yield. The techniques covered should appear quite familiar to the reader because they closely relate to the analytical approaches in earlier chapters.

Bond Values

Valuing a bond is normally fairly straightforward. A typical bond issued by a corporation is a simple debt instrument. Its basic provisions generally entail a series of contractual semiannual interest payments, defined as a fixed rate based on the bond's stated par (face) value (usually $1,000). The legal contract, or *indenture*, promises repayment of the principal (nominal value) at a specified maturity date a number of years in the future. The basic characteristics of defined interest payments and repayment stipulations are encountered in most normal debt arrangements. Complicating aspects are sometimes found in provisions such as conversion into common stock at a predetermined exchange value, or payment of interest only when earned by the issuing company. We'll review some of these specialized features briefly.

A bond's basic value rests on the investor's assessment of the relative attractiveness of the expected stream of future interest receipts and the prospect for eventual recovery of the principal at maturity. Of course, there's normally no obligation for the investor to hold the bond until maturity because most bonds can be readily traded in the securities markets. Still, the risk underlying the bond contract must be considered here in terms of the issuing company's future ability to generate sufficient cash with which to pay both interest and principal. The collective judgment of security analysts and investors about the issuing company's prospects of doing this will influence the price level at which the bond is publicly traded, and the bond is likely to be rated by financial services like Moody's and Standard & Poors and placed in a particular risk category relative to other bonds.

To determine a bond's value, we must first calculate the present value of the interest payments received up to the maturity date and add to this the present value of the ultimate principal repayment. You'll recognize this method as comparable with the process of calculating the present value of capital expenditures in Chapter 6. The discount rate applied is the risk-adjusted rate that represents the investor's own standard of measuring investment opportunities within a range of acceptable risk.

For example, an investor with an 8 percent annual return standard would value a bond with a coupon interest rate of 6 percent annually significantly lower than its par value. The calculation is shown in Figure 9–1. The investor's annual return standard of 8 percent is equivalent to a semiannual standard of 4 percent, a restatement for purposes of calculation that's necessary to match the semiannual interest payments paid by most bonds.

The resulting value, $832.89, represents the maximum price our investor should be willing to pay—or the minimum price at which the investor should be willing to sell—if the investor normally expects a return (yield) of 8 percent from this type of investment. This particular bond should therefore be acquired only at a price considerably below (at a discount from) par. Note that the stated interest rate on the bond is relevant only for determining the semiannual cash receipts in absolute dollar terms.

FIGURE 9–1
Bond Valuation

Date of analysis:	July 1, 1994		
Face value (par) of bond:	$1,000		
Maturity date:	July 1, 2008		
Bond interest (coupon rate):	6% per year		
Interest receipts:	$30 semiannually		

	Total Cash Flow	Present Value Factors, 4 Percent*	Present Value
28 receipts of $30 over 14 years (28 periods)	$ 840	16.663 (× $30)	$499.89
Receipt of principal 14 years hence (28 periods)	1,000	0.333	333.00
Totals	$1,840		$832.89

*From Tables II and I (Chapter 6), respectively.

Actual valuation of the bond and the cash flows it represents depends on the investor's opportunity rate (return standard). In other words, the desired yield determines the price, and vice versa. This relationship also applies, of course, to the market quotations for publicly traded bonds. The quoted price, or value, is a function of the current yield collectively desired by the many buyers and sellers of these debt instruments.

If our investor were for some unrealistic reason satisfied with the very low annual yield of only 4 percent from holding the same bond (equivalent to 2 percent per six-month period), the value to the investor would rise considerably above par, as shown in Figure 9–2. Under these assumed conditions, the investor should be willing to pay a premium of up to $212.43 for the $1,000 bond because the personal return standard is lower than the stated interest rate. If the investor's own standard and the coupon interest rate were to coincide precisely, the value of the bond would, of course, match exactly the par value of $1,000.

In fact, any bond's quoted market price will tend to approach the par value as it reaches maturity because at

FIGURE 9-2
Bond Valuation with Lower Return Standard (4 percent per year)

	Total Cash Flow	Present Value Factors, 2 Percent*	Present Value
28 receipts of $30 over 14 years (28 periods) ...	$ 840	21.281 (× $30)	$ 638.43
Receipt of principal 14 years hence (28 periods) .	1,000	0.574	574.00
Totals	$1,840		$1,212.43

*From Tables II and I (Chapter 6), respectively.

that point the only representative value will be the imminent repayment of the principal—assuming, of course, that the company is financially able to pay as the amount becomes due.

Bond Yields. A related but common problem for the analyst or investor is the calculation of the yield produced by various bonds when quoted prices differ from par value. The key to this analysis again is the relationship of value and yield as discussed already. The technique used is a present value calculation that in effect determines the internal rate of return of the cash flow patterns generated by the bond over its remaining life.

The method is identical to that used for assessing the cash flows of any business investment proposal. The key difference in the data is that the individual investor's calculations are based on pretax cash flows that must be adjusted in each case by the investor for the personal tax situation. Other minor differences are the cash incidence in a semiannual pattern, and the form in which bond prices (the net investment) are quoted. Published prices are normally stated as a percentage of par. For example, a bond quoted at 103⅜ has a price of $1,033.75.

Bond yield tables have long been employed to determine a bond's internal rate of return (yield). While today's computers and calculators have financial routines that allow direct calculation, we'll nevertheless take a quick look at a yield table if only to help the reader understand the examples by visual inspection of the relationships. Bond yield tables are finely graduated present value tables that list the whole potential range of stated interest rates, subdivided into fractional progressions of as little as $\frac{1}{32}$ of a point. They're far more detailed than the present value tables in Chapter 6.

For example, Figure 9–3 shows a small segment of such a yield table, in this case for a bond with a coupon interest rate of precisely 6 percent. The columns show the number of six-month periods remaining in the life of the bond, while the rows display the yield to maturity or a price, given the number of periods to maturity. The yield to maturity simply refers to the yield obtained by the investor if the bond is actually held until its par value is repaid at the maturity date. If the investor were to sell at an earlier date, the market price of the bond received at that time would be substituted for par value in calculating the return. As a result, the yield achieved for the period up to the date of sale may differ from the

FIGURE 9–3
Bond Yield Table (sample section for a 6 percent rate)

	Price Given Years or Periods to Maturity					
Yield to Maturity	13 Years (26 periods)	13½ Years (27 periods)	14 Years (28 periods)	14½ Years (29 periods)	15 Years (30 periods)	15½ Years (31 periods)
3.80%	1.224 043	1.230 661	1.237 155	1.243 528	1.249 782	1.255 919
3.85	1.218 284	1.224 709	1.231 012	1.237 196	1.243 263	1.249 215
3.90	1.212 559	1.218 793	1.224 907	1.230 904	1.236 787	1.242 557
3.95	1.206 868	1.212 913	1.218 841	1.224 654	1.230 354	1.235 944
4.00	1.201 210	1.207 068	1.212 812*	1.218 443	1.223 964	1.229 377
4.05	1.195 585	1.201 260	1.206 821	1.212 273	1.217 616	1.222 853
4.10	1.189 993	1.195 486	1.200 868	1.206 142	1.211 310	1.216 375
4.15	1.184 434	1.189 747	1.194 952	1.200 051	1.205 046	1.209 940
4.20	1.178 908	1.184 043	1.189 073	1.193 999	1.198 823	1.203 549
4.25	1.173 414	1.178 374	1.183 230	1.187 985	1.192 642	1.197 201

*This example was used in Figure 9–2 (slight difference due to rounding of present value factors). Note that prices are given in the form of a 7-digit multiplier, which is applied against a $1,000 par value.

yield to maturity if the bond were trading above or below par. We can quickly find the bond's yield to maturity at any given purchase price in the bond yield tables.

Conversely, it's also possible to find the exact price (value) that corresponds to any particular desired yield to maturity. Our example of the 6 percent bond used in the previous section (Figure 9–2) is represented on the 4 percent yield line and in the 28-period column of the bond yield table segment reproduced in Figure 9–3. Bond yield tables provide a visual impression of the progression or regression of prices and yields which is, of course, based on their mathematical relationship. A programmed calculator goes through the same steps and formulas used to generate the tables.

Yield to maturity can be approximated by using a shortcut method if neither a programmed calculator nor a bond table is handy. If we assume that our 6 percent bond was quoted at a price of $832.89 on July 1, 1994 (which was the result of our earlier calculation), the discount from the par value of $1,000 is $167.11. The investor will thus not only receive the coupon interest of $30 for 28 periods, but will also earn the discount of $167.11 if the bond is held to maturity and if the repayment of $1,000 is received.

The shortcut method approximates the true yield by adjusting the periodic interest payment with a proportional amortization of this discount. The first step reflects the common accounting practice of amortizing discounts or premiums over the life of the bond. In our example, the $167.11 discount is therefore divided by the remaining 28 periods, and the resulting periodic value increment of $5.97 is added to the periodic interest receipt of $30. The adjusted six-month earnings pattern is now $35.97 per period.

The next step relates the adjusted periodic earnings of $35.97 to the average investment outstanding during the remaining life of the bond. The price paid by the investor is $832.89, while the investment's value will rise to $1,000 at maturity. The average of the two values is one half of the sum, $916.45. We can then calculate the *periodic* yield to maturity (based on the six-month interest period) by relating the periodic earnings of $35.97 to the average investment outstanding, or we can find the *annual* yield to maturity by relating two six-months earnings amounts of $35.97 each to the average investment:

$$\text{Yield} = \frac{2 \times \$35.97}{\$916.45} = 7.85\% \text{ per year}$$

This result is slightly below the precise yield of 8 percent per year on which our original calculation was built. The averaging shortcut will always introduce some error because it imperfectly simulates the progressive present value structure. As yield rates and the number of time periods increase, larger errors will result. Yet the rough calculation provides a satisfactory result for use as an initial analytical check.

Had a premium been involved (i.e., had the purchase price been above the par value of the bond), the shortcut calculation would, in contrast, reduce the periodic interest earnings by the proportional amortization of the premium. The second example discussed in the previous section (Figure 9–2) posed such a condition.

The result would appear as follows, again representing a close approximation of the true 4 percent solution:

$$\text{Yield} = \frac{(\$30.00 - \$7.59)2}{(\$1,212.43 + \$1,000) \div 2} = 4.05\% \text{ per year}$$

In summary, bond yield calculations involve a fairly straightforward determination of the internal rate of return of future cash flows generated by the bond investment at a known present price. As in the case of a business capital investment, a trade-off of current outlays for future cash flows under conditions of uncertainty is involved. Yield and value are mathematically related and this relationship can be utilized to locate either result in pre-set bond yield tables, or to solve the analysis directly with a programmed calculator or personal computer.

Bond Provisions and Value. The simple value and yield relationships discussed so far are, of course, affected by the specific conditions surrounding the company and its industry, and also by additional provisions in the specific bond indenture itself. The issuer's ability to pay must be assessed through careful analysis of the company's earnings pattern and projections of expected performance. The techniques in the early chapters of this book are helpful in this process. Ability to pay is a function of the projected cash flows and how well these flows cover debt service of both interest and principal. Sensitivity analysis based on high and low estimates of performance can be useful here.

Variations in the bond indenture agreement will also affect the value and the yield earned. We'll refer only to the major types of bond variations here. *Mortgage bonds* are secured by specific assets of the issuing firm. Because of this relationship, the bondholders have a cushion against default on the principal. As a result of the reduced risk, the coupon interest rate offered with mortgage bonds may be somewhat lower than that of unsecured debenture bonds and reduce the yield to the investor. *Income bonds* are at the other extreme on the risk spectrum because they're not only unsecured, but also pay interest only if the company's earnings reach a specified minimum level. Their yield levels will be correspondingly high.

Convertible bonds, as we've already observed, add the attraction of the holders' eventual participation in the potential market appreciation of common stock for which the bond can be exchanged at a set price. Therefore the coupon rate of interest may be somewhat lower than that of a straight bond. As we discussed in Chapter 8, the value of convertible bonds is affected by (1) the market's assessment of the likely performance of the common stock, (2) the gap between the stipulated conversion price and the current price of the common stock, and (3) the coupon interest it pays semiannually.

Normally, the conversion price is set higher than the prevailing market value of the common stock at the time of issue to allow for expected value growth of the common stock over time. Conversion is essentially at the investor's discretion when found advantageous, although the indenture usually stipulates a time limit as a well as the right of the issuing company to call the bonds for redemption at a slight premium price after a certain date, thus forcing the investor to act. As common share prices approach and surpass the conversion price, the bond's value will rise above par because of the growing value of the equivalent common shares it represents.

A fairly recent phenomenon in the bond markets is the appearance of so-called *junk bonds* extensively promoted by some investment bankers to support company takeovers, using very high levels of debt, or for so-called *leveraged buyouts* by groups of managers or investors that similarly use extremely high financial leverage to finance the purchase of the company involved. These securities are in effect *subordinate* to (ranking below) the claims of other creditors in case of default and are sold under often highly risky circumstances because the amount of indebtedness involved in some of these transactions exceeds what's normally considered a prudent level. The yields provided by these unsecured instruments are usually commensurate with the high risk perceived by investors, and defaults aren't uncommon.

Many other modifications and provisions are possible to tailor bonds of various types to the issuing company's needs and to the prevailing conditions in the securities markets. The many variations in bond provisions and their impact on value and yield call for careful judgments that go beyond the direct analytical techniques we discussed. We repeat that the calculations described are but the starting point, and no hard-and-fast rules exist for weighing mechanically all aspects of bond valuation. In the final analysis, value and yield must be adjusted with due regard to the investor's economic and risk preferences, in line with the specific objectives in owning debt instruments. The references at the end of the chapter cover these aspects in greater detail.

Preferred Stock Values

By its very nature, preferred stock represents a middle ground between debt and common equity ownership. The security provides a series of cash dividend payments, but normally has no specific provision (or expectation) for repayment of the par value of the stock. However, at times preferred stock carries a call provision, which allows the issuing company to retire part or all of the stock during a specific time period by paying a small premium over the stated value of the stock.

While the investor enjoys a preferential position over common stock with regard to current dividends and also to recovery of principal in the case of liquidation of the enterprise, preferred dividends may not be paid if company performance is poor. Such an event will, of course, affect the stock's value adversely.

Preferred dividends, like common dividends, are declared at the discretion of the board of directors and may not be made up if missed unless the preferred issue carries specific legal requirements to the contrary. Such provisions, for example, may call for *cumulating* past unpaid dividends until the company can afford to declare dividends of any kind. At other times, particularly in new companies, preferred stocks may carry a *participation* feature, which requires the board of directors to declare preferred dividends higher than the stated rate if earnings exceed a stipulated minimum level. But these two special situations are only infrequently encountered.

The task of valuing preferred stock, therefore, has to be based on less definite conditions than was the case with bonds because the only reasonably certain element is the stated annual dividend, which was set as a percentage of stated value. For example, an 8 percent preferred stock usually refers to a $100 share of stock that's expected to pay a dividend of $8 per year, most likely in quarterly installments, a pattern normally matching that for common stocks. The investor is faced with valuing this stream of prospective cash dividends. If the price paid for a share of preferred stock was $100, and the stock is held indefinitely, the yield under these circumstances would be 8 percent, assuming that the company is likely to be able to pay the dividend regularly.

If the price was more or less than the stated value, the yield could be found by relating the amount of the dividend to the actual price per share:

$$\text{Yield} = \frac{\text{Annual dividend per share}}{\text{Price paid per share}}$$

If the investor could expect to sell the stock at $110 five years hence, the exact yield can be determined by using either present value techniques or the shortcut methods discussed earlier in the section on bonds.

However, estimating a future disposal value involves a good deal of conjecture. In contrast to bonds, preferred shares have no specific maturity date or par value to be paid at maturity. The actual price of a preferred stock traded in the securities markets depends both on company performance and on the collective value the securities markets place on the given preferred issue. In turn, this price level reflects the risk/reward trade-off demanded for the whole spectrum of investments at the time. The value range will depend not only on the respective risk premiums assigned to individual securities, but also on the inflationary expectations underlying the economy which are reflected in the risk-free rate on which risk premiums are based. Value may be a little easier to estimate if the stock carries a mandatory call provision applicable at a specific future date and price, especially if the date of analysis is close to that time.

When we look at preferred stock values from the viewpoint of investing, we should use the investor's own return standard to arrive at the maximum price the investor should be willing to pay for the stock, or the minimum price at which the investor should be willing to sell. We simply relate the stipulated dividend rate to our investor's required return—which is relevant for the level of risk implicit in the preferred issue—to arrive at the answer. If the return standard were 9 percent against which to test the 8 percent preferred, we would determine the investor-specific value as follows:

$$\text{Value per share} = \frac{\text{Stated dividend rate}}{\text{Required return}} = \frac{0.08}{0.09} = \$88.89$$

If the investor were satisfied with only a 7 percent return, the value would be

$$\text{Value per share} = \frac{0.08}{0.07} = \$114.28$$

The judgments that remain to be made, of course, relate to any uncertainty in the future dividend pattern, and any likely material change in the future value of the stock due to either changing market conditions or a scheduled call for redemption at a premium price.

Preferred Stock Provisions and Value. As in the case of bonds, there are many modifications in the provisions of preferred stocks that may affect their value in the market. We mentioned earlier that some preferred stocks, particularly in newly established companies, contain a *participation* feature, which entitles the preferred holder to higher dividends if corporate earnings exceed a set level. This feature can favorably affect the potential yield and thus the valuation of the stock, depending on how likely it is that the company will reach this higher earnings level.

A much more common feature, similar to some bonds, is *convertibility*, the possibility of changing the preferred ownership position into that of common stock, as discussed in Chapter 8. As in the case of convertible bonds, however, the value of this feature can't be calculated precisely. Yet, as the price of common stock reaches and exceeds the stated conversion price, the price of the convertible preferred stock will tend to reflect the market value of the equivalent number of common shares. Before this point is reached, the convertible preferred stock's value will be largely considered the same as regular preferred stock's value and will be based essentially on the stated dividend. Convertibility is generally accompanied by a call provision, at a premium price, which enables the company to force conversion when conditions are right.

In summary, the challenge of preferred stock valuation also goes beyond the simple techniques we've shown. In the end, decisions should be made only after careful assessment of the relative attractiveness of the specific features and conditions surrounding a particular company's preferred stock.

Common Stock Values

The most complex valuation problem is encountered when we turn to common stock because by definition, common stock represents owners' residual claim on the total performance and outlook of the issuing corporation. We found this to be true when we examined the cost of capital from the point of view of the corporation in Chapter 7.

Common stock valuation is especially difficult because it involves full ownership risks, yet permits claims on both assets and earnings only after all other claims have been satisfied. An investment in common stock thus involves sharing both the risks and the rewards. This heightens the uncertainty about potential dividend receipts and the amount of recovery of the "principal." As a consequence, measurement techniques have to deal with variables subject to a high degree of judgment.

The rewards of successful common stock ownership are several: *cash dividends* (and sometimes additional *stock distributions* in lieu of cash), *growth in recorded equity* from growing earnings (which in part are reinvested by management), and past and prospective *cash flow performance* with the resulting potential appreciation (or decline) of the stock's market price. As we observed in Chapter 7, many practical and theoretical issues surround the interpretation and measurement of these elements. Here we'll focus on ways of developing reasonable approximations of common share values and, similarly, approximations of the yield an investor derives from a common stock investment.

Earnings and Common Stock Value. The simplest way to approach the valuation of a share of common stock is to estimate the likely future level of earnings per share, and to capitalize these earnings at an appropriate discount rate that reflects return expectations within the scope of the investor's personal risk preference.

The formulation is

$$\text{Value per share} = \frac{\text{Earnings per share (projected)}}{\text{Discount rate (investor's expectation of return)}}$$

We recall from our discussion of the cost of capital, however, that there are serious practical shortcomings in using projected earnings to measure shareholder expectations. Unless a company continually pays out all of its earnings in the form of dividends—which we know from Chapters 2 and 3 to be quite unlikely, especially for a growing company that requires reinvestment of at least some of its earnings—the stream of projected earnings isn't at all representative of the benefits in fact received by the shareholder. Moreover, the formula is static unless any potential growth or decline in earnings is built in. Finally, there's the basic problem of forecasting the earnings pattern itself for both the company and its industry.

A more specific approach to estimating common share value is to capitalize expected dividends. The size, regularity, and trend in dividend payout to shareholders have an important effect on the value of a share of common stock, being elements of shareholder value creation. Yet there's also a degree of uncertainty about the receipt of any series of future dividends. Not only will such dividends depend on the firm's ability to perform successfully, but also dividends are declared at the discretion of the corporate board of directors.

No general rule applies in this area—dividend policies can range from no cash payment at all to regular payments of 75 percent or more of current earnings. At times, dividends paid may even exceed current earnings because the company is unwilling to cut the current dividend per share during a temporary earnings slump. Most boards of directors see some value in the consistency with which dividends are paid, and major adjustments in the size of the dividend, up or down, are only made reluctantly.

The approach to valuation via dividends involves projecting the expected dividends per share and discounting them by the return standard appropriate for the investor. Several major issues arise here.

First, the current level of dividends paid is likely to change over time. For example, in a successful, growing company the dividend is likely to grow as well. The problem is to make the projection of future dividends realistic, as past performance is the only guide. If a company has been paying a steadily growing dividend over many years, an extrapolation of this past trend may be reasonable, but must be tempered by subjective judgments about the outlook for the company and its industry. Companies with more erratic patterns of earnings and dividends, however, pose a greater challenge.

The second issue is the method of calculation. The most common format is the so-called *dividend discount model* or *dividend growth model,* which we'll cover next in its simplest form. The formula is a restatement of the dividend approach we used as one way of calculating the cost of equity in Chapter 7. In that approach we defined the cost of common equity as the ratio of the current dividend to the current market price plus the expected rate of growth of future dividends. Here, instead of solving for the cost of equity—which is the investor's expectation of return—we solve for the value or price of the stock:

$$\text{Value per share} = \frac{\text{Current dividend}}{\text{Discount rate (investor's expectation of return)} - \text{Dividend growth rate}}$$

This particular formula is based on the idea that the value of a share of stock is the sum of the present values of a series of growing annual dividend payments, discounted at the investor's return expectation for this class of risk. But it implies an ongoing series of payments in perpetuity, and it also implies a constant annual rate of growth in the dividend payment. The formula also permits using the less realistic assumption of a constantly declining dividend.

However, it's important to note that this model would give an invalid answer for a company paying dividends that grow as fast or faster than the discount rate because then the denominator would become zero or even negative. Clearly, under such a happy condition the investor's return expectation should be reexamined and raised, or the stock should be considered outside the investor's risk/reward spectrum.

The dividend discount model is related mathematically to an annuity formula that assumes a constant growth rate and constant discount rate. The valuation it provides implicitly includes any appreciation in the future market value of the stock that's due to management's reinvestment of the retained portion of the growing earnings that made the increase in dividends possible. This condition holds because in the model the stock's market value at any future time is defined as the present value at that point of the ensuing stream of growing dividends.

The simplifying assumption of a constant rate of growth in dividends can be modified if a more erratic pattern of future dividends is expected. The calculation then becomes a present value analysis of uneven annual cash flows up to a selected point in the future. If the analyst wishes to assume that the dividend growth rate will become stable at some future time, the basic formula can then be inserted and its result discounted to the present. We must realize, of course, that forecasting a precise pattern of dividends is problematic under most circumstances; therefore, the analyst should look for reasonable approximations.

The two measures just discussed don't take into account the general trends and specific fluctuations in the securities markets. Obviously, values of specific shares can't be independent of movements in the securities markets as a whole, which are caused by economic, industry, political, and myriad other factors. Therefore, the economic returns a company achieves on the resources invested and managed tend to be recognized in the *relative market value* of its shares, that is, relative to share values of its competitors and within the context of overall market movements. Moreover, the value of a company's shares reflects the collective performance assessments by security analysts and institutional investors, and the resulting demand for, or lack of interest in, those shares. While important, these considerations are beyond the scope of this book.

Common Stock Yield and Investor Expectations. Chapter 3 presented two simple yardsticks for measuring the owners' return on investment in common stock. One of these was the *earnings yield,* a simple ratio of current or projected earnings per share to the current market price. The other was an inverse relationship, the so-called *price/earnings ratio.* As we pointed out, these simple ratios are static expressions based on readily available data and should only serve as temporary rough indicators of the real investor's yield created by a company's economic performance, that is, the cash flow pattern generated and projected.

The two measures are useful mainly for a comparative analysis of companies or industry groupings, but must be supplemented by more insights if the analyst wishes to approximate the actual economic yield of a stock. Any serious examination of value or yield relative to the shareholder's expectations should use more sophisticated techniques—such as the capital asset pricing model (CAPM)—that take into account market risk, specific company risk, portfolio considerations, and investors' risk preferences.

A great deal of research has improved our understanding of the relative performance of common stocks within the movements of the security markets. This has resulted in refined definitions of the *systematic risk* underlying a diversified portfolio of stocks traded and the *unsystematic (avoidable) risk* of a particular security. As we discussed in Chapter 7, the CAPM relates the relative risk of a security to the risk of the market portfolio through a calculated factor, β, which indicates the difference in the risk characteristics of the stock versus the risk characteristics of the portfolio. These are defined in terms of the historical trend in returns earned over and above the *risk-free return* from the safest type of investment, such as long-term U.S. government bonds.

Thus, the expected yield of a particular common stock is the sum of the risk-free return plus a risk premium, which is the risk premium earned in the total portfolio of stocks, adjusted by the inherent riskiness of the particular security. We described the formula in Chapter 7:

$$\text{Yield} = R_f + \beta(R_m - R_f)$$

where

R_f is the risk-free return.

β is the particular stock's covariance of variability in returns (the specific measure of riskiness).

R_m is the average return expected on common stocks.

Fortunately, the β for publicly traded companies is readily available in financial services such as Value Line. Indications of the risk-free rate prevalent at the time and estimates of the return from groups of common stocks are also available in published sources.

We've only touched on some of the techniques used to determine value and yield for common stocks. Much more practical and theoretical insight is needed to deal confidently with the complex issues involved. The references at the end of this chapter provide greater depth.

Other Considerations in Valuing Common Stock. The book value per share of common stock is often quoted in financial references and company reviews. As we've observed, this figure is the recorded residual claim of the shareholder as stated on the balance sheet. Book value is an accumulation of past values and doesn't reflect economic value in the form of potential earnings or dividends. Only under unusual circumstances will book value per share be reasonably representative of anything approximating the economic value of a share of common stock.

This might be true, for example, if a company either has just been started or is about to be liquidated. Under normal conditions, however, book value per share will become increasingly remote from current values because changes in the values of existing assets are rarely, if ever, reflected in an adjustment to the books of account. The *book to market* ratio discussed in Chapter 3 is used as a rough indicator of this divergence, and a book value that's close to or even exceeds market value may suggest that the issuing company is underperforming, a situation that could invite takeover attempts by aggressive investors or corporations.

Market values of common stocks have been treated lightly in our discussion because a book on financial analysis techniques isn't the place in which to explore workings of the securities market. Suffice it to say here that if the following several basic conditions are met, quotations of a stock in the securities market can reasonably be assumed to represent the underlying economic value based on a firm's current and prospective performance.

- The stock should be traded frequently and in fairly sizable volume.
- Share ownership should ideally be widespread so that trading doesn't involve moving large blocks of shares between a small number of concerned parties.
- The stock should be publicly traded on one or more exchange or be part of the increasingly important over-the-counter market.

Even if all of these conditions are met, a stock's market value at any point may not necessarily reflect the company's true potential because external factors (such as changes in the economy, market conditions, publicity about the company and its industry, or takeover attempts) may affect the price at which the stock is traded. To help them understand this context, analysts study the range within which market values have moved, preferably over at least one year, and chart prices' behavior relative to market averages and composite averages for the industry grouping. One example is the historical and projected charting found in the Value Line company analyses.

Specialized Valuation Issues

In Chapter 7 we discussed the main aspects of rights and warrants from the perspective of the issuing company. We'll now turn briefly to illustrating the value of these specialized forms of financing to the investor.

Rights values arise from the fact that these securities entitle the holder to purchase common shares at a price often significantly below the prevailing market price. For example, an investor holding five common shares has received five rights which represent the opportunity to purchase one new share of common at $30. The current market value of the existing common stock is $40. Our investor's initial position is:

Number of shares	5
Number of rights	5
Value of five shares @ $40	$200
Subscription price	$30

After exercising the rights and paying $30 to the company, the shareholder's position will be:

Number of shares	6
Value of investment	$230.00
Investment per share	$38.33
Value of a right	$1.67*

*(Old value − New value)

The market value of the company's shares after all rights have been exercised will in fact approximate $38.33 because the new shares were offered at a significant discount, in the ratio of one new share for each five old shares held. When a rights offering is announced, the shares of the company will trade *cum rights* (with rights) from the effective date (holder-of-record date) until the specified date at which the stock becomes *ex rights* (trades without rights). At that time a decline in price reflecting the value of the now separate rights will take place.

To the investor, the value of each right is therefore the proportionate discount provided by the rights offering, as related to the ratio of old and new shares. Rights are often traded in the market at the approximate level of the calculated value. Both the value of common stock ex rights and the value of rights themselves will, of course, be influenced by general movements in the securities markets that are independent of the particular company's circumstances.

Warrants have value directly related to the market price of the common shares of the company. Unlike rights, warrants aren't issued proportionally to all common shareholders, but are most frequently attached to issues of new debt and occasionally to new issues of common. Moreover, warrants tend to have expiration dates far longer than rights, and in some cases have no expiration at all. In effect, warrants are options entitling the holder to purchase a new share of common at a fixed exercise price for an extended period of time.

The value of the warrant therefore will be directly related to the difference between the exercise price and the expected market value of the common during the usually lengthy exercise period. If the common stock continually trades at or below the exercise price, the value of the warrant will be zero. If the market value of the common rises above the exercise price—especially if it's expected to grow in the future during the remainder of the exercise period—the warrant's value will rise in concert.

VALUING AN ONGOING BUSINESS

It's frequently necessary to find the total value of a business as an ongoing entity, especially when its purchase or sale is being considered, but also to determine changes in value over time. The wave of acquisitions, mergers, and hostile takeovers in the 1980s involved thousands upon thousands of such valuations. A similar type of valuation may be used when a company, for purposes of internal restructuring, disposes of certain product lines or operating divisions. The buyers may be other companies, groups of investors, or even the existing management who may want to acquire the division financed through a leveraged buyout, employing high proportions of unsecured debt.

Regardless of the form of the purchase, sale, or restructuring, both the buyer and the seller need to arrive at a reasonable approximation of the economic value of the business as a going concern. At the same time, both owners and managers have a continuing interest in the current and expected value of the business even if no sale or merger is contemplated. Managing for economic value has become a critical focus in recent years.

We'll first discuss the basic concepts of *valuing business cash flows*, which apply to most valuation situations. Next we'll turn to the more specialized cases of *restructuring* and the values driving corporate takeovers, and end the chapter with a review of the ultimate management obligation of creating *shareholder value*, the concept with which we started the book.

Valuing Business Cash Flows

In essence, an ongoing business represents a series of future cash flows. Thus, the present value methods discussed in Chapter 6 are applicable here, just as if the analyst were calculating the desirability of a capital investment project. This calls for a transformation of past and projected earnings performance into a net cash flow framework.

To begin with, the operating earnings of the business must be forecast for a reasonable number of years in the future. The relevant definition of operating earnings for this purpose is earnings before interest, but after taxes, that is, EBIT (1 − tax rate), as discussed in Chapter 8. The reason for using tax-adjusted EBIT is that we're looking for the cash flows generated *before* any financing considerations—just as we did when analyzing capital expenditures in Chapter 6.

The projection of the expected earnings pattern calls for a variety of assumptions and judgments. The simplest way to project, of course, would be to consider the current level of earnings as constant. Under most circumstances, however, such a simplification wouldn't be realistic. If operating earnings can be expected to grow or decline, or to follow a pronounced cyclical pattern, we must make a year-by-year projection for as far in the future as possible. Any significant nonoperating earnings after applicable taxes, such as investment income, should be recognized and added in every period, as they represent part of the value of the total company.

The second step is to convert the operating earnings pattern into cash flows, by adjusting the aftertax earnings result for depreciation and amortization write-offs and for deferred taxes, as we discussed in Chapters 3 and 6.

The third step is to determine the future capital outlays deemed necessary to support both the present level of earnings and any anticipated changes in operations. These include outlays for property, plant and equipment, major spending programs such as R&D (research and development) projects, and incremental working capital requirements.

To some extent, such estimates are quite speculative, yet it's normally unrealistic to assume that earnings of an ongoing business will continue even at current levels. Unquestionably, there will have to be periodic infusions of capital for replacement and upgrading of existing equipment, not to mention the requirements to support growth expectations, as discussed in Chapter 2. As we observed then, a simplifying assumption commonly used to project these capital expenditures is that to maintain the present level of earnings, each year an amount close or equal to annual depreciation must be reinvested. The estimated amount of outlays for expansion or new products and services and their effect on earnings are dealt with as separate, distinct capital outlays and their ensuing cash inflows in the years in which they're expected to occur. We made such an assumption in the business models in Chapters 1 and 5.

The final step in valuing an ongoing business involves truncating the analysis after an appropriate number of years and deriving a terminal value (market value) for the business at that point. By definition, this terminal value would be the sum of the present values of all future cash flows from that point on. But the difficulty of forecasting operations beyond the end of the chosen analysis period calls for finding a shortcut answer for the terminal value.

A common way of dealing with the problem is to use a simple earnings multiple at that point, that is, to set the value of the business in year 6 or 10, or whatever cutoff point is desired, at 8, 10, or 15 times the aftertax earnings in that year. The multiple chosen will depend on the nature of the business and the trends in the industry it represents. Because of the power of discounting, such an approximation of terminal value will generally suffice.

In a generalized format, this approach appears as:

Cash Flow Element	Year 1	Year 2	Year 3	Year i	Year j
Aftertax operating earnings*	+	+	+	+	+
Add: Write-offs and other noncash items	+	+	+	+	+
Less: Capital investments (including working capital)	−	−	−	−	−
Plus: Terminal value					+
Net cash flows	y_1	y_2	y_3	y_i	y_j

*Plus any significant *nonoperating* earnings after taxes.

The resulting annual net cash flows, also referred to as *free cash flow*, represent the cash available to the company to support its obligations to the providers of the long-term funds (i.e., the payment of interest, dividends, and potential repayment of debt or even repurchase of its own shares).

Once the annual pattern plus the terminal value has been *discounted* at the appropriate return standard—normally the weighted cost of capital—the resulting net present value represents a fair approximation of the value of the total business. The quality of the result depends, of course, on the quality of the estimates used in deriving it. The analyst should employ sensitivity analysis to test the likely range of outcomes.

It will be useful to demonstrate visually how this present value relates to a company's capital structure. What we've developed by discounting the net cash flow stream and the assumed terminal value is the approximate fair market value of the company's *capitalization*. Figure 9–4 demonstrates that the total recorded value of a business is the sum of its working capital, fixed assets, and other assets, which are financed by the combination of long-term debt and equity. The present value

FIGURE 9–4

Present Value of Business Cash Flows and the Capital Structure

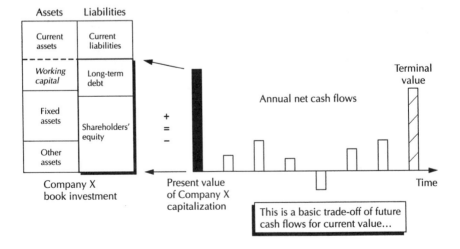

approach has enabled us to express this accounting value in current economic terms—a present value that may be higher or lower than the recorded values on the balance sheet. Only by coincidence will the two values be precisely equal.

It should be evident that to arrive at the market value of the shareholders' equity requires that we subtract the value of the long-term debt from the present value result, which was the total market value of the business, also called *value of the firm* or *enterprise value*. We must be careful to determine the value of long-term debt, not in terms of the recorded values on the balance sheet, but rather in terms of the current yields prevailing for debt of similar risk, as we discussed earlier in this chapter.

Thus, if current interest rates are higher than the stated rates for the company's debt, the value of the debt will be lower than recorded, and vice versa. By observing this principle, we remain consistent with the weighted average cost of capital yardstick applied in discounting the cash flow pattern, a measure that contains the cost of incremental debt, as we recall from Chapter 7. A similar deduction must be made for any preferred stock contained in the capital structure.

We've now achieved a direct valuation of the company's common equity by means of an economic approach that's superior to the simpler devices discussed in the common stock section of this chapter. This concept is the basis for much of the analytical work underlying modern security analysis, where the importance of cash flow analysis has overshadowed most other methodologies.

In a multibusiness company, the approach can be refined by developing operating cash flow patterns for each of the business units, and discounting these individual patterns at the corporate cost of capital or, if the businesses differ widely in their risk/reward conditions, by applying different discount standards that reflect these differences. In recent years, the concept of testing the present value of individual business units to determine the relative contribution to the corporation's total value has become widely accepted.

Yet given the nature of the estimates underlying the analysis, there's nothing automatic about the application of such values in an actual transaction involving the sale of a company or any of its parts. Different analysts and certainly buyers and sellers will use their own sets of assumptions in developing their respective results. There will also be efforts to test the analytical results against comparable transactions to the extent that they're available and relevant. The actual value finally agreed upon in any transaction between a buyer and a seller will depend on many more factors, not the least of which is the difference in the return expectations of the parties involved and their negotiating stance and skills.

Shortcuts in Valuing an Ongoing Business. In the previous example, an earnings multiple was used to derive the terminal value for the business. This multiple simply indicated what a particular level of current or projected earnings was "worth" at the end point of the analysis. Closely related to the price/earnings ratio, this rule of thumb is often applied to quickly value the company, and the result can be an "opener" in initial negotiations. Never precise, the earnings multiple is derived from rough statistical comparisons of similar transactions and from a comparative evaluation of the performance of the price/earnings ratios of companies in the industry.

When the measure is turned into a ratio of estimated earnings to value, it provides a rough estimate of the rate of return on the purchase or selling price, assuming that the earnings chosen are representative of what the future will bring. When taken as only one of the indicators of value within a whole array of negotiating data, the earnings multiple and the related crude rate of return have some merit.

Other shortcuts in valuing an ongoing business involve determining the total market value of common and preferred equity from market quotations—in itself somewhat of a challenge in view of stock market fluctuations—and adjusting this total for any long-term debt to be assumed in the transaction. One issue involved in this approach is the question of how representative the market quotations are depending on the trading pattern and volume of the particular stock. At times, when no publicly traded securities are involved, the business's book value is examined as an indicator of value. Needless to say, the fact that recorded values don't necessarily reflect economic values can be a significant problem.

All of these results may at one time or another be entered into the deliberations, but considerable judgment must be exercised to determine their relevance in the particular case. In most situations, the discounted cash flow approach will be the conceptually most convincing measure.

Value in Restructuring and Combinations

This section will apply the concepts of cash flow analysis of an ongoing business and related measures to the specific issue of restructuring a company for higher value, or for seeking higher value in a combination of two or more companies.

Restructuring and Value. The opportunity to restructure arises from the recognition by management or by interested outside parties that a *value gap* exists between the value actually being created by a company, and the potential value achievable under changed circumstances. This value gap, in simple terms, is the difference between the present value of the projected cash flows under existing conditions, and the present value of a different and usually higher cash flow pattern from the restructured company. The attraction in a corporate takeover is for the acquirer to realize the potential benefits implicit in the value gap. Depending on the circumstances, the value gap can support very sizable premiums in the price bidding usually encountered in takeover situations—even though the actual results may in fact fall short of the premiums paid in the heat of the contest.

It's beyond the scope of this book to develop all aspects of the rationale and the special considerations and techniques employed by corporate takeover specialists, leveraged buyout consultants, and investment bankers using instruments such as junk bonds to restructure companies large and small. Instead, we'll briefly discuss the economic rationale and basic analytical approach to determining the value gap. For this purpose, the most common reasons that explain the value gap should be listed first.

Underperformance by parts or all of a company is likely to be the most important cause of lowered values. In thousands of situations, the historical record and projected performance by existing management using existing strategies and policies were demonstrated to be inferior to those of comparable businesses. Such a record is usually directly reflected in relative share price levels. Whether restructuring is initiated by the board of directors from within, or through friendly or hostile initiatives by outsiders, the aim is to raise lagging performance and cash flow expectations. Revision of business strategies, improved cost effectiveness and technology, reduction of unnecessary expenses, and more aggressive management of the company's resources are commonly used to achieve such results.

Disposal of selected lines of business is an extension of the improvement strategies just mentioned. Here the considerations may involve the sale of poor performers, and reinvesting the proceeds in more promising parts of the company, distributing the cash to owners in the form of special dividends, or even repurchasing shares. Successful businesses may also be sold with the idea of realizing the economic gains from such a "star" and using the proceeds to fund remaining potential successes. Another consideration is to more sharply focus management's attention on lines of activity it can competently manage for long-term success. Not to be overlooked is the fact that proceeds from the sale of part of a company can help finance a takeover.

Eliminating redundant assets is often used to free economic value that tends to remain hidden, such as unused real estate, investments, and even excessive amounts of cash bearing only minimal returns. The restructuring analysis in effect focuses on separating those economic values that are necessary to carry on the desired activities, while cashing in on all resources not relevant to the core purposes of the new company.

It should be clear that the point of view of restructuring is to develop in essence a breakup value of the company under study, carefully examining each business unit and all major assets held, and looking for ways of not only improving operating cash flows but also realizing the economic values of resources that can be stripped away without affecting the chosen direction.

From an analytical standpoint, the approach is similar to the present value cash flow valuation discussed earlier. The main difference is that a set of estimates is used that identifies specific enhancements in the cash flow pattern, as well as disposal values from businesses or redundant resources.

If our earlier analysis can be stated as

$$\text{Value} = \text{PV (Free cash flow + Terminal value)}$$

then the restructuring approach can be stated as

$$\text{Value} = \text{PV (Free cash flow + Terminal value)} + \text{PV (Enhancements)}$$
$$+ \text{PV (Disposal proceeds} - \text{Cash flow lost from disposals)}$$

and the value gap will be the difference between the two results. A key attraction to the restructurer is, of course, obtaining control of the higher cash flows involved.

It should be noted that two other aspects enter the picture. If a company changes hands in a restructuring, the depreciation basis for the assets involved is usually increased because of the higher values involved in the transaction. Such an increase in the tax shield effect will enhance cash flow because income taxes paid are reduced. Also, if the restructuring introduces higher financial leverage, as is usually the case, the impact on return on shareholders' equity should be favorable, even though the cash flow valuation may be adversely affected. The valuation changes because as the risk exposure increases, the cost of debt in the company's weighted cost of capital will rise, causing the discount standard to rise—thereby lowering the present value.

Combinations and Synergy. Another form of restructuring is found in the combination of two or more hitherto independent companies. The rationale often claimed for acquisitions and mergers is that economic benefits from synergy are expected to occur. While many empirical studies have cast doubt on whether business combinations are always as mutually beneficial as hoped, it's logical to assume that joining two separate businesses, particularly in the same industry, will tend to bring about some operating efficiencies.

Examples might include more fully utilizing manufacturing facilities or warehousing space, eliminating duplicate railway tracks or delivery routes, or consolidating certain activities, such as marketing and selling, support staffs, and administration. Many of these benefits can also be expected when complementary companies or even those in different businesses are combined.

The impact of synergy can be felt in two major ways. The more *direct* benefits are identifiable cash flow improvements, that is, lower expenses that result from consolidation and reduction of facilities and staffs, and higher contribution from improved market position and coverage. The specific levels of such cash flow benefits must be estimated when an acquisition or merger is considered. Such estimates will, of course, vary in quality depending on how quantifiable the opportunities for improvements are. There are also likely to be tax shield and leverage effects as we discussed in the previous section.

A more *indirect* benefit is that the stock of the combined company may become more attractive to investors and will achieve a higher market price, reflecting improved cash flows. Security analysts and the investment community generally expect combinations considered synergistic to bring about not only a more profitable company, but possibly one poised for faster growth, one with a stronger market position, or one subject to lesser earnings fluctuations as the cycles of the individual businesses could offset each other. This reassessment may in time lower the company's risk premium, lower its cost of capital, and also improve the expected price/earnings ratio.

Possible profit improvements resulting from a business combination can be displayed to the extent that they're quantifiable. To do this the analyst uses two sets of pro forma income statements. One set shows the projected net profits and cash flows from each company separately, while the other reflects the combined company and includes the envisioned improvements. These statements then become the basis for comparative ratio analysis, for calculating value with various methods, including present value analysis, and for highlighting the estimated annual amount of synergistic effect included in the second set of statements.

At times it may be useful to determine separately the present value of all the synergistic cash flow benefits contained in the combined pro forma statements. This present value can then be used as a rough guide in negotiating the terms of the merger, as the value of these benefits may have to be considered in setting the value premium the acquirer has to pay. In the end, the basis for valuation is likely to be a combination of present value analysis, rules of thumb, and the effect of a large variety of conditions, both tangible and intangible.

Combinations and Share Values. When an exchange of common stock is involved in an acquisition or merger agreement, the valuation challenge is extended beyond the economic valuation of the cash flow patterns themselves. The issue of valuing two different securities arises, as well as the issue of having to find an appropriate ratio of exchange that reflects the shares' respective values. Moreover, in most cases the acquirer has to pay a significant premium (between 15 and 25 percent is the usual range) over the objective value of the acquired company.

This premium will, of course, affect the actual ratio of exchange of shares agreed on. While in the end a numerical solution is applied, the underlying values and the premium will be the result of extensive negotiation and a certain amount of "horse trading."

As the two stocks are valued, any differences in the quality and breadth of trading in the securities markets can be an important factor. If, for example, a large, well-established company acquires a new, fast-growing company, the market value assessment of the acquirer's stock is likely more reliable than that of the acquired company, whose stock may be thinly traded and unproven. But even if they had comparable market exposure, the inherent difference in the nature and performance of the two companies may exhibit itself in, among other indicators, a pronounced difference in price/earnings ratios. In effect, this means one company's performance is valued less highly in the market than the other. This difference will influence valuation of the stocks and the final price negotiated.

We'll demonstrate just a few key calculations needed to arrive at the basis of exchange, using a simplified example. Let's assume that Acquirer Corporation and Candidate, Inc., have the following key dimensions and performance data at the time of their merger negotiations:

Key Data	Acquirer Corporation	Candidate, Inc.
Current earnings	$50,000,000	$10,000,000
Number of shares	10 million	10 million
Earnings per share	$ 5.00	$ 1.00
Current market price	$60.00	$15.00
Price/earnings ratio	12X	15X

Negotiations between the management teams have reached a point where, after Candidate has rejected several offers, Acquirer now considers a price premium of about 20 percent over the current market value of Candidate's stock necessary to make a deal. This calls for an exchange ratio of $18/$60, or about 0.3 shares of Acquirer stock for each share of Candidate stock. The impact on Acquirer would be as follows, at the combined current levels of earnings that include no synergistic benefits:

	Acquirer Corporation
Combined earnings	$60,000,000
Number of shares (10.0 + 3.0 million)	13 million
New earnings per share	$4.62
Old earnings per share	$5.00
Immediate dilution	$0.38

Under these conditions, Acquirer would suffer an immediate dilution of 38 cents per share from the combination. Yet the fact that Candidate's stock had a higher price/earnings ratio suggests that the smaller company enjoys desirable attributes which may include high growth in earnings or technologically protected position.

Acquirer must therefore consider two points. First, are Candidate's earnings likely to grow at a rate that will close the gap in earnings per share relatively quickly, aided by any synergistic benefits available now? Second, is the inclusion of Candidate likely to change the risk/reward characteristics of the combined company so as to improve the price/earnings ratio—and thus help overcome the dilution?

In our example, the earnings gap to be filled is 13

million shares times 38 cents, or almost $5 million in annual earnings—just to return to the current level of Acquirer's earnings per share. How much in synergistic benefits can be expected? Perhaps the ratio of exchange has to be reconsidered in this light? But would the smaller company even be interested in being acquired at less than a 20 percent premium over market, a not uncommon inducement?

Note that if we assume a reversal of the price/ earnings ratios in the example, both the terms of the offer and the reported performance of the combined companies would change dramatically. At 15 times earnings, Acquirer's price would be $75 per share, while at 12 times earnings, Candidate would sell at $12 per share. Given a 20 percent acquisition premium for Candidate's stock, the exchange ratio would be $14.40/ $75.00, or 0.192 shares of Acquirer for each share of Candidate. This would call for 1.92 million new shares of Acquirer, and the new earnings per share would amount to $60,000,000 − $11,920,000, or $5.03 per share, a slight net improvement even before any synergistic benefits are realized.

In this changed situation, both parties would be better off immediately, simply because we assumed the price/earnings ratios to be reversed. It's possible, of course, that a company acquired at a premium—which has caused the combined earnings per share to drop initially—may more than offset the gap with higher growth and synergistic benefits later. This would depend on the relative size of the two companies as well as on the value and exchange considerations discussed.

This is but one simplified example and therefore only a quick glimpse of the nature of the deliberations involved in exchanges of stock. At the same time we've attempted to alert you to the many issues underlying the valuation process in mergers and acquisitions. Analysis of such transactions always involves careful projections of the separate and combined earnings and cash flow patterns, the calculation of dilution, and an assessment of the likely risk/reward market response (in effect, a potential change in the β) as an input to the negotiation process.

Managing for Shareholder Value

We now return to the primary concept we established at the beginning of this book, namely, that the basic obligation of any company's management is to make investment, operating, and financing decisions that will enhance shareholder value over the long term. Our discussion of valuing business cash flows and the issues involved in restructuring strongly suggest that management should periodically reexamine the policies and strategies followed to test whether its basic obligation of creating shareholder value is being met. Recall that increasing shareholder value depends on making economic investments that exceed the investors' return standard as well as managing existing resource investments for cash flow results that similarly exceed investor expectations.

Despite the upheavals caused by the takeover boom of recent years, the most beneficial aspect has been the widespread rediscovery of management fundamentals— even if under threat of dismissal by hostile raiders. In fact, testing the efficiency with which all resources are employed and the relative contribution from various business segments with an objective "outside" orientation has become commonplace in many companies. One could argue that this should have been commonplace all along because the economic basis of all business decisions should have been recognized.

In recent years a number of valuation methodologies have been developed that are based on linking past and expected cash flow patterns to the market value of a company as a whole and to the relative price level of its common shares. Referred to as *value management,* the approach is used by various consulting firms to establish a linkage between management actions and shareholder value results. Moreover, such programs relate cash flow thinking to management incentives, and they're designed to provide a coherent set of economic principles that should guide a company's planning processes, investment policies, financing choices, and operational decisions toward increasing shareholder value.

The most sophisticated and empirically grounded methodology of this kind has been developed by HOLT Value Associates, now a subsidiary of The Boston Consulting Group. Its value-based management system is founded on translating a company's financial results through a variety of adjustments into a current dollar cash flow return on investment (CFROI) measure, which expresses the company's economic performance. This concept, when applied to expected cash flows and combined with projected growth in the company's asset base, can be used to calculate the company's market value by applying a market-based investors' return standard. The model recognizes the adjusted cash flow contributions from existing assets and combines them with new investment cash flows, all on a comparable economic basis.

In effect, a company's financial data are transformed into a consistent economic "project" cash flow view which, when discounted at an empirically derived investors' return standard, permits calculation of the relative market value of the company's capitalization. In most cases, the calculated share values not only track very closely with historical price patterns but also become solid predictors for expected value if the assumed cash flows are realized in the future. The model is a highly integrated and sophisticated application of the economic cash flow principles we've discussed throughout this book.

Figure 9–5 shows a useful overview diagram tying together the various concepts we've discussed. It's designed to help you visualize the link between manage-

FIGURE 9–5
An Overview of Shareholder Value Creation

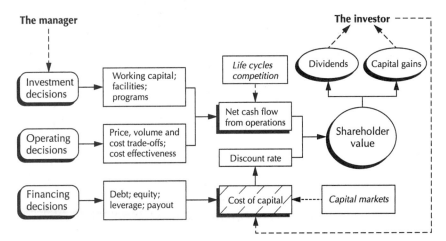

ment decisions and shareholder value. The diagram shows the three basic types of decisions on the left and identifies their key impacts.

The combination of investment and operating decisions generates cash flow from operations after taxes, while the financing decisions will influence the company's capital structure and the development of its weighted cost of capital.

Applying the cost of capital—or an expected investor return—as a discount rate to the cash flow from operations, or free cash flow, determines the shareholder value, as we discussed earlier. At the same time, product life cycles, competition, and many other influences will affect the size and variability of the cash flow from operations. The capital market will influence the investor's return expectation.

Alternatively, the last part of the diagram recognizes that shareholder value can also be viewed as being driven by a combination of cash dividends and realized capital gains when seen through the eyes of the shareholder. We remember from Chapter 3 that total shareholder return (TSR) was defined as the combined return from dividends and capital gains over a period of time. This alternative view, however, can't be divorced from the basic driving forces of the business, the cash flow patterns, for it's positive free cash flow that will permit the company to pay dividends in the first place, and that will also boost the shares' market value, enabling the investor to realize capital gains.

What are the implications of this overview? Note that we've once more returned to a systems view of the corporation, driven by the same basic management decisions, but stressing the cash flow patterns that are the economic underpinning of performance and value. All financial analysis techniques and methodologies in the end are related to the business system as viewed here and in Chapter 1.

The basic message of managing for shareholder value is nothing more than management's obligation to base all of its investment, operating, and financing decisions of an economic (that is, cash flow) rationale and to manage all resources entrusted to its care for superior economic returns. Over time, consistency in this approach will generate growing shareholder value and growth in share price performance, relative to the movements of the overall stock market.

If this sounds fundamental, it's intended to, for the challenge of the 1990s is competitive survival by managing better in a world arena—where economic fundamentals are gaining dominance over ideology. Financial analysis in its many forms, as it was introduced in Chapter 1 and specifically explained in the remainder of this book, is an essential tool for analytically oriented persons of any viewpoint as they judge the performance and outlook of any business.

KEY ISSUES

The following is a recap of the key issues raised directly or indirectly in this chapter. They're enumerated here to help you keep the techniques discussed within the perspective of financial theory and business practice.

1. The challenge of valuation involves the dual problems of forecasting the economic benefits derived from an asset, and of selecting an economic standard with which to measure these benefits.

2. Value takes many forms, but in the end valuation in business must rest on an attempt to express an economic risk/reward trade-off in the form of cash flows committed and cash flows generated.

3. Investors approach the valuation of an investment proposition in terms of their individual risk preferences. Thus, market values are a function of individual and collective risk assessments.

4. Valuation techniques are essentially assessment tools that attempt to quantify the available objective data. Yet such quantification will always remain in part subjective and in part subject to forces beyond individual parties' control.

5. While the securities markets provide momentary indications, the value of a common stock at any time is a combination of residual claims, future expectations, and assessments of general and specific risk, subject to economic and business conditions and the decisions of management and the board of directors.

6. Valuation is distorted by the same elements that distort other types of financial analysis: price-level changes, accounting conventions, economic conditions, market fluctuations, and many subjective intangible factors.

7. Valuing a business for sale or purchase is one of the most complex tasks an analyst can undertake. It calls for skills in projection of earnings and cash

flows, assessment of risk, and interpretation of the impact of combining management styles, operations, and resources.

8. Shareholder value creation is the ultimate result of successful investments, operations, and financing carried out by management within an economic framework. However, the link between a company's current and prospective performance in these areas and the market value of its common stock at a particular time isn't necessarily direct or directly measurable because of the combination of forces acting on the stock market.

SUMMARY

In this chapter we've brought together a whole range of concepts and techniques to provide you with an overview of how to value assets, securities, and business operations. To set the stage, we discussed key definitions of value and then took the viewpoint of the investor assessing the value of the three main forms of securities issued by a company. After covering both value and yield in these situations, we expanded our view to encompass the value of an ongoing business. Our purpose was to find ways of setting the value in transactions such as sale of a business, restructuring, or the combination of companies in the form of a merger or acquisition.

We found that methods were available for deriving such values, but that the specific assumptions and the background of the transaction added many dimensions to the basic calculations. Finally, we reviewed the concept of managing for shareholder value, returning to a systems overview that linked management decisions on investment, operations, and financing to the present value of a business, and in turn linked shareholder value to dividends and capital gains. Ultimately, value will always remain partially subjective, and be settled in an exchange between interested parties, but managing for economic performance and value was seen as the basic obligation of management.

SELECTED REFERENCES

Boston Consulting Group. *Value Based Management: A Framework for Managing Value Creation.* Chicago: Boston Consulting Group, 1993.

Brealey, Richard, and Stewart Myers. *Principles of Corporate Finance.* 3d ed. New York: McGraw-Hill, 1988.

Copeland, Tom; Tim Koller; and Jack Murrin. *Measuring and Managing the Value of Companies.* New York: John Wiley & Sons, 1990.

Pratt, Shannon P. *Valuing a Business: The Analysis and Appraisal of Closely Held Companies.* 2nd ed. Homewood, Ill.: Dow Jones-Irwin, 1989.

Rappaport, Alfred. *Creating Shareholder Value.* New York: Free Press, 1986.

Rock, Milton R. *The Merger and Acquisition Handbook.* New York: McGraw-Hill, 1987.

Rosen, Lawrence R. *The Dow Jones-Irwin Guide to Calculating Yields.* Homewood, Ill.: Dow Jones-Irwin, 1985.

Van Horne, James C. *Financial Management and Policy.* 9th ed. Englewood Cliffs, N.J.: Prentice Hall, 1991.

Weston, J. F., and Eugene Brigham. *Essentials of Managerial Finance.* 10th ed. Fort Worth, Tex.: Dryden Press, 1993.

SELF-STUDY EXERCISES AND PROBLEMS

(Solutions are provided in Appendix VI)

1. Using the present value tables in Chapter 6, develop the value (price) of bonds with the following characteristics:

   a. A bond with a face value of $1,000 carries interest of 8 percent per year, paid semiannually. It will be redeemed for $1,075 at the end of 14 years. At what price would the bond yield a return of 6 percent? A yield of 10 percent?

b. A bond with a face value of $1,000 carries interest of 8.5 percent per year, paid semiannually. It's callable at 110 percent of face value beginning October 1, 2003, and will be redeemed (unless called) on October 1, 2013. What price on October 1, 1994, would yield a prospective investor a return of 6 percent? What price would yield 9 percent? (Use interpolation.)

2. Develop the approximate yield (return) of bonds with the following characteristics:

a. A bond with a face value of $1,000 carries interest at 7 percent per year, paid semiannually on January 15 and July 15. It will be redeemed at 110 percent on July 15, 2005. The market quotation on July 15, 1994, is 124⅛. What's the approximate yield to an investor who purchases the bond on this date? What's the exact yield given in an appropriate bond table?

b. The same bond is quoted at 122½ on September 1, 1994. In addition to the market price, accrued interest is paid by the purchaser if the trade takes place between interest dates. What's the exact yield given in an appropriate bond table?

c. A bond with a face value of $500 carries interest at 8 percent per year, paid annually. It will be redeemed at par on March 1, 2015. The bond was purchased on August 20, 1994, for $487.50, including accrued interest. What's the approximate yield? What's the exact yield, using an appropriate bond table or a computer?

3. Develop and discuss the value of individual rights to subscribe to shares of stock under the circumstances of (a) and (b), and calculate the subscription price in (c).

a. A company is offering its common stockholders the right to subscribe to one share of common at $65 for each 12 shares held. At the time of the offering the common is trading at $89. What's the likely market value of the common going to be after the offering period (ex rights)?

b. A company is offering its common stockholders the right to purchase one share of 7 percent convertible preferred at 82 for each six shares of common stock held. A reasonable expectation is that the preferred will be trading at 105, once issued. What would the rights value be if the offer were made for each four shares of common held?

c. If the value of a right is expected to be $2, and the market price is expected to be $123 after exercise of the rights, what's the subscription price under a subscription ratio of 11:1?

4. The following information is available about two different common stocks, Company A and Company B:

	Company A	Company B
Earnings per share	$2.50	$7.25
Dividends per share	1.00	5.00
Growth in earnings	8%	4%
Price range	$26–$20	$60–$56
β	1.3	0.8
Risk-free return	7.0%	7.0%
Expected return, S&P 500	13.5%	13.5%

On the assumption that the companies' growth rates will continue, develop an estimate of the value of the common stock and its yield for each. Discuss.

5. The following estimates about the next five years' performance of GHI Company have been provided to you. Based on this information and the current data available to you, calculate the company's value as a going business, assuming that the expected return from such a business investment would be 12 percent after taxes. Test the present value calculation against other yardsticks of value. Discuss.

	GHI Company Projections ($ millions)				
	Year 1	Year 2	Year 3	Year 4	Year 5
Projected earnings (after taxes)	$2.7	$2.9	$3.2	$3.6	$4.0
Projected investments (including working capital)	$0.5	$2.5	$1.5	$1.5	$2.0
Projected depreciation	$1.0	$1.1	$1.4	$1.6	$1.8

The terminal value at the end of the period can be estimated at between 10 and 12 times earnings. The company's earnings for the past year were $2.5 million, and the price/earnings ratio for its industry is currently 11.0.

6. The MNO Company's stock was closely held, and the volume of stock traded over the counter represented only a small fraction of the total shares outstanding. You've been asked to develop as many valuation approaches as possible in preparation for the disposition of a 25 percent block of common stock held by the estate of one of the founders. The estate's executor will be interested in the possible viewpoints to be taken in arriving at a fair value. The following data have been made available for the purpose:

MNO COMPANY
Balance Sheet, December 31, 1994
($ thousands)

Assets

Current assets:

Cash	$ 230	(working balance, $150)
Marketable securities	415	(held for payment of taxes and investment in equipment)
Accounts receivable	525	(94% collectible, net of expenses)
Inventories	815	(quick disposal value two thirds of book, normal sale 95%)
Total current assets	1,985	
Fixed assets	1,715	(quick sale value $225, replacement value $2,500)
Less: Accumulated depreciation	820	
Net fixed assets	895	
Prepaid expenses	40	(insurance, licenses, etc.)
Goodwill	175	(based on previous acquisitions)
Organization expense	20	(legal fees, taxes)
Total assets	$3,115	

Liabilities and Net Worth

Current liabilities:

Accounts payable	$ 370	($350 current, $20 overdue)
Notes payable	125	(due 60 days hence)
Accrued liabilities	290	(wages, interest, etc.)
Accrued taxes	150	(income taxes, withholding)
Total current liabilities	935	
Mortgage payable	175	(80% of fixed assets as security)
Bonds, net of sinking fund	520	(unsecured)
Deferred income taxes	55	
Reserve for self-insurance	110	(contingency surplus reserve)
Preferred stock	300	(7% preferred, 3,000 shares)
Common stock	525	(52,500 shares, $10 par)
Capital surplus	110	(excess paid in for common)
Retained earnings	385	(accumulated earnings less dividends)
Total liabilities and net worth	$3,115	

The company's β is estimated at 1.2 while the spread between a risk-free return of 7 percent and S&P 500 returns is expected to be about 6 percent.

Operating History, MNO Company

	1990	1991	1992	1993	1994	3-31-95*
Profit after taxes (000) ...	$92	$110	$126	$139	$118	$34
Depreciation	62	63	66	70	72	19
Earnings per share	1.75	2.10	2.40	2.65	2.25	0.65
Dividends per share	1.20	1.60	1.60	1.80	1.80	0.45
Market price, high	31⅜	33¼	39⅞	34⅛	29¾	30⅞
Market price, low	13⅞	19¾	23⅝	22⅛	19¼	19⅜
Market price, average	22⅝	26½	31¾	28⅛	24½	25⅛
Industry price/earnings ratio	14×	15×	16×	12×	11×	—

*Quarter.

Develop valuation approaches based on book values, market values, past trends, and projections (no significant changes are expected in the operations of the company and the industry), taking into account redundant assets and limited trading of the stock. Stipulate your assumptions and list additional information you would consider necessary for a recommendation. Discuss your findings.

7. Two companies are discussing a potential merger. Company A has a price/earnings ratio of 12 ×, with current EPS of $8, a dividend of $2, and a market price range of $90 to $100, with a recent price of $98. Ten million shares are outstanding. Company B has a price/earnings ratio of 20 ×, and is growing at twice the 6 percent rate of Company A. Its current EPS are $3, it pays no dividend, and its market price is ranging between $45 and $70. One million shares are outstanding. Company A is assessing the impact of a potential offer to Company B at a price of $65, as compared to Company B's current price of $54. Calculate the appropriate measures to assess the impact of these terms, and discuss potential implications.

APPENDIX I
GLOSSARY OF
KEY CONCEPTS*

Accelerated depreciation Patterns of *depreciation* write-offs that place larger proportions into the early years of an *asset*'s book life, rather than into the later years, either for accounting or for tax deduction purposes.

Accounting earnings The difference between recognized *revenues* and *expenses* during an accounting period, based on generally accepted accounting principles.

Accounts payable (payables) Obligations owed to trade creditors and suppliers as incurred in the normal course of business; also called *trade credit*.

Accounts receivable (receivables) Obligations owed by customers and other parties as incurred in the normal course of business.

Accruals Recognition of *revenues* or *expenses* when earned or incurred, without regard to the actual timing of the cash transactions; used in the accrual method of accounting.

Acid test A stringent measure of *liquidity* relating current cash *assets* (cash, cash equivalents, and receivables) to *current liabilities*.

Activity-based analysis A form of *economic analysis* that develops the

---

*Items shown in italics are defined separately.

specific *costs* and *benefits* generated by an activity, product line, or business segment.

Aftertax cash flow Cash generated from *operations* or from an *investment* net of income taxes, derived by adding back noncash charges like *depreciation* to aftertax earnings.

Aftertax value Net *revenue*, net *cost*, or net *investment* after adjusting for the effect of applicable income taxes.

Allocation An assignment or distribution of *costs* or *revenues* to products, activity centers, or other entities using a common basis.

Amortization A periodic charge reflecting the decline in the recorded value of an *intangible asset* over a specified number of years.

Annualized net present value The transformation of a *net present value* into an equivalent series of annual values over the life of the project, used in judging the proposal's margin of *risk*.

Annuity A uniform series of payments or receipts over a specified number of periods.

Asset A physical or intangible item of value to a company or an individual.

Asset turnover An expression of the effectiveness with which *assets* generate sales, defined as the ratio of *net sales* to total assets.

Balance sheet A *financial statement* reflecting the recorded values of all *assets*, *liabilities*, and *owners' equity* at a point in time.

Balloon payment A significant *principal* payment due at the end of the term of a financial obligation.

Bankruptcy A legal process of disposing of the *assets* of a business or individual to satisfy creditors' claims in total or in part, and protecting the debtor(s) from further legal action.

Benefit (cost/benefit) The positive element in an *economic trade-off* which relates *economic earnings* to *economic costs* in an *investment*, *operating*, or *financing* decision.

Beta (β) A calculated form of expressing the specific (systematic) risk of a company's *common stock* relative to the stock market as a whole. (Cf. *volatility*.)

Bond A financial instrument representing a form of corporate *long-term debt* issued to investors; a variety of different types of bonds exist.

Bond rating A published ranking of a *bond* developed by financial organizations to express its relative soundness on a defined scale.

Book value The recorded value of an *asset* or *liability* as reflected in the *financial statements* of a company or individual.

Book value of equity The recorded value of *owners' equity* on a company's *balance sheet*, representing the owners' residual claim on the *assets*.

Break-even analysis Determining the level of sales at which a company will just recover *fixed* and *variable costs;* a zero-profit condition.

Breakup value The value realized from separating the parts of a multibusiness company and disposing of them individually.

Burden The combination of interest charges and current *principal* payments required by a financial obligation.

Burden coverage The ratio of periodic *income* before taxes to the corresponding amount of *burden,* adjusted for income taxes; a test of the ability to service a *debt* obligation.

Business risk The risk inherent in the *cash flows* from *investments* and *operations,* apart from the risk inherent in the form of *financing* used.

Call provision A provision permitting the issuing company to redeem in part or in total a *bond* or *preferred stock* issue at a date determined by the company.

Capital The *funds* committed to an enterprise in the form of ownership *equity* and long-term *financing.*

Capital budget A selected group of *investment* projects approved in principle for implementation, pending individual approval, and related closely to a company's business strategies.

Capital investment A relatively long-term commitment of funds to a project expected to generate positive net *cash flows* over time.

Capital rationing The allocation of limited *investment* funds to a selection of investment projects smaller than all currently acceptable projects; a fairly common condition.

Capital structure The relative proportions of different sources of *capital* used in the long-term funding of the *investments* and *operations* of a company.

Capitalization The sum of all long-term sources of *capital* of a company, also derived by subtracting *current liabilities* from total *assets.*

Cash accounting A method of accounting in which *revenues* and *expenses* and all other transactions are recognized when cash changes hands, in contrast to the *accrual* method of accounting.

Cash budget A periodic projection of cash receipts and cash disbursements over a specified length of time. (Cf. *cash flow forecast.*)

Cash flow The positive (inflow) or negative (outflow) movements of cash caused by an activity over a specific period of time.

Cash flow analysis An economic method of analysis that employs the positive (inflow) and negative (outflow) movements of cash caused by an activity to determine the relative desirability of the activity; usually involves *discounted cash flow* methodology.

Cash flow cycle The periodic movement of cash through an enterprise, caused by *investment, operating,* and *financing* decisions.

Cash flow forecast A periodic forecast of cash movements through an enterprise, recognizing sources and uses of funds.

Cash flow from operations Cash generated or used by a business over a specified period of time; usually derived by adjusting aftertax profit for *noncash* charges and noncash receipts.

Cash flow statement A *financial statement* listing the cash impact of the activities of a business over a specified period of time, separating the *cash flows* into the areas of *operations, investments,* and *financing.*

Collection period The average number of days over which *accounts receivable* are outstanding, either in total or by defined categories; a measure of the effectiveness with which customer *credit* is managed.

Common stock (common shares) Securities representing a direct ownership interest in a corporation and a residual claim on the *assets.*

Common-size financial statements A ratio analysis of *balance sheets* and *income statements* in which all elements are represented as a percentage of *assets* or *net sales,* respectively. Used in analyzing trends and in comparing statements from different companies.

Comparables Selected *assets* or business entities chosen by analysts to establish comparability with an asset or business being valued; used in determining the *fair market value* in the absence of market transactions.

Compounding The process of calculating the growing value of a sum of money over time, caused by the periodic interest earned and by the reinvestment of such interest.

Constant-dollar analysis The adjustment of financial magnitudes for inflation to reflect a common dollar value basis (using dollar values of a specified point in time), and the use of these adjusted values in accounting or *economic analysis.*

Consumer price index (CPI) An index provided by the U.S. government that represents the periodic change in the cost of a selected group of items purchased by consumers; used as a measure of *inflation.*

Contribution analysis A method of analysis that determines the relative excess of revenue over variable costs of product lines, business segments, and activities, and judges the contribution made toward meeting *fixed costs,* overhead, and *profits.*

Conversion ratio The stated number of *common shares* or other securities into which a *convertible security* may be exchanged.

Conversion value The *market value* represented by the *common* *shares* or other *assets* into which a *convertible security* may be exchanged.

Convertible security   A financial security that may be exchanged into another security or *asset* with a prescribed *conversion ratio* at the option of the holder.

Cost   The transaction value at which an *asset* was acquired; also, any periodic *expense* recognized against matching periodic *revenue.*

Cost of capital (weighted average cost of capital, hurdle rate)   The weighted average of the aftertax cost to a company of all forms of long-term financing used; employed as a minimum standard for the return to be earned on new *investments.*

Cost of debt   The *cost* to a company of employing *debt,* developed from the aftertax interest charges of various forms of debt.

Cost of equity   The *cost* to a company of employing common shareholders' funds, developed from the investors' expectations about the return from holding such shares, usually in the form of dividends and capital gains.

Cost of goods (services) sold (cost of sales)   The total of all *costs* and *expenses* incurred in producing or accquiring goods or services for sale.

Coupon rate   The stated interest rate specified on the interest coupons attached to *bonds,* as contrasted with the *yield* obtained on a bond, which relates the coupon rate to the *market value* of the bond.

Covenant   Provision in the *bond* agreement specifying restrictions or other requirements that the issuer has to observe to maintain the bond's *credit* rating.

Coverage   Relationship of fixed requirements, such as interest or *burden* connected with *debt,* to operating income before or after taxes. (Cf. *times interest earned, times burden covered.*)

Credit (creditworthiness)   The recognized ability of an individual or company to assume indebtedness with the prospect of properly servicing such *debt.*

Cumulative preferred stock   A form of *preferred stock* that carries the provision that any unpaid dividends accumulate for later payment, and must be paid in full before common dividends may be declared.

Current asset   Any *asset* on the *balance sheet* with a short-term expectation of being turned into cash, such as cash, *receivables,* and inventories; usually considered as having a one-year time horizon or less.

Current liability   Any *liability* on the *balance sheet* with a short-term maturity, usually payable within one year, such as *accounts payable* and accrued taxes.

Current portion of long-term debt The proportion of a long-term *liability* that is due and payable within one year.

Current ratio A common measure of *liquidity* that relates the sum of *current assets* to the sum of *current liabilities.*

Current-dollar accounting The adjustment of historical financial magnitudes for inflation to reflect current-dollar values (adjusting for price changes) and the use of these adjusted values in accounting or economic analysis. (Cf. *constant-dollar analysis.*)

Current-value basis The restatement of the recorded values of selected *assets* in current dollar terms to reflect price changes. (Cf. *current-dollar accounting.*)

Cutoff rate The minimum *rate of return* (*hurdle rate*) that *capital investment* projects have to meet, usually based on the *cost of capital* or a judgmentally adjusted standard.

Cyclical variations The impact on a company's *funds flows* from the operational changes caused by business cycles.

Day's sales A measure of the credit quality of *accounts receivable*, which expresses outstanding receivables in terms of average daily *sales*; can be compared with the *credit* terms under which sales were made.

Debt (liability) An obligation to pay amounts due (and interest if required) under specified terms, or to provide goods or services to others.

Debt to assets A ratio relating outstanding *debt* obligations (usually *long-term debt* but at times all types of debt) to total *assets*; used as a measure of *financial leverage.* (Cf. *debt to equity.*)

Debt to capitalization A ratio relating *long-term debt* to a company's *capitalization*; used as a measure of *financial leverage* as found in the *capital structure.* (Cf. *debt to equity.*)

Debt to equity A ratio relating outstanding *debt* obligations (usually *long-term debt* but at times all types of debt) to *shareholders' equity*; used as a measure of *financial leverage.*

Default Failure to make a payment on a *debt* obligation when due.

Deferred taxes A provision for income tax *liabilities* or income tax *assets* recorded on the *balance sheet*, arising from timing differences between recognized tax liabilities in a company's accounting system and tax liabilities reported to the tax authorities.

Deflation A decline in general price levels. (Cf. *inflation.*)

Depreciation The decline in an *asset*'s value, from use or obsolescence, that's recognized in the accounting system and for income tax purposes as a periodic allocation (*write-off*) against income of a portion of the original *cost* of the *asset.* (Cf. *accelerated depreciation, noncash charges.*)

Dilution The proportional reduction of *earnings per share* or *book* *value* per share from an increase in the number of shares outstanding, either from a new issue or from conversion of *convertible securities* outstanding.

Discount rate   The earnings rate used in calculating the *present value* of future *cash flows* using the *discounting* process.

Discounted cash flow   The *discounting* methodology employed in determining the economic attractiveness of *capital investment* projects.

Discounted cash flow rate of return (DCF)   The *earnings* rate (*yield*) that equates a project's cash inflows and outflows over its economic life; also called *internal rate of return.*

Discounting   The process of calculating the reduced value of a future sum of money in proportion to the opportunity of earning interest and the distance in time of payment or receipt. (Cf. *compounding, present value.*)

Disinvestment   The act of disposing of *assets* or whole business segments, caused by a reassessment of the strategic fit of these assets; the opposite of *investment.*

Diversification   The process of investing in a number of unrelated or partially interdependent *assets* or activities to achieve a more stable *portfolio.*

Dividend coverage   Relationship of the amount of common and/or preferred dividends to aftertax *earnings* of a company; a test of the ability of the company to pay the current level of dividends.

Dividend discount model   A valuation method for *common stock* that employs the *present value* of expected future dividends and any change in the expected level of dividends.

Dividend payout   A ratio relating the amount of dividends distributed to the aftertax *earnings* of a corporation to derive the percentage of earnings paid to shareholders.

Dividend yield   The current return to shareholders from dividends received over a specified period, derived by dividing dividends per share by the current average market price of the *stock.* (Cf. *yield.*)

Dynamic analysis   A method of analyzing business decisions that incorporates the effect of likely changes in key variables, as contrasted with fixed assumptions. (Cf. *sensitivity analysis.*)

Earnings (income, net income, profit, net profit)   The difference between all recorded *revenues* and all related *costs* and *expenses* for a specified period, using generally accepted accounting principles.

Earnings before interest and taxes (EBIT)   An expression of a company's earning power before the effects of financing and taxation; used in a variety of *financial analyses.*

Earnings per share (EPS) The proportional share of a corporation's *earnings* that can be claimed by each share of *common stock* outstanding, derived by dividing aftertax earnings after payment of preferred dividends by the average number of common shares outstanding during the period. (Cf. *fully diluted earnings per share.*)

Earnings yield The current return to shareholders from *earnings* recorded for a specified period, derived by dividing periodic earnings by the *stock*'s current or average market price. (Cf. *yield.*)

Economic analysis The development of the economic impact of a business decision that determines the actual *trade-off* between *economic costs* and *benefits* independent of accounting conventions.

Economic benefit The consequence of a decision that causes an ultimate increase in present and future *cash flows.*

Economic cost The consequence of a decision that causes an ultimate reduction in present and future *cash flows.*

Economic earnings (loss) The net result of a *trade-off* between *economic benefits* and *economic costs.*

Economic life The time over which a current or future *investment* can be expected to provide *economic earnings*, which is independent of the physical life of any *assets* involved.

Economic return A measure of the earnings power of an *investment* in terms of net *cash flows* generated by the *capital* committed. (Cf. *discounted cash flow.*)

Economic trade-off The comparison of the *economic benefits* and *economic costs* caused by a business decision.

Economic value The *net present value* of all future *economic benefits* and *costs* expected from an existing or prospective *investment.*

Enterprise value The *net present value* of all estimated future *cash flows* to be generated by a business.

Equity (owners' equity, net worth, shareholders' equity) The recorded ownership claim of common and preferred shareholders in a corporation as reflected on the *balance sheet.* Also defined as total *assets* less all *liabilities.*

Equivalence A point of indifference at which the *present value* of future *cash flows* reflects the return expectations of a prospective investor.

Expected return A weighted average of alternative outcomes of an *investment*, using the respective probabilities as weights.

Expense A periodic offset against *revenue* recognized under generally accepted accounting principles, representing either a direct cash outlay or an *allocation* or *accrual* of past and future outlays.

Fair market value (FMV) The price for an *asset* on which two rational parties with sufficient information would agree in the absence of negotiating pressure.

Financial Accounting Standards Board (FASB) The official rule-making institute of the accounting profession, which is privately funded by the profession.

Financial analysis The process of determining and weighing the financial impact of business decisions.

Financial flexibility The ability to maintain alternative choices for raising additional *capital* while preserving a *capital structure* appropriate to the risks and conditions of a company's business.

Financial growth plans A model of future financial flows that tracks the results of key *investment, operational,* and *financing* dimensions under a variety of assumptions about strategies, policies, and business conditions.

Financial leverage The magnifying (or diminishing) effect on *return on equity* from the use of *debt* in the *capital structure,* caused by introducing fixed interest charges against the returns obtained from the incremental funds invested. (Cf. *operating leverage.*)

Financial model The representation in a computer program of key financial dimensions of a business system for purposes of simulating the impact of management decisions. (Cf. *financial growth plans.*)

Financial statements Key periodic statements prepared under generally accepted accounting principles, which represent the financial condition of a company *(balance sheet), the operating results (operating statement),* the changes in funds flows *(funds flow statement),* and the changes in *owners' equity* (statement of changes in *owners' equity*).

Financial system A dynamic representation of the key elements and relationships governing *investments, operations,* and *financing* of a business entity. (Cf. *financial model.*)

Financing The provision of *funds* from internal or external sources to fund the *investments* and *operations* of a business.

First-in, first-out (FIFO) A method of accounting for inventory in which the oldest item is assumed to be used or sold first. (Cf. *last-in, first-out.*)

Fixed assets Any *asset* on the *balance sheet* considered to have a life or usefulness for a business in excess of one year, such as land, buildings, and machinery. (Cf. *current assets.*)

Fixed costs Any *cost* that doesn't vary with changes in the volume of operations over time.

Fixed-income security Any security that provides an unchanging stream of interest or dividends to the holder over its life.

Foreign exchange exposure The potential loss from an unexpected change in currency exchange rates affecting *investments* or *operations*.

Free cash flow   The net *cash flow* available to a company after providing for all acceptable new *investments* to support its strategy, before any dividend payments or changes in *financing*.

Fully diluted earnings per share   *Earnings per share* which are calculated on the assumption that all outstanding *convertible securities* and *warrants* have been converted into the appropriate number of common shares, raising the denominator and reducing *earnings per share*.

Funds   A general term denoting means of payment, often equated with cash.

Funds flow   The movement of *funds* of all types through a business over time, ultimately resulting in changes in cash.

Funds flow statement   A *financial statement* prepared to display the *funds* movements in a business over a specified period of time, separated into sections on *operations, investment, financing*, and cash balances.

Going-concern value   The *net present value* of the expected future *cash flows* generated by a business from its normal operations. (Cf. *economic value, enterprise value*.)

Gross margin   The difference between *net sales* and *cost of goods sold* (or *cost of services provided*), generally expressed as a ratio of this difference divided by net sales.

Growth/decline variations   The impact on a company's *funds* flows from the operational changes caused by growth or decline in the volume of business.

Hedge   A strategy to neutralize the risk of an *investment* by engaging in offsetting contracts whereby potential gains and losses will cancel each other.

Historical cost principle   An accounting principle requiring the recording of transactions and the maintenance of recorded values at the actual level incurred, regardless of any subsequent changes in the value of the *assets* or *liabilities* involved.

Hurdle rate   A minimum standard for the return required of an *investment*, used in selecting from among alternative investment choices.

Income   The difference between the *revenues* and the matching *costs* and *expenses* for a specified period. (Cf. *earnings*.)

Income statement (operating statement, profit and loss statement)   A *financial statement* reporting the periodic *revenues* and matching *costs* and *expenses* for a specified period, and deriving the *income* for the period.

Incremental analysis A method of analysis that focuses on the changes caused by a business decision.

Inflation An increase in general price levels.

Inflation premium The increased *return on investment* required to compensate the holders for expected inflation.

Insolvency The condition where an individual's or company's *liabilities* exceed the realizable value of the *assets* held.

Interest coverage Relationship of periodic interest expense to operating *income* before or after taxes, used to judge a company's ability to pay interest charges. (Cf. *times interest earned*.)

Internal rate of return (IRR) The *discount rate* that equates the cash inflows and cash outflows of an *investment* project, resulting in a *net present value* of zero. (Cf. *rate of return, yield*.)

Inventory turnover A ratio that relates ending inventory or average inventory to the *cost of goods sold* for a specified period of time; used in judging the effectiveness with which inventories are controlled.

Inventory valuation Any adjustment to recorded inventory values to correct for differences between historical *costs* and current prices, also affecting *cost of goods sold*.

Investment The commitment of *funds* for purposes of obtaining an *economic return* over a period of time, usually in the form of periodic *cash flows* and/or a *terminal value*.

Investment value The value of a *convertible security* based strictly on its characteristics as a *fixed-income security*, without regard to its conversion provision.

Junk bond Any *bond* issued by corporations with risk characteristics higher than what's normally rated as investment-grade risk (normal risk exposure).

Last-in, first-out (LIFO) A method of accounting for inventory in which the newest item is assumed to be used or sold first. (Cf. *first-in, first-out*.)

Leasing The process of contracting for the use of *assets* owned by others over a specified period of time, in exchange for a stipulated pattern of periodic payments.

Leverage The magnifying effect from volume changes on *profits* caused by fixed elements in a company's *cost* structure, or the magnifying effect from profit changes on *return on equity* caused by *fixed-cost debt* obligations in the *capital structure*. (Cf. *financial leverage, operating leverage*.)

Leveraged buyout (LBO) The acquisition of a business by investors using a high percentage of *debt* carried by the business itself.

Liability An obligation to pay a specified amount or to perform a service; at times also the recognized potential obligation to pay or perform a service (contingent liability).

Liquid asset An *asset* that can be rapidly converted into cash without suffering a significant reduction in value, usually classified as a *current asset.*

Liquidation The process of terminating a business entity by selling its *assets*, paying off its *liabilities*, and distributing any remaining cash to its owners.

Liquidation value The estimated value of a business based on *liquidation* of its *assets.*

Liquidity The degree to which a company is readily able to meet its current obligations from *liquid assets.* (Cf. *acid test, current ratio.*)

Long-term debt Any *debt* obligation of a company with a maturity of more than one year.

Managerial economics The methodology underlying the analysis and resolution of the *economic trade-offs* involved in making management decisions.

Marginal costs (revenues) Increments of *costs* and *revenues* attributable to changes in a variable affecting an issue being decided.

Market to book value The relationship between the current market price of *common stock* and its recorded *book value*, a ratio often used in judging the performance of a company's *stock.*

Market value The value of an *asset* as determined in an unconstrained market of multiple buyers and sellers, such as a securities exchange.

Market value of equity The combined value of all *common shares* of a company at current market prices. (Cf. *book value of equity.*)

Market value of firm The *market value* of a company's *equity* plus the market value of its *debt.*

Monetary asset Any *asset* defined in terms of units of currency, such as cash and *accounts receivable.*

Multiple hurdle rates A set of minimum return standards in a company that are used to judge the desirability of *investments* in activities or lines of business with widely different risk characteristics.

Mutually exclusive alternatives Alternative *investments* for achieving the same objective, although only one can be undertaken.

Net assets Total *assets* less *current liabilities*, as recorded on the *balance sheet.*

Net income (loss) The difference between periodic *revenues* and matching *costs* and *expenses.* (Cf. *earnings, net profit, profit.*)

Net investment The commitment of new *funds* to an *investment* project, net of any funds recovered due to the decision to invest, adjusted for tax implications.

Net present value (NPV)   The difference between the *present values* of cash inflows and outflows from an *investment*, representing the net gain or loss in value expected relative to the earnings standard applied.

Net profit   The difference between periodic *revenues* and matching *costs* and *expenses*. (Cf. *earnings, net income, profit.*)

Net sales   Total *revenue* from sales for a specified period, less adjustments such as returns, allowances, and sales discounts.

Net worth   The recorded value of *shareholders' equity* on the *balance sheet.*

Nominal amount   Any quantity not adjusted for changes in the purchasing power of the currency in which it's recorded. (Cf. *real amount.*)

Noncash item   An *expense* or *revenue* recognized in the accounting process that doesn't represent a *cash flow* during the period, such as *depreciation* or unrealized income or gains.

Operating cash flows   The net *cash flow* caused by the operations of a business during a specified period.

Operating funds   *Funds* required to support current operations, such as *working capital* items.

Operating leverage   The magnifying (or diminishing) effect of volume changes on *profits* caused by the *fixed costs* in the company's operations.

Operating statement (income statement)   A *financial statement* reporting the *revenues* and matching *costs* and *expenses* for a specified period, and deriving the *net income.*

Operational analysis   The various methods of analyzing the specific and comparative aspects of a company's operating performance.

Operations   The activities in a company that support the basic purpose of the business, generating *revenues* and managing related *costs* and *expenses* for profitable results.

Opportunity cost   *Economic benefits* forgone by selecting one alternative course of action over another.

Opportunity rate of return   A rate of return standard reflecting the long-term level of returns expected in a business, often based on a company's *cost of capital.*

Option   A contractual opportunity to purchase or sell an *asset* or security at a predetermined price, without the obligation of doing so.

Over-the-counter market (OTC)   A market network among security dealers that permits electronic trading of securities not listed on a formal securities exchange.

Owners' equity   The recorded value of *preferred* and *common* shareholders' claims against the *assets* on a company's *balance sheet;*

also, the proprietors' recorded claims in the case of an unincorporated business or partnership. (Cf. *equity, shareholders' equity.*)

Paid-in capital   The recorded amount of *capital* provided by shareholders on the *balance sheet,* as contrasted with *retained earnings.*

Par value   The *nominal* value established by the issuer of a security, as contrasted with the *market value* of the security. In the case of a *bond,* the issuing company will pay the par value at maturity.

Payables   See *accounts payable.*

Payables period   A translation of *accounts payable* into the days of average purchases outstanding at a point in time; used as an indicator of the effectiveness with which *trade credit* is employed.

Payback period   The period of time over which the *cash flows* from an *investment* are expected to recover the initial outlay.

Perpetuity   A series of level periodic receipts or payments (*annuity*) expected to last forever.

Plug figure   A common term used to represent an unknown variable in a financial analysis, such as the amount of *financing* required in a pro forma projection. (Cf. *pro forma statement.*)

Portfolio   A set of diverse *investments* held by an individual or a company.

Preferred stock   A special class of capital stock, usually with a dividend provision, that receives a form of preference over *common stock* in its claims on *earnings* and *assets.*

Present value   The value today of a future sum or series of sums of money, calculated by *discounting* the future sums with an appropriate rate.

Present value payback   The point in the *economic life* of an investment project at which the cumulative *present value* of *cash inflows* equals the present value of the *cash outflows.*

Price to earnings (P/E)   The relationship of the market price of a share of *stock* to the most recent *earnings per share* over 12 months; used as a rough indicator of what investors are willing to pay for $1 of a company's *earnings.*

Primary earnings per share   A company's *earnings per share* calculated on the basis of all *common shares* actually outstanding, without regard to any *convertible securities* or *warrants* yet to be converted. (Cf. *fully diluted earnings.*)

Principal   The original amount of a loan or *bond,* also called face value, on which the rate of interest to be paid is based.

Private placement   The sale of securities to a selected group of investors rather than through a *public offering.*

Profit   The difference between periodic *revenues* and matching *costs* and *expenses.* (Cf. *earnings, net profit.*)

Profit center   A portion of a business in which *revenues, costs,* and *expenses* can be recognized separately, allowing the activity to be managed for *profit* performance.

Profitability index (PI)   A measure of *investment* desirability, defined as the *present value* of all cash inflows expected over the *economic life* of a project divided by the present value of the cash outflows.

Pro forma statement   A projected *financial statement* reflecting the financial impact of a set of assumed conditions for a specified future period.

Projection   A forecast of the quantitative implications of a set of assumed conditions.

Public issue (public offering)   The sale of newly issued securities to the public through underwriters. (Cf. *private placement.*)

Purchasing power parity   A condition in which commodities in different countries cost the same amount when prices are expressed in a given currency, due to expected adjustments in foreign exchange rates.

Quick ratio (acid test)   A stringent measure of *liquidity* relating current cash *assets* (cash, cash equivalents, and *receivables* to *current liabilities*).

Quick sale value   The value of an *asset* or business when assumed to be sold under hurried conditions, resulting generally in a lower valuation than *market value.*

Range of earnings chart (EBIT chart)   A graphic representation of the related changes in *earnings before interest and taxes (EBIT)* and *earnings per share* under various financing alternatives.

Rate of return   The level of *earnings* attained or expected from an *investment* over a period of time. (Cf. *yield.*)

Ratio analysis   The use of a variety of ratios in analyzing the financial performance and condition of a business from various viewpoints, such as managers', owners', and creditors'.

Real amount   Any quantity that has been adjusted for changes in the purchasing power of the currency in which it's recorded. (Cf. *nominal amount.*)

Realized income   *Earnings* or gains that are recognized as the result of a transaction, as contrasted with earnings or gains that exist on paper only.

Receivables   See *accounts receivable.*

Recovery value (terminal value)   The value of any *assets* or future *profits* expected to be realized at the end of the *economic life* of an *investment,* net of taxes.

Redundant assets   Any *assets* held by a company that don't contribute returns appropriate for the lines of business principally engaged in; these are candidates for *disinvestment* (divestiture).

Relevant costs Identifiable *cost* or *expense* elements that are expected to change in response to a decision being analyzed.

Relevant revenues Identifiable *revenue* elements that are expected to change in response to a decision being analyzed.

Residual profits A measure of *profit center* performance, defined as *income* less the estimated annual *cost* of the *capital* supporting the profit center.

Retained earnings (earned surplus) The cumulative amount of past and current *earnings* retained and reinvested in a corporation, instead of being distributed to shareholders in the form of dividends.

Return on assets (ROA) The relationship of annual aftertax *earnings* to total *assets* (average or ending balance), used as a measure of the productivity of a company's assets. At times aftertax earnings are adjusted for interest to eliminate the impact of *financing*.

Return on capitalization (invested capital) (ROC) The relationship of annual *earnings* before interest, after taxes to the *capitalization* (average or ending balance); used as a measure of the productivity of a company's invested *capital* regardless of the amount of *financial leverage* employed. (Cf. *return on net assets.*)

Return on equity (net worth) (ROE) The relationship of annual aftertax *earnings* to the recorded *shareholders' equity.* Used as a measure of the effectiveness with which shareholder funds have been invested.

Return on investment (ROI) The relationship of annual aftertax *earnings* to the *book value* (average or ending balance) of the *asset,* business, or *profit center* generating these earnings. Used as a measure of the productivity of the *investment.* (Cf. *return on assets.*)

Return on net assets (RONA) The relationship of annual *earnings* before interest, after taxes to total *assets* less *current liabilities* (*net assets*) (average or ending balance), used as a measure of the productivity of a company's invested *capital* regardless of the amount of *financial leverage* employed. (Cf. *return on capitalization.*)

Revenue (sales) The recorded incidence of a sale of goods and/or services as recognized in the accounting system.

Risk allowance A provision for risk in an analysis, such as lowering a project's expected *cash flows* or using a *risk-adjusted return standard.*

Risk analysis A process of integrating risk dimensions into an analysis, such as using *sensitivity analysis* or modeling outcomes that have been adjusted by probabilistic methods.

Risk aversion A subjective unwillingness to accept a given level of risk unless a significant *economic trade-off* can be realized.

Risk-adjusted return standard (discount rate, hurdle rate, cost of capital)   A minimum *discount rate* that has been adjusted upward to include a specified risk premium.

Risk-free interest rate   The assumed *yield* obtainable on a guaranteed security in the absence of *inflation.*

Risk premium   The increased *return* required from an *investment* to compensate the holder for the level of risk involved.

Sales (revenue)   The recorded incidence of a sale of goods and/or services as recognized in the accounting system.

Seasonal variations   The impact on a company's *funds* flows from the operational changes caused by seasonal business conditions.

Secured creditor   A creditor whose claim is backed by the pledge of a specified *asset,* whose proceeds will go to the creditor in case of *liquidation.*

Securities and Exchange Commission (SEC)   The regulatory body established by the federal government to oversee securities markets.

Senior creditor   Any creditor with specific claims on *income* or *assets* that rank ahead of that of general (unsecured) creditors.

Sensitivity analysis   The process of testing the impact on the results of an analysis from changes in one or more of the input variables.

Sequential outlays   One or more future *investment* outlays expected during the *economic life* of an investment project, which should be taken into account in judging the project's overall desirability.

Shareholder return   The *economic return* to shareholders in the form of dividends and capital gains or losses from *share price appreciation* or declines realized during a specified period.

Shareholders' equity   The recorded value of the residual claims of all shareholders as reflected on the *balance sheet.*

Share price appreciation   The change in the *market value* of preferred and common shares over time.

Shelf registration   The filing, under *SEC* rules, of a general-purpose prospectus outlining possible financing plans for up to two years, to speed up the actual issue when the timing is considered appropriate.

Short-term liabilities   *Debt* obligations due within 12 months of the date of a *balance sheet.* Generally listed under *current liabilities.*

Simulation   The process of modeling the potential outcomes of a financial plan or *investment* proposal, taking into account alternative assumptions about key variables and policies, and calculating the results using computer programs.

Sinking fund   A separate pool of cash into which periodic payments are made for the future redemption of an obligation.

Solvency   The condition of an individual or company in which obligations can be paid when due.

Sources and uses statement   A *financial statement* that separates all *funds* inflows and outflows for a given period of time, derived from changes in *balance sheet* accounts and supplemented with *operating statement* data.

Spot market   A market in which prices of securities or commodities are determined for immediate transactions.

Spread   The difference between the issue price of a new security and the net amount received by the issuing company, caused by underwriting commissions and *expenses*.

Standard deviation   A statistical measure of variability.

Statement of changes in financial position   A variation of the *funds flow statement* focusing on changes in *working capital* for the period.

Stock   General term used in referring to *common stock*; also applied to *preferred stock*.

Stock option   A contractual arrangement allowing selected corporate employees to purchase a specified number of shares at a set price within a specified period of time; used as an incentive for key personnel.

Straight-line depreciation   A pattern of *depreciation* write-offs that charges level amounts during the *asset*'s book life, for either accounting or tax deduction purposes.

Subordinated creditor   A creditor whose claim is specifically designated as ranking below the claims of other creditors of a company.

Sunk cost   A past outlay of *funds* that can't be recovered or changed by a current or future decision, and that's irrelevant in the analysis of future actions.

Sustainable growth rate   The rate of growth in *equity* or *sales volume* that a company can maintain without changing its *return on assets, asset turnover, debt to equity*, and *dividend payout*, and while keeping its *capital structure* proportions at their current levels.

Synergy   The assumed *economic benefits* to be obtained from a successful combination of two businesses due to increased efficiency, economies of scale, and mutual reinforcement of business effectiveness.

Tax shield   The impact on a company's income tax obligations from a change in a tax-deductible expense, such as *depreciation* or interest, defined as the amount of change times the applicable tax rate. It assumes that the company has sufficient taxable income to offset the change in the *expense*.

Terminal value (recovery value) The value of any *assets* or future *cash flows* expected to be realized at the end of the *economic life* of an *investment*, net of taxes.

Time lags The elapsed time between the recorded incidence of a transaction and its actual cash impact.

Time value of money The *discounted* or *compounded* value of a sum of money over a specified period of time, using a specified discount or compound rate. (Cf. *present value.*)

Times burden covered The relationship of the amount of *burden* during a period to *earnings* before interest and taxes. Used as a measure of a a company's ability to service its *debt.*

Times interest earned The relationship of the amount of periodic interest expense to *earnings* before interest and taxes. Used as a measure of a company's ability to make regular interest payments.

Total shareholder return (shareholder return) The *economic return* to shareholders in the form of *dividends* and capital gains or losses from *share price appreciation* or decline realized during a specified period.

Trade credit Credit extended to a company in the course of normal business operations by its suppliers. (Cf. *accounts payable.*)

Trade-off The process of judging the relative advantage or disadvantage from making a decision that involves identified *economic benefits* and *costs.*

Trade payables Amounts owed to a company's suppliers of goods and services. (Cf. *accounts payable.*)

Transfer price An internally established price level at which units of a company trade goods or services with each other.

Trend analysis A method of analysis that applies judgmental or statistical methods to historical series of data for the purpose of judging performance or making informed projections of future conditions.

Uncommitted earnings per share (UEPS) *Earnings per share* adjusted for the effect of future *sinking fund* payments and other repayment provisions, used in judging alternative financing possibilities.

Underwriter Investment banker or a group (syndicate) of investment bankers used by a corporation in marketing new securities issues to the public, guaranteeing a specific price to the issuing company. (Cf. *public offering.*)

Unrealized income (gain) *Earnings* or gains that are recognized on paper without the benefit of a transaction, as contrasted with earnings or gains that are realized through actual transactions. (Cf. *realized income.*)

Variable cost Any *cost* or *expense* that varies with operating volume over a specified period. (Cf. *fixed cost.*)

Volatility The risk introduced by past and expected fluctuations in a company's *earnings*, often expressed as β (*beta*).

Warrant A financial instrument issued to investors giving them the option to purchase additional shares at a specified price. Usually issued in connection with a new security issue.

Weighted average cost of capital Overall *cost of capital* derived by weighting the respective *costs* of different parts of a company's *capital structure* by their proportions.

Working capital (net working capital) The difference between *current assets* and *current liabilities* as recorded on the *balance sheet*, representing the amount of *operating funds* that are financed by the company's *capital structure.*

Working capital cycle The periodic transformation of *working capital* components into cash inflows and outflows.

Write-offs Accounting entries that allocate portions of past outlays into appropriate operating periods, such as *depreciation* and *amortization.*

Yield The *rate of return* earned by an *investment*'s cash inflows and outflows during a specified period. (Cf. *internal rate of return.*)

Yield to maturity The *internal rate of return* earned by a *bond* when held to maturity.

APPENDIX II
SOME INTERNA-
TIONAL ISSUES
IN BUSINESS
ANALYSIS

In Chapter 3 we developed the principles of performance analysis and stressed the need for management to derive an economic return from the resources entrusted to them. The analysis involved such measures as profit margins, return on assets, and return on net worth, seen from different points of view. We also related the various measures within a system of ratios to show the different levers management can use to improve the profitability of the business and to create shareholder value. We will briefly discuss some of the challenges generally encountered in measuring multibusiness companies, and then turn to the particular issues arising from operating with different national currencies.

GENERAL PERFORMANCE ANALYSIS CHALLENGES

Performance measures work best when applied to a total business entity, where investment, operations, and financing are collectively controlled and managed by a management team. It's possible to derive both return on investment (ROI) and return on equity (ROE)—the latter allowing for the effect of financial leverage. Recall the expanded formula for return on equity,

$$ROE = \frac{\text{Net profit}}{\text{Sales}} \times \frac{\text{Sales}}{\text{Assets}} \times \frac{\text{Assets}}{\text{Assets} - \text{Liabilities}}$$

where the first element represents operations, the second element investment, and the third financial leverage. Also, as we discussed in Chapter 9, various cash flow analysis approaches can be applied to judge the performance and the value of the company.

Complications arise when the measures are applied to segments of a multi-unit company, where individual units are responsible for investment and operations only, and financing remains a corporate headquarters function. In this case, the units are normally measured on a return on investment basis only, employing concepts such as return on total assets (ROA), return on net assets (RONA), or return on average assets employed (ROAA), modified to suit the needs of the particular company. The management of financial leverage doesn't enter in here. Recall the formula for return on assets

$$ROA = \frac{\text{Net profit}}{\text{Sales}} \times \frac{\text{Sales}}{\text{Assets}}$$

which when applied to an operating unit relates the unit's net profit (before or after taxes) to the unit's sales and its identifiable assets. Again, we can use cash flow measures to judge the performance and the value of business units, but these require a variety of adjustments to make sure that all relevant cash flow elements have been considered, and that the appropriate return standards are applied.

Further complications arise when units within a large corporation supply goods and services to each other. The most difficult aspect is the issue of setting appropriate transfer prices for the value of the goods and services moving between units of the corporation. At times, readily available, clearly established market prices can be used to value these transfers. More often than not, however, transfer prices have to be set through negotiation or even by corporate decree. There are no entirely satisfactory approaches to resolving this often vexing issue, which cannot only cause serious distortions in the results of individual units, but—even more significantly—may distort the decisions of unit managers and cause them to over- or underinvest, or to suboptimize their operations.

INTERNATIONAL PERFORMANCE ANALYSIS CHALLENGES

The issue of measuring the performance of a business becomes particularly challenging when operations extend into the international arena, either when divisions are operating entirely within a foreign country, or when organizational entities perform transactions in several currencies. In the former situation, the division usually can be viewed as a rather independent entity—albeit operating with a foreign currency—while in the latter case, the flow of goods and services across borders introduces significant measurement problems. All of the measurement issues we mentioned earlier usually apply to foreign operations as well, but in addition there's the problem of measuring the impact of absolute and relative changes in the different currencies involved.

Foreign Subsidiaries Operating in a Single Country

The simplest case involves a wholly-owned subsidiary, which for all practical purposes acts as part of the host country, and which keeps its books and financial statements in the local currency. The key measurements in which the U.S. parent company will be interested are current earnings performance and the valuation of the subsidiary.

Given that all transactions and cost accounting steps are carried out in the local currency, the calculation of earnings performance through various ratios will be internally consistent and unaffected by currency fluctuations and exchange rates. Whether the subsidiary operates in German marks, English pounds, or Brazilian cruzeiros, performance measures will indicate the effectiveness with which the subsidiary's assets are employed, and various ratios used to measure performance will give appropriate readings.

Since the U.S. parent company will also be interested in viewing the level of earnings as expressed in U.S. dollars, particularly for purposes of consolidating the earnings, exchange rates must be brought into play. We can represent the situation in the form of some simple formulas, revisiting the discussions of Chapters 3 and 5. If we simulate the subsidiary's earnings in dollars $(E_\$)$ by denoting unit price (P), variable costs (C), fixed costs (F), unit volume (V), and exchange rate (R), and denote all relevant components in terms of the foreign currency (f), the simple equation is

$$\text{Subsidiary } E_\$ = R \left[(P_f - C_f) \, V - F_f \right]$$

Clearly the exchange rate R affects all financial terms in the formulation, and the dollar earnings reported will be a function of the level of exchange between the dollar and the foreign currency involved. There's nothing the subsidiary management can do about the exchange rate, which may fluctuate wildly or may be very stable. The subsidiary's earnings as such aren't affected—only their expression in dollar terms will be altered. The U.S. parent, on the other hand, may be quite affected by rising or falling exchange rates which will change the subsidiary's dollar earnings.

When we wish to develop the dollar return on investment (return on assets) of the subsidiary (ROI_s), the only additional item needed to complete the formula is the amount of the subsidiary's assets denoted in the foreign currency (A_f):

$$ROI_s = \frac{R\ [(P_f - C_f)\ V - F_f]}{R \times A_f} = \frac{(P_f - C_f)\ V - F_f}{A_f} = ROI_f$$

Note that the exchange rate R drops out of the equation and the return on investment in dollar terms is equivalent to the return in foreign currency terms. As we stated earlier, ratio analysis performed on an entity with consistent accounting in a single currency will provide meaningful results independent of exchange rate concerns. Only the distortions inherent in the accounting system itself, as discussed in Chapters 2 and 3, will affect the stated amount of the division's assets.

The implications of this discussion are rather straightforward. The management of a subsidiary operating as a unit completely within a given country can be judged by using all standard ratios expressed in the local currency. But the inclusion of the subsidiary's foreign currency earnings in consolidated U.S. financial statements will be affected by any movement in the dollar exchange rates, as will the recording of foreign assets in U.S. dollar terms. The U.S. parent's financial statements may have to be adjusted frequently to account for exchange rate differences alone.

Distortions arising from significant inflationary trends will affect a foreign subsidiary in much the same way as businesses experienced inflation in the United States during the 1970s. In essence, recorded asset values will tend to be understated over time. To the extent that inflationary conditions in the foreign country exceed U.S. levels, it may be desirable to revalue the foreign subsidiary's balance sheet elements for analysis purposes to make sure that ratios derived from the statement are internally consistent.

Valuation of the subsidiary in cash flow terms can be done by expressing the expected cash inflows in the foreign currency and discounting these to arrive at the present value, as we did in Chapter 9. Note that the issues of price, volume, and cost as well as terminal value will remain consistent through the use of the foreign currency in which they occur. All of the issues surrounding the estimates of future conditions in markets, costs, economic developments, and so on will apply here as they would in the United States. The final result can then be translated into U.S. dollars at the prevailing exchange rate, if desired.

Subsidiaries Operating across Foreign Borders

A more common consequence of the continued expansion of international trade is the need for a corporate entity to do business in several countries and in their respective currencies. Now the issue of exchange rates begins to loom large, for both earnings calculations and performance measures will be affected by the mix of currencies on the company's books. Let's take the simplified example of a so-called cross-border subsidiary that imports goods from the U.S. parent company and sells these goods within the foreign country in which it operates. Let's further assume that the U.S. parent requires payment for the goods in dollars, while the subsidiary quotes and sells the goods in the local currency. Moreover, all other costs of the subsidiary will be incurred in the local currency as well.

We can again write the equation for the dollar earnings of the subsidiary $(E_\$)$, taking into account the fact that its variable costs are incurred in dollars:

$$\text{Subsidiary } E_\$ = R \left[(P_f - \frac{C_\$}{R}) V - F_f\right]$$

This equation simply describes the subsidiary's condition in which prices and fixed costs have to be converted into dollars, while variable costs are already incurred in dollars.

The complications that can arise from this situation are apparent. No longer does the exchange rate simply apply to earnings as it did in the case of the single-country subsidiary. Now the exchange rate additionally affects a highly significant cost element in the subsidiary's cost structure. Any movement in the exchange rate during a period of operations will directly affect the subsidiary's cost of goods sold. For example, if the foreign currency weakens from four units per U.S. dollar to six, the subsidiary has suffered a 50 percent increase in its cost of goods sold because it must obtain dollars for payment to its U.S. parent that have become 50 percent more expensive. This could severely affect the subsidiary's competitive position in the local market unless it can readily pass on this price increase. An opposite effect will, of course, occur if the exchange rate moves in favor of the local currency, such as from four units per U.S. dollar to three.

Exchange rate movements' impact on the subsidiary's performance measures depends on a number of factors. If significant price movements in the subsidiary's cost of goods sold due to the U.S. dollar exchange rate don't affect its market position because it can adjust the price of the goods based on the change in cost—a highly unrealistic assumption—the performance ratios are likely to be unaffected. In reality, changes in the cost of goods sold will normally impact the subsidiary's ability to compete locally, and attempts to price according to cost will not only affect the volume of units sold, but also change operational costs because of these volume changes.

It's not possible to develop a simple formula approach here, because the total operating system of the subsidiary will be affected in largely unpredictable ways. For example, any attempted price changes are likely to be less than proportional to the change in the cost of goods sold, in order to minimize the competitive impact. Market reactions to these price changes will largely depend on the subsidiary's market position, the quality and price of competitive goods, the availability of competitive substitutes from sources not subject to similar exchange rate fluctuations, and so on. It will usually be best to model the major dimensions of the subsidiary's business system and to simulate a variety of assumptions about price, volume, and cost changes.

The basic calculation in Figure II–1 shows the type of analysis that will help gauge the effect on the subsidiary's earnings and ROA under several assumed conditions. Clearly, more specific knowledge about local market conditions would have to be applied to refine the range of estimates, and more of the underlying variables would have to be modeled to obtain a clearer picture of the impact of currency exchange rates.

FIGURE II–1

IMPACT ON SUBSIDIARY EARNINGS AND ROA USING
SEVERAL ASSUMED EXCHANGE RATE CONDITIONS

		Current Period		
Variable	Prior Period	Constant Exchange Rate	Dollar Strengthens	Dollar Weakens
Exchange Rate (R)	$0.25	$0.25	$0.17	$0.33
(U.S. dollars/foreign currency)				
Selling price per unit (P_f)	f50.00	f55.00	f75.00	f50.00
Purchased cost per unit (C_s)	$10.00	$10.00	$10.00	$10.00
Purchased cost per unit (C_f)	f40.00	f40.00	f60.00	f30.00
Number of units sold (V)	1,000	1,000	750	1,100
Subsidiary assets (A_f)	f30,000	f30,000	f36,000	f27,000
Earnings, ROI in foreign currency:				
Revenues	f50,000	f55,000	f56,250	f55,000
Cost of goods sold	40,000	40,000	45,000	33,000
Fixed costs	5,000	5,000	5,000	5,000
Earnings	5,000	10,000	6,250	17,000
ROI	17%	33%	17%	63%
Earnings in U.S. dollars	$1,250	$2,500	$1,063	$5,610

This set of assumptions reflects conditions in two time periods, with exchange rates allowed to move significantly in the current period from the conditions of the prior period. The foreign selling price was assumed to increase slightly in the current period under stable exchange rates (second column). The impact of this 10 percent price increase is a doubling of foreign earnings from f5,000 to f10,000, and a parallel doubling of the dollar earnings. Note that the ROI reflects this doubling as well.

As the dollar strengthens in the third column, the foreign purchase cost per unit jumps 50 percent, and the subsidiary tries to increase the price to recover the extra cost. This is likely to depress the volume sold—here it's assumed to drop by 25 percent. Higher-cost inventories will also increase the subsidiary's asset base by an assumed f6,000. While earnings in the foreign currency decline by 37.5 percent, the ROI is cut in half because of the impact of higher-cost inventories on the asset base. The dollar earnings, however, suffer an even greater decline due to the strengthening of the dollar exchange rate.

The fourth column reflects a weakening of the dollar, which makes U.S. goods cheaper to import. In fact, the cost to the subsidiary drops to 50 percent of the stronger dollar condition in the third column. We assume that the subsidiary will pass on much of this in the form of a lower price, which raises the number of units sold by 10 percent, to 1,100. Revenues are now the same as in the case of the stable exchange rate in the second column. Note, however, the impact of the reduction in costs on the foreign earnings, which soar to f17,000 and are reflected in the ROI of 63 percent—which in turn is boosted by the drop in assets due to lower-cost inventories. In addition, the weaker dollar exchange rate escalates the dollar earnings to more than twice the level of the second column, an increase of 124 percent!

It should be clear from this highly simplified example that we must thoroughly analyze the dynamics of the foreign markets and conditions in addition to assessing the mere reflection of currency exchange rates as changes occur. You're invited to trace through a variety of assumptions in this simple model to gain further insight into the dynamics at play.

More complexity is introduced when differing inflation rates in various countries are taken into account. As was experienced in the United States during the 1970s, inflationary conditions don't necessarily increase operating earnings proportionately, as the price of inputs like materials, labor, and fuel don't necessarily move in concert. Thus a detailed analysis of the impact of foreign operations requires much more insight than this brief exposure could provide.

We should briefly mention another aspect of foreign currency transactions here. Companies engaged in buying, selling, and operating in various foreign currencies will use, whenever possible, the concept of *hedging* to protect themselves from even temporary exposure to currency fluctuations. In simple terms, hedging involves the simultaneous purchase or sale of foreign currency contracts that offset the amounts of the commercial transaction undertaken. For example, if a U.S. company sold goods into a foreign market and expects to be paid in the foreign currency some 30 or 60 days hence, the company's treasurer may execute a simultaneous contract to sell an equivalent amount of foreign currency at that time, but based on today's exchange rate. Such a currency contract—called a *forward trade*—exemplifies a common transaction in the worldwide market for currencies. The purpose of currency hedging is in effect to lock in the prevailing exchange rate and to avoid the risk of fluctuations. Again, there are many more aspects of foreign currency management than we can cover in a book of this scope. Readers should turn to specialized materials on these subjects for in-depth coverage.

APPENDIX III
BASIC INFLATION
CONCEPTS

Throughout this book we've referred to inflation's distorting effects on financial decisions and analysis. In this appendix we'll offer a brief commentary on the basic nature of the often misunderstood phenomenon of inflation. Financial transactions are carried out and recorded with the help of a common medium of exchange, such as U.S. dollars. Variations in this medium will affect the numerical meaning of these transactions. But we know that underlying the transactions are economic trade-offs; that is, values are given and received. We must be careful not to confuse changes in economic values with changes in the medium used to effect and account for these transactions. We'll examine the ramifications of this statement in several contexts here.

PRICE LEVEL CHANGES

The economic values of goods and services invariably change over time. The reason for this is as basic as human nature: The law of supply and demand operates, in an uncontrolled market environment, to increase the value of goods and services that are in short supply, and to decrease the value of those available in abundance. This shift in relative values takes place even in a primitive barter economy that doesn't utilize any currency at all. The ratio of exchange of coconuts for beans, for example, will move in favor of coconuts when they're scarce, and in favor of beans when these are out of season. Many seasonal agricultural products go through a familiar price cycle, reflecting their temporary unavailability, on to the first arrivals in the marketplace, and eventually to an abundance before they become unavailable again. The phenomenon isn't limited to seasonal goods, however. Natural resources go through cycles of availability, be it from the need to set up the infrastructure to exploit new sources as old ones expire, or from extreme concerted actions such as OPEC's moves in the 1970s and 80s that upset world oil prices through the cartel's control of over half the world's oil production.

We know that the economic value of manufactured goods is similarly subject to the law of supply and demand. For example, as new technology emerges in the market (such as the first digital watches or compact disc players), the price commanded by the early units will be well above prices charged later on, after many suppliers have entered the market and competed for a share of consumer demand. The same is true of all goods and services for which there are present or potential alternative suppliers, domestic or international.

Our point here is that the economic value underlying personal, commercial, and financial transactions is determined by forces that are largely independent of the monetary expression in which they're recorded. As we'll see, an analysis of price level changes ideally should separate the change in price levels caused by shifts in economic value from those caused by changes in the currency itself. Accurate separation of the two is difficult in practice, but necessary for understanding the meaning of financial projections.

MONETARY INFLATION

Another phenomenon affecting transaction values is any basic change in the purchasing power of the currency. There are many reasons underlying the decline or strengthening of a currency's value as a medium of exchange. One of the most important factors causing inflationary declines in purchasing power is the amount of currency in circulation relative to economic activity. If the government raises the money supply faster than required to accommodate the growth in economic activity, there will literally be more dollars chasing relatively fewer goods and services, and thus the stated dollar prices for all goods and services will rise—even though basic demand for any specific item may be unchanged.

This description is oversimplified, of course. A great many more factors affect currency values. One is the impact of government deficits and how they're financed. Another is the value of the dollar relative to other currencies and the impact of exchange rates on international trade, as we observed in Appendix II. In addition, international money flows and investment in response to more attractive investment opportunities cause shifts in the values of national currencies over and above the effects of the individual countries' fiscal and economic conditions. Union negotiations, wage settlements, and cost of living adjustments in wages, pensions, and social security are also related to changing currency values. Every nation's central bank—the Federal Reserve bank in the case of the United States—is vital in the process because its policies affect both the size of the money supply and interest rates. These in turn affect government fiscal policies, business activity, international trade and money flows, and so on. And ultimately, serious declines in the value of a currency can also affect the basic supply and demand of goods and services, as, for example, customers and businesses buy ahead to beat anticipated price increases.

The point here isn't to systematically analyze inflation and its causes, but rather to make the basic distinction between economic and monetary changes influencing price levels. Suffice it to say that price level changes due to monetary effects are largely the ones that distort economic values of personal and commercial transactions. If monetary conditions remained stable (that is, if the amount of currency in circulation always matched the level of economic activity), price level changes would only reflect changes in economic values—something we've agreed is at the core of management's efforts to improve the owners' economic condition. Because monetary stability is an unrealistic expectation, however, the challenge remains to make the analysis of the actual conditions affecting prices and economic values truly meaningful.

NOMINAL AND REAL DOLLARS

Business and personal transactions are expressed in terms of *nominal* dollars, also called current dollars, that reflect today's prices, unadjusted or altered in any way. For accounting purposes, nominal dollars are used every day to record transactions. However, when dollar prices change over time, the amounts recorded in the past no longer reflect current prices, either in terms of the underlying economic values or in terms of the value of the currency at the moment.

To deal with changes in the value of the currency, economists have devised *price indexes* intended to separate, at least in part, monetary distortions from fluctuations in economic value. Such an index is constructed by measuring the aggregate change in the prices of a representative group of products and services as a surrogate for the change in the value of the currency. Yet we already know that any goods and services chosen for this purpose are themselves also subject to changes in supply and demand apart from mere currency fluctuations. But there's no direct way to measure changes in currency values as such. Inevitably, therefore, the price index approach involves mixing demand/supply conditions and currency values, and the only hope is that the selection of goods and services employed in a given index is broad enough to compensate somewhat for the underlying demand/ supply conditions.

The *consumer price index*, a popular index of inflation, is calculated in this fashion. It's based on frequent sampling of the prices of a "market basket" of goods and services purchased by American consumers, including food, housing, clothing, and transportation. The composition and weighting of this basket is changed gradually to reflect changing habits and tastes, although there's much room for argument about how representative the selection is. Another popular index, applicable to business, is the *producer price index,* based on a representative weighted sampling of the wholesale prices of goods produced. Other indexes deal with wholesale commodity prices and a variety of specialized groupings of products and services.

The broadest index in common use is applied to the gross national product as a whole, the so-called *GNP deflator,* which expresses the price changes experienced in the total range of goods and services produced in the U.S. economy. Based on broad statistical sampling, the current level of the GNP deflator is announced frequently throughout the year in connection with other economic statistics about business and government activity. All of these indexes are prepared by calculating the changes in prices from those of a selected base year, which is changed only infrequently to avoid having to adjust comparative statistical series whenever the base year is changed.

The price indexes are used to translate nominal dollar values in government statistics and business reports into *real dollar values.* This involves converting nominal dollar values to a chosen standard so that past and present dollar transactions can be compared in equivalent terms. For example, to compare this year's economic performance to last year's, we may choose to express current economic statistics using last year's dollars as the standard. Last year's dollars are then called real, and today's data are expressed in these "real" terms. To do this, we simply adjust today's dollars by the amount of inflation experienced since last year. If inflation this year was 4.5 percent over last year as expressed in the GNP deflator, every nominal dollar figure for this year would be adjusted downward by 4.5 percent. The result would be an expression of this year's results in terms of real dollars which are based on the prior year.

A real dollar is thus simply a nominal dollar that has been adjusted to the price level of a particular stated base year, using one of the applicable price indexes. The base chosen can be any year, as long as past or future years are consistently stated in terms of the currency value for the base year. In fact, real dollars are often called *constant dollars*, a name that simply recognizes that they're derived from a constant base. The process of adjustment has the following effect: During inflationary periods, the real dollars for the years preceding the base year will be adjusted upward, while the real dollars of future years will be adjusted downward. The reverse is true, of course, if the period involves deflation instead.

To illustrate, let's assume that the following price developments took place during a five-year period. We're using the producer price index (PPI). This index was constructed on the basis of Year 0. In the following table, we've set Year 3 as the base year for our analysis.

	Year 1	Year 2	Year 3	Year 4	Year 5
Producer price index (Year 0)	1.09	1.15	1.21	1.25	1.33
Producer price index (Year 3)	0.90	0.95	1.00	1.03	1.10
Real value of $100 (Base Year 3)	$111	$105	$100	$97	$91

Note that two steps were involved. First, the producer price index had to be adjusted for our chosen base, Year 3; that is, the index had to be set at 1.00 for Year 3 and then all index numbers were divided by the value of the index for the base year, which is 1.21. (The index could, of course, have been constructed on any other year because an index measures price changes year by year from whatever starting point is chosen.) The next step was to divide the adjusted index values on the second line into the nominal dollars of each year. We chose to use the amount of $100 for all years, but the process applies, of course, to any amount of nominal dollars in any one of the years. Using a single round figure permitted us to illustrate the shifts in value with a same dollar amount.

The example clearly shows that a dollar's purchasing power in Year 4 versus Year 3 declined by 3 percent. The implication from a business point of view is that a company must increase its nominal earnings power by 3 percent to keep up with inflation in the prices it must pay for goods and services. Anything less than that will leave the owners worse off.

This simple process allows us to convert nominal dollars into inflation-adjusted real dollars. Problems arise in choosing the proper index for a business situation, and also from the fact that the index embodies changes in economic value as well as in currency value, as we discussed earlier. Much thought has been expended on refining the process of inflation adjustment, but in the end the judgment about its usefulness depends on the purpose of the analysis and the degree of accuracy desired.

APPLICATIONS OF INFLATION ADJUSTMENT IN FINANCIAL ANALYSIS

Restatement of company data or projections in real dollar terms is at times useful to assess whether the company's performance has kept up with shifts in currency values. Such restatement may be used to value a company's assets and liabilities, or to show the real growth or decline in sales and earnings. As we observed, publicly traded companies are obligated to include an annual inflation-adjusted restatement of key data in their published shareholder reports.

Much effort goes into adjusting financial projections for inflation, particularly in the area of capital investment analysis. There are no truly satisfactory general rules for this process, however. When an analyst must project cash flows from a major capital investment, the easiest approach continues to be projection in nominal dollars, taking into account expected cost and price increases of the key variables involved, tailored specifically to the conditions of the business. The discount standard applied against the projection is also based on nominal return expectations that, of course, embody the inflationary outlook.

To refine the analysis, many companies prepare projections in real dollars, attempting to forecast the true economic increases or decreases in costs and prices. Then an appropriate inflation index is applied to the figures to convert them into nominal dollars. The problem is, however, that the margin between revenues and costs may widen unduly, simply because the same inflation index is applied to the larger revenue numbers and to the smaller cost numbers. Often arbitrary adjustments have to be made to keep the margin spread manageable.

Another approach involves developing projections expressed in real dollars and discounting these with a return standard that has also been converted into real returns. The result will be internally consistent as far as the project is concerned. However, the result is not readily comparable with the current overall performance of the business—recorded and expressed in nominal dollar terms—unless the company has also found a way to convert and measure ongoing performance in real dollar terms. Some companies are beginning to experiment with such restated reports and measures, but the approach involves a massive effort, in terms of both data preparation and education of personnel generating and using the projections and performance data. It's instinctively easier to think about business in nominal dollars than real dollars, and progress refining these processes is being made only gradually. The complexities are such that the financial and planning staffs of companies wishing to use a real dollar approach face a lengthy conceptual and practical conversion problem.

IMPACT OF INFLATION

To restate quickly, the basic impact of inflation—and the much less common opposite situation, deflation—is a growing distortion of recorded values on a company's financial statements, and an ongoing partial distortion of operating results. Accounting methods discussed in Chapters 1 and 2 are designed to make the effect of the inflationary distortion at least consistent. In terms of cash flows, inflation distorts a company's tax payments if the taxes due are based on low historical cost apportionment, and it results in a cash drain if dividends are higher than they would be if real-dollar earnings were considered, to name two examples. Inflation also affects financing conditions, particularly the repayment of principal on long-term debt obligations. But as we observed before, the mediating influence of interest rates—which respond to inflation expectations—tends to prevent windfalls for the borrower looking to repay debt with "cheap" dollars. Normally, over the long run, distortions from inflation affect lenders and borrowers alike. Relative advantages gained by one over the other are only temporary.

Overall, the subject of inflation adjustments continues to evolve in financial analysis. It's unlikely that totally consistent methods that are generally applicable will be found.

APPENDIX IV
OBJECT-ORIENTED
FINANCIAL
ANALYSIS: AN
INTRODUCTION*

The practice of financial analysis has been immeasurably enhanced in recent years through the continuing evolution of computer-aided approaches in the form of electronic spreadsheets and computer-based financial models of various types. These devices have not only eased the analyst's computational task, but have also opened up a wide range of sensitivity analyses and testing of alternatives heretofore not possible.

At the same time, however, computer-aided financial analysis in its present form has remained essentially a passive, if powerful, processing tool that leaves most of the formatting, choice of data, specification of linkages, and computational instructions up to the analyst—in other words, it relies on the professional "knowledge base" of the individual to control the process in full. Once such knowledge has been applied in a specific analysis, it's usually difficult—because of the passive nature of spreadsheet methodology—to retrieve and examine the many choices made by the analyst, especially if another person wishes

---

*The materials in this appendix are based on work done by Lee Hecht, chairman and cofounder of Modernsoft, Inc., and are reproduced here with permission of the company.

to use or expand work already done. Moreover, significant changes in a large number of variables may become so cumbersome for the analyst to track that setting up an entirely new analysis may be preferable, but at the cost of giving up valuable continuity.

The advent of cost-effective personal computers and workstations with massively improved computational speed and internal memory has made it possible to develop entirely new approaches to computer-aided financial analysis and decision support. One of the most promising of these is a system of object-oriented financial analysis, management, and decision support being developed by Modernsoft, Inc., of Palo Alto, California. The software framework employed is called *FinancialWorkbench*™ (FWb™), which embodies interactive, knowledge-based, object-oriented design concepts.

Modernsoft takes the approach that most financial situations, large or small, can be modeled as collections of interacting financial objects. In addition, the FWb™ system provides a set of financial object "building blocks"—called *classes*—which are selected and sometimes specialized by the user to represent, at the desired level of detail, the essential elements of the situation and their interactions. For all practical purposes, objects can be created to represent any of the elements and interactions that might be needed in analyzing and managing a financial situation or in making a financial decision.

Once the financial objects have been created and classified, the FWb™ system enables the analyst to perform, in an interactive fashion, consistent financial analyses on this "model" with few constraints, all the while building and preserving the interlinked knowledge base that underlies the situation. Thus FWb™ extends beyond mere computation into an *active sharing* of knowledge and experience between the analyst and the system. Its core is the concept of employing financial objects as the permanent carriers of relevant financial and other knowledge, representing a base of information that's expandable to any amount of detail desired.

Financial objects and their inherent knowledge can support a significant portion of the active analytical effort of the analyst. Not only is the individual's knowledge base interactively pooled with the knowledge base already embodied in the financial software, but this combined knowledge base used in solving a problem also remains freely accessible at all times as the analysis progresses. The various financial objects in effect become active parts of an interlinked financial systems model (such as was broadly illustrated in Chapter 1), which can be viewed, accessed, and analyzed as a "living entity," and which responds instantly and consistently to any changes in data or assumptions. This integrative capability is especially important in highly complex analytical situations, where tracking linkages under existing spreadsheet constraints would be cumbersome. Successful application of object-oriented financial analysis will enable analysts to perform far more comprehensive, innovative, and insightful analytical tasks than heretofore possible.

FINANCIAL OBJECTS—BASIC CONCEPT

Since financial objects and their classes are the essential feature of this analytical approach, it will be useful to illustrate the nature of financial objects on the basis of a simple example. Most real-world situations are so complex that a "complete" financial analysis isn't practical because the number of interacting elements is usually enormous. It's possible, however, to abstract the essential elements and their interactions and thus to "model" the basic situation, gradually adding complexity as needed for meaningful results. For purposes of illustration we've chosen a highly simplified break-even analysis to focus on the nature of financial objects. The principles demonstrated here apply, of course, to much more sophisticated and complex situations.

PotCo produces and sells cooking pots for a price of $10 per unit. Each pot requires $5 in direct production costs. All other PotCo expenses are $100,000 annually. The president of PotCo wants to know how many pots have to be sold annually to break even. One possible collection of objects that can be used to model this straightforward situation is illustrated in Figure IV–1.

Having defined this basic set of objects, the interaction among the individual objects can be shown as follows in Figure IV–2. The various relationships are, of course, not limited to break-even analysis alone, and the analyst can exploit this established knowledge base for other analytical tasks. Once the relationships have been specified, they remain easily accessible and demonstrable within the system, but they can also be modified for any purpose.

The simple model represented here can then be used to calculate the annual break-even volume by specifying an annual profit of $0 as an analytical inquiry, and the analyst can also modify key variables to explore the sensitivity of the result to different assumptions.

FWb™ provides for the creation of any number of objects with properties that correspond to accounting terms (e.g., revenue, asset, liability) and physical objects (e.g., unit of product, corporate jet, bank loan) encountered in a broad range of real-world financial situations. It's possible to provide knowledge and data support for most kinds of financial decisions by describing each situation in terms of some relevant group of objects, establishing the various interactions

FIGURE IV-1
Basic Objects for Break-Even Analysis

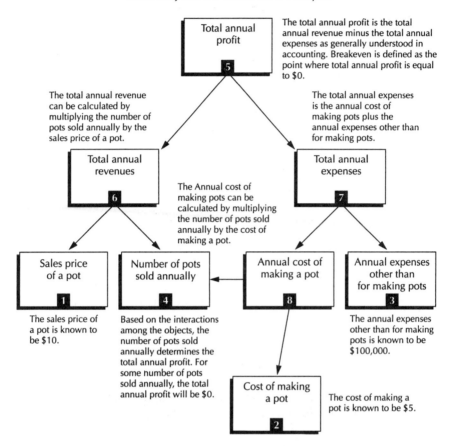

among these objects, and using the extensive set of analytical techniques embedded in the system to manipulate them.

Although objects created in FWb™ can be quite general, all objects must have some aspect that's financial in nature. This is necessary because FWb™ uses financial knowledge to understand, organize, reason about, and engineer the objects created by the user. Knowledge that's not strictly financial can be added to objects to provide additional dimensions along which analysis and engineering can be performed. Because all objects must have at least one financial dimension, objects used in FWb™ are normally referred to as *financial* objects.

Using a set of specific *classes* provided by FWb™ as the building blocks for analysis, the user proceeds to select the proper class for each financial object. Once an object has been classified, it automatically inherits a number of properties that are embodied in its class as

520

FIGURE IV-2
Interaction among Objects

Each of these objects "interacts" directly with one or more
other objects. Notice that object 4 is physical, namely the
number of pots that are sold in a year, while all of the
other objects are abstract financial concepts.

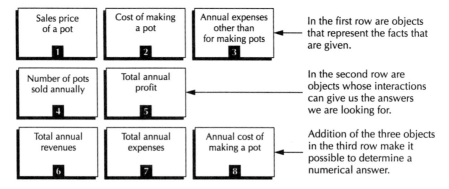

Sales price of a pot **1**	Cost of making a pot **2**	Annual expenses other than for making pots **3**	In the first row are objects that represent the facts that are given.
Number of pots sold annually **4**	Total annual profit **5**		In the second row are objects whose interactions can give us the answers we are looking for.
Total annual revenues **6**	Total annual expenses **7**	Annual cost of making a pot **8**	Addition of the three objects in the third row make it possible to determine a numerical answer.

part of the existing knowledge base in the system. The specific knowledge contained in a class allows the system to recognize an object, for example, as revenue for financial purposes, as individual subcategories of revenue and their preferred sequencing, and the attendant requirement to sum these individual revenues appropriately for specific reports and so on. In this way, the individual knowledge and experience that the analyst draws on in choosing the appropriate class becomes included in each financial object and remains there to be used from then on for any purpose, together with any additional aspects stipulated by the analyst.

As the user works through an analysis, FWb™ automatically generates a substantial amount of information about the financial situation, which then remains available both to the analyst and to the system as part of the knowledge base. In many cases this new knowledge will be automatically applied via calculations or consistency checks as the analysis progresses, thereby enabling the analyst to complete the tasks at hand more efficiently and with greater internal consistency.

The main potential for object-oriented financial analysis lies in the enormous expansion of the analyst's capabilities through an *on-line interface* of knowledge and information heretofore not realizable via existing methods and software packages. This methodology frees the analyst from the drudgery of repetitive inputs, formulation of instructions, and attempts at tracking the assumptions and results of complex analyses. In a broader sense, object-oriented financial analysis brings about the realization of "live financial modeling"—free from the massive internal systems development tasks usually associated with anything but rudimentary spreadsheet techniques. The scope of financial concepts and techniques discussed in this book is thus being harnessed for analysts in a way that their main effort can be concentrated on carefully structuring the decisional problems and the points of view from which they're to be resolved—which is a validation of the basic message about the orientation of financial analysis given at the beginning of this book.

APPENDIX V
SOURCES OF
FINANCIAL
INFORMATION

While this book's orientation is techniques of financial analysis, many of the applications we've discussed implied the use of information beyond that stipulated or available directly. Thus, you must be familiar with at least the main sources of financial information to obtain the necessary input for analysis. For this reason we've devoted this appendix to a brief review of common data sources; where required we give guidelines for interpretating the financial data presented. The information provided gives you the background needed to make more sophisticated decisions about company performance, new financing, temporary borrowing, investments, credit, capital budgeting, and so on.

Again, in keeping with the nature of this book, this appendix is meant only as an introduction to sources of current financial, periodic financial, and background company and business information. Additional references for further study and data are provided at the end of this appendix.

CURRENT FINANCIAL INFORMATION

The most common and convenient way to keep abreast of financial developments is through the daily financial pages of national, metropolitan, and regional newspapers. The most complete and widely read financial coverage is found in *The Wall Street Journal* and *The New York Times*, which contain detailed information on securities and commodity markets; news, feature articles, and statistics on economic and business conditions; news and earnings reports for individual companies; dividend announcements; currency, commodity, and trading data; and a great deal of coverage of international business and economic conditions. Major U.S. and Canadian dailies also carry key financial and economic data, but their coverage and emphasis vary greatly. Smaller and regional papers often provide only selected highlights tailored to the area and the readership.

The bulk of the materials shown in the financial pages involve securities transactions and current financial data. This information isn't entirely self-explanatory. We'll describe the meaning of some of the abbreviations and symbols used in *The Wall Street Journal* listings for stock transactions (traded on exchanges and over the counter), bond transactions, and other key financial data. Other newspapers generally present data in a fairly comparable fashion, but in less detail.

Stock Quotations

Stock Exchanges. Transactions made on organized exchanges— New York Stock Exchange (NYSE), American Stock Exchange (AMEX), and several regional exchanges—and the electronic network of the National Association of Securities Dealers (NASDAQ) generally include the kind of information shown in Figure V–1. It shows the day's transactions in 12 stocks out of the 2,552 individual stocks traded on the New York Stock Exchange on Monday, June 14, 1993, as reported the next day in *The Wall Street Journal.* The total volume of shares traded for the day was about 210 million, an average volume in a year in which daily volumes well over 275 million were quite common and in which a slow day involved trading volumes under 175 million shares. Daily trading statistics for the NYSE, AMEX, and NASDAQ are summarized in *The Wall Street Journal* under overall headings "Stock Market Data Bank" and "The Dow Jones Averages."

The first stock listed in Figure V–1, Abitibi, had a high value of 13¾ and a low of 10¼ over the previous 52 weeks. (This is the range in which the shares closed at the end of the trading day in the previous 12 months, but not including the closing value of June 14, 1993.) The quotations are given in dollars per share and fractions of a dollar not smaller than ⅛ ($0.125). Abitibi paid dividends at the annual rate

FIGURE V–1

New York Stock Exchange—Sample of Stock Transactions,
Monday, June 14, 1993

52 Weeks					Yield	P/E	Sales in				Net
High	Low	Stocks	Sym.	Div.	%	Ratio	100s	High	Low	Close	Change
13¾	10¼	Abitibi g	ABY	0.5	...	...	5	11⅛	11⅛	11⅛	−⅛
x 50⅜	24½	Alza	AZA	...	...	27	1799	26¾	26	26	+½
8¾	7	Cigna High	HIS	.90 a	10.6	...	356	8⅝	8½	8½	−⅛
30¼	16¼	Glaxo Hldg	GLX	.85 e	4.6	14	9973	18½	18¼	18⅜	+¼
▲ 88⅞	50¼	Hewlett Pk	HWP	1.00 f	1.1	25	9152	89¼	86⅞	87½	+1¼
s 38¼	30⅛	Honeywell	HON	.89	2.5	14	5392	36⅞	35⅛	35¾	−⅞
n 25½	24½	IBM dep. pf		.13 p	.5	...	2035	25⅛	25	25	−⅛
▼ 43⅜	31¼	Liz Clabrn	LIZ	.45 f	1.5	13	8807	31⅜	29¾	30⅞	−½
46¾	29⅞	Raychem	RYC	.32	.7	dd	642	45⅞	44¾	44⅞	−⅞
2⅞	¹⁵⁄₁₆	vj Std. B Paint	SBP	...	...	...	27	2⅜	2¼	2⅜	...
n ▲ 22¾	21¼	Svc Mastr wi		...	...	10	10	23	22¾	23	+¼
45	34⅞	US West	USW	2.14 f	4.8	15	2355	44⅜	44⅛	44¼	−⅛

of $.50 during the period (based on the last quarterly declaration). The special symbol "g" indicates that Abitibi, a major pulp and paper company headquartered in Canada, paid its dividends in Canadian dollars.

The next column shows the company's symbol, **ABY**, used in the electronic stock quotations flashed all over the world. Next is the dividend yield based on the current market quotations, while the following column reports the price/earnings ratio based on current reported earnings (12-month period) and current price levels. Abitibi's yield and P/E aren't shown on that day because few shares were traded, but they're listed for most other companies.

The day's transactions in Abitibi stock totaled only 500 shares, as indicated in the eighth column, where sales are listed in multiples of 100 shares. This is because stocks are ordinarily traded in round lots of 100 shares, while fewer than 100 shares is considered an odd lot, and brokers usually charge a premium for trading in the latter.

The next four columns indicate the stock's price movements based on actual transactions during June 14, 1993. Trade in Abitibi reached a high for the day of $11.125 and a low of $11.125. Why are the figures the same? There may have been only one or two transactions. Note that there were spreads between highs and lows in the other, more heavily traded stocks. The net change of −$.125 in Abitibi's last column indicates the difference between its price at the close of trading on June 14 and the price at the close of the previous trading day.

Unless otherwise indicated, the transactions listed involve common stocks. If a preferred stock is traded, the symbol "pf" is added right after the name. In our example the **IBM** issue traded is a preferred stock. The dividend quoted for preferred stock is the annual rate, as is the case with common stock. In the case of IBM, however, the dividend of $0.13 represents the initial dividend, indicated by the symbol "p" and yielding about 0.5 percent. The symbol ahead of the 52-week high and low columns (▲) indicates that the stock has reached a new 52-week high, while the inverse of this arrow (▼) indicates a new 52-week low. Standard Brands Paint, where the symbol "vj" ahead of the name indicates a state of bankruptcy, isn't paying any dividends at all. The price range of Standard Brands Paint and the current high and low indicate its severe difficulties.

A number of additional symbols and abbreviations are commonly used and explained briefly in footnotes on the financial pages of most papers. A number of these are shown in our sample listing. For example, an "n" ahead of IBM's and Service Master's 52-week high/low range indicates that this is a new issue on the exchange. An "s" in the same place, as in the case of Honeywell, denotes a stock dividend or stock split of more than 25 percent within the past 52 weeks. An "x" in that position, as shown with Alza Corporation, indicates that the stock is trading ex dividends or ex rights, that is, a very recently declared dividend or rights issue will no longer accrue to the purchaser on this date.

An "e" with the dividend rate, as in the case of Glaxo Holdings, signals that a cash dividend was paid but that no regular dividend rate exists. An "f" (as with Hewlett-Packard, Liz Claiborn, and US West) indicates a regular annual dividend that was increased at the last board meeting. Other symbols are used to show extra dividends ("a") as with Cigna High, an initial dividend ("p") as with the IBM issue, and ("b"), the annual rate of cash dividends plus a stock dividend.

Apart from notations for dividend exceptions, symbols are also used to show when a company's P/E ratio can't be calculated because a deficit was reported for the period ("dd") as was the case with Raychem Corporation. Other notations include a company's calling for redemption of a particular stock ("cld"), various conditions of rights and warrants (which represent options to purchase additional shares), and anticipatory quotations of a new issue on a when-issued basis ("wi"). Service Master's stock represents such advance trading. Also, a "z" indicates that total sales transactions for the day involved fewer than 100 shares.

The individual listings of stock transactions in *The Wall Street Journal* are supplemented by various summaries of overall trading figures in the so-called "Stock Market Data Bank." One of these is the list of the day's most active stocks. On June 14, 1993, the stock with by far the highest turnover of shares among the 2,552 stocks listed for the NYSE was the bankrupt ("vj") LTV Corporation (10.5 million shares), closing at ⅛, with no change from the prior day.

Another market summary—the "Diary" for the past two trading days and for trading one week ago, covering the NYSE, NASDAQ, and AMEX—showed that on June 14, 1993, among the 2,552 different issues traded on the NYSE, 946 advanced and 960 declined, leaving 646 issues unchanged. The number of new highs achieved was 47, while there were 34 new lows—reflecting the fairly flat market in mid-June 1993. The volume of advancing issues slightly outpaced declining issues by 97 million to 87 million in the total trading volume of 210 million shares. The diary also lists price percentage gainers and losers for the day, which on June 14, 1993, were Southdown (up 15.8 percent) and RMI Titanium (down 20.0 percent). Among the volume percentage leaders, Patriot Preferred took first place at 116,000 shares, which represented a surging 1,320 percent increase over its average trading volume during the past 65 days.

Also included are graphic displays of four months of the movements of the Dow Jones averages, for industrials, transportation, and utilities, and a table of the opening, closing, and hourly values of the averages for five trading days. For example, on Monday, June 14, 1993, the Dow Jones Industrial Average closed at 3,514.69, up 9.68 from Friday, June 11. Briefer listings of other major market indicators (such as the Standard & Poor's 500 Index, the NASDAQ Composite Index, and the London and Tokyo indexes) are shown in an overview table. These and other indicators collectively provide an impression of the market's "mood" and direction.

Quotations of transactions on the American Stock Exchange are similar. Transactions on regional exchanges, such as the Pacific Stock Exchange in San Francisco and the Midwest Stock Exchange in Chicago, are often listed together with the most important quotations on the major Canadian stock exchanges in Toronto and Montreal. These transactions are quoted in less detail. Normally, only the number of shares traded, the high and low prices, and the closing prices with changes from the previous close are listed. At times the quotations are limited to volume and closing prices only.

Reference was made earlier to the various stock price averages, which are popular and important clues to the stock market's behavior in general. These averages are calculated daily and in some cases continuously from on-line data bases. The averages are followed by analysts, investors, and financial managers who interpret market movements to decide on purchase or sale of securities, or to assess various types of new securities. Because the various averages involve a selected and relatively small number of stocks, their upward or downward movement over time isn't necessarily a predictor of the likely movement of any particular stock or of the overall market.

As discussed earlier, there are many factors underlying the value and market position of a particular security, the most important being the current and prospective operating circumstances of the company and the cash flows generated in response to these. The market's atmosphere and general economic conditions will certainly influence the particular stock's behavior, but we must caution against the adage that a "rising tide lifts all ships in the harbor" (a gross oversimplification of stock market behavior). The limitations of stock indexes are those of averages in general, which can only be broad indicators of a likely trend against which all particulars of a security have to be compared.

The most commonly quoted and publicized stock price averages are the Dow Jones averages of 30 industrial, 20 transportation, and 15 utility stocks, and the composite average of all those 65 securities. The Dow Jones Industrial Average contains most well-known companies in the United States, such as IBM, General Motors, General Electric, Woolworth, Du Pont, and Procter & Gamble. Because it's heavily weighted toward these "blue-chip" securities—many of which have performed poorly in the past decade—the Dow Jones average isn't particularly applicable for analysis of securities of lesser known companies, specialized "growth situations," and conglomerates.

The New York Times average of 50 stocks includes 25 transportation issues and 25 industrial stocks. This average is also somewhat weighted in favor of blue chips. The Standard & Poor's averages— composite indexes of 425 industrial stocks, 50 utilities, and 25 transportation companies, and a combination of all these averages in the S&P 500—are more broadly based and more closely approximate the average price level of all stocks listed on the New York Stock Exchange because the S&P 500 includes about one quarter of the issues actively traded there.

As pointed out before, the various stock averages, including daily ranges and average price levels, are available for each trading day. Because transactions are electronically tracked, the current level of these averages is always available almost instantaneously during the trading day. Continuous adjustments are made for stock splits, stock dividends, and many changes in the corporate structure of the companies in the index. Some references at the end of this appendix detail how the indexes are calculated.

NASDAQ National Market Issues. A huge volume of securities is traded outside the organized exchanges in an auction market consisting of hundreds of security dealers and individuals in all parts of the country. They're electronically linked via extensive computer networks. This *over-the-counter (OTC) market* is an amazingly flexible arrangement which allows trading between prospective buyers and sellers of such securities as government bonds, state and municipal bonds, stocks and bonds of smaller and newer companies, bank stocks, mutual funds, insurance companies, small issues, and infrequently traded issues.

On Monday, June 14, 1993, the NASDAQ Composite Index climbed 3.22, or .46 percent, to 696.41. Decliners topped gainers 1,345 to 1,323 on a total volume of 208 million shares, just about equivalent to the NYSE's volume. Financial listings for the NASDAQ national market issue transactions are similar to stock exchange transaction listings, except that notations indicating special conditions are incorporated into the four- or five-letter listing symbol. If a fifth letter is used, its special meaning is keyed to a symbol explanation below the NASDAQ listing.

Figure V–2 from the June 15, 1993, *Wall Street Journal* provides a sample listing of eight NASDAQ quotations for June 14, 1993. The format is the same as that for the New York Stock Exchange listings in Figure V–1 except that the symbol denoting the company is composed of four letters.

The notations with NASDAQ transactions are the same as for the New York Stock Exchange quotations. Three additional symbols occur in our sample of companies. The "j" with the Hibernia dividend indicates that a dividend was paid this year, but that at the last dividend meeting a dividend was omitted or deferred. The "i" after the Kahler dividend indicates the amount declared or paid after a stock dividend or stock split. The "cc" in Olympic's P/E ratio column indicates that the P/E ratio is 100 or more.

Foreign Exchanges. Some of the larger newspapers carry limited quotations from major foreign stock exchanges. Trading of internationally recognized securities on the Paris, London, Tokyo, or Frankfurt stock exchanges is reported in the currency of the country involved. At times, the financial pages may contain current stock averages for foreign countries, supplemented by accounts of major activities there. *The Wall Street Journal* presents the Dow Jones World Stock Indexes, which reflect market trends in major regions of the world. Closing prices and changes from the prior trading day are provided for many industrial groupings and for major regions such as the United States, the Americas, Europe, and Asia-Pacific.

Mutual Funds. Mutual funds are professionally managed investment pools. A share of a mutual fund represents an investment in a portfolio of different securities, which may be oriented toward a variety of investment objectives such as earnings or capital appreciation. These funds have gained in importance in recent years so mutual fund trading is quoted in most major newspapers. Price ranges are provided by the National Association of Securities Dealers. The quotes normally show the investment objectives (Inv. Obj.) of the fund, which are defined in 27 categories, including capital appre-

FIGURE V–2
NASDAQ National Market, Sample of Stock Transactions,
Monday, June 14, 1993

52 Weeks		Stocks	Sym.	Div.	Yield %	P/E Ratio	Sales in 100s	High	Low	Close	Net Change
High	Low										
s 16⅞	7¹¹⁄₁₆	Adac Labs	ADAC	.48	3.8	13	1980	12⅞	11¾	12¾	+1
n 15	7¼	Celebrity	FLWR	...	...	...	41	8¾	8	8¾	+⅝
n ▼ 12	10¼	Equinox Sys	EQNX	...	...	...	357	10½	9½	9⅝	−⅞
16¾	5¾	Hibernia Svg	HSBK	.35 j	...	6	18	13¾	12¾	13¾	+1
s 6	2⅜	Kahler	KHLR	.02 i	.4	dd	7	5⅛	4⅞	5⅛	+⅜
8¾	4⅝	Olympic Fnl	OLYM	...	...	cc	292	5¾	5⅜	5¾	+⅜
13	9¼	Roanoke Elec	RESC	.48 a	3.8	18	74	12¾	12	12⅝	+⅝
s ▲ 6⅜	1⅞	Siskon Gold A	SISK	...	...	...	499	6½	6⅛	6½	+⅜

ciation (CAP) and growth and income (G&I) for stock funds, short-term (BST) and high-yield taxable (BHI) for taxable bond funds, and intermediate-term (IDM) and high-yield municipal (HYM) for municipal bond funds. Next is given the net asset value per share (NAV), then an offering price including net asset value and the maximum sales charge, followed by the change in net asset value (NAV) from the previous day. Finally, the total return is provided for the year to date and for the past four weeks, along with a standard ranking (R) in terms of the gains achieved.

A variety of mutual fund indexes developed by Lipper are quoted to show daily trends in major categories, such as growth funds, small company growth funds, and gold funds.

Options.   Options (which are essentially contracts to buy or sell a security on a future date and at a stipulated price) are traded on various exchanges and are listed in terms of closing prices for "puts" (sales prices) and "calls" (purchase prices) for several months in the future. This specialized market has grown rapidly in recent years as has the market for commodity futures, which similarly represent contracts for future sales and purchases of certain commodities and are quoted in the financial pages.

Option quotations provide the volume during a given day, the exchange the put or call was traded on, the last trade in dollars plus fractions, the net change from the prior trading day, the closing price, and the "open interest" (options outstanding) from the prior trading day.

Bond Quotations

The three major types of bonds—corporate, state and municipal, and federal government—represent a huge market involving both the organized exchanges and the NASDAQ market. In fact, the overwhelming majority of government bonds of both types are traded in the NASDAQ market, while the majority of corporate bond issues are traded on the stock exchanges.

It will be useful to discuss how bond transactions are listed. Figure V–3 shows a listing for the NYSE; trading on other exchanges is handled similarly.

The first line gives not only the name of the issuing company, but also the coupon interest rate and the maturity date by the last two digits of the year. Thus, the first line is an American Telephone and Telegraph issue with a stated interest rate of 8½ percent and due date of 2022. Note that the issue is trading at a price above par to yield 7.6 percent, a yield more in keeping with the lower long-term interest conditions of 1993 compared to 1992, when the bond was issued.

The most important difference to remember vis-à-vis stock quotations is that bonds are quoted in percentages of par value, expressed in fractions no smaller than one eighth of a percent. For example, the AT&T bonds closed at a price of 106⅞, which represents $1,068.75 for each $1,000 of par value. Sales volumes are given in thousands of dollars because $1,000 is the most common denomination of a single bond. In contrast to stocks, only the closing price and the change from the prior day's closing price are listed.

The symbols used with the individual bonds parallel those discussed earlier. For example, "vj" with the LTV and National Gypsum bonds indicates these two companies' state of bankruptcy. Note the extremely low quotations in both cases, despite the high coupon interest rate in the case of LTV, reflecting the poor outlook for regular payment of interest. No yield is given for the LTV bond, suggesting that interest isn't being paid. The National Gypsum bond is a zero-interest issue ("zr")—as is the Grace bond—which means that the bond is sold at a discount deep enough to provide the investor at maturity with both recovery of principal and an earnings yield commensurate with interest rate conditions. The symbol "cv" with Champion and Zenith indicates that the bond is convertible into common stock.

Note that the 6½ percent Champion bond is trading at a yield of only 6.1 percent (6.50 ÷ 106.88), which signals that the price reflects the underlying value of the Champion common stock into which it's convertible, and not just the coupon interest. The "f" with the LTV bond means that the issues is being traded "flat," that is, without any claim for current unpaid interest. The low price reflects this precarious position. The "dc" with the International Paper bond denotes that the bond is selling at a deep discount, while the "cld" with the Pacific Northwest Telephone issue indicates that the bond has been called for redemption by the company.

A slightly different method is used to list current quotations for government agency bonds and miscellaneous securities traded over

FIGURE V–3
New York Stock Exchange Bond Transactions, Monday, June 14, 1993
(volume $32,190,000)

Bonds	Current Yield	Volume	Close	Net Change
Am T&T 8½ 22	7.6	33	106⅞	+⅛
Champ 6½ 11	cv	30	106	−1
Grace zr 06	...	45	37¼	−¼
I Pap dc 5⅛ 12	6.6	48	78	+1⅛
vj LTV 10⅜ 99f	...	50	22	...
vj NtGyp zr 04	...	395	2¼	+⅜
PNWT 9 cld	...	5	104⁷/₃₂	−¹/₃₂
Zenith 6¼ 11	cv	85	69¾	+⅛

the counter. Again we'll use an example from *The Wall Street Journal* for the trading day of Monday, June 14, 1993. Figure V–4 gives quotes for U.S. Treasury bonds, U.S. Treasury bills, Federal Home Loan Bank bonds, and World Bank bonds.

We find that the securities are listed in terms of bid and asked quotations, which represent the price desired for purchase or sale on the trading day but don't necessarily denote specific transactions. Another important difference reflected in this example is the custom of quoting prices in percentage of par value, this time stated in terms of fractions of a percent in 32ds of a point. Thus, a quote of 99:19 means a price of $99^{19}/_{32}$ percent or $995.94 per $1,000 of par value. The final column shows the yield to maturity, which reflects the return on investment earned at the current price if the bond is held to its maturity date and redeemed at par.

Note that the yield on the 10¾ percent Treasury bond due in 2005 is well below the relatively high coupon rate, while the 5½ percent bond due in April 2000 is yielding 5.56 percent, very close to the coupon rate. These differentials reflect the relatively low interest levels prevailing in 1993, which were far below the inflation-driven conditions of the late 1970s and early 1980s. The low yield on the 9 percent bond is due to the fact that it's about to be redeemed in February 1994.

U.S. government securities as well as other debt instruments will be affected by the general outlook for interest rates. U.S. government securities will tend to yield a lower return than most corporate and other public bonds because the likelihood of default is extremely remote and the purchaser is normally looking for a safe investment with an assured long-term or short-term yield. Also, they generally are exempt from state income taxes.

FIGURE V–4
Government Agency and Miscellaneous Securities Quotations,
Monday, June 14, 1993
(over the counter)

Rate	Maturity	Days to Maturity	Bid	Asked	Bid Change	Ask Yield
U.S. Treasury bonds and notes (n):						
9	Feb 94		103:20	103:22	...	3.36
10¾	Aug 05		138:17	138:21	+3	6.18
5½	Apr 00 n		99:19	99:21	+3	5.56
U.S. Treasury bills:						
	Sep 09, '93	85	3.05*	3.03*	...	3.09
	May 05, '94	323	3.32*	3.30*	−0.02	3.42
Federal Home Loan Bank:						
4.50	9-95		99:23	99:27	...	4.57
9.30	1-99		116:10	116:18	...	5.80
World Bank Bonds:						
12.38	10-02		141:13	141:21	...	6.38
5.88	7-97		102:15	102:23	...	5.13

*Discount rates.

As we found in the case of the stock market quotations, bond market listings are supplemented by a variety of reports on the volume of trading, bonds averages, summaries of advancing and declining conditions, highs and lows for the year, and so on. Again, these provide the investor with a general feel for the daily movements of the bond markets and interest rate conditions. The most commonly used averages are the Dow Jones Bond Averages (20 bonds, including 10 public utilities and 10 industrials), Merrill Lynch Corporate Debt Issues, and Lehman Brothers U.S. Securities Indexes. Bond averages are calculated in percentages of par, as were the quotations themselves.

On Monday, June 14, 1993, the NYSE bond volume was $32,190,000 for all issues, with the 20-bond average falling slightly to 107.47, down 0.08 from the prior trading day. Issues traded numbered 445, of which 176 staged advances, 150 declined, and 119 remained unchanged. New highs for the year were achieved by 28 issues, and new lows by 3 issues.

Other Financial Data

Most papers list, in one form or another, so-called leading, coincident, and lagging business and economic indicators—such as indexes of industrial production, freight car loadings, prices, output in the automotive industry, and steel production—both in feature stories and in tabular form. When supplemented by reports of earnings and dividend declarations of individual corporations, news about corporate management, analysis and announcement of new financing, and industry analysis, this information can provide a broad background for financial analysis.

Among the more specialized data in the financial pages are listings of transactions in the *commodities markets*. Commodities include a great variety of basic raw materials such as cotton, lumber, copper, and rubber as well as foods such as coffee, corn, and wheat. The best-known exchange for commodity trading is the Chicago Board of Trade. More specialized exchanges include the New York Cotton Exchange or international exchanges such as the London Metal Exchange. Commodities may be traded on a *spot* basis; that is, the commodity is purchased outright at the time. Commodities *futures* are also traded. These are contracts to buy or sell a commodity at a specified price at some point in the future. The commodities market is far too varied to describe here, but we should take a quick look at how commodities are quoted.

The information on commodities trading provided by most sources usually involves opening and closing transactions as well as highs and lows for the trading day and the season. Changes from the previous trading day are also often listed. A variety of indexes are available, such as the Dow Jones Spot Index, Dow Jones Futures Index, and Reuters United Kingdom Index. A company whose operations depend to a large extent on raw materials traded in a spot or futures market can be severely influenced by fluctuations in spot or futures prices. Because fluctuations in commodities markets can be severe, traders in these markets often *hedge*. This involves arrangements to *both* buy and sell the same commodity, which will "cover" the trader for shifts in prices. References at the end of this appendix provide detailed information on commodities trading.

Foreign Exchange

Most newspapers list the major currencies of the world in equivalents of U.S. dollars. Normally the quotations represent selling prices of bank transfers in the United States for payment abroad, and quotations are given for the current trading day as well as for the previous day. Also, prices for foreign bank notes are often quoted in equivalents of U.S. dollars on both buying and selling bases.

PERIODIC FINANCIAL INFORMATION

Apart from the financial data contained in daily newspapers, a wealth of information is provided by various financial, economic, and business periodicals. Furthermore, readily available reference works contain periodic listings and analyses of financial information oriented toward the investor and financial analyst. The advent of the computer has made possible the rapid collection and analysis of company and economic data, and collective information can now be obtained on-line through data base access or in hard copy on a timely basis. The most important sources of periodic financial and business information are discussed next.

Magazines

Major Periodicals. For general business coverage, *Business Week* remains one of the most useful and widely read publications. It covers current developments in business and economics, both national and international. It analyzes major events and reports on individual companies, stock markets, labor, business education, and so on with a selective listing of economic indicators as well as a special index of business activity.

For more detailed coverage of stock quotations, security offerings, banking developments, and financial, industrial, and commodity trends, the *Commercial and Financial Chronicle* is the most comprehensive source available. The *Wall Street Transcript* analyzes securities of a great variety of individual companies, on both financial and economic bases, and assesses the technical basis of stock market charts. It discusses major corporate presentations to security analysts about past performance and future plans, and features roundtable discussions on industry groups by security analysts.

Barron's covers business trends in terms of individual companies as well as major industries, and provides much information about corporate securities. The section "Stock Market at a Glance" is a useful and detailed picture of the securities markets. *Fortune* offers biweekly comments on national economic trends. It profiles major U.S. and international executives in addition to giving detailed articles on industry, company, and socio-economic trends. The magazine's annual listing and ranking of the Fortune 500 (the best-performing U.S. companies) and similar listings of banks and major foreign companies are useful references.

Semimonthly *Forbes* magazine takes the investor's viewpoint, providing detailed and searching analyses of individual companies and their managements. The annual January issue, which reviews the performance of major U.S. industries, is an excellent source of information on industry trends and ranks companies by a series of criteria.

For an international outlook, the weekly British magazine *The Economist* surveys international and United Kingdom developments in politics, economics, and business, and discusses U.S. developments in depth. It can be considered an international *Business Week,* as can *World Business.*

Economic and business trends are covered in considerable detail in publications of major commercial banks such as the *National City Bank Monthly Letter* and *New England Letter* of the First National Bank of Boston. The various Federal Reserve banks' general bulletins and regional bulletins contain regional economic data.

The bimonthly *Harvard Business Review* (a highly regarded forum for discussion of management concepts and tools) includes financial insights from practitioners and academicians for an extensive world-wide readership of business executives. Several other major business schools publish journals of similar orientation.

Dun's Review presents trade indexes, data on business failures, and key financial ratios in addition to articles about industry and commerce. *Nation's Business,* a publication of the U.S. Chamber of Commerce, presents general articles on business subjects. The *Federal Reserve Bulletin* contains much statistical data on business and government finances, both domestic and international. The *Survey of Current Business* also provides extensive business statistics.

Detailed stock exchange quotations and data about many *unlisted securities* (those not traded on a recognized exchange), foreign exchange, and money rates are contained in the *Bank and Quotation Record.* The quarterly *Journal of Finance* presents articles on finance, investments, economics, money, and credit, including international aspects of these topics.

Other Periodicals.   Many specialized periodicals are published by trade associations and banking, commercial, and trading groups too numerous to mention. Also useful are the great variety of U.S. government surveys and publications, statistical papers provided by the United Nations and its major agencies, and the various analyses and reviews in academic journals. The end of this appendix lists several books that provide detailed guidelines on and descriptions of the type of information available from various sources.

Listed below are some major periodicals that deal directly with, or relate to, corporate finance. Many other relevant publications are also available. Some publications are specialized and oriented toward a specific community of interest; others deal with financial conditions in foreign countries. The titles are largely self-explanatory:

Banker's Magazine	*Financial Executive*
Corporate Financing	*Financial Management*
Credit and Financial Management	*Financial World*
Finance	*Journal of Banking and Finance*
Financial Analysts Journal	*Journal of Commerce*

Management Accounting
   (U.S. and British editions)
Managerial Finance

Mergers and Acquisitions
National Tax Journal
World Financial Markets

Financial Manuals and Services

The most popular and best-known set of financial manuals and services is provided by Moody's, with Standard & Poor's a close second. Moody's publishes several volumes: *Industrials; Banks and Finance; Insurance; Public Utilities; Transportation; Municipals; and Government;* *OTC* (over the counter); and *International.* These manuals are published each year and contain up-to-date key historical data, financial statements, securities price ranges, and dividend records for a large number of companies, including practically all publicly held corporations. Moody's manuals are updated through semiweekly supplements with detailed cross-references.

Moody's *Quarterly Handbook* gives one-page summaries of key financial and operating data for major publicly held corporations. Furthermore, Moody's weekly stock and bond surveys analyze market and industry conditions. Besides its semiweekly *Dividend Record*, a semimonthly *Bond Record* contains current prices, earnings, and ratings of most important bonds traded in this country.

Standard & Poor's publications include the *Standard Corporation Records.* This financial information about a large number of companies is published in loose-leaf format and is updated through daily supplements. A useful S&P publication, the *Analysts Handbook*, provides industry surveys with key financial data on individual companies and some industries. Standard & Poor's other services include several dealing with the bond market, weekly forecasts of the security markets, securities statistics, and a monthly earnings and stock rating guide.

Financial services similar to Moody's and Standard & Poor's are provided by *Fitch's Corporation Manuals* and by more specialized manuals such as *Walker's Manual* of Pacific Coast securities. An almost overwhelming flow of information, judgments, and analyses of individual companies from an investor's standpoint is provided by the major brokerage houses. Furthermore, services available to individuals on a subscription basis provide up-to-date financial analyses and evaluations of individual companies and their securities. The most important among these services are *Value Line, United Business Service, Babson's,* and *Investor's Management Sciences.* The Value Line investment survey provides ratings and reports on companies, with selections and opinions for the investor, while Investor's Management Sciences concentrates on providing a great deal of standardized statistical information as the basis for making analytical judgments. *Dun &*

Bradstreet's credit information services help in evaluating small or unlisted companies. On-line data bases make important information about companies listed on stock exchanges available instantly through various service providers.

BACKGROUND COMPANY AND BUSINESS INFORMATION
Annual Reports

The most commonly used reference source about the current affairs of publicly held corporations is the annual report furnished to shareholders. The formats used by individual corporations vary widely from detailed coverage (that may even include current corporate, industry, and national issues) to a bare minimum disclosure of financial results. Nevertheless, the annual report is generally an important direct source of financial information. Because the disclosure requirements of the Securities and Exchange Commission (SEC), the recommendations of the accounting profession, and state laws have become more and more demanding over time, the analyst can usually count on annual reports presenting a fairly consistent set of data.

Government Data

More specific details about company operations can often be found in the annual statement that corporations must file with the SEC in Washington, D.C. This information is filed on Form 10-K and is available upon request for public inspection. Furthermore, when a corporation wants to issue new securities in significant amounts or alter its capital structure in a major way, the detailed proposal that must be filed with the SEC, the *prospectus*, is generally a more complete source of company background data than is the normal annual report. It will cover the history of the company, ownership patterns, directors and top management, financial and operating data, products, facilities, and information regarding the intended use of the new funds.

If a company is closely held (most of the shares are held by founders, their families, and key employees) or too small to be listed by the key financial services, information about its financial operations can often be obtained from the corporation records departments of the states in which the company does business. Again, these reports are open to the public for inspection.

Trade Associations

Trade associations are a prime source of information about their respective industries. A great deal of statistical information is available annually or more often and covers products, services, finances, and performance criteria applicable to the industry or trade group. Often financial and performance data are grouped by types and sizes of firms to make overall statistics on the industry more applicable to a particular operation. Trade associations include the American Electronics Association, American Paper Institute, and National Lumber Manufacturers Association to name but a few. Sources for listings and addresses of these associations and their publications can be found in the references at the end of the appendix.

Econometric Services

Many forecasts of U.S. and international economic conditions are available to the financial analyst. Based on so-called *econometric* models developed by a variety of academic institutions and economic advisory services, these forecasts of the U.S. economy and more recently of other countries' economies as well can provide valuable clues regarding the likely movement of the country's economy within which financial conditions must be viewed. Among the widely quoted and used econometric models are those developed by the Wharton School at the University of Pennsylvania, Data Resources Inc., and Chase Econometric Associates. Many corporations subscribe to such forecasting services and use the projections in their operational and financial planning. Increasingly, corporate and academic economists are testing their own assumptions about economic trends with the help of econometric models. Another feature of these services is the growing variety of on-line data bases containing a vast array of statistical and financial information for immediate access.

While we've merely touched on the major sources of specific or general information on financial business affairs, the reader is encouraged to make use of the sources discussed as well as the references at the end of this appendix. In addition, a great deal of information is available from various business libraries in corporations, colleges, and universities as well as from local institutions. The problem facing a financial analyst, whether student or professional, isn't a lack of data; rather, it's selecting what's truly relevant.

SELECTED REFERENCES

Clasing, Henry K., Jr. *The Dow Jones-Irwin Guide to Put and Call Options.* Rev. ed. Homewood, Ill.: Dow Jones-Irwin, 1978.

Daniells, Lorna M. *Business Information Sources.* Rev. ed. Berkeley: University of California Press, 1985.

Gould, Bruce G. *The Dow Jones-Irwin Guide to Commodity Trading.* Rev. ed. Homewood, Ill.: Dow Jones-Irwin, 1981.

Lehmann, Michael B. *The Dow Jones-Irwin Guide to Using The Wall Street Journal.* Homewood, Ill.: Dow Jones-Irwin, 1990.

Levine, Sumner N., ed. *Dow Jones-Irwin Business Almanac.* Homewood, Ill.: Dow Jones-Irwin, 1982.

Novallo, Annette. *Information Industry Directory.* 14th ed. Detroit: Gale Research, 1993.

Pierce, Phyllis S., ed. *The Dow Jones Averages 1885–1990.* Homewood, Ill.: Business One-Irwin, 1991.

Ruder, William, and Raymond Nathan. *The Businessman's Guide to Washington.* New York: Collier Books, 1975.

Way, James, ed. *Encyclopedia of Business Information Sources.* 9th ed. Detroit: Gale Research, 1992.

APPENDIX VI
SOLUTIONS TO
SELF-STUDY
PROBLEMS
PLUS QUESTIONS
FOR DISCUSSION

This appendix contains solutions to all problems at the end of Chapters 2 through 9. A series of questions for discussion is provided following each chapter's solutions. These questions should help stimulate your thoughts about key aspects of the chapter and serve as a basis for group discussions.

CHAPTER 2

Solutions to Problems

1.

CBA COMPANY
Changes in Balance Sheet ($ thousands)

Assets		Liabilities	
Cash	$ (12.2)	Accounts payable	$ 11.8
Marketable securities	10.0	Notes payable	90.0
Accounts receivable	(8.8)	Accrued expenses	2.9
Inventories	60.7	Total current liabilities	$104.7
Total current assets ..	49.7		
Land	–0–	Mortgage payable	$ (15.2)
Plant and equipment (net) .	19.6	Common stock	5.0
Total fixed assets	19.6	Retained earnings	(17.0)
		Total net worth	$ (27.2)
Other assets	8.2	Total liabilities and	
Total assets	$ 77.5	net worth	$ 77.5

Funds Flow Statement, 1994

Sources		Uses	
Depreciation	$ 32.2*	Loss from operations	$ 2.0*
Decrease in cash	12.2	Dividends paid	15.0†
Decrease in accounts receivable	8.8	Increase in securities	10.0
Increase in accounts payable	11.8	Increase in inventories	60.7
Increase in notes payable	90.0	Investment in plant	51.8‡
Increase in accrued expenses	2.9	Increase in other assets	8.2
Increase in common stock	5.0	Decrease in mortgage	15.2
Total	$162.9	Total	$162.9

The results were built up from:

* Taken from 1994 operating statement.

† Change in retained earnings matches the combination of loss from operations ($2,000) on the 1994 operating statement and dividends paid ($15,000). No extraordinary items appear and no assumptions are necessary.

‡ Since net plant and equipment increased by $19,600, and the only known element affecting the account is depreciation ($32,200), the amount of investment must have been the sum of these amounts ($51,800).

Observations

The biggest single use is a drastic rise in inventories, even though sales volume changed little. Are inventory controls failing? Dividends were wisely cut as profits plummeted. The key funds source was borrowing (short-term) of $90 which provides more than half of funds needs. Sizable capital investment (almost twice depreciation) points to optimistic future plans—any problems in sight? Is the company beginning to lean on suppliers? (Accounts payable is up somewhat.) Is equity capital called for?

2. *a.* ABC Company

Beginning balance, retained earnings (12/31/93)		$167,300
Less:		
Net loss for 1994 (incl. loss from abandonment)	$14,100	
Common dividends paid	12,000	
Inventory adjustment	24,000	
Amortization of goodwill, patents	15,000	65,100
Ending balance, retained earnings (12/31/94)		$102,200

Funds Flow Items

Sources		Uses	
Depreciation	$21,400	Net *operating* loss	$ 10,100
Total	$21,400	Loss from abandonment	4,000
		Dividends paid	12,000
		Investment in fixed assets	57,500
		Amortization	15,000
		Inventory adjustment	24,000
		Total	$122,600

Depreciation (noncash) should be reflected as a source as it reduced operating profit/loss; loss conditions don't change in basic character. Loss from abandonment can be separated from profit/loss; it was offset by reduction in assets. A gain could be shown as a separate source, offset by the increase in cash.

Amortization and inventory adjustments are assumed to have been earned surplus reductions here; they can be separated out as shown, as they've been offset by a decrease in patents and inventories, or they can be eliminated on both sides of the statement.

b. **DEF Company**
The layout of the data is:

	Beginning Balance	Additions	Reductions	Ending Balance	Change
Gross property and fixed assets	$8,431,500*	$1,250,500*	$1,252,000†	$8,430,000*	$(1,500)
Accumulated depreciation .	3,513,000†	1,613,000*	1,252,000‡	3,874,000*	361,000
Net property and fixed assets	$4,918,500	$ (362,500)	$ –0–	$4,556,000	$(362,500)
					(Result)

The result is built up from:
* Given information.
† Forced figures.
‡ Assumption that fully depreciated assets were abandoned.

Observations
Any assumption about a gain or loss on sale and/or abandonment would be handled as in Item 2a. Any disposition of partially depreciated assets would cause greater "reductions" in assets than in accumulated depreciation, which in turn would raise the derived asset additions.

c. **XYZ Company**
The layout of the data is:

	Beginning Balance	Additions	Reductions	Ending Balance	Change
Gross fixed assets	$823,700*	$236,100†	{$ 2,500‡ 110,000*	$947,300	$123,600
Accumulated depreciation	N.A.	78,500*	{ 2,500‡ 81,000*	N.A.	(5,000)*
Net fixed assets	$ N.A.	$157,600	$ 29,000†	$ N.A.	$128,600
		(result)			(result)

The result was built up from:
* Information available.
† Forced figures.
‡ Assumption that fully depreciated assets of $2,500 were written off.

Gain on sales of assets:

Recorded value	$110,000
Accumulated depreciation	81,000
Book value	$ 29,000
Cash received	45,000
Gain on sale	$ 16,000

Funds Flow Items

Sources		Uses	
Depreciation	$ 78,500		
Net write-off of assets ...	29,000*	Investments	$236,100
	$107,500		

* Could be split into gain ($16,000) and cash received ($45,000).
Note that sources and uses net out to $128,600.

3.

FED COMPANY
Funds Flow Statement, 1994

Sources		Uses†	
Net income	$ 6*	Increase in accounts	
Depreciation	26*	receivable	$ 5
Increase in deferred		Increase in notes	
income taxes	2	receivable	20
Gain from sale of asset	4†	Increase in inventories	7
Decrease in cash	12	Investment in plant and	
Overdraft	4	equipment	38†
Decrease in securities	18	Increase in prepaids	2
Increase in accounts payable	24	Decrease in notes payable ..	30
Increase in accrued expenses	9	Decrease in secured notes	
Increase in preferred stock ..	4	payable	20
Increase in common stock and		Dividends (preferred and	
capital surplus	20	common)	7
Total	$129	Total	$129

The results were built up from:

* Taken from 1994 operating statement.

† The fixed property conditions are as follows:

	Beginning Balance	Additions	Reductions	Ending Balance	Change
Gross property and expenses	$268	$38 ⟵	$ 23	$283	$15
Accumulated depreciation ...	157	26	23	160	3
Net property and expenses	$111	$12	$-0-	$123	$12

The key element is the forced figure of $38, which is based on the stated assumptions. The gain from sale of assets in the retained earnings account should be reflected as a source, just like net income.

Patent and other amortization of $3 is adjusted for in the retained earnings account; thus it is not a funds item.

544

Observations

Key funds movements revolve around capital investments and financing. Repayments of short- and long-term notes and credit demands from customers make up better than half of the funds uses. Some new equity has come in, but not enough. The company is running out of cash and stretching payables.

A short-term solution only. (Working capital items could be lumped in one figure, of course.)

A funds flow statement by area of management concern highlights these findings:

Operating inflows:		
Net sales	$ 1,237	
Increase in accounts payable	24	
Increase in accrued expenses	9	
Increase in deferred income taxes	2	
Total operating inflows	$+1,272	
Operating outflows:		
Cost of goods sold (excluding depreciation)	$ 896	
Selling and administrative	297	
Income taxes	5	
Increase in accounts receivable	5	
Increase in notes receivable	20	
Increase in inventories	7	
Increase in prepaids	2	
Total operating outflows	$−1,232	
Net operating inflows		$+40
Financial inflows:		
Increase in preferred stock	$ 4	
Increase in capital stock and surplus	20	
Decrease in securities	18	
Gain on sale of assets	4	
Total financial inflows	$ +46	
Financial outflows:		
Repayment of notes payable	$ 30	
Repayment of secured notes	20	
Interest on debt	7	
Total financial outflows	$ −57	
Net financial outflows		$−11
Investment outflows:		
Additions to plant and equipment	$ 38	
Cash dividends paid	7	
Total investment outflows		$−45
Net outflows from operations, financing, and investment		$−16
Analysis of cash impact:		
Beginning cash balance		+12
Ending cash balance		$− 4

This format clearly shows the important financial and investment movements, which leave operations strapped.

4. ZYX Company

A variety of funds flow statements are possible here:

From peak to trough of season (two seasons).

From peak to peak, or trough to trough.

From April to April, or any other month.

Two-year span, July to July, to provide a long-term perspective.

Samples of these possible funds flow statements are:

	1/31/94 to 4/30/94	1/31/95 to 4/30/95	4/30/93 to 1/31/95	1/31/93 to 1/31/95	4/30/93 to 4/30/95	7/31/93 to 7/31/95
Sources of Funds						
Profit from operations	$ 10	$ 17	$ 67	$ 77	$ 84	$172
Depreciation	6	7	21	27	28	54
Decrease in cash	—	—	1	—	—	5
Decrease in receivables	191	237	—	—	—	11
Decrease in inventories	184	253	—	—	33	—
Decrease in other assets	1	—	—	—	—	—
Increase in payables	—	—	85	67	—	16
Increase in notes	—	—	342	48	—	45
Increase in common	—	—	25	25	25	25
Total sources	$392	$514	$541	$244	$170	$328
Use of Funds						
Capital investments	$ 48	$ 50	$—	$ 48	$ 50	$ 98
Increase in cash	17	13	—	16	12	—
Increase in receivables	—	—	260	69	23	79
Increase in inventories	—	—	220	36	—	—
Increase in other assets	—	—	3	2	3	2
Decrease in payables	18	91	—	—	6	—
Decrease in notes	294	342	—	—	—	—
Decrease in mortgage	—	—	10	10	10	20
Dividends paid	15	18	48	63	66	129
Total uses	$392	$514	$541	$244	$170	$328

Observations

This strong seasonal pattern from January to April shows up vividly in the peak to trough and trough to peak comparisons, where receivables and inventories are matched with payables and sizable short-term notes. There's a lag effect in buildup of inventories and receivables, as expected. Growth shows up in like-to-like comparisons, with no undue strains. This is a good example of the effect of careless placement of funds flow analysis over alternative time periods.

Questions for Discussion

1. Differentiate between cash flow and funds flow. What is "cash flow from operations"?
2. In what ways does a funds flow statement correspond to the operating statement for a period? In what ways does it differ? Can the two be readily reconciled?
3. In what ways are the concepts of debit and credit related to funds uses and sources? On the basis of a simple balance sheet, derive the principles of this relationship. Discuss.
4. Does a sizable profit for a period necessarily mean an increase in a company's cash account? If not, why not?
5. Does a company whose operations are shrinking always throw off cash? If not, why not? What assumptions must be made?
6. Why is depreciation a "source of funds" when it's clear that a mere bookkeeping entry is involved?
7. If a company incurred an operating loss for a period, is depreciation still treated as a funds inflow?
8. What's the tax impact of depreciation? Are there any funds movements involved?
9. Why is it necessary to "reverse" such transactions as write-down of goodwill and amortization of patents?
10. What is the funds impact of accelerated depreciation, and why?
11. By what criteria is the selection of the proper time period for funds flow analysis made? Can you derive any rules?
12. What are the major ways in which inflation distorts the funds flow picture? Should adjustments be made?

CHAPTER 3

Solutions to Problems

1. a. $\dfrac{\text{Net profit}}{\text{Sales}} = 11.4\%;\ \dfrac{\text{Sales}}{\text{Assets}} = 1.34$

$\text{Assets} = \dfrac{\text{Sales}}{1.34}$ (Sales > Assets); Sales = 1.34 × Assets

Thus

$$\dfrac{\text{Net profit}}{\text{Assets}} = \dfrac{\text{Net profit}}{\dfrac{\text{Sales}}{1.34}} = 11.4\%(1.34) = 15.28\%$$

If we assume no debt in the capitalization, then net worth equals capitalization. Thus

$$\frac{\text{Net profit}}{\text{Capitalization}} = \frac{\text{Net profit}}{\text{Net worth}} = \frac{1}{.67} \times \frac{\text{Net profit}}{\text{Assets}}$$

Return on net worth is

$$\frac{15.28}{.67} = 22.8\%$$

A faster asset turnover means a smaller asset base and smaller capitalization relative to sales. Thus return figures go up.

b. Gross margin is 31.4 percent; thus the cost of goods sold of $4,391,300 must represent sales of

$$\frac{\$4,391,300}{1.0 - .314} = \$6,401,312$$

Net profit must be 9.7 percent of $6,401,312, or $620,927. Total assets must be derived from

$$\frac{\text{Sales}}{\text{Assets}} = .827; \text{ Assets} = \frac{\text{Sales}}{.827} = \frac{\$6,401,312}{.827} = \$7,740,401$$

Return on capitalization must be

$$\frac{\text{Net profit}}{\text{Assets} - \text{Current liabilities}} = \frac{\text{Net profit}}{.79 \text{ (Assets)}} = \frac{\$621,927}{6,114,917} = 10.15\%$$

c. Changes in current ratio and effect on working capital:

$$\text{Current ratio: 2.2 to 1} = \frac{\$573,100}{\$260,500}$$

(The $260,500 is derived from the relationship.)
Working capital: $573,100 - $260,500 = $312,600

(1) Payment of accounts payable:

Decrease in cash $67,500
Decrease in payables $67,500

Both current assets and current liabilities are reduced by the same amount; this improves current ratio but leaves working capital unaffected:

$$\frac{\$573,100 - \$67,500}{\$260,500 - \$67,500} = \frac{\$505,600}{\$193,000} = 2.62 \text{ to } 1$$

This is a common action taken by small companies at year-end to improve their current ratio.

548

(2) Collection of note:

Increase in cash $33,000
Decrease in notes receivable $33,000

Both elements are within current assets; thus there's no net effect on either the current ratio or the working capital.

(3) Purchase on account:

Increase in inventory $41,300
Increase in payables $41,300

Both current assets and current liabilities are increased; thus the opposite effect of exercise (1), with working capital unaffected:

$$\frac{\$573,100 + \$41,300}{\$260,500 + \$41,300} = \frac{\$614,400}{\$301,800} = 2.04 \text{ to } 1$$

(4) Dividend payment:

Decrease in cash $60,000
Decrease in accrued dividends $42,000
Decrease in retained earnings ..... $18,000 (no effect)

The effect on the two elements is uneven; thus changes occur in both the current ratio and working capital:

$$\frac{\$573,100 - \$60,000}{\$260,500 - \$42,000} = \frac{\$513,100}{\$218,500} = 2.35 \text{ to } 1$$

The current ratio is slightly improved, while working capital drops by $18,000.

(5) Machine sale:

Increase in cash .... $ 80,000
Decrease in fixed assets .... $202,000 (no effect)
Decrease in accumulated
  depreciation .... $112,000 (no effect)
Loss on sale of assets .... $ 10,000 (no effect)

The only effect is an increase in current assets, which increases both the ratio and working capital:

$$\frac{\$573,100 + \$80,000}{\$260,500} = \frac{\$653,100}{\$260,500} = 2.51 \text{ to } 1$$

The current ratio rises to 2.51, while working capital improves by $80,000.

(6) Sale of merchandise:

Increase in receivables $109,700*
Decrease in inventory .... $ 73,500
Increase in retained earnings ...... $ 36,200 (no effect)

*Derived from $\dfrac{\$73,500}{1.0 - .33}$ = $109,700.

There's a net increase in current assets, which improves the current ratio and working capital:

$$\frac{\$573,100 + \$109,700 - \$73,500}{\$260,500} = \frac{\$609,300}{\$260,500} = 2.34 \text{ to } 1$$

The current ratio rises to 2.34, while working capital improves by $36,200.

(7) Write-offs:

Decrease in inventory .... $ 20,000
Decrease in goodwill .... $ 15,000 (no effect)
Decrease in retained earnings ..... $ 35,000 (no effect)

There's a reduction of current assets, which affects both the current ratio and working capital:

$$\frac{\$573,100 - \$20,000}{\$260,500} = \frac{\$553,100}{\$260,500} = 2.12 \text{ to } 1$$

The current ratio drops slightly to 2.12, while working capital is reduced by $20,000.

d. Days' receivables and payables:

$$\frac{\text{Net sales}}{\text{Days}} = \frac{\$437,500}{90} = \$4,861 \text{ per day}$$

$$\frac{\text{Purchases}}{\text{Days}} = \frac{\$143,500}{90} = \$1,594 \text{ per day}$$

$$\text{Days' receivables} = \frac{\text{Accounts receivable}}{\text{Daily sales}}$$

$$= \frac{\$156,800}{\$4,861} = 32.3 \text{ days}$$

$$\text{Days' payables} = \frac{\text{Accounts payable}}{\text{Daily purchases}}$$

$$= \frac{\$69,300}{\$1,594} = 43.5 \text{ days}$$

The company's collections are fairly slow in view of the discount period of 10 days, while its payments are slightly faster than needed against the 45-day terms.

Inventory turnover:

$$\text{Average inventory: } \frac{\$382,200 + \$227,300}{2} = \$304,750$$

Turnover on sales:

$$\frac{\text{Average inventory}}{\text{Sales for quarter}} = \frac{\$304,750}{\$437,500} = 69.7\% \text{ (quarterly)}$$

or

$$\frac{\text{Average inventory}}{\text{Annual sales}} = \frac{\$304,750}{(\$437,500)} = 17.4\% \text{ (annualized)}$$

or

$$\frac{\text{Sales for quarter}}{\text{Average inventory}} = \frac{\$437,500}{\$304,750} = 1.44 \text{ times (quarterly)}$$

or

$$\frac{\text{Annual sales}}{\text{Average inventory}} = \frac{4(\$437,500)}{\$304,750} = 5.74 \text{ (annualized)}$$

Turnover on cost of sales:

$$\frac{\text{Average inventory}}{\text{Cost of sales for quarter}} = \frac{\$304,750}{\$298,400} = 102.1\% \text{ (quarterly)}$$

$$\frac{\text{Average inventory}}{\text{Annual cost of sales}} = \frac{\$304,750}{4(\$298,400)} = 25.5\% \text{ (annualized)}$$

or

$$\frac{\text{Cost of sales for quarter}}{\text{Average inventory}} = \frac{\$298,400}{\$304,750} = .98 \text{ times (quarterly)}$$

or

$$\frac{\text{Annual cost of sales}}{\text{Average inventory}} = \frac{4(\$298,400)}{\$304,750} = 3.92 \text{ times (annualized)}$$

Turnover on ending inventory:

$$\frac{\text{Ending inventory}}{\text{Cost of sales for quarter}} = \frac{\$227,300}{\$298,400} = 76.2\% \text{ (quarterly)}$$

or

$$\frac{\text{Cost of sales for quarter}}{\text{Ending inventory}} = \frac{\$298,400}{\$227,300} = 1.31 \text{ times (quarterly)}$$

The cost of sales figures are more useful as a rule. Ending inventory should be used in relation to the quarterly cost of sales if there are significant seasonal swings. Annualization on a simple "4×" basis is problematic if a strong seasonal or growth/decline pattern is suspected.

2. ABC Company
The various ratios are grouped by point of view:

a. Management's view:

	1993	1994
Cost of goods sold	70.4%	70.6%
Gross margin	29.6%	29.4%
Profit margin	5.7%	5.4%
Profit before interest and taxes	10.7%	10.8%
Profit after taxes, before interest	5.8%	5.8%
Selling and administrative expenses	15.0%	14.4%
Employee profit sharing	4.1%	4.4%
Other income	.2%	.2%
Tax rate	46.0%	46.0%
Contribution	N.A.	N.A.
Gross asset turnover $\left(\dfrac{\text{Assets}}{\text{Sales}}\right)$	59.5%	64.6%
Net asset turnover $\left(\dfrac{\text{Assets}}{\text{Sales}}\right)$	39.4%	44.4%
Ending inventory turns $\left(\dfrac{\text{Cost of sales}}{\text{Inventory}}\right)$	5.2×	4.8×
Days' receivables	51.1 days	60.7 days
Days' payables (cost of sales)	34.0 days	37.0 days
Net profit to total assets	9.6%	8.3%
Net profit to capitalization	14.4%	12.1%
Net profit before interest and tax to total assets	18.0%	16.8%
Net profit before interest and tax to capitalization	27.2%	24.4%
Net profit after tax, before interest, to total assets	9.7%	9.0%
Net profit after tax, before interest, to capitalization	14.6%	13.2%

b. Owner's view:

	1993	1994
Net profit to net worth (including deferred tax)	15.1%	16.3%
Net profit to common equity (w/o deferred tax)	15.2%	16.7%
Earnings per share	$3.69	$4.61
Cash flow per share	$6.48	$8.38
Dividends per share	$ .54	$ .59
Dividend coverage—earnings	6.8×	7.8×
Dividend coverage—cash flow	11.9×	14.2×

c. Lender's view:

	1993	1994
Current ratio	2.1:1	2.2:1
Acid test (excluding advances)	1.3:1	1.4:1
Total debt to assets	35.7%	48.7%
Long-term debt to capitalization	3.0%	25.3%
Total debt to net worth	55.5%	95.0%
Long-term debt to net worth	3.1%	32.9%
Interest coverage (pretax)	70×	13×
Cash flow before taxes—interest coverage	98×	18×
Full interest coverage ($8.5 million)	—	11×

552

Observations

A slight worsening is shown in operating performance, at the same effective tax rate, which makes 1993 the better year. More investment has been committed both in working capital and fixed assets—collections are slowing, inventories are up, and profits on assets are down by every measure.

Leverage has improved the profit on net worth, however, and earnings per share are up sharply. No problems exist in covering dividends on interest, even if a full year's interest is assumed.

Comparisons should be made with companies in similar product lines, particularly on capital structure, return on net worth, and coverages. High-low analysis of good and bad years should highlight risk of earnings fluctuations. A two-year static picture isn't enough for good perspective.

Questions for Discussion

1. Explain the relationships of the four basic financial statements. Which statement encompasses the results of all decisions? Why?

2. Why does the balance sheet have to balance at all times? What does the statement signify?

3. What are the key factors that allow comparison of industry ratios to the ratios of an individual company?

4. List several accounting practices that can result in changes in the ratios that measure profitability. What's their effect?

5. List several accounting practices that can result in changes in the ratios that measure liquidity and debt exposure. What's their effect?

6. What measurement issues arise when two different divisions of a company are compared on the basis of management ratios, given widely divergent conditions in age, markets, and costs?

7. A commonly used ratio from the standpoint of the lender is "times interest earned." How meaningful is this ratio in assessing the quality of the indebtedness involved?

8. Does operating cash flow represent the majority of funds movements caused by operations? If not, why not?

9. What key questions would you ask if you were a banker reviewing a loan request from a small, rapidly growing company?

10. What's the impact of inflation on ratio analysis? What key distortions can be expected, and in which ratios?

11. What are the major problems encountered in the process of adjusting for inflation?

12. If you were general manager of a division, which key ratio would you choose to be evaluated on for your unit's financial performance, and why? What conditions would you stipulate?

CHAPTER 4

Solutions to Problems

1. *a.* Change in credit policy:
   Forty days' sales developed as follows:

$$\text{Daily sales: } \frac{\$9,137,000}{360} = \$25,381/\text{day}$$

18 days' sales: 18 × $25,381 = $ 456,858
40 days' sales: 40 × $25,381 = $1,015,240

Increase in receivables: $ 558,382

Sixty days' sales:

60 days' sales: 60 × $25,381 = $1,522,860

Increase in receivables: $1,066,002

Observations
Funds need increase with 40 days is over $500,000. Cash flow per year available from operations is only $305,000. Likely the company must secure other funds. Need is doubled if policy is changed to 60 days.

b. Inventory consignment:
   Average inventory: $725,000.

$$\text{Current turnover: } \frac{\text{Cost of goods sold}}{\text{Average inventory}} = \frac{.83 \times \$9,137,000}{\$725,000} = 10.5 \text{ times}$$

$$\text{Turnover slowdown: } \frac{\text{Cost of goods sold}}{7.0} = \frac{\$7,583,700}{7.0} = \$1,083,400$$

Inventory increases by $1,083,400 less $725,000 = $ 358,400

$$\text{Turnover increase: } \frac{\text{Cost of goods sold}}{11.0} = \frac{\$7,583,700}{11.0} = \$ 689,400$$

Inventory decreases by $725,000 less $689,400 = $ 35,600

Observations
Funds needs change as indicated. The company likely will require increased production operations to achieve higher supply (about 5 percent), and also some increased purchases,

which will provide some funds through higher payables. But the slowdown must be financed by other funds sources.

c. Change in payment terms:
Company now has 10 days' purchases outstanding:

$$\text{Payables} = \frac{\text{Purchases}}{360} \times 10 = \frac{\$5,316,000}{36} = \$147,667.$$

Change in terms means 5 more days' extension, which provides funds of $73,833 (1/2 of above) for no additional cost.

Observations
Company earns 2 percent now to pay 20 days sooner; it will earn 2 percent to pay 30 days sooner (from day 15 to day 45). Annual interest thus 12 times 2% = 24%. If company can obtain funds for less, it's desirable to discount. (See Chapter 7.)

d. Capital expenditures and dividends:

Funds need	$125,000 for equipment
Plus 60% of $131,000 = ...	79,000
Total	$204,000

Against cash from operations:

Profits	$131,000
Depreciation	174,000
Total	$305,000

Observations
Can be handled by internal funds unless significant changes in working capital needs occur (such as in earlier examples).

e. Sales growth:
10 percent increase in sales ($913,700) requires:

Funds for receivables: 18 days of increased sales	$ 45,700
Funds for inventories: 10 percent increase	72,500
Funds from payables: 10 days of increased purchases	(14,800)
Total funds need	$103,400
Against additional profits of 10% (assume no efficiency of scale):	$ 13,100

Observations
Unless there are significant improvements in operations, the increase in sales requires funds of about $90,000. This makes dividends and capital expenditures under (d) barely possible from internal funds, and leaves no room for inefficiency.

2.

ABC COMPANY
Pro Forma Operating Statement
For the Year Ended October 31, 1996
($ thousands)

	Amount		Percent	
Net sales	$4,350		100.0%	
Cost of goods sold:				
Labor	$1,044		24.0	
Materials	631		14.5	
Overhead*	862		19.8	
Depreciation	143		3.3	
	2,680		61.6	
Gross profit	$1,670		38.4	
Selling expense	430		9.9	
General and administrative	352	782	8.1	18.0
Profit before taxes		$ 888		20.4
Income taxes (46%)		408		9.4
Net income		$ 480		11.1%

*$743 + $45 + $74.

Observations

A slight increase in the rate of profit is due to higher efficiency in labor and overhead, which combine to overcome a rise in selling expense.

3.

DEF COMPANY
Pro Forma Balance Sheet
December 31, 1996

Cash	$ 150,000	(desired level)
Receivables	348,300	(12 days on $10.45 mil.)
Inventories*	1,044,600	(as calculated below)
Total current assets	$1,542,900	
Land, buildings, etc.	$ 478,500	(plus $57,000)
Accumulated depreciation	248,700	(plus $31,400)
	$ 229,800	
Other assets	21,700	(no change)
Total assets	$1,794,400	
Accounts payable	$ 648,300	(24 days' purchases)
Note payable—bank	468,900	(plug figure—up by $43,900)
Accrued expenses	63,400	(no change)
Total current liabilities	$1,180,600	
Term loan—properties	$ 110,000	(minus $10,000)
Capital stock	200,000	(no change)
Paid-in surplus	112,000	(no change)
Retained earnings	191,800	($184,400 + $19,900 − $12,500)

Pro Forma Balance Sheet (concluded)

Total liabilities and net worth	$1,794,400

*Beginning inventory	$ 912,700
Purchases	9,725,000
	$10,637,700
Cost of goods sold	9,593,100 (91.8% of $10,450,000)
Ending inventory	$ 1,044,600

Observations

The main difference appears to be a rise in inventories that requires about $130,000, while receivables drop slightly. Appar-
ently sales are leveling off or dropping. (If 12 days' sales are
assumed outstanding in 1996, sales for the year must have been
$10,836,000, while purchases keep going up.) Repayment of
note and high dividend payout cause need for extra borrowing
(plug figure) of about $44,000 even if cash is drawn down to
$150,000.

4.

XYZ COMPANY
Cash Budget for Six Months
October 1995 through March 1996
($ thousands)

	Oct.	Nov.	Dec.	Jan.	Feb.	Mar.	Total
Cash receipts:							
Collections from credit	$ 215	$ 245	$ 265	$ 385	$ 345	$ 505	$1,960
Cash sales	385	345	505	325	290	360	2,210
Total receipts	$ 600	$ 590	$ 770	$ 710	$ 635	$ 865	$4,170
Cash disbursements (see breakdown of purchases below):							
Cash purchases ..	$ 61	$ 54	$ 29	$ 32	$ 45	$ 48	$ 269
Credit purchases— 10 days (less 2% discount) ..	218	220	146	121	160	184	1,049
Credit purchases— 45 days	257	266	286	205	153	192	1,359
Salaries and wages	146	131	192	124	110	137	840
Operating expenses	108	97	141	91	81	101	619
Cash dividend ...	—	—	40	—	—	—	40
Federal income tax	—	—	—	20	—	—	20
Mortgage payment	7	7	7	7	7	7	42

	Oct.	Nov.	Dec.	Jan.	Feb.	Mar.	Total
Total cash disbursements	$ 797	$ 775	$ 841	$ 600	$ 556	$ 669	$4,238
Net cash receipts (disbursements) ...	$(197)	$(185)	$ (71)	$ 110	$ 79	$ 196	$ (68)
Cumulative net cash flow	$(197)	$(382)	$(453)	$(343)	$(264)	$ (68)	
Analysis of cash requirements:							
Beginning cash balance	$ 95	$(102)	$(287)	$(358)	$(248)	$(169)	
Net cash receipts (disbursements) .	(197)	(185)	(71)	110	79	196	
Ending cash balance	$(102)	$(287)	$(358)	$(248)	$(169)	$ 27	
Minimum cash balance	75	75	75	75	75	75	
Cash requirements ...	$ 177	$ 362	$ 433	$ 323	$ 244	$ 48	

Observations

In spite of sizable cash needs, which reach a peak of $433,000 in December, the pattern of cash movements winds up not far below the minimum cash balance six months hence. Seasonal short-term borrowing is indicated here to cover inventory buildup and lag in collection pattern.

5. Pro forma statements developed from data given:

Initial cash	$250,000
Less: Equipment	175,000
	$ 75,000
Organization expenses	15,000
Cash remaining	$ 60,000

ZYX CORPORATION
Breakdown of Monthly Purchases

Terms	Aug.	Sept.	Oct.	Nov.	Dec.	Jan.	Feb.	Mar.
Cash	N.A.	$45	$61*	$54	$29	$32	$45	$48
2/10, n/30	N.A.	60/60/60*	81*/81*/82	71/71/72	38/39/39	42/43/43	60/60/60	64/64/64
n/45	145/145*	112*/113	153/152	134/133	72/73	80/80	112/113	120/120
Total	—	$450	$610	$535	$290	$320	$450	$480

*Due for payment in October. (September purchases are reconstructed from $60 amount to 2/10, n/30, which must be one third of 40 percent of total purchases.)

ZYX CORPORATION
Pro Forma Operating Statement
Six Months Ended July 31, 1995
($ thousands)

Sales revenue	$2,400	(6 × $400,000)
Cost of goods sold:		
Labor	$ 360	(6 × $ 60,000)
Materials purchased	750	(6 × $125,000)
Rent	111	(6 × $ 18,500)
Overhead	456	(6 × $ 76,000)
Depreciation	36	(6 × $ 6,000)
Amortization	3	(6 × $ 500)
Total	$1,716	
Less: Prepaids	$ 12	
Inventories	205	
	$ 217	1,499
Gross margin		$ 901
Selling and administrative expenses		330 (6 × $ 55,000)
Profit before taxes		$ 571
Taxes at 40%		228
Aftertax profit		343

ZYX CORPORATION
Pro Forma Balance Sheet
July 31, 1995
($ thousands)

Cash	$ 40	(minimum balance)
Accounts receivable	600	(45 days' sales)
Inventories	205	(given)
Total current assets	$ 845	
Equipment	$175	
Less: Depreciation	36	139
Prepaid items	12	(given)
Patents	47	(net of amortization)
Organization expense	15	(given)
Total assets	$1,058	
Accounts payable	$ 125	(30 days' purchases)
Accrued expenses	15	(1 week's wages)
Accrued taxes	228	(from operating statement)
Total current liabilities	$ 368	
Capital stock ($1 par)	300	(given)
Retained earnings	343	(from operating statement)
	$1,011	
Plug figure	47	(funds need 7/31/95)
Total liabilities and net worth	$1,058	

Observations

The figures appear quite optimistic; no allowance is made for start-up problems. Profitability thus seems excessive. There are likely to be greater funds needs early in the period, as collections lag and production problems appear. Also, if taxes have to be pre-paid, a major funds source will be affected. Moreover, growth will require additional funds:

```
10 percent increase in sales requires:
    10% increase in receivables, inventories .......................  $80
    Less: 10% increase in payables, accruals .......................   34
                                                                      ────
                                                                      $46
    10% increase in cash flow from operations ......................   38
    Need  ..........................................................  $ 8
                                                                      ════
```

This need will increase drastically if any key assumptions are off.

6.

ABC SUPERMARKET
Cash Budget
For Six Months Ended June 30, 1995
($ thousands)

	Jan.	Feb.	Mar.	Apr.	May	June	Total
Receipts:							
Cash sales	$200.0	$190.0	$220.0	$200.0	$230.0	$220.0	$1,260.0
Cash from sale of property ..	—	—	6.0	6.0	6.0	—	18.0
Rental income	—	—	.3	.3	.3	.3	1.2
Total receipts .	$200.0	$190.0	$226.3	$206.3	$236.3	$220.3	$1,279.2
Disbursements:							
Purchases recorded	$150.0	$142.5	$165.0	$150.0	$172.5	$165.0	$ 945.0
Payment for purchases (15-day lag)	$159.0	$146.3	$153.7	$157.5	$161.3	$168.7	$ 946.5
Salaries (12% of sales)	24.0	22.8	26.4	24.0	27.6	26.4	151.2
Other expenses (9% of sales)	18.0	17.1	19.8	18.0	20.7	19.8	113.4
Rent	3.5	3.5	3.5	3.5	3.5	3.5	21.0
Income taxes ..	2.0	—	2.0	3.5	—	2.0	9.5
Note payment .	—	3.0	—	—	5.0	—	8.0
Repayment to principals ...	3.0	—	3.0	—	3.0	—	9.0
Payment on fixtures	—	12.0	12.0	12.0	12.0	—	48.0

	Jan.	Feb.	Mar.	Apr.	May	June	Total
Total disbursements ...	$209.5	$204.7	$220.4	$218.5	$233.1	$220.4	$1,306.6
Net cash flow ..	$ (9.5)	$ (14.7)	$ 5.9	$ (12.2)	$ 3.2	$ (.1)	$ (27.4)
Cumulative net cash	$ (9.5)	$ (24.2)	$ (18.3)	$ (30.5)	$ (27.3)	$ (27.4)	
Analysis of cash requirements:							
Beginning cash balance	$ 42.5	$ 33.0	$ 18.3	$ 24.2	$ 12.0	$ 15.2	
Net cash flow ..	(9.5)	(14.7)	5.9	(12.2)	3.2	(.1)	
Ending cash balance	$ 33.0	$ 18.3	$ 24.2	$ 12.0	$ 15.2	$ 15.1	
Minimum cash balance	20.0	20.0	20.0	20.0	20.0	20.0	
Cash need (excess)	$ (13.0)	$ 1.7	$ (14.2)	$ 8.0	$ 4.8	$ 4.9	

Observations

The cash pattern indicates excess funds needs in four out of the six months if a $20,000 minimum balance is desired. The greatest funds need is in April 1995, but even by the end of the period no cleanup of required borrowing will have been achieved.

7.

XYZ COMPANY
Cash Budget by Month
Six Months Ended March 31, 1996
($ thousands)

	Oct.	Nov.	Dec.	Jan.	Feb.	Mar.	Total
Cash receipts:							
Collections (see next table) ..	$2,608	$2,092	$2,983	$2,400	$2,567	$2,708	$15,358
Cash disbursements:							
Payments for purchases (see below) ..	712	663	650	650	650	650	3,975
Wages	215	215	215	215	215	215	1,290
Other expenses	420	420	420	420	420	420	2,520
Selling and administrative expense	326	345	343	368	330	342	2,054
Note repayments	—	750	—	—	750	—	1,500
Interest	—	—	—	300	—	—	300
Dividend payments ...	25	—	—	25	—	—	50

	Oct.	Nov.	Dec.	Jan.	Feb.	Mar.	Total
Tax payment . .	—	—	—	375	—	—	375
Total disbursements	$1,698	$2,393	$1,628	$2,353	$2,365	$1,627	$12,064
Net cash receipts (disbursements)	$ 910	$ (301)	$1,355	$ 47	$ 202	$1,081	$ 3,294
Cumulative cash flow	$ 910	$ 609	$1,964	$2,011	$2,213	$3,294	

Collection Pattern—Sales

Timing	Aug.	Sept.	Oct.	Nov.	Dec.	Jan.	Feb.	Totals
Oct. 1–10	$ 641							
Oct. 11–20	642							$2,608
Oct. 21–31	642	$ 683*						
Nov. 1–10		683						
Nov. 11–20		684						$2,092
Nov. 21–30			$ 725					
Dec. 1-10			725					
Dec. 11–20			725	$ 766*				$2,983
Dec. 21–31				767				
Jan. 1–10				767				
Jan. 11–20					$ 816			$2,400
Jan. 21–31					817			
Feb. 1–10					817			
Feb. 11–20						$ 875		$2,567
Feb. 21–29						875		
Mar. 1–10						875		
Mar. 11–20							$916	$2,708
Mar. 21–31							917	
Totals	$1,925	$2,050	$2,175	$2,300	$2,450	$2,625	—	

*Change in collection pattern assumed.

Accounts Receivable

Sept. 30, 1995:	August sales	$1,925	
	September sales	2,050	
		$3,975	(60 days)
Dec. 31, 1995:	⅓ of November sales	$ 767	
	December sales	$2,450	
		$3,217	(40 days)
March 31, 1996:	⅓ of February sales	$ 917	
	March sales	2,850	
		$3,767	(40 days)

562

Purchase pattern: Forty-five days' payables throughout; thus there's a lag of 3/2 months.

Pro forma statements developed from data given and calculated:

XYZ COMPANY
Pro Forma Income Statements
Three Months Ended 12/31/95 and Six Months Ended 3/31/96
($ thousands)

	1995 3 Months	1995/96 6 Months
Sales	$6,925	$15,150 (given)
Cost of sales	4,848	10,605 (70 percent of sales)
Gross margin	$2,077	$ 4,545
Selling and administrative	$1,014	$ 2,054 (from cash budget)
Interest	75	150 (developed)
	$1,089	$ 2,204
Profit before taxes	$ 988	$ 2,341
Income taxes	494	1,171 (50 percent of profit)
Net income	$ 494	$ 1,170 (to balance sheet)

XYZ COMPANY
Pro Forma Balance Sheets
December 31, 1995 and March 31, 1996
($ thousands)

	12/31/95	3/31/96
Cash	$ 2,704 (+$1,964)	$ 4,034 (+$3,294)
Accounts receivable	3,217 (see above)	3,767 (see above)
Raw materials	2,200 (see below)	1,675 (see below)
Finished goods	6,081 (see below)	4,833 (see below)
Plant and equipment (net)	7,081 (−$129 depr.)	6,952 (−$258 depr.)
Other assets	1,730 (no change)	1,730 (no change)
Total assets	$23,013	$22,991
Accounts payable	$ 975 (45 days)	$ 975 (45 days)
Notes payable	3,370 (−$750)	2,620 (−$1,500)
Accrued liability	3,444 (see below)	3,521 (see below)
Long-term debt	5,250 (no change)	5,250 (no change)
Preferred stock	1,750 (no change)	1,750 (no change)
Common stock	5,000 (no change)	5,000 (no change)
Earned surplus	3,224 (−$25, +$494)	3,875 (−$50, +$1,170)
Total liabilities	$23,013	$22,991

Inventory Analysis

	12/31/95	3/31/96
Raw Materials:		
Beginning balance	$ 2,725	$ 2,725
Purchases @ $650/month	1,950	3,900

Inventory Analysis *(concluded)*

	12/31/95	3/31/96
	$ 4,675	$ 6,625
Withdrawals @ $825/month	2,475	4,950
Ending balance	$ 2,200	$ 1,675
Finished Goods:		
Beginning balance	$ 6,420	$ 6,420
Materials @ $825/month	2,475	4,950
Wages @ $215/month	645	1,290
Other expenses @ $420/month	1,260	2,520
Depreciation @ $43/month	129	258
	$10,929	$15,438
Cost of goods sold reported	4,848	10,605
Ending balance	$ 6,081	$ 4,833

Assume interest of $300 covers one year. Thus, by 9/31/95, $225 must have been accrued. Also, assume liabilities to accrue until paid in cash.

Accrued Liabilities

	12/31/95	3/31/96
Beginning balance	$ 2,875	$ 2,875
Accrued interest	75	150
Accrued taxes (income statement)	494	1,171
	$ 3,444	$ 4,196
Interest payment	—	(300)
Tax payment	—	(375)
Balance shown	$ 3,444	$ 3,521

Observations

The key change is the transformation of receivables and inventories into cash, due to the change in policies. Note the dramatic drop in inventories by 3/31/96, *if* the policies work as expected. No funds needs arise during the period, and the main collection impact is felt in October and December. If collections don't come in as expected, $1,833 will be deferred and not available by 3/31/96, and $1,533 by 12/31/95:

Receivables 12/31/95	$3,217
60 days	4,750
Difference	$1,533

Receivables 3/31/96	$3,767
60 days	5,600
Difference	$1,833

Management must make sure inventories go down, and this depends on quality and nature of goods on hand.

Questions for Discussion

1. As we can balance a pro forma balance sheet with a plug figure representing cash or a loan, must we be very careful with accounting conventions?

2. Given the freedom to project pro forma balance sheets and plugging them in the end, what limitations are there to this freedom? Explain.

3. Name key assumptions that have to agree for both a pro forma balance sheet and the matching pro forma operating statement.

4. Differentiate between a cash budget and a pro forma operating statement.

5. Should depreciation ever appear on a cash budget? If not, does it have any direct impact?

6. Must a cash budget and a corresponding set of pro forma statements always tie together so that they can be reconciled?

7. Differentiate between an operating budget (sales, manufacturing, service) and a cash budget.

8. Is it permissible to show an increase in finished goods inventories on a pro forma balance sheet, while at the same time reflecting a production level less than current unit sales in the cost of goods sold area of the operating statement?

9. In what ways is a pro forma funds flow statement helpful to understand projected conditions?

CHAPTER 5

Solutions to Problems

1. ABC Corporation

   Break-even point calculation:
   Price per unit $5.50
   Variable costs per unit $3.25
   Contribution $2.25

   Fixed costs: $360,000.

   Units required to recover fixed costs with contribution:

   $$\frac{\$360,000}{\$2.25} = 160,000 \text{ units}$$

a.   Leverage

Profit Effect from Volume Increases (20%)			Profit Effect from Volume Decreases (20%)		
Units	Profit	Change	Units	Profit	Change
160,000	$ 0	—	160,000	$ 0	—
192,000	72,000	infinite	128,000	(72,000)	infinite
230,400	158,400	120.0%	102,400	(129,600)	80.0%
276,480	262,080	65.5%	81,920	(175,680)	39.8%
331,776	386,496	47.5%	65,536	(212,544)	21.0%

Note the declining rate of change as we move away from the break-even point.

b.   Changes in conditions:
Price drop of 50 cents:
Change in contribution from $2.25 to $1.75:

$$\text{Break-even point: } \frac{\$360,000}{\$1.75} = 205,715 \text{ units}$$

Cost increase of 25 cents—variable:
Change in contribution from $2.25 to $2.00:

$$\text{Break-even point: } \frac{\$360,000}{\$2.00} = 180,000 \text{ units}$$

Cost increase of $40,000—fixed:
Change in fixed cost from $360,000 to $400,000:

$$\text{Break-even point: } \frac{\$400,000}{\$2.25} = 177,778$$

c.   Changing conditions by operating level:
Calculations must be made step by step to take account of changing conditions:

(1) Contribution from first 150,000 units:

Price $5.50
Variable costs 3.25
     Contribution   .... $2.25 × 150,000 = $337,500

(2) Contribution from next 25,000 units:

Price $5.50
Variable costs 3.00
     Contribution   .... $2.50 × 25,000 = $62,500

The break-even point will lie between 150,000 and 175,000 units, since the combined contribution of $400,000 exceeds fixed costs by $40,000. Thus the break-even point is based on fixed cost remaining after 150,000 units, i.e., $22,500 ($360,000 − $337,500).

$$\frac{\$22,500}{\$2.50} = 9,000 \text{ units added to } 150,000, \text{ or } 159,000 \text{ units}$$

The contribution from units after 175,000 units and after 190,000 does not come into play unless fixed costs were raised earlier.

ABC CORPORATION
Break-Even Chart

Original condition and price drop

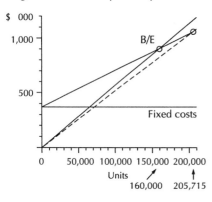

Original condition and variable cost increase

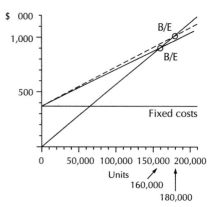

Original condition and fixed cost increase

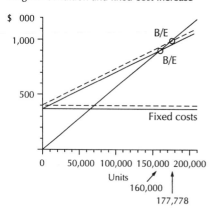

Original condition and step-wise changes

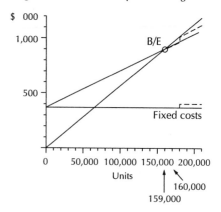

2. Financial leverage
    a. For $i = 5\%$ and $R = 8\%$:
        No debt: $r = 8\%$
        25% debt: $0.08 + 25/75(.08 - .05)$; $r = 9\%$
        50% debt: $0.08 + 50/50(.08 - .05)$; $r = 11\%$
        75% debt: $0.08 + 75/25(.08 - .05)$; $r = 17\%$
    b. For $i = 6\%$ and $R = 5\%$:
        No debt: $r = 5\%$
        25% debt: $0.05 + 25/75(.05 - .06)$; $r = 4.7\%$
        50% debt: $0.05 + 50/50(.05 - .06)$; $r = 4\%$
        75% debt: $0.05 + 75/25(.05 - .06)$; $r = 2\%$

Observations

The leverage effect is less dramatic as the difference between interest rates paid and return on assets earned decreases. Still, at high leverage, a more than proportional push on **ROE** is achieved, as Figure 5–6 in the chapter suggests. The negative leverage resulting from poor performance achieved by investing the capital is just as powerful as in the positive case.

3. Five-year financial plan ($ thousands)

	Year 1	Year 2	Year 3	Year 4	Year 5	Revised Year 5
Capital structure						
Debt as a percent of capitalization	20%	20%	33%	33%	33%	43%
Debt	$ 300	$ 309	$ 638	$ 664	$ 706	$1,059
Equity	1,200	1,235	1,277	1,330	1,413	1,413
Net assets (capitalization)	$1,500	$1,544	$1,915	$1,994	$2,119	$2,472
Profitability (after taxes):						
Return on net assets ...	8%	9%	10%	10%	10%	11%
Amount of profit	$120	$139	$192	$199	$212	$272
Interest rate (after taxes)	4.5%	4.5%	5.0%	5.0%	5.0%	4.5%
Amount of interest	$ 14	$ 14	$ 32	$ 33	$ 35	$ 48
Profit after interest and taxes	$106	$125	$160	$166	$177	$224
Earnings disposition:						
Dividend payout	2/3	2/3	2/3	1/2	1/2	2/3
Dividends paid	$ 71	$ 83	$107	$ 83	$ 88	$149
Reinvestment	$ 35	$ 42	$ 53	$ 83	$ 89	$ 75
Financing and investment:						
New debt, old ratio	9	10	26	42	44	56
New debt, new ratio ...	—	319	—	—*	—	—
New investment	$ 44	$371	$ 79	$125	$133	$131

	Year 1	Year 2	Year 3	Year 4	Year 5	Revised Year 5
Results (end of year):						
Net return, net assets ..	7.1%	8.1%	8.4%	8.3%	8.4%	9.1%
Return on equity	8.8	10.1	12.5	12.5	12.5	15.8
Growth on equity	2.9	3.4	4.2	6.2	6.3	5.3
Growth in earnings	—	17.9	28.0	3.8	6.6	34.9
Earnings per share	$0.53	$0.62	$0.80	$0.83	$0.88	$1.12
Dividends per share	$0.36	$0.42	$0.54	$0.42	$0.44	$0.74

*For revised year 5, this item should be $353.

Observations

The results displayed are self-explanatory and show a rising level as both operating and financial conditions are changed. The higher dividend payout in the revised Year 5 situation causes a drop in equity growth, even though operating conditions are more favorable.

Questions for Discussion

1. Derive a simple formula to express the break-even point in relation to volume and cost.
2. What influence does depreciation, as a fixed cost, have on a company's break-even characteristics?
3. Draw parallels and distinctions between operating and financial leverage, and cite examples from your own experience.
4. Why isn't it possible, at the same time, to have high growth in equity and a high dividend payout?
5. What are the key levers management can apply to bring about high growth in equity?
6. What relevant growth areas can you name as modeling targets, and why are they relevant?
7. Is it realistic to assume a continuous rollover of debt in the growth model? Are there any likely limitations?
8. What are the potential lags involved in attaining sustainable growth targets, such as were discussed in Chapter 2?
9. How does funds flow analysis relate to the business systems diagram (Figure 1–4) in Chapter 1?
10. Which are the most important assumptions in a growth model?

CHAPTER 6

Solutions to Problems

1. *a.* Net present value at 10 percent and 16 percent (factors from Table I in Chapter 6):

Amounts		PV Factors at 10%	Present Value	PV Factors at 16%	Present Value
$10,000	×	.909	$ 9,090	.862	$ 8,620
15,000	×	.826	12,390	.743	11,145
15,000	×	.751	11,265	.641	9,615
20,000	×	.683	13,660	.552	11,040
15,000	×	.621	9,315	.476	7,140
10,000	×	.564	5,640	.410	4,100
5,000	×	.513	2,565	.354	1,770
			$63,925		$53,430
Outlay			60,000		60,000
Net present value			$ 3,925		$ (6,570)

b. Internal rate of return (yield):
Must be between 10 and 16 percent; closer to the lower end.
Trial at 12 percent (factors from Table 6–I):

Amounts		PV Factors at 12%	Present Value
$10,000	×	.893	$ 8,930
15,000	×	.797	11,955
15,000	×	.712	10,680
20,000	×	.636	12,720
15,000	×	.567	8,505
10,000	×	.507	5,070
5,000	×	.452	2,260
			$60,120
Outlay			60,000
Net present value			120

c. Even cash flows:
$13,000 per year at 10 percent (factor from Table II):

$13,000 × 4.868 = $63,284
Net investment = 60,000
Net present value = $ 3,284

d. Cash flows to yield 16 percent:
Annualize the investment of $60,000 at 16 percent:

$$A = \frac{PV}{f}$$

$$= \frac{\$60,000}{4.039} = \$14,855$$

The required amount over seven years is slightly under
$14,900.

e. Net present values at 10 and 16 percent, given recovery of
$10,000:

Recovery of $10,000 at end of year 7 (factors from Table I):

$$\text{at 10 percent: } \$10,000 \times .513 = \$5,130$$
$$\text{at 16 percent: } \$10,000 \times .354 = \$3,540$$

Original values in *a*:

At 10 percent: $3,925 plus recovery of $5,130 = $9,055
At 16 percent: $(6,570) plus recovery of $3,540 = $(3,030)

IRR must now be somewhat under 16 percent since net present value turns negative below that rate.

f. Cash flows to yield 16 percent, given recovery of $10,000:
Present value of recovery at 16 percent: $3,540 (from *e*)
Present value of investment:

Outlay less present value of recovery:

$$\$60,000 \text{ less } \$3,540 = \$56,460$$

Cash flows required based on annualizing present value of investment (see *d*):

$$A = \frac{\$56,460}{4.039} = \$13,979$$

Note that the recovery of $10,000 in Year 7 reduced required cash flows by about $900 per year. This can, of course, be shown directly by developing the annual equivalent of the recovery:

$$A = \frac{\$3,540}{4.039} = \$876$$

2. **ABC Company**

Net investment: 64% of $1,500,000 = $960,000
Past research and development: Not relevant here.

Profit improvement:

Year 1: 64% of $200,000	=	$ 128,000
Year 2: 64% of $300,000	=	192,000
Year 3: 64% of $600,000	=	384,000
Year 4: 64% of $500,000	=	320,000
Year 5: 64% of $400,000	=	256,000
Total		$1,280,000
Average yearly amount	....	$ 256,000

Measures calculated (000 omitted):

a. Payback (on average amount):

$$\frac{\$960}{\$256} = 3.75 \text{ years—Almost 4 years on actual pattern}$$

b. Return on investment:

$$\frac{\$256}{\$960} = 26.7 \text{ percent—Can't calculate on actual pattern}$$

c. Average return:

$$\frac{\$256}{\$480} = 53.3 \text{ percent—Can't calculate on actual pattern}$$

d. Net present value (at 12 percent):

Based on average: 3.605 × $256 (Table II)	= +$922,800
Outlay	− 960,000
Net present value	−$ 37,120

Based on actual pattern (factors from Table I):

Amounts		PV Factors		Present Value	Cumulative
$128,000	×	.893	=	$114,304	$114,304
192,000	×	.797	=	153,024	267,328
384,000	×	.712	=	273,408	540,736
320,000	×	.636	=	203,520	744,256
256,000	×	.567	=	145,152	889,408
				+$889,408	

Outlay .... − 960,000

Net present value .... −$ 70,592

(Note that the actual pattern causes worsening of the result!)

e. Present value index:

$$\text{Based on average: } \frac{\$922,880}{960,000} = .96$$

$$\text{Based on pattern: } \frac{\$889,408}{960,000} = .93$$

f. Internal rate of return:
Due to the closeness of the present value results, the IRR is approximately 12 percent in either case, slightly lower on the average basis, and somewhat lower on the actual pattern.

g. Present value payback:
Just about five years; a little less on the average basis, a little more on the pattern.

h. Annualized net present value (factors from Table II):

$$\text{Based on average: } \frac{+\$37,120}{3.605} = +\$10,297 \text{ each year}$$

$$\text{Based on pattern: } \frac{-\$70,592}{3.605} = -\$19,582 \text{ each year}$$

Observations

The project barely meets current standards. If the data had been available *before* the R&D expenditures were made, the expenditures then and now shouldn't be made. If no other preferable investments are available now, however, the investment is OK since past outlays are *sunk* costs.

3. Trustee of major estate:
    Net investment: $100,000 in *a* and *b*.
    Yield:

a.
$$\text{Yield factor: } \frac{\$100,000}{\$16,500} = 6.06$$

In Table II, on the eight-year line this corresponds to a yield of about 7 percent if a rough interpolation is made.

b.
$$\text{Yield factor: } \frac{\$100,000}{\$233,000} = .429$$

In Table I, on the 11-year line this corresponds exactly to a yield of 8 percent. Thus, the second proposition is preferable.

Net present value (6 percent):

a. Benefits: 8 × $16,500.
    Present value of benefits: 6.210 × $16,500 (Table II) = $102,465.
    Net present value: +$2,465.

b. Benefits: Lump sum in 11 years is $233,000.
    Present value of benefits: .527 × $233,000 (Table I) = $122,791.
    Net present value: +$22,791.

Observations

If a higher discount factor were used, the results would be reversed since proposition (*a*) provides continuous early benefits. The question of risk looms large here—11 years is a long time. Also, some students argue that reinvestment of the cash flows makes (*a*) preferable—they must be convinced that the effect has been taken into account in the discount procedure. It's worthwhile to calculate with the class a *compounding* of all cash flows to 11 years to prove this point. The question of changing earnings opportunities over time should be posed.

4. **DEF** Company

Net investment: $52,800.
Life: Eight years, no salvage.
Depreciation: $6,600/year straight-line.

Annual operating cash flow:

Net labor and material savings	$12,100
Less depreciation	6,600
	$ 5,500
Taxes at 36%	1,980
Aftertax savings	$ 3,520
Add back depreciation	6,600
Operating cash flow	$10,120

a. Payback:

$$\frac{\$52,800}{\$10,120} = 5.2 \text{ years}$$

b. Return on investment:

$$\frac{\$10,120}{\$52,800} = 19.2\%$$

c. Average return:

$$\frac{\$10,120}{\$26,400} = 38.3\%$$

d. Net present value (at 12 percent):

Present value of operating cash flow:

4.968 × $10,120 (Table II):	= +$50,276
Present value of net investment	− 52,800
Net present value	−$ 2,524

e. Present value index:

$$\frac{\$50,276}{\$52,800} = .95$$

f. Internal rate of return: Approximately 11%.
g. Present value payback: Just about eight years. A small gap exists. There's no cushion.
h. Annualized net present value:

$$\frac{-\$2,594}{4.968} = -\$508 \text{ each year}$$ (This shows the annual gap that has to be overcome to meet the standard!)

Observations

   This example introduces depreciation and its importance as a tax shield. This is an opportunity to demonstrate various ways of calculating the tax shield effect. Accelerated depreciation available under the tax laws would tend to boost considerably the benefits of the project in the early years. You should work through different depreciation patterns and develop present values using Tables I and II.

5. XYZ Corporation

Past investment: $3.75 million (sunk).
Net investment data:

Original outlay: $6,300,000.
Recovery in 12 years: $1,260,000 (book value).
Working capital:
Initial .... $1,500,000.
Recovery in 12 years .... $1,250,000.
Promotion expenditure ($1.0 million × .64): $640,000 (aftertax).
Life of proposition: 12 years.
Profit improvements:

	Years 1–3	Years 4–8	Years 9–12	Total
Profit improvement	$1,900	$2,200	$1,300	$21,900
Less: Depreciation	420	420	420	5,040
	$1,480	$1,780	$ 880	$16,860
Tax at 36% (rounded)	533	640	317	6,070
	$ 947	$1,140	$ 563	$10,790
Add back depreciation	420	420	420	5,040
Operating cash flow	$1,367	$1,560	$ 983	$15,830

Present value analysis at 12 percent:

Time Period	Investments	Operating Cash Flows	PV Factors at 12%*	Present Values	PV Factors at 15%*	Present Values
0 }	−$6,300 −$1,500 −$ 640		1.000	−$8,440	1.000	−$8,440
1 2 3		+$1,367/yr.	2.402	+ 3,284	2.283	+ 3,120
4 5 6 7 8		+$1,560/yr.	4.968 −2.402 2.566	+ 4,003	4.487 −2.283 2.204	+ 3,438
9 10 11 12		+$ 983/yr.	6.194 −4.968 1.226	+ 1,205	5.421 −4.487 .934	+ 918
12 }†	+$1,260 +$1,250		.257	+ 645	.187	+ 469
Net present values				+$ 697		−$ 495

*From Table II, except year-end of Year 12, which is from Table I.
†Year end.

Net present value at 12 percent is about $700,000, indicating a better-than-standard result. In fact, the recovery of working capital and book values of equipment in Year 12 could be forgone and the project would still meet standards.

Present value index at 12 percent:
Based on initial investment:

$$\frac{\$9,137}{\$8,440} = 1.08$$

Based on net investment:

$$\frac{\$8,492}{\$7,795} = 1.09$$

Present value payback:
Just about 12 years because the recovery represents the excess present value.

Internal rate of return (IRR):
By trial and error a little under 14 percent. (See PV analysis above.)

Annualized net present value:

$$\frac{\$697}{6.194} = \$122,500 \text{ per year (narrow margin for error)}$$

Observations
Project is close to standard; it shows problems of handling uneven cash flows. Can't recover past (sunk) R&D. Therefore similar future projects will be of doubtful value to the company.

6. **ZYX COMPANY**

Net Investment

Original machine	$32,000	
Current book value	$25,600	
Market value	15,000	(relevant)
Loss on sale	$10,600	
Tax savings on loss @ 36%	3,816	(relevant)
Net loss	$ 6,784	
Net investment	$55,500	
Value in eight years	$ 1,500	

Calculation of Net Investment

New machine	$55,500
Less cash on old	15,000
	$40,500

Calculation of Net Investment *(concluded)*

Less tax savings 3,816

Initial investment $36,684

To be adjusted for recoveries in Year 8.

Comparison of Lives

Only eight years are comparable. If the new machine lasted longer, its life would have to be cut off for purposes of comparison.

Operating Savings and Benefits

	Old Machine	New Machine	Annual Difference
Operating savings—current volume:			
Labor	$ 24,000	$ 16,000	$ 8,000
Materials	96,000	92,000	4,000
Overhead (200% of labor)	48,000	32,000	(not applicable)
	$168,000	$140,000	$12,000
Contribution—additional volume:			
30,000 units @ $.95		$ 28,500	
Less: Labor @ $.08		(2,400)	
Materials @ $.46		(13,800)	
Selling and promotion		(5,500)	6,800
Total savings and contribution			$18,800
Depreciation	$ 3,200	$ 6,750*	(3,550)
Taxable benefits			$15,250
Taxes at 36%			5,490
Aftertax benefits			$ 9,760
Add back depreciation			3,550
Aftertax cash flow			$13,260

* $55,500 new machine
  −1,500 scrap
  $54,000 ÷ 8 = $6,750/year

Payback:

$$\frac{\$36,684 - \$1,500}{\$13,260} = 2.65 \text{ years}$$

Return on investment:

$$\frac{\$13,260}{\$35,184} = 37.7\%$$

Net present value:

Time Period	Amounts	PV Factor 16%	Present Values
0	−$36,684	1.00	−$36,684
1–8	+$13,260/yr.	4.344	+$57,601
8	+$ 1,500	.305	+$ 458
	Net present value		+$21,375

Present value index:

• Net investment basis:

$$\frac{\$57,601}{\$36,684 - \$458} = 1.59$$

• Without terminal value:

$$\frac{\$57,601 + \$458}{\$36,684} = 1.58$$

Present value payback:
This is determined through use of the annuity table:

$$\text{Annuity factor} = \frac{\$36,226}{\$13,260/\text{yr.}} = 2.732$$

Interpolation in the 16 percent column of Table II indicates a little under four years is required. The terminal value could be a problem if it were significantly larger than assumed here, because it has been discounted for receipt in Year 8, which is much later than the payback period of 4 years. If precision is required, year-by-year trial-and-error approaches can be made.

Annualized net present value:

$$\frac{\$21,375}{4.344} = \$4,920$$

This is a sizable cushion for error in the performance estimates.
Internal rate of return (IRR):
Trial and error necessary; result is about 32%.

Time Period	Amounts	PV Factors at 35%	Present Values	PV Factors at 30%	Present Values
0	−$36,684	1.000	−$36,684	1.000	−$36,684
1–8	+$13,260/yr.	2.598	+$34,449	2.925	+$38,786
8	+$ 1,500	.091	+$ 136	.123	+$ 184
			−$ 2,098		+$ 2,286

Observations

This is the best example, among the ones provided, with which to practice your mastery of problem structure, differential costs, different lives, and accounting allocations. Questions could be raised concerning a 10-year life of the new machine, and also whether the product is worthwhile per se—which is the assumption on which the differential cost analysis rests. The improvement could merely raise product profitability from poor to mediocre!

7. UVW Company

Net investment: $275,000.
Life: 12 years.
Operating cash flows:

Amount	Probability	Expectation
$15,000	.05	$ 750
35,000	.15	5,250
45,000	.40	18,000
50,000	.25	12,500
60,000	.15	9,000
	1.00	$45,500

a. Net present value at 10% (on expectation):

Investment outlay	−$275,000
12 years at $45,500 (6.814)	+ 310,040
Net present value	+$ 34,960

This is also approximately the same as the net present value based on the most likely outcome ($45,000):

Investment	−$275,000
6.814 × $45,000	306,630
Net present value	+$ 31,630

b. Annualized net present value:

• On expectation:

$$\frac{\$34,960}{6.814} = \$5,130$$

• On most likely value:

$$\frac{\$31,630}{6.814} = \$4,640$$

In either case there's a sizable cushion against estimating error.

c. Internal rate of return:

$$\frac{\$275,000}{\$45,500} = 6.044; \text{ or } \frac{\$275,000}{\$45,000} = 6.111$$

Yield over 12 years is about 12 percent (12-year life in Table II) in either case.

d. Minimum life at $45,000/year:

$$\frac{\$275,000}{\$45,000} = 6.111 \text{ at } 10\%$$

This requires a little under 10 years (10 percent column in Table II), a cushion of about 2 years.

e. Minimum cash flow to achieve 10%:

$$\frac{\$275,000}{6.814} = \$40,360 \text{ per year for 12 years}$$

The chances of achieving this level of cash flow are better than 80 percent. Is this good enough?

Observations

This example serves to illustrate analysis by elements of probabilistic reasoning, holding a lot of assumptions stable. It appears that the project has a reasonable chance of success, but the final answer rests on the judgment of the people involved.

Questions for Discussion

1. Define the difference between cash flows, differential costs, and relevant costs.
2. Why should we study the various alternatives before making a capital investment decision?
3. Are sunk costs always to be ignored in capital investment analysis? Can't such a practice lead to financial difficulties?
4. Do past investments in large support facilities count when considering production investments that will make use of this unused capacity?
5. Do accounting allocations ever become relevant in investment analysis?
6. Define the difference between present value payback and annualized net present value.
7. What's the difference between an annualized net present value and an annuity?
8. Why might the internal rate of return (yield) provide two answers at the same time?

580

9. Why is it necessary to adjust for uneven lives in alternative capital investments when discounting reduces the importance of future cash flows anyway?

10. Is it possible to make an annual charge for working capital in a capital investment proposal, in lieu of specifying an outflow for the amount of working capital at point zero and an inflow for its recovery at the end of the past year?

11. Differentiate between capital budgeting and capital investment analysis. Which additional questions need to be resolved in the former?

12. Which aspects of capital investment analysis and capital budgeting lend themselves to modeling?

CHAPTER 7

Solutions to Problems

1. GHI Company

Calculations of cost of capital:

Existing debt:	12% × (1 − .36) =	7.7%
Incremental debt:	10% × (1 − .36) =	6.4%
Existing preferred:		14.0%
Incremental preferred:		12.0%
Common equity:		

Earnings basis: $\dfrac{\$\,9.50}{\$77.00} = 12.3\%$

Dividend basis: $\dfrac{\$\,4.50}{\$77.00} + 7\% = 12.8\%$

CAPM: $k_e = 9\% + 1.25\,(15.0 - 9.0) = 16.5\%$

Observations

We need to define the purpose of the analysis, and the figures by themselves are only the beginning. The cost of common equity shows a large differential between the shortcuts and the CAPM approach. It would be useful to be able to review recent company performance. Apparently the risk premium implicit in the β suggests that more volatility can be expected.

2. KLN Company

Weighted cost of capital:
Existing conditions:

Debt cost 7.0(1 − .46) 3.78%
Preferred cost 6.00%
Common equity cost—(CAPM 7.5 + 1.2 [13.5 − 7.5]) 14.70%

Incremental conditions:

Debt cost 11.0(1 − .46) 5.94%
Preferred cost 9.00%
Common equity (CAPM) 14.70%

Assignment of weights:
Book value basis:

Debt	$250	35.8%
Preferred	50	7.1
Common equity	400	57.1
	$700	100.0%

Market value basis:

Debt (7.0/11.0 × 250)	$159	23.0%
Preferred (6.0/9.0 × 50)	33	4.8
Common equity $50/share	500	72.2
	$692	100.0%

Weighted cost (incremental):

	Book Value		Market Value	
Debt	35.8% × 5.94 =	2.13%	23.0% × 5.94 =	1.37%
Preferred	7.1 × 9.00 =	0.64	4.8 × 9.00 =	0.43
Common equity	57.1 × 14.70 =	8.39	72.2 × 14.70 =	10.61
	100.0%	11.16%	100.0%	12.41%

Weighted cost (existing):

	Book Value		Market Value	
Debt	35.8% × 3.78 =	1.35%	23.0% × 3.78 =	0.87%
Preferred	7.1 × 6.00 =	0.43	4.8 × 6.00 =	0.26
Common equity	57.1 × 14.70 =	8.39	72.2 × 14.70 =	10.61
	100.0%	10.17%	100.0%	11.74%

Observations

The range of results is narrow, within two percentage points. If we ignore the book value basis as not relevant, the market value results are even closer. If any use is made of the concept for future investments, the existing conditions aren't relevant either. Thus, the weighted cost is about 12 percent, perhaps a little higher.

Questions for Discussion

1. Why can't we speak of *"the* cost of capital" as an absolute figure?

2. What indirect costs can be ascribed to a long-term loan or to a convertible debenture?
3. Why are shareholder expectations important in developing the cost of common equity when the company has no control over the behavior of the stock market?
4. If beta, as defined in the CAPM, isn't a fully satisfactory measure of risk, what alternative concepts can you suggest?
5. How important is the choice of weights in developing the weighted cost of capital as a minimum return standard?
6. If weighted cost of capital is a useful standard with which to assess prospective returns from new capital investments, how should the return on existing investments be judged?
7. If a company's financial policies are changing (e.g., the use of leverage increases), does this mean its return requirements must change also?
8. If you were president of a multidivision company with rather different businesses, how would you answer the argument that some divisions should use lower return standards than others?
9. How critical is it that a capital investment project exactly meet the weighted cost of capital standard? What questions would you ask?
10. What major elements would you consider in developing a broad allocation of capital to the rather different divisions of a company? Which would be most important?

CHAPTER 8
Solutions to Problems

1. *a.*

ABC CORPORATION
Per Share Analysis
($ thousands, except per share amounts)

	Old Level	New Level
EBIT	$ 14,700	$ 17,400 (118%)
Interest (same)	1,100	1,100
Profit before taxes	$ 13,600	$ 16,300
Taxes at 34%	4,625	5,540
Profit after taxes	$ 8,975	$ 10,760
Number of common shares	300,000	350,000
Earnings per share	$ 29.91	$ 30.74
Sinking fund	$ 900	900
Sinking fund per share	$ 3.00	$ 2.57
Uncommitted earnings per share	$ 26.91	$ 28.17
Depreciation per share	$ 7.50	$ 6.43
Cash flow per share	$ 37.41	$ 37.17

Immediate dilution: $\dfrac{\$8,975,000}{350,000}$ − $29.41   = ($3.77) dilution (12.8%).

Net dilution (strengthening): $30.74 − $29.41 = $1.33 strengthening (4.5%).

b. $5.0 million preferred stock (10%)
or $5.0 million debentures (9%), due in 15 years.

Per Share Analysis
($ thousands, except per share amounts)

	Preferred		Debentures	
	Old Level	New Level	Old Level	New Level
EBIT	$ 14,700	$ 17,400	$ 14,700	$ 17,400
Interest—old	1,100	1,100	1,100	1,100
Interest—new	—	—	450	450
Profit before taxes	$ 13,600	$ 16,300	$ 13,150	$ 15,850
Taxes at 34%	4,625	5,540	4,475	5,390
Profit after taxes	$ 8,975	$ 10,760	$ 8,675	$ 10,460
Preferred dividends	500	500	—	—
Profits to common	$ 8,475	$ 10,260	$ 8,675	$ 10,460
Number of common shares	300,000	300,000	300,000	300,000
Earnings per share	$ 28.25	$ 34.20	$ 28.92	$ 34.86
Sinking fund	$ 900	$ 900	$ 900	$ 900
Sinking fund per share	$ 3.00	$ 3.00	$ 3.00	$ 3.00
Uncommitted earnings per share	$ 25.25	$ 31.20	$ 25.92	$ 31.86
Depreciation per share	$ 7.50	$ 7.50	$ 7.50	$ 7.50
Cash flow per share	$ 35.75	$ 41.70	$ 36.42	$ 42.36

Immediate dilution:

Preferred: $28.25 − $29.91 = (1.06); $\dfrac{\$1.66}{\$29.91}$ = 5.9% dilution

Debentures: $28.92 − $29.91 = ($.99); $\dfrac{\$.99}{\$29.91}$ = 3.4% dilution

Net dilution (strengthening):

Preferred: $34.20 − $29.91 = $4.29; 14.3% strengthening
Debentures: $34.86 − $29.91 = $4.95; 16.5% strengthening

c. Comparative cost of capital:
Common stock:
$5 million represents 50,000 shares, or $100 per share, far
below the current average price of $130. EPS required to
keep stockholders as well off as before: $29.91. Thus, the ap-
parent "cost" of this issue is

$\dfrac{\$29.91}{\$100.00}$ = 29.9% after taxes, a very low P/E ratio, indeed.

584

Based on the **CAPM**, the cost of common stock is

$$8.0 + 1.4\ (14.5 - 8.0) = 17.1\%\ \text{after taxes}$$

This is obviously a risky company, from which the market is demanding a high risk premium.

- Preferred stock: 10% after taxes.
- Debentures: 5.9% after taxes.

Observations

Note the apparent attractiveness of the new investments, and the leverage effect of lower-cost preferred or debt. (The example has been exaggerated with a low P/E to make the differences more apparent.)

2. **XYZ Corporation**
   a. Comparative cost of capital:
      (1) Determine the **EBIT** level:

EPS (current)	$12.50
Number of common shares	1,000,000
Profit to common	$12,500,000
Preferred dividends (existing)	1,500,000
Profit after taxes	$14,000,000
Taxes (46%)	11,925,000
Profit before taxes	$25,925,000
Bond interest (existing)	2,500,000
EBIT	$28,425,000

   (2) Determine profit to common at current **EBIT** level:

	Common	Preferred
EBIT	$28,425	$28,425
Interest	2,500	2,500
Profit before taxes	$25,925	$25,925
Taxes (46%)	11,925	11,925
Profit after taxes	$14,000	$14,000
Preferred dividends	1,500	4,200
Profit to common	$12,500	$ 9,800
Number of shares	1,240,000	1,000,000
EPS	$10.08	$ 9.80

   (3) Determine profit to common needed to maintain current **EPS**:

	Common	Preferred
EPS	$12.50	$12.50
Number of shares	1,240,000	1,000,000

	Common	Preferred
Profit to common	$15,500	$12,500
Profit to common—current EBIT	12,500	9.800
Incremental profit (after taxes)	$ 3,000	$ 2,700
Incremental investment	$30,000	$30,000
Specific cost of capital	10.0%	9.0%
Specific cost before taxes	18.5%	16.7%

The cost of preferred stock is the same as the stated dividend rate, of course, assuming the stock was issued at par.

(4) Calculation of cost of common equity based on CAPM:

$$k_e = 8.0 + 1.2 \,(13.0 - 8.0)$$
$$= 8.0 + 6.0 = 14.0\%$$

b. Equivalency between common and preferred alternatives:

Formula: $\dfrac{(E - i)\, .54 - p}{n}$

$$\underset{\text{(common)}}{\dfrac{(E - \$2,500)\, .54 - \$1,500}{1,240}} = \underset{\text{(preferred)}}{\dfrac{E - \$2,500)\, .54 - \$4,200}{1,000}}$$

$$540E - 1,350,000 - 1,500,000 = 669.6E - 1,674,000 - 5,208,000$$
$$129.6E = 4,032,000$$
$$E = 31,111$$

Earnings equivalency thus is at $31,111,000 EBIT. Earnings per share/dividend per share equivalency:

EPS needed for $8.00 dividend	$8.00
Number of common shares	1,240,000
Profit to common	$ 9,920,000
Preferred dividends	1,500,000
Profit after taxes	$11,420,000
Taxes (46%)	9,728,000
Profit before taxes	$21,148,000
Interest	2,500,000
EBIT for $8.00 dividend	$23,648,000

c. Leverage effect of preferred alternative:

	Level 1	Level 2	Level 3	Level 4
EBIT (current $28,425)	$10,000	$15,000	$22,500	$33,750
Interest	2,500	2,500	2,500	2,500
	$ 7,500	$12,500	$20,000	$31,250
Taxes (46%)	3,450	5,750	9,200	14,375
	$ 4,050	$ 6,750	$10,800	$16,875

	Level 1	Level 2	Level 3	Level 4
Preferred dividend	4,200	4,200	4,200	4,200
Profit to common	$ (150)	$ 2,550	$ 6,600	$12,675
Common shares	1,000,000	1,000,000	1,000,000	1,000,000
EPS (current $12.50)	$ (.15)	$ 2.55	$ 6.60	$12.68
Percent increase in EBIT	50%	50%	50%	
Percent increase in EPS	Infinite	159%	92%	

This is a highly leveraged situation, but the rate of increase drops as earnings move away from the EBIT break-even level (coverage of fixed charges = zero EPS, or EBIT level of $10.28 million).

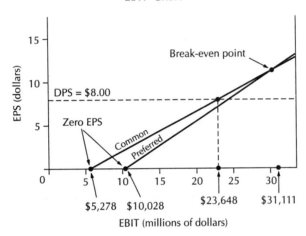

XYZ CORPORATION
EBIT Chart

Observations

Again, some exaggeration is used to make the points involved. The example can be used for a good drilling of concepts—by working the data in both directions.

3.

DEF COMPANY
EPS Calculations
($ thousands, except per share amounts)

	Common		Preferred		Debentures	
	Current*	Low	Current*	Low	Current*	Low
EBIT	$42,000	$22,000	$42,000	$22,000	$42,000	$22,000
Interest—old	1,200	1,200	1,200	1,200	1,200	1,200
Interest—new	—	—	—	—	$ 4,250	$ 4,250
Profit before taxes ..	$40,800	$20,800	$40,800	$20,800	$36,550	$16,550
Taxes (46%)	18,768	9,568	18,768	9,568	16,813	7,613
Profit after taxes	$22,032	$11,232	$22,032	$11,232	$19,737	$ 8,937

	Common		Preferred		Debentures	
	Current*	Low	Current*	Low	Current*	Low
Preferred dividend —old	1,800	1,800	1,800	1,800	1,800	1,800
Preferred dividend —new	—	—	4,750	4,750	—	—
Profit to common	$20,232	$ 9,432	$15,482	$ 4,682	$17,937	$ 7,137
Number of common shares (millions)	3.0	3.0	2.0	2.0	2.0	2.0
EPS	$6.74	$3.14	$7.94	$2.34	$8.97	$3.57
SFPS	$ .33	$ .33	$ .50	$ .50	$1.50	$1.50
UEPS	$6.41	$2.81	$7.24	$1.84	$7.47	$2.07
Dividend coverage (EPS)	3.37 ×	1.57 ×	3.87 ×	1.17 ×	4.49 ×	.79 ×

*Current EBIT plus incremental earnings on new capital.

Dilution Data

	Common	Preferred	Debentures
EBIT (old)	$34,000	$34,000	$34,000
Interest	1,200	1,200	5,450
Profit before taxes	$32,800	$32,800	$28,550
Taxes (46%)	15,088	15,088	13,133
Profit after taxes	$17,712	$17,712	$15,417
Preferred dividends	1,800	6,550	1,800
Profit to common	$15,912	$11,162	$13,617
Number of shares (millions)	3.0	2.0	2.0
EPS (old = $7.96)	$ 5.30	$ 5.58	$ 6.81

Immediate dilution:

    Common: $7.96 − $5.30 = $2.66; drop of 33.4%
    Preferred: $7.96 − $5.58 = $2.38; drop of 29.9%
    Debentures: $7.96 − $6.81 = $1.15; drop of 14.4%

Net dilution (strengthening):

    Common: $7.96 − $6.74 = $1.22; drop of 15.3%
    Preferred: $7.96 − $7.74 = $(.22); drop of 2.8%
    Debentures: $7.96 − $8.97 = $(1.01); drop of 12.7%

Cost of capital (after taxes):

    Common: $7.96 per share for $50.00—apparent "cost" = 15.9%*
    Preferred: 9.5 percent stated rate   = 9.5%
    Debentures: 9.5 percent before tax (1 − .46) × 8.5%   = 4.6%
        *Based on the CAPM, the cost of common is 7.5 + 1.2(14.0 − 7.5) = 15.2%.

Break-even points:

• Common versus preferred:

$$\frac{(E - 1,200).54 - 1,800}{3,000} = \frac{(E - 1,200).54 - 6,550}{2,000}$$
(common)   (preferred)

$1,080E - 1,296,000 - 3,600,000 = 1,620E - 1,944,000 - 19,650,000$

$540E = 16,698,000; \ E = 30,922; \ \text{EBIT} = \$30,922,200$

- Common versus debentures:

$$\frac{(E - 1,200).54 - 1,800}{3,000} = \frac{(E - 5,450).54 - 1,800}{2,000}$$

$1,080E - 1,296,000 - 3,600,000 = 1,620E - 8,829,000 - 5,400,000$

$540E = 9,333,000; \ E = 17,283; \ \text{EBIT} = \$17,283,300$

- Dividend coverage:
  Shown in the EPS calculations above.

Zero EPS:

- Common:

  $(E - 1,200).54 - 1,800 = 0; \ .54E - 648 - 1,800 = 0; \ E = \$4,533,300$ EBIT.

- Preferred:

  $(E - 1,200).54 - 6,550 = 0; \ .54E - 648 - 6,550 = 0; \ E = \$13,329,600$ EBIT.

DEF COMPANY
EBIT Chart

- Debentures:

$(E - 5,450).54 - 1,800 = 0; .54E - 2,943 - 1,800 = 0; E = \$8,783,300$ EBIT.

Observations

The example allows full treatment of the technical aspects of the three alternatives, and the display is useful in its exaggeration. Please review the key points beyond those represented by the figures, which are also necessary for choice. Otherwise the data are self-explanatory.

Questions for Discussion

1. List the key conditions that would affect the relative importance of the areas of cost, risk exposure, flexibility, timing, and control.
2. Why is it important to look ahead to the potential next stage of financing when deciding the choice among current alternatives for new funds?
3. Relate the weighted cost of capital of a company to the costs of the respective alternatives for incremental funds. Are they based on the same reasoning?
4. How does the immediate dilution of earnings caused by alternative ways of raising additional funds relate to the return standards required for new investments?
5. Why are calculations of the comparative cost of alternative financing choices based on the proceeds and not on the face value?
6. What are the key assumptions underlying the EBIT chart, and under what conditions is it necessary to redraw the lines?
7. How does prospective inflation affect the choice among alternative methods of raising additional funds?
8. When leasing is an alternative, what are the key considerations that would make it attractive?
9. Is there such a thing as an ideal long-term capital structure, and should blocks of incremental capital be tailored to fit such a structure?

CHAPTER 9

Solutions to Problems

1. Bond price examples:
   a. Price at 6%:

Principal due after 28 periods at 3%, plus premium of $75
(using preprogrammed calculator) $1,075 × 0.437 .... $ 469.78
PV of 28 semiannual interest payments of $40, at 3% per
period (factor from calculator) $40 × 18.764 ....   750.56
Price to yield 6% per annum $1,220.34

Price at 10%
$1,075 × 0.255 (Table I in Chapter 6) .... $ 274.12
$40 × 14.898 (Table II in Chapter 6) 595.92
Price to yield 10% per annum .... $ 870.04

b. Price at 6%:

Principal due after 44 periods at 3% if not called:
$1,000 × 0.31 (interpolation, Table I) .... $ 310.00
44 semiannual interest receipts of $42.50:
$42.50 × 24.0 (interpolation, Table II) 1,020.00
Price to yield 6% per annum $1,330.00

If called at 110 on 10/1/03:
Principal plus call premium due after 24 periods at 3%:
$1,100 × 0.50 (interpolation, Table I) .... $ 550.00
24 semiannual interest receipts of $42.50:
$42.50 × 16.9 (interpolation, Table II) 718.25
Price to yield 6% per annum $1,268.25

c. Price at 9%:

$1,000 × 0.13 (interpolation, 4.5%) .... $ 130.00
$42.50 × 18.7 (interpolation, 4.5%) 794.75
Price to yield 9% per annum .... $ 924.75

If called:
$1,100 × 0.33 (interpolation, 4.5%) .... $ 363.00
$42.50 × 14.3 (interpolation, 4.5%) 607.75
Price to yield 9% per annum .... $ 970.75

2. Bond yield examples:

a. No interest accrued because the interest date coincides with
the purchase date.

Market price 7/15/94 .... $1,241.25
Redemption price 7/15/05 ....   1,100.00
                                                  $2,341.25
Average investment (1/2) $1,170.63

Number of periods: 28.
Interest per period: $35.00.
Amortization of premium: $141.25 ÷ 28 = $5.04.
Average periodic income: $35.00 − $5.04 = $29.96, or $59.92 per year.

Yield: $\dfrac{\$59.92}{\$1,170.63} = 5.12\%$

Exact yield from bond table: 4.65%

b. Exact yield from bond table: 4.85%.

c. Annual interest: $40.00.
    Accrued interest on August 20, 1994:

$$5 \text{ months} + 20 \text{ days} = 170 \text{ days}$$

or

$$\frac{170}{360} \times \$40 = \$18.89$$

Net price on August 20:

$$\$487.50 - \$18.89 = \$468.61$$

Market price 8/20/94	$468.61
Redemption price 3/1/15	500.00
	$968.61
Average investment (1/2)	$484.30

23½ (approximately) periods of interest @ $40.00.
Amortization of discount: $31.39 ÷ 23.5 = $1.34.
Annual income: $40.00 − $1.34 = $38.66.

Approximate yield: $\dfrac{\$38.66}{\$484.30} = 7.98\%$

Exact yield from bond table: 8.62%

3. Value of rights and subscription price:
   a. Market value ex rights:

   Subscription price (S) = $65.00
   Market price (M) = $89.00
   Number of rights (N) = 12

The following relationship holds where R = value of a right:

$$R = \frac{M - S}{N + 1}; \; R = \frac{89 - 65}{13} = \$1.85$$

The market value ex rights will be approximately $89.00 − 1.85 = $87.15, reflecting the removal of the rights value.

   b. Rights value for purchase of convertible preferred:

   Value of preferred (V) = $105.00
   Subscription price (S) = $ 82.00
   Number of rights (N) = 6

The following relationship holds where R = value of a right:

$$R = \frac{V - S}{N^*} = \frac{105 - 82}{6} = \$3.83$$

*Number of common shares isn't affected.

if $N = 4$, $R = \$5.75$

c. Subscription price:

Market price $(M) = \$123.00$
Number of rights $(N) = 11$
Value of a right $(R) = \$2.00$

$$R = \frac{M - S}{N + 1}; \quad 2 = \frac{123 - S}{12}; \quad S = \$99.00$$

4. Calculation of common stock value:

a. Expected yield using the CAPM:

Company A: $7.0 + 1.3(13.5 - 7.0) = 7.0 + 8.45 = 15.45\%$
Company B: $7.0 + 0.8(13.5 - 7.0) = 7.0 + 5.2 = 12.2\%$

b. Valuation (dividend discount model):

Company A: $P = \dfrac{D}{I - g} = \dfrac{\$1.00}{.154 - 0.08} = \$13.50$

Company B: $P = \dfrac{\$5.00}{0.122 - 0.04} = \dfrac{\$5.00}{.082} = \$61.00$

c. Other yardsticks:

	Company A	Company B
Earnings yield:	$\dfrac{\$2.50}{\frac{1}{2}(26 + 18)} = 11.4\%$	$\dfrac{\$7.25}{\frac{1}{2}(60 + 56)} = 12.5\%$
Dividend yield:	$\dfrac{\$1.00}{\$22.00} = 4.5\%$	$\dfrac{5.00}{\$58.00} = 8.6\%$

Observations

Company A is the more volatile company, while it is growing faster. The market is apparently awarding it a premium at the moment. It would be useful to check out public expectations about the company's future performance. Company B seems stable and properly priced; no surprises are expected here.

5. Valuation of GHI Company as an ongoing business:

Calculation of Present Values

	Year 1	Year 2	Year 3	Year 4	Year 5	Terminal Value
Earnings after taxes	$2.7	$2.9	$3.2	$3.6	$ 4.0	—
Add: Depreciation	1.0	1.1	1.4	1.6	1.8	—

	Year 1	Year 2	Year 3	Year 4	Year 5	Terminal Value
Aftertax cash flow	$3.7	$4.0	$4.6	$5.2	$ 5.8	—
Less: Investments	0.5	2.5	1.5	1.5	2.0	—
Net cash flow	3.2	1.5	3.1	3.7	3.8	$40.0
Present value factors (from Table I)	.893	.797	.712	636	.567	.567
Present values	$2.86	$1.20	$2.21	$2.35	$ 2.15	$22.68
Cumulative	$2.86	$4.06	$6.27	$8.62	$10.77	$33.45

Based on current P/E ratio, the company is worth about 11 × $2.5 million ($27.5 million). Building in the projected growth raises the value.

Observations

Quality of estimates is a question, as is the choice of the discount rate. If the rate is raised, the value drops, of course. We would need to know more about financial condition, debt to be assumed, nature of business, and so on. Many more questions must be asked. This is just the start.

6. MNO Company valuation:

Book value (based on balance sheet):

Common equity:	
Common stock	$ 525
Capital surplus	110
Earned surplus	385
Total	$1,020
Number of shares	52,500
Book value per share	$19.43

If we assume surplus reserves and deferred taxes to be part of equity, the total rises to $1,185, and the value per share to $22.57. The redundant cash is minimal in this picture and should probably be applied to accounts payable.

Liquidation value:

Assets	Fast Liquidation	Normal Sale
Cash	$ 230	$ 230
Securities	415	415
Receivables (94%)	494	494
Inventories (2/3; 95%)	543	774
Fixed assets	225	225+
Prepaids (assume 25%)	—	10
Goodwill	—	—
Organization expense	—	—
Total	$1,907	$2,148

Assets	Fast Liquidation	Normal Sale
Less:		
Current liabilities	$ 935	$ 935
Mortgage payable	175	175
Bonds	520	520
Preferred stock	300	300
Total deduction	$1,930	$1,930
Value of common	$ (23)	$ 218
Per share	$ (.44)	$ 4.15

Market value:

Most recent: $25⅛, but thinly traded.
Based on average of past 3 years: $28⅛.
Based on recent industry P/E of 11: $.65 × 4 × 11 = $28.60.
Based on average P/E of 13: $.65 × 4 × 13 = $33.80.
Based on long-term profit growth, EPS should be about $3.00, and P/E of 11 would be $33.00.

Observations

Because no forced liquidation is intended, the value should be based on a going concern concept, and the main argument should be on the breadth of the market, the use of industry P/E ratios, and so on.

Additional information should be sought about nature of the industry, long-term product trends, profitability of similar companies, dividend policies of other companies, product line changes and threats, competitive abilities, and so on.

7. Potential merger:

	Company A	Company B
P/E ratio	12X	20X
Earnings per share	$8.00	$3.00
Dividends per share	$2.00	none
Aftertax earnings	$80.0 million	$3.0 million
Price range	$90 to $100	$45 to $70
Current price	$98.00	$54.00 ($65.00 offered)
Growth rate	6% per year	12% per year
Number of shares	10 million	1 million

a. Exchange ratio:

65 ÷ 98 = ⅔ share of A for 1 share of B = 667,000 shares

b. Impact on earnings:

$80.0 million plus $3.0 million = $83.0 million
10.0 million shares plus 667,000 = 10,667,000 shares
$83.0 ÷ 10,667,000 = $7.78 per share (22¢ dilution)

c. Impact on dividends: Each share of Company B now receives the equivalent of $1.33 per share in dividends versus none before.

d. Impact on earnings growth: Three years hence the situation is expected to be:

Company A @ 6 percent growth will earn $95.3 million ($9.53 EPS).

Company B @ 12 percent growth will earn $4.2 million ($4.20 EPS).

Total company earnings thus will grow to $99.5 million, and EPS will be $99.5 ÷ 10,667,000 = $9.33.

Observations

The dilution in earnings of 22 cents immediately isn't likely to be overcome in the foreseeable future inasmuch as in three years the earnings per share of the combined company will be 20 cents *lower* than what Company A alone could have achieved. On the other hand, synergy, if any, hasn't been considered. In view of the sizable annual dividends now paid them, the holders of Company B stock might perhaps consider a somewhat lower offer.

Questions for Discussion

1. Differentiate between economic value and market value. Are both concepts absolute?

2. Is value in the eye of the beholder or can conditions be quantified sufficiently to allow objective choices?

3. Discuss the relationship between yield and value. Are both concepts based on the same conditions?

4. Is it possible to allow specifically for the effect of such provisions as participation, convertibility, callability, and other special covenants in valuing preferred stocks or bonds?

5. Why should we attempt to value an ongoing business via cash flow analysis when in the end the decision is based on many other factors as well?

6. List major considerations affecting valuation in an inflationary environment.

7. If price/earnings ratios are so important in setting the ratio of exchange in a merger based on a share swap, how can such a volatile measure give reasonable indications of value?

8. Synergy is an argument for business combinations, but it's hard to measure and achieve. Why?

9. With vast increases in computer capabilities, will valuation likely become more quantified?
10. If there's so much uncertainty in estimates of future cash flows, why does it make sense to apply even more sophisticated valuation formulas?

INDEX